COGNITIVE DEVELOPMENT IN THE SCHOOL YEARS

COGNITIVE DEVELOPMENT IN THE SCHOOL YEARS

EDITED BY ANN FLOYD

A HALSTED PRESS BOOK

JOHN WILEY & SONS
New York

Selection and editorial material
copyright © The Open University 1979

Published in the USA
by Halsted Press, a Division
of John Wiley & Sons Inc.
New York

Library of Congress Cataloging in Publication Data

Main entry under title:

Cognitive development in the school years.

'A Halsted Press book.'
Includes index.
    1. Cognition in children — Addresses, essays, lectures.
2. Piaget, Jean, 1896-   — Addresses, essays, lectures.
3. Educational psychology — Addresses, essays, lectures.
I. Floyd, Ann.
BF723.C5C63   155.4'24   78-9155
ISBN 0-470-26429-2

Typeset by Leaper & Gard Ltd, Bristol
Printed and bound in Great Britain

CONTENTS

Section Four: Educational Applications

COGNITIVE DEVELOPMENT IN THE SCHOOL YEARS

SECTION ONE: PIAGET IN PERSPECTIVE

Introduction

It is only appropriate that a volume such as this should begin with an attempt to assess Piaget's lasting contribution to our understanding of cognitive development in the school years. Despite very diverse views on the significance of his work, Piagetian concepts are very widely found in this field of research. Sometimes they are interpreted in the Genevan way, other times they are modified, refined or extended, and still other times they are heavily criticised. But they still feature, as you will see from the collection of readings in this volume.

The two chapters in the first part of the Reader were written by people who have had many years of experience of working with Piagetian concepts. At the same time, neither of them is wholly uncritical of Genevan thinking. Certainly they are both in a position to make informed judgements as to what aspects of Piaget's work are likely to be of lasting value. And in doing so they both acknowledge that in addition to these more enduring aspects the indebtedness of contemporary research to the whole corpus of Piagetian work is considerable. It has so often acted as a stimulus to thinking about child development, even when particular results have been questioned and methods criticised.

The first chapter is written by Kenneth Lovell, who has made a considerable study of the development of scientific and mathematical concepts in children. It begins with a reminder that Piaget's work on developmental psychology was initially motivated not so much by the intrinsic interest of this field as by a desire to find out how knowledge is acquired. Was this by purely adding more and more items of information to a relatively fixed framework for storing such items, or in addition to this process, does the framework itself develop in the direction of being able to absorb an increasing number of types of information? The study of cognitive development could throw considerable light on this question, and it led Piaget to try to find out whether the difference between children's thinking and the thinking of adults lay solely in the amount of information available, or whether it also involved qualitative differences in the processing of this information.

Lovell's chapter continues with a short historical sketch of Piaget's work leading into an account of his current position on a number of issues. This is followed by a discussion of some of the comments and criticisms that have been made by other researchers, and in the light of all this Lovell gives his own view as to which aspects of Piaget's work are likely to be of lasting value. Finally he briefly considers the other chapters in this collection insofar as these have a bearing on the issues he has been discussing.

The second chapter is written by Jan Smedslund who has spent many years working in the Piagetian framework. He has now come to consider that this has some major weaknesses which he outlines in his chapter. In particular, he is concerned that the Piagetian approach concentrates on too narrow a range of skills and that this often leads to distortion of the true picture of an individual child's development level. Nevertheless, he considers that several aspects of Piaget's work do have a lasting value and he states what he considers these to be.

The other three sections in this Reader give further consideration to many of the issues raised here. Sections 2 and 3 contain a variety of examples of research into cognitive development, Section 2 being concerned with children in the primary school years and Section 3 with those of secondary school age. Finally, Section 4 looks at the ways in which the education of these children has been or could be influenced by such understanding of child development as we have.

1 SOME ASPECTS OF THE WORK OF PIAGET IN PERSPECTIVE

Kenneth Lovell

Source: specially written for this volume.

1. The Scope of His Work

When the history of twentieth century developmental psychology is written it is likely that the name of Piaget will stand, like the body of a giant, head and shoulders above all the others. His work is so fundamental that most papers now published in the field of child psychology refer to his views in some way or other. Note, however, that Piaget may not regard himself as an expert developmental psychologist. He is more likely to look upon himself as the founder of a particular branch of psychology, namely genetic epistemology. This is an important point, for while thousands of persons around the world regard him as an outstanding child psychologist, it is his own conception of his aims which gives the vital key to his life's work. He became a developmental psychologist in order to find out how knowledge is constructed. In short he wanted to know if knowledge results from the accumulation of small bits of information or whether there must already be a mental structure or reference frame inside which some new piece of knowledge can be meaningful.

For more than fifty years he and his colleagues have reported a mass of observations on aspects of child and adolescent developments and from these he has elaborated important hypotheses relating to the growth of knowledge. He used the clinical or 'critical' method of individually interviewing children, and thereby attempted to build a bridge between his early love of biology and his enduring passion of epistemology. Piaget and his colleagues have published more than forty books and a much larger number of articles. Further, his work has generated an enormous amount of research by other workers — a true sign of the greatness of his own efforts. The compilation of Piagetian research by S. and C. Modgil (1976), which is in eight volumes and includes some 3,500 references, gives some idea of the extent of the research by the Genevans and others to the end of 1975.

His work may be divided up into four broad periods. First the period up to about 1930 in which the empirical data was obtained wholly by verbal methods. This period includes his classic studies of the language and thought of the child, and the moral judgement of the child. Piaget later admitted (Piaget, 1953) that his method of studying logic in the child was much too verbal at first. The second period involved his observations of his own children, and from these he developed his views on the origins of intelligence and the construction of reality (Piaget, 1936, 1937). Indeed in this phase it was the study of the sensori-motor phase of his own children's development that provided much of the basis for his theoretical work (Piaget, 1947).

Some of the best known of Piaget's work occurred in the third phase in which he studied the move from pre-operational thought to concrete operational thought and from the latter to formal operational thought. Here we have the many and well known studies of conservation, classification, seriation; together with the growth of understanding of number, space, geometry, time, chance and others. In this period he was investigating, because of his epistemological interests, the origins of the concepts with which we structure the world. Without doubt it is the studies of this period which have greatly coloured the teacher's view of the work of Piaget. Much, but not all of this work in this period, is briefly summarised by Piaget and Inhelder (1969).

The fourth period of his work extends to the present time. In this period we find the many volumes of Etudes d'Epistemologie Genetique (written with the help of others) as well as books on structuralism,[†] memory and intelligence, mental imagery and thinking, causality, on the growth of the child's conceptualisation of his own actions, and a further volume dealing with the problem of equilibration[†] (Piaget, 1975).

We have already indicated Piaget's philosophical interests, namely how knowledge comes to be constructed. A brief word now is given on his philosophic stance. Of Genetic Epistemology he writes, 'The fundamental hypothesis of genetic epistemology is that there is a parallelism between the progress made in the logical and rational organisation of knowledge and the corresponding psychological processes' (Piaget, 1970a, p. 13). Put more simply, what he calls genetic epistemology is the study of how knowledge has progressed from early simple forms to more complex and indeed, more powerful constructs. To pursue this study, genetic epistemology employs three broad sources of data. First, the study of the cognitive development of the child through investigating the slow construction of his basic conceptualisations (rather than the build-up of particular skills or the acquisition of specific pieces of information). A second source is the history of science, from the viewpoint of how one level of knowledge gave way to a higher level. The important point here is what it is in the one theory held that paved the way for the creation of new scientific knowledge. A third source resides in formal models of the state of some specific piece of scientific knowledge at a given point in time. Such models assume or presuppose experimentally determined regularities; on the other hand such models also allow the discovery of new relations between regularities. However, these formal models are mainly structural models and therefore have limitations from the point of view of genetic epistemology or developmental psychology, for these require process models, that is, frameworks which model the processes which move the knowledge from one stage to the next.

Thus, if Piaget's philosophical interest is in knowledge construction, his philosophical viewpoint involves a form of structuralism.[†] His critics have often pointed out that he, like everyone else, looks at evidence from 'a point of view', and that there could be other conceptual frameworks elaborated to cover the same ground. This argument is accepted, but it is pointed out that in the natural sciences too, it is not unusual for alternative frameworks to be elaborated to explain the evidence. Other critics object to his work because of the non-observable and non-measurable nature of the main concepts which he employs such as schemes,[†] assimilation,[†] accommodation.[†] True, many of these do not lend themselves to clear hypotheses which experimental evidence can support or refute. On the other hand many of his ideas are testable.

It has been assumed in this section that readers already have some knowledge of at least some areas of his work. This brief historical treatment is to give no more than a sketch of the vast scope of his work over more than fifty years, and merely to indicate the philosophy that informed it.

2. The Present Position of Piaget on Some Issues

It is a great mistake to think that Piaget considers his theory to be either complete or all embracing. Rather it is constantly being modified either by himself or others. Indeed, he has referred to himself as 'one of the chief "revisionists of Piaget" ' (Piaget, 1970a, p. 703 footnote). Again in a special issue of *Archives de Psychologie* published in 1976 in honour of his eightieth birthday he himself wrote, 'I have the conviction, illusory or well founded . . . and only the future will tell whether this conviction is partly true or only the result of my obstinate pride . . . that I have laid bare a more or less evident general skeleton which remains full of gaps so that when these gaps will be filled the articulations will have to be differentiated but the general lines of the system will not be changed.'[1] We cannot, of course, be sure how much the general lines of the theory will have to be changed in the future, but we can speak of some changes that have been made in his own views on specific issues over the period, say 1958 to 1978. It must be remembered that in many areas of the natural sciences too, for instance physics, theories elaborated twenty or thirty years ago have had to undergo many changes since then. Below there is a brief discussion of just four issues on which Piaget has changed his mind in recent years. Space does not permit further discussion.

Equilibration is perhaps Piaget's most important, yet most controversial, concept and we begin by considering this. In a recent book on this subject (Piaget, 1975) he points out that his earlier writings on this subject were quite inadequate. Some forty years ago he intuitively formulated his ideas that cognition was a self-regulatory or self-referential system. In such a system interactions between different parts of the system interact with interactions between other parts, this wholeness of the system giving it its stable properties. In biological organisms there are certainly simultaneous interactions between, say, perception and action which maintain an internal equilibrium. For Piaget, cognition shares with biological organisations this self-regulatory quality which establishes whatever levels of activity that have to be maintained for equilibrium, and thus the interactions of interactions.

Now if such systems merely compensated for perturbations and re-established a pre-existing equilibrium, one would merely be maintaining the status quo. Piaget argues that cognitive systems do not operate in this fashion. Rather they operate, as it were, in an ever widening spiral fashion. This reflects the ability of the systems to deal with more and more disturbances which arise from both inner reflection and outside contradictions as the child's experience of the world grows. The widening spiral also reflects the ability of the systems to integrate disturbances into wider and more powerful structures as, for example, when early concrete operations are slowly replaced by later concrete operations and when the latter gradually give way to formal operations. That is to say, not only does the compensation of perturbations get the system back to an equilibrium state but it attains a higher order of equilibrium. Piaget is now particularly concerned (Piaget, 1975) to be able to give an account of the development of this widening spiral, or some account of what he calls 'equilibration majorante' or 'augmentative equilibrium'.[2] This contrasts with his earlier interest which lasted over many years in giving more weight to a structural description of the main stages of equilibration as in concrete and formal operational thought.

This change in outlook leading Piaget to give a new account of the mechanisms of equilibration has led him to change, slightly, the observational and experimental methods employed. There is now an even closer look at individual children, and more attention paid both to the experimental situation and to the dialogue with the child. These changes are reflected in his work on correspondences discussed below.

While Piaget's views on the processes of equilibration have changed he remains as firmly as ever an interactionist. While for the empiricist, discovered knowledge was already an existence in external reality, and for the naturist or apriorist forms of knowledge were predetermined inside the subject, for Piaget the cognitive structures involved in knowing are given neither in the object nor in the person, but in the interaction between them.

A second important change in Piaget's outlook concerns his views on the role of correspondences and morphisms[†] in cognitive growth. As is well known he holds the view that knowledge involves essentially systems of transformations. We can only know something if, and only if, we can construct and transform it. Although he did not invent this viewpoint he has held to it consistently. However, more recently, he has become interested in correspondences as well as transformations. This is linked to his current interest in the child's growth in understanding of the mathematical concept of category.

Transformations can be arranged in the manner in which they follow on from one another. In correspondences, however, there is no transformation. Here we are comparing terms or states as they are. One can of course compare transformations, for a transformation produces a state, but in making the comparison, as such, there is no further transformation. We can find examples of correspondences at every level of intellectual growth (Piaget, 1976). For example, he argues that at the sensori-motor level each assimilation into a specific scheme is a correspondence. Thus if the infant when touching one hanging rattle to make it swing sees another similarly hanging, he will make a correspondence between the second and the first and set the second one swinging too. At the operational level it is not just a case of assimilating through physical action whatever can be perceived; rather there is now a mental action and thus a *necessary* correspondence. For example, every direct operation (say, addition) corresponds to an inverse operation (subtraction).

In the last few years the Genevans have been experimenting to establish the relationships between correspondences and transformations. This new work cannot be discussed in any detail but one experiment (Piaget, 1976) will indicate that their findings change some of their earlier views. Consider the well known experiment in which two balls of plasticine are judged by the child to be equal in amount. A piece of plasticine is taken off one of the balls and the young child is asked if there is now the same amount of plasticine in the ball. Young children invariably answer correctly. Then the piece is put back on the other side of the ball and the child again appropriately questioned. Once more they answer correctly. This process goes on until the same sausage shape is obtained as when the plasticine in the traditional experiment is rolled. The interesting thing is that with this 'taking off' and 'adding on' process, 75 per cent of five-and-a-half-year-olds conserve giving correct answers like 'You took the piece away but put it back again so it's OK'. Moreover the conservation is stable because if the classic experiment is carried out and the ball rolled into a sausage, conservation is still maintained and good reasons are given.

Piaget's view now is that rapid learning has taken place because use was made of the correspondence of the isomorphism[†] between what was taken off and what was replaced (see the paper by Inhelder, Sinclair and Bovet later in this book). This new type of conservation experiment focuses the pupil's attention on the fact that whenever there is one correspondence there must be the other. In another sense here we have an experimental situation that emphasises the functional aspects of transformations. Now at the operational level there are, as stated earlier, necessary correspondences between every direct operation and its inverse. Piaget is thus giving emphasis to correspondence as an aid in cognitive development, at the same time, of course, maintaining the importance of transformations in knowing.

The relationship between language and thought is another issue about which Piaget seems to have changed his mind in recent years. His views in the late 1950s are given by Inhelder and Piaget (1958).[3] In general terms we may say that he had often stated that language was not a sufficient condition for the formation of intellectual operations. Similar views were held in the early 1960s. Again we find him saying in respect of younger children (Duckworth, 1964): 'The level of understanding seems to modify the language that is used, rather than vice versa . . . Mainly language serves to translate what is already understood . . .' In 1967 we find Sinclair-De-Zwart (1967), a colleague of Piaget at Geneva, giving details of fresh studies carried out by her. In essence she stated that up to and including the level of concrete operational thought, logical structures determine the nature of the linguistic structures rather than the other way round. Language may play a role in the growth of such thought; language can, so to speak, prepare an operation; language helps in the selection, storage and retrieval of information; but it does not play a central role in the elaboration of concrete operational structures.

In the early 1960s, Piaget (1963) had a more open mind about the role of language in the elaboration of formal operational thought. In respect of the structures of such thought he wished to reserve his judgement on the role language played, whether it was 'truly conservative or merely indirect and supportive'. However, by 1970 Piaget seems to make language less dependent on cognition for its structure (see Ferriero, 1971). There is no longer the emphasis that cognitive operations (or pre-operations) direct language or language acquisition, rather than the other way round. The view now held is that both cognitive, linguistic and non-linguistic structures (such as those involving imagery) derive from a more abstract logical system of regulations and organisations common to all domains. Linguistic structures may well be affected by cognitive structures and vice versa through this more general abstract system. This allows both cognitive and linguistic structures to influence one another and at the same time for each to have a degree of autonomy. The partial autonomy of the linguistic structures suggests that it may be possible under certain circumstances to construct operational structures by verbal means; the suggestion having already been experimentally confirmed in the case of conservation.

A fourth change in outlook may be briefly noted. By the late 1960s Piaget and his colleagues came to the view that by the later part of the pre-operational period of thought, say, five to seven years, children's thinking did in fact possess some kind of logic. But it is a semi-logic compared with the thinking of the concrete operational period for it does not possess the property of reversibility. Thus we find Piaget *et al.* (1968a) describing their work on *identities*. These are essentially qualitative in nature in that the child recognises that an object is the 'same thing' even when its appearance, form or size changes; as for example, when a piece of straight wire is twisted to form 'spectacles'. In other words the wire is still the same entity as before, although the child will not yet conserve its length (a quantitative invariant).

Piaget *et al.* (1968b) also maintain that children of this age have some understanding of functions in the sense of grasping that the value of a depends on the value of b, or $a = f(b)$. Using apparatus a child is able to relate, say, changes in the length of a spring to changes in the weights attached to it. But the changes the child notes are only qualitative correspondences in respect of objects or situations, in the sense that changes in one object tend to be associated with changes in another. The functional relationship is only qualitative and there is no precise quantitative relationship.

These identities and functions reflect the young child's increasing awareness of associations, consistencies and invariants in his world, thereby rendering it a more predictable place to live in. This is an important step for him.

3. Some Comments on, and Criticisms of, Piaget's Theory

It will be appreciated that the present writer must be highly selective in respect of the issues chosen for discussion in this section. We begin by mentioning two questions raised in a recent publication which bear on his theoretical position and then discuss some of the experimental evidence which either amplifies or runs contrary to some of his views.

Mention has already been made of a book by Piaget on Structuralism (Piaget, 1971). In a recent publication entitled *Structure and Transformation* edited by Riegel and Rosenwald (1976) there is a comprehensive description of the basic principles of the structuralist paradigm. However, while Piaget considers himself a structuralist his views differ at times from those of the contributors to this recent volume. For example, he writes 'If it be true that all structures are generated, it is just as true that generation is always a passing from a simpler to a more complex structure, this process, according to the present state of knowledge being endless.' This is strictly in keeping with the structuralist paradigm which argues that as the individual changes — as for example in middle and old age — so does reality for the individual, and in turn as reality changes so does the individual. Yet in Piagetian theory, structural development stops at mid-adolescence when the INRC[†] structure is elaborated, and so the contributors ask for new conceptualisations by Piaget about changes of structure in adulthood.

In studying cognitive development one frequently encounters the term 'stages'. This is used in two ways. First, to indicate the increase in understanding of some specific idea. Thus Lovell (1971) and Thomas (1975) indicate the stages through which pupils pass in their increasing understanding of the concept of mathematical function. Second, the term is used by Piaget to indicate the increasing ability of pupils to solve tasks which demand more and more complex logical mathematical operations for their solutions. It is in this sense that the term is used, and briefly discussed, in this chapter. But in later papers in this book it is also used in the first sense as, for example, in the paper by Graham which deals with stages of moral judgement. It must, of course, be made clear that the 'stage' of thinking as used in the second sense of the term, underpins the 'stage' at which pupils are in understanding some specific idea (the first sense of the term).

We next consider an important issue in the four to seven year-old period. A very large number of training studies have taken place in an effort to accelerate the growth of children's thinking mainly from pre-operational to concrete operational thought. Various techniques have been used in, say, conservation training: for example, conflict-equilibration[†] (proposed by the Genevans themselves because of their theory); constituent structure training (the child is trained in one of the constituent skills held by Piaget to be critical to conservation training); verbal rule instruction (verbally presented rules are coordinated with experimental manipulations); and a number of others. All these differing approaches have shown that operations can be trained and this seems to be the case whether strong or weak criteria are used to test for operational thinking.

It might be thought these findings are at variance with Piaget's teaching. This is now only partly true for the Genevans themselves have, in recent years, carried out a number of training studies and come to the same broad conclusions (Inhelder, Sinclair and Bovet, 1974). The argument now is whether such training is effective unless there are at least some of the relevant constituents present. The Genevans, for example, argue that when training is successful there is evidence of partially attained structures before the training begins, and are uncertain what happens when the child is completely pre-operational. It must be admitted, of course, that there are difficulties in defining precisely the behavioural manifestation of cognitive structures. However, since learning takes place using methods not necessarily based on conflict-equilibration this does leave Piaget with a problem his theory has not resolved.

A number of workers such as Bruner, Bryant, Gelman and others argue that many cognitive functions such as, say, conservation, are available to the child much earlier in life and are not constructed in the five to seven year period as indicated by Piaget. The child is said to be unable to give evidence of these constructions or use them because of, say, conflict among alternative hypotheses, failure to remember initial conditions, or for other reasons. Some of the relevant studies by these workers have been criticised, but even assuming their validity, these workers have still to explain how the cognitive functions originally arose and make clear how experience changed the strategies the young child used. Moreover, the views of these workers do not necessarily deny Piaget's views on the need for progressive construction.

Finally it should be noted that far fewer training studies have been carried out at the interface between concrete and formal operational thinking. To date the number would be something in excess of twenty (cf. Siegler, 1977). Moreover, as far as this writer knows, none, to date, has followed up the effects of such training for longer than four months after training ceased. Thus our knowledge of the effects of training at this interface is limited.

When we consider concrete and formal operations more broadly a number of issues arise. First, Piaget is sometimes criticised for apparently holding the view that 'stages' are found in cognitive growth; and that such growth is discontinuous rather than continuous. In reply to the attack on stages as such, it must be stated that he is not an empiricist with 'stages out there' to be discovered. Rather he set up tasks which demanded for their solution increasingly complex logical-mathematical operations which were relevant to his philosophical position, and children progressed through 'stages' as they showed an improvement in solving the tasks. In respect of the discontinuity/continuity argument he has clearly stated that the research techniques and tasks used restrict the number of identifiable intermediate steps that can be detected. Thus we can never be sure whether discontinuity or continuity best describe the phenomena being studied since the number of intermediate steps can never be complete or exhaustive (Piaget, 1960). Rather he takes the view that within an open system we find phases of relative stability, as in the case of concrete and formal operational stages, punctuated by unstable periods of transition. In connection with this issue the longitudinal study of average grade school pupils by Neimark (1974) using an information processing approach should be considered. She tested pupils twice a year over at least three years in respect of their problem solving strategies. The task was novel, language free (except for the instructions), and involved simple patterns of black and white on card. Thus to pupils in a developed society the task could be regarded at least as content-familiar. Her findings suggest two qualitatively different levels of approach corresponding to concrete and formal operations, the move from the lower to higher level proceeding through discrete steps. This was also true, with advancing age, using a cross-sectional approach. However, nothing that has been written in this paragraph necessarily implies that the concept of stages will be of lasting value.

Second, Piaget's notion of *structure d'ensemble*† has been questioned. The completed elaboration of such structures could not, of course, be expected before the end of the relevant developmental period. But if at the end of, say, the concrete operational period there was established empirically an asynchronism among the constituents of a *given concept*, his notion of *structure d'ensemble*† would be in great jeopardy. There is some evidence (cf. Hooper and Sipple, 1975) that in the age range five to seven and a half years or so the development of classificatory abilities may sometimes lag behind rational abilities, contrary of course to Piagetian theory. But in pupils aged nine to twelve years the position is by no means clear. After a review of the relevant literature, Hooper and Dihoff (1975) made a thorough study of synchrony† in this age range. In order to avoid possible criticisms of their data analysis they used multi-dimensional scaling, clustering and factor analytic procedures. They concluded that, on the basis of their evidence, developmental synchrony[†] cannot yet be abandoned, but this does not preclude asynchrony being established in the future. At the level of formal operations there is no evidence as yet for a unitary concept even at 17 to 18 years of age; indeed there is some evidence against it. The question of synchrony must not, of course, be confused with that of horizontal decalage (the same structure applied to adjoining cognitive areas), or oblique decalage (Inhelder, Sinclair and Bovet, 1974).

At this point it must be made clear that some psychologists are quite opposed to Piaget's notion of operatory structures. Instead they prefer to regard the acquisition of a particular piece of knowledge as dependent on the learning of a set of skills which are then practised and perhaps combined into new combinations. Such skills will most likely arise from the cumulative learning of prior skills. However, the skills or the new combinations of skills are then activated and used by individuals when perhaps they are suitably motivated by the task and appropriately cued into it. When considering this viewpoint one must remember that the question of the 'narrowness' or 'width' of the intellectual skill must be considered. A skill could be narrow in the sense that it enabled the individual to assimilate a particular piece of knowledge but did not transfer to new knowledge. On the other hand an intellectual skill could be wide enough to be an operation and thus a part of an operatory structure. For psychologists who take a narrow view of intellectual skills it is obvious that the question of synchrony of the constituents of an operatory structure does not arise.

Third, there is the important question of whether the required strategies of thought will be invoked to solve a given task when the same strategies are indeed used by the individual in the solution of other problems. By the early 1960s it was known (cf. Lovell, 1961) that there were only moderately sized correlations between the level of responses to tasks given by Inhelder and Piaget (1958). This is an issue which traditional Piagetian theory has not seriously considered at the level of formal operations.

Piaget and Inhelder (1969) certainly maintain that concrete operations are not content-free and are thus subject to variability due to stimulus differences. When Inhelder and Piaget (1964) gave a classificatory task involving pictures of animals the task was found to be much harder than when beads or flowers were used. Their rationale was that children are more familiar with beads and flowers. This may well be true, but it is likely to be only part of the story.

At the level of formal thought Inhelder and Piaget (1958) consider that the content of the problem is subordinate to the form of the relations in it. This is not the case in fact. The response which a child or adult gives to the task depends on the social context of the task and the meaning that the task has for him in his world. So it is not just a question of familiarity with the content, although that certainly plays a part.

There is now much evidence to support the view just expressed. For example, the work reported by Wason and Johnson-Laird (1972), or Wason (1977) shows that reasoning is affected by the content of the problem and in a systematic way. Indeed most people realise that the content of a problem which they have to solve in everyday life affects the ease with which they solve it. The studies reported by Luria (1976), also Cole and Scribner (1974), show that the types of concept formed (functional relational[†] rather than categoric[†] concepts) and the ability to use specific strategies in reasoning, do depend upon the content of the problem and the meaning it has for the individual. Again Tulkin and Konner (1973) report hypothetico-deductive thinking among Kalahari bushmen in relation to animal tracking. Yet if the same bushmen were suddenly taken into a physics laboratory and asked to solve a problem involving, say, the separation of variables — an analogous task — it is most unlikely that hypothetico-deductive thinking would be available until after a long period of study which would give meaning to the task and provide familiarity with the variables.

The problem of the availability of reasoning skills in diverse situations is an important issue for psychology and education. There is now much evidence that, in Britain and elsewhere, three-year-old children from some homes use language less often to report on past experiences and predict the future, to give explanations, to justify behaviour and to reflect on feelings, compared with children from professional homes. The former children more often use language to communicate the 'here and now' events. By seven years of age these working class children when talking to peers, can make as long and as complex sentences as children from professional homes, but their families less often encourage them to make comparisons, to recall the past, anticipate the future, to look for similarities and differences, and to offer 'logical' explanations (Tough, 1977). Because of this children from different families enter school with a different set of meanings or constructions about the world.

In some families then, in Britain or in any other country, the life style is such that thinking is more frequently rooted in the perceptible or tangible, the concrete, the practical. But there is by no means a one-to-one relationship between this kind of life style and socio-economic status.

Some families of limited income do encourage their children to think of possibilities and hypothetical situations, thus divorcing themselves more often from the tangible and concrete, to subject themselves to more long-term planning, to reflect on their actions and the likely outcomes, and to think and find solutions to problems for themselves rather than have them transmitted merely by rule or routine sequence. Many professional familes do this too: some do not. But studies of language use, also of concept formation and reasoning in a number of countries, suggest that family life style, as defined, has implications for cognitive development.

Children from families where there is no attempt to move them from thinking in terms of the immediate present may sometimes be better at assessing the perceptual cues of objects or situations. Moreover, we must never belittle such thinking; it may be appropriate for certain life styles. But they have a greater tendency to use functional relational concepts, and they have more difficulty in handling verbal-logical relations where the form of the argument is divorced from the content — as is often the case in formal schooling. The reasoning of everyone is, of course, affected to some extent by knowledge of, and familiarity with, the content; but certain life styles make it easier for the pupil to handle verbal logical relations independent of content. Life styles which do not help the children in this way, put children at something of a disadvantage in formal schooling in a developed or developing society. These differences in family life styles are found in all countries, regardless of whether their economic system is capitalist or socialist. Much could be done by families (often regardless of income) to help their children acquire and use in diverse situations, those thinking skills which are now increasingly demanded by developed and developing societies throughout the world.

Piaget's failure to consider content and meaning in his traditional theory of formal operations is well expressed by Halford (1972) when he points out that Wason's work had shown that: 'If adults have what Piaget calls formal operational thought, then Piaget does very little to specify the conditions under which this will be observed.' While human reasoning is no doubt rule governed, its rules are not those of traditional propositional logic and the appropriate calculus has not yet been formulated.

Fourth, we have already explained that there are difficulties over the problem of stages. It remains to be seen to what extent Piaget's more recent views on equilibrium (Piaget, 1975) can provide a satisfactory and generally agreed account of the processes involved in the transition between stages. In other words, will it indicate the strategies children adopt in response to the changing child-environment interaction? An information processing approach may also help in the teasing out of the steps in cognitive development. The most frequently used models now used in information processing are probably the production system models made possible by using computers. Well known workers in this field are Klahr and Wallace (1975) and Baylor *et al.* (1973). All information processing approaches are well concerned with a detailing of the processes of reasoning and concept formation, a detailing that Piagetian theory has lacked. But to date it must be said that information processing is of limited value for the teacher (although of value to the researcher) for it is time consuming to tease out the micro-processes, and there is limited experience of teaching the processes found and establishing the outcomes of such teaching.

4. Aspects of Piaget's Work Likely to be of Lasting Value

Much could be written on this topic but the writer's judgement must be summarised briefly. Some of the points listed below overlap to some extent, but they do separately suggest some of Piaget's work and ideas are likely to be of long term value.

1. The sheer amount of factual knowledge established which shows at least some of the broad outlines of cognitive development. This in no sense implies that Piaget's notion of stages will be of permanent value. Nor does it set approval on the theoretical framework he elaborated, but the framework did enable him to get a mass of data.

2. His strong approval, through use, of an age-long approach, namely, the clinical method. Although this method has marked strengths, it also has weaknesses. But in Piaget's hands it has been very productive in many areas of cognition. Moreover, it has been adopted, as a result of Piaget's influence, by innumerable research workers in studying pupils' ideas in areas of knowledge not covered by him. It will continue to be used in this way for a long time.

3. The extensive research that has been generated, and will go on being generated, by Piaget's research. Some studies involve testing his results, some developing new lines of research based on his ideas. Eventually this research will lead to new and lasting knowledge even if the findings are at variance with his.

4. Piaget's emphasis on organisation, for without this there can be no adaptation. From this follows, for him, the importance of cognitive organisation. This means that new knowledge will be internalised and structured, and in time will determine the strategies used in future encounters with the environment. This is a very different stance from that

of linking particular behaviours with specific aspects of the environment and specific learned skills.

5. The position Piaget adopts in respect of the progressive construction of knowledge resulting from the interactions between subject and objects. If new knowledge is not progressively constructed by the individual himself, with the aid of teaching, action, observation, the use of materials and/or language, and social interaction, as required, it remains imperfectly understood. This view does not necessarily lend support to what is broadly known as 'discovery learning' in certain educational circles.

6. His perspective which maintains that knowledge is constructed out of the interaction between the person and reality, for the cognitive structures involved in knowing are given neither in the object, nor in the person, but in the interaction between them. While he may not have been the first person to advance this general view, he did relate this to the idea of decentration and its relation to objectivity. For example, Piaget (1950) wrote: 'It is impossible at any level to separate the object from the subject. Relations exist between the two only, but these relations may be more or less centered or decentered, and it is this inversion of direction which makes up the transition from subjectivity to objectivity.'

7. The importance given to the role of cognitive conflict as a means of bringing about improved cognitive adaptation and hence a higher level of thinking. [This is not to deny the place of verbal rule learning. One way in which such learning may act is through being able to mobilise unintegrated structures through generating conflict.] In the school situation his notion of cognitive conflict argues that the curriculum or task presented to the pupil should demand cognitive skills slightly more advanced (+1 level) than those available in order to induce conflict.

8. Just one detailed study (Piaget, 1977) may perhaps be mentioned where the insights obtained are likely to be of lasting value. This relates to the time lag between a child having the requisite strategies or programmes to carry out an action (e.g. walking on all fours) and being able to reflect on his actions and describe what he is doing. The cognisance, or act of becoming conscious of an active scheme (i.e. of a repeatable and generalisable action), or of an internalised scheme for that matter, is a pre-requisite for generalisation and for tackling new problems in which the same strategies are involved.

It is likely to be a long time before the lasting insights which Piaget has produced together with those established by others, can be brought together into a theory which subsumes or replaces his own. In the special issue of the *Archives de Psychologie* already mentioned he writes: 'When a theory succeeds another theory the first impression is often that the new theory contradicts the older and eliminates it. But later research often shows that more has to be retained of the older theory than could be foreseen. The better theory turns out to be the one that retains most of the preceding theories.' It is in this light that we should regard Piaget's work. It is not that he has been proved wrong or right. An effort has been made in this chapter to show that he is incorrect in respect of some matters while other aspects of his work are likely to have lasting value. His theory will certainly have to be amended but it is too early yet to say what form the new one will take.

5. Comments on the Papers which follow this Chapter

The first seven papers deal with the Primary years. The first is by Smedslund who has worked with Piaget but who has become critical of many of his views. He questions Piaget's notion of operatory structures, and seems to wish to replace them through the progressive building of skill upon skill and concept upon concept in terms of the learning obtained within the culture. Objection is also made to Piaget's peripheral attention to the social context of a task and the meaning it has for the child; that is, his failure to consider 'the person in the total situation'. Carey also takes the view that the cumulative acquisition of particular skills, their practice, and the learning of new combinations of them, can provide a basis for particular achievements. Moreover she argues a case for there being no basic linguistic or cognitive differences in people's problem solving potential or thinking. However, there is no mention of the fact that the child's experience in the home and environment might affect the ease or difficulty of applying an acquired cognitive skill in diverse situations. The alternative to this, and the one Carey seems to prefer, is that the number of such skills, to use Carey's own phrase, is 'staggeringly large'; indeed for her each piece of knowledge could be thought of in this way.

Bryant's paper may be considered in three broad parts. In the first his data suggest to him that when errors occur in inference problems given to young children, they are most likely to be the effect of memory failure. Furth (1977) disputes this. Using a modified repetition of Bryant's procedure he argues that the performance of young children was not related to the operative knowing of the rule of transitivity, but to a cumulative combining of figurative memory. The second part of Bryant's contribution considers the problems which the Kendlers set to young children and he again concludes that failure to solve them tells us nothing of their inferential ability. In the third he concedes that although the young child can make inferences when the essential information is given, he is unable to do so when he has to obtain the relevant information before the inference is made.

Of the studies carried out by Inhelder *et al.* into the learning and development of cognition, they regard the one given in this book, which involves the training procedure for the conservation of length, to be one of the most instructive in highlighting developmental processes in action. The chapter points up two connected issues. First, the relation between the operatory structures involved in the conservation of number which involves discontinuous units, and those involved in the conservation of continuous quantity, namely length. Second, how the child comes to construct the concept of length, also of measurement in one dimension.

Graham's paper focuses on children's moral awareness, moral thinking, or moral judgement; it does not deal with moral behaviour although there may well be a link between judgement and behaviour. The paper deals briefly with the work of Piaget and Kohlberg, and then discusses the further studies that have stemmed from both, including those involved in training. But there remains the problem of the variation in level of moral judgements across situations. It looks as if social context and the meaning of the situation to the individual are again of significance, and it could be that social learning as well as cognitive development may each have something to contribute to moral judgement. A very different paper is that by Fischbein. The results obtained by him in respect of the child's grasp of chance and necessity might well be expected with the apparatus used; and the conclusions put forward by him are plausible. But careful thought needs to be given to the study involving the effect of instruction on the quantitative estimation of odds, just as careful thought needs to be given to the results obtained by Fischbein *et al.* (1970). Both the present study and the 1970 study provide interesting data concerning the shifts in strategies brought about by training. But in both studies it remains unclear as to how close the questions set to obtain the results reported, were to the questions set in the teaching. Indeed, these results would be more convincing if a transfer task had been used.

Hagen *et al.* are concerned in the changes in strategies, with age, which children use to improve memory. Studies from pre-school to adolescence show that in respect of memory, there are changes in the way data are acquired, organised and retrieved. This paper discusses the relevant studies, and raises, and to some extent discusses, the fact that young children can perform many activities of memory when encouraged to do so by an adult but rarely do so on their own. The authors presume that the child's awareness of himself as an active, strategy using organism has its own developmental course. It might be added that this presumption is entirely in keeping with Piaget's views of the child's increasing decentration and of his being increasingly able to look in on and monitor his own thinking.

The next five papers deal with pupils in the secondary school years. Piaget makes some concessions to social context and meaning by admitting that adolescents and young adults are likely to be able to apply formal operations in their areas of aptitude and professionalisation.

The paper by Lunzer gives a very critical reappraisal of Piaget's notion of formal reasoning. He discusses the pupil's slowly increasing ability 'to accept a lack of closure'. In simple language this means the slow improvement shown by pupils in weighing the evidence and refraining from coming, at once and in a single step, to an answer which seems clear to them but which is incorrect. Then he deals with multiple interacting systems. Put differently, this means the pupils show ability to move from being able to handle a two-variable system (in which there is one dependent and one independent variable), to being able to handle a three or more variable system in which there are two or more independent variables. In one of the examples given he also deals with the important question of abstraction, suggesting that with age many pupils can reach a third level of abstraction and detach themselves from concrete referents in certain situations. Such skills are likely to be necessary but not sufficient for advanced thinking although one or more of them may not be involved in any one problem. Lunzer also deals with the problem of logical inference, bringing in issues I have already discussed, such as the importance of context; also that the propositional calculus does not adequately model human thinking.

Peel outlines what he considers to characterise the move from elementary to more developed forms of thinking in the secondary school years. In respect of some of the data he discusses the move from being able to particularise to being able to generalise and abstract. Other data refer to the move from descriptive-repetition to imaginative-explanation of data. But as with Piaget's model, Peel is not yet able to indicate under what conditions or in what circumstances the more advanced forms of thinking will be in evidence. Then follows a paper by Rhys describing his work in the field of Geography. Pupil responses were evaluated using a scale whose principal features are given in Table 12.1, and which generally follow in the Peel tradition. He finds, as we all do, that the level of pupil response varies from question to question. The article by Da Silva suggests that when pupils are asked, in the context of historical passages, to elucidate the meaning of an unknown word, they respond by giving an increasingly adequate definition as age increases. Moreover, the improved definitions are linked with increasing intellectual maturity.

The final batch of papers deals with some applications of what is known of cognitive development. Harlen gives some account of the work of the 'Project in Learning Science'. On studying this paper readers may wish to reflect on two points. First, if one is working within a Piagetian tradition there should not be an exact match between task and cognitive development. Rather the task should be at the +1 level to induce conflict as was explained earlier. Second, Harlen proposes goals such as perseverance, open-mindedness, willingness to cooperate and the like. These may indeed be goals. However, even in the restricted context of science lessons the strength of such characteristics is likely to fluctuate for a child according to the meaning the particular tasks have for the child, and to the social situation. Teachers would be likely to give a rating which took into account his variability on a particular characteristic in science lessons, although there is no certainty that such a rating would hold outside of science lessons. Psychologists who are expert in the field of personality assessment (cf. Mischel, 1968) warn us that the idea of highly generalised behavioural consistencies, apart from intelligence, have not been demonstrated, and the concept of broad response predispositions is untenable.

Shayer's article describes the results of an analysis of the conceptual demands of the Nuffield 'O' level Physics course. It suggests that there was more of a match between these demands and the levels of thinking reached by children, especially in the first three years of the course, than had been the case in the first version of the Chemistry course, and in the Biology course.

The final paper in this volume deals with Mathematics learning. It opens with a consideration of some types of learning and of the relationships between the types. Then follows a discussion on how valuable Piagetian theory is for understanding pupil difficulties and pupil progress. At times the theory is, as expected, found to be wanting. Readers may, however, wish to consider the suggestion advanced in respect of the solution of the equation $x + 5 = 8 - 3x$. If x and $3x$ are operated on as generalised numbers, does this demand second degree operations in the Piagetian sense, and hence formal operations?

It will be appreciated that in this chapter no comments have been made on Piaget's work in the field of perception, which is also an aspect of cognition.

Notes

1. Translated from the French.
2. So translated by Sinclair-De-Zwart of the University of Geneva.
3. Translated into English 1964.

References

Baylor, W. (1973), 'An Information Processing Model of Some Seriation Tasks', *Canadian Psychologist*, 14, pp. 167-96

Cole, M. and Scribner, S. (1974), *Culture and Thought* (Wiley, London)

Duckworth, E. (1964), 'Piaget Rediscovered', in Ripple, R.E. and Rockcastle, V.N. (eds.), *Piaget Rediscovered* (Cornell University School of Education)

Ferriero, E. (1971), *Les relations temporelles dans le langage de l'enfant* (Librairie Droz, Geneva)

Fischbein, E. *et al.* (1970), 'Comparison of Ratios and the Chance Concept in Children', *Child Development*, 41, pp. 377-89

Furth, H.G. (1977), 'The Operative and Figurative Aspects of Knowledge in Piaget's Theory', in Geber, B.A. (ed.), *Piaget and Knowing* (Routledge and Kegan Paul, London)

Halford, G.S. (1972), 'The Impact of Piaget on Psychology in the Seventies', in Bodwell, P.C. (ed.), *New Horizons in Psychology*, vol. 2 (Penguin, Harmondsworth)

Hooper, F. and Dihoff, R.E. (1975), *Multidimensional Scaling of Piagetian Task Performance* (Wisconsin Research and Development Centre for Cognitive Learning, Madison)

Hooper, F. and Sipple, T.S. (1975), *An Investigation of Matrix Task, Classificatory and Seriation Abilities* (Wisconsin Research and Development Centre for Cognitive Learning, Madison)

Inhelder, B. and Piaget, J. (1958), *The Growth of Logical Thinking from Childhood to Adolescence* (Routledge and Kegan Paul, London)

Inhelder, B. and Piaget, J. (1964), *The Early Growth of Logic in the Child* (Routledge and Kegan Paul, London)

Inhelder, B., Sinclair, H. and Bovet, M. (1974), *Learning and the Development of Cognition* (Routledge and Kegan Paul, London)

Klahr, D. and Wallace, J.C. (1975), *Cognitive Developments: An Information Processing View* (Lawrence Erlbaum Associates, New York)

Lovell, K. (1961), 'A Follow-up Study of Inhelder and Piaget's *The Growth of Logical Thinking*', *Brit. J. Psychol.*, 52, pp. 143-54

Lovell, K. (1971), 'Some Aspects of the Growth of a Concept of a Function', in Rosskopf, M.F. *et al.* (eds.), *Piagetian Cognitive Development Research and Mathematical Education* (National Council of Teachers of Mathematics, Washington)

Luria, A.R. (1976), *Cognitive Development* (Harvard University Press, London)

Mischel, W. (1968), *Personality and Assessment* (Wiley, London)

Modgil, S. and Modgil, C. (1976), *Piagetian Research: Compilation and Commentary* (National Foundation for Educational Research, Windsor)

Neimark, E.D. (1974), 'Intellectual Development During Adolescence', in *Child Developmental Research*, vol. 4 (University of Chicago Press, London)

Numero special en hommage à Jean Piaget (1974), *Archives de Psychologie*, no. 171, p.44

Piaget, J. (1936), *The Origins of Intelligence in Children* (Routledge and Kegan Paul, London, translated into English 1953)

Piaget, J. (1937), *The Construction of Reality in the Child* (Routledge and Kegan Paul, London, translated into English 1955)

Piaget, J. (1947), *The Psychology of Intelligence* (Routledge and Kegan Paul, London, translated into English 1950)

Piaget, J. (1950), 'Introduction à l'epistemologie genetique, II. La pensée physique' (Presses Universitaires de France, Paris)

Piaget, J. (1953), *Logic and Psychology* (Manchester University Press, Manchester)

Piaget, J. (1960), 'The General Problems of the Psychobiological Development of the Child', in Tanner, J.M. and Inhelder, B. (eds.), *Discussions in Child Development*, vol. 4 (Tavistock Publications, London)

Piaget, J. (1963), 'Le langage et les operations intellectuelles', in J. de Ajuriaguerra *et al.* (eds.), *Problemes de psycho-linguistique* (Presses Universitaires de France, Paris)

Piaget, J. (1970a), *Genetic Epistemology* (Columbia University Press)

Piaget, J. (1970b), 'Piaget's Theory', in Mussin, P. (ed.), *Manual of Child Psychology*, vol. 1 (Wiley, London)

Piaget, J. (1971), *Structuralism* (Routledge and Kegan Paul, London)

Piaget, J. (1975), *L'equilibration des structures cognitive* (Presses Universitaires de France, Paris)

Piaget, J. (1976), 'On Correspondence and Morphisms', *The Genetic Epistemologist* (May issue)

Piaget, J. (1977), *The Grasp of Consciousness* (Routledge and Kegan Paul, London)

Piaget, J. and Inhelder, B. (1969), *The Psychology of the Child* (Routledge and Kegan Paul, London)

Piaget, J. *et al.* (1968a), *Epistemologie et psychologie de l'identité* (Presses Universitaires de France, Paris)

Piaget, J. *et al.* (1968b), *Epistemologie et psychologie de la fonction* (Presses Universitaires de France, Paris)

Riegel, K.F. and Rosenwald, G.C. (1976) (eds.), *Structure and Transformations: Developmental and Historical Aspects* (Wiley, London)

Siegler, R.S. (1977), 'Formal Operational Reasoning', *The Genetic Epistemologist* (October issue)

Sinclair-De-Zwart, H. (1967), *L'acquisition du langage et développement de la pensée sous-systèmes linguistiques et opérations concrètes* (Dunod, Paris)

Thomas, H.L. (1975), 'The Concept of Function', in Rosskopf, M.F. (ed.), *Children's Mathematical Concepts* (Teachers College Press, London)

Tough, J. (1977), *The Development of Meaning* (George Allen and Unwin, London)

Tulkin, S.R. and Konner, M.J. (1973), 'Alternative Conceptions of Human Functioning', *Human Development*, 16, pp. 33-52

Wason, P.C. (1977), 'The Theory of Formal Operations', in Geber, B.A. (ed.), *Piaget and Knowing* (Routledge and Kegan Paul, London)

Wason, P.C. and Johnson-Laird, P.N. (1972), *Psychology and Reasoning: Structure and Content* (Batsford, London)

2 PIAGET'S PSYCHOLOGY IN PRACTICE

Jan Smedslund

Source: *Br. J. Educ. Psychol.*, 47 (1977), pp. 1-6.

Summary. As a result of eight years' experience of Piagetian research and subsequent work as a practising psychologist, certain aspects of Piaget's theories are criticised. In particular the existential status of operatory structures, the relation between logicality and understanding, and the representativeness of the tasks are questioned. Piagetian theory is seen as forcing the psychologist to adopt an artificially detached and one-sidedly cognitive attitude towards children, and to focus interest entirely on very abstract aspects of performance. While accepting the historical importance of Piaget's contributions, it is argued that the limitations and constraints implicit in the theory seriously threaten its usefulness in practical situations.

Introduction

In this paper I will regard the psychology of Piaget not primarily as it is embodied in books or articles, but as leading to a form of practice involving mainly certain types of diagnostic encounter with children. In other words, I will be primarily concerned with what Piagetian psychologists *do*, rather than with how they write and talk *about* things. Starting from a consideration of this practice, I will then proceed to draw certain theoretical conclusions.

My first encounter with Piagetian psychology in practice occurred in the attic of École International in Geneva in the autumn of 1957. I still remember vividly the excitement of being free to *converse* with my subjects and particularly being free to ask for their *explanations*. As a well trained experimental psychologist I had up to that time been mainly confined to marks on sheets of paper as my data. Given my empiricist background I was also much intrigued and impressed by the children's apparent belief in the *necessity* of certain relations, and in their later dealings with what is merely *possible*. Altogether, I felt somehow liberated from a metatheoretical straitjacket. Some, but not all, of the discrepancy between what I felt to be legitimate research interests and the phenomena of my everyday life was removed.

Including my year in Geneva, I spent altogether about eight years doing research within the Piagetian framework. During that time I visited and worked in between 50 and 70 schools, kindergartens and nursery schools in Switzerland, USA, and Norway. More than 1,400 children participated in my published experiments and I saw hundreds of others during informal explorations and pilot studies.

Very gradually, I became aware of what I think are some major weaknesses inherent in this research tradition, which restrict its usefulness for practical purposes. As this became clear to me, I left the Piagetian theoretical framework and moved on towards other modes of understanding. I take this occasion to try to summarise very briefly both my main criticisms of Piaget's psychology as a type of practice, and those aspects of this practice which I still regard as valuable.

Critique of Piagetian Practice

In my work with children I eventually came to wonder about three aspects of our encounters, namely the existential status of Piagetian operatory structures, the relation between logicality and understanding, and the representativeness of the tasks. In other words, I became concerned about what I now see as respectively some ontological, epistemological and pragmatic aspects of Piaget's position.

The Existential Status of Piagetian Operatory Structures

My conversations and dealings with children never quite convinced me that their behaviour could be adequately described as reflecting the presence or absence of certain operatory structures. Partly, this was a matter of intuitive impression. I found that I could not deal with the children as if they had such operatory structures in the same natural and confident way that I dealt with them as being conscious, as perceiving, thinking and feeling, and utilising the words of everyday language. The preoccupation with structure and the distinction between form and content alienated me from my subjects, just as did the artificiality of the tasks, to be discussed later.

As I accumulated experimental data and read the publications of others, my doubts further increased. The empirical evidence did not provide much direct support for the existence of operatory structures. All kinds of discrepancies crop up with children of all ages and with adults, and with all kinds of concepts and structures. A child behaves in one way in one situation and in another way in another situation which may appear strictly equivalent to the first situation as far as task structure is concerned. In general, logical task structure does not seem to be a good predictor of behaviour across situational variations. This does not apply only to children but to adults as well. (See, for example, Wason and Johnson-Laird, 1972, and Wason, 1976.)

In Piaget's system the concept of horizontal decalage and resistance of the situation is invoked to explain such discrepancies. This concept has a relatively feeble explanatory power, since there are few generally reliable indicators of degree of resistance of new situations to an alleged operatory structure. Nevertheless, Piaget seems to hold some hope for future developments in this area (Piaget, 1962).

However, my objections to Piaget's logical formalism had deeper roots than the sense of alienation from the children that it brought me, and the weak and inconclusive experimental support it could muster. I became increasingly uneasy with the conception of operations as internalised versions of certain very general sensory-motor acts. The act of uniting or bringing together is such an act as well as its opposite, the act of separation or bringing apart. The assumption of such very general actions seems to reflect an *a priori* ontological position of *conceptual realism*. There are two main symptoms of this in Piaget's writings. The first is his treatment of resistance of the object or situation as a real psychological factor. One can only speak of resistance in this context if one presupposes the existence of that which is resisted, namely, the operatory structure. The other symptom is the terminology in which the operative structures are described. There are said to exist only a few of these structures, such as the additive and multiplicative 'groupings' of classes and relations. Each of one of them, such as *the* additive 'grouping' of classes, is supposed to be activated in all those infinitely numerous situations which have the corresponding structure, but nothing else, in common. If the child does not behave in accordance with the structure, this is explained by assuming too strong resistance from the situation.

Piaget's assumption of the existence of such purely structural entities as the additive grouping of classes, etc., is unacceptable to me, because it implies that human beings can function abstractly, i.e. out of context and independently of content. Everyday experience, as well as numerous experiments, show that this is not the case.

The alternative to Piaget would be to regard only children's concrete activities in concrete situations as real. This would involve no distinction between form and content and would eliminate the need for a concept of resistance, since there would be nothing to resist. The explanation of why the child behaves in a given way in a given situation would have to be *historical*. An example of this was a little boy in one of my pilot studies who failed in most of the tasks, but was superb in the task of measuring length. The boy's father turned out to be a carpenter, and the boy had been allowed to watch and help his father many times.

Piaget's theory characterises children of various ages on the basis of purely structural criteria. What generalised descriptions of children can be produced if one takes an alternative position? The answer is that one can predict the sequence of many acquisitions (*a*) from knowledge of the organisation of the various tasks (some skills and concepts are presupposed by other skills and concepts, etc.), and (*b*) from knowledge of the institutionalised sequences of instruction in a given culture. Prediction of characteristics of children of various ages across cultures has to be very uncertain, and rely on whatever general similarities in experiences there may be and perhaps on some general characteristics of maturation linked with the species.

In summary, I gradually came to regard Piaget's abstract formalism as counterintuitive, as somewhat alienating in practice, and as without sufficient scientific foundation.

The Relation between Logicality and Understanding

During the prolonged debates about criteria for the presence or absence of certain structures, notably conservation and transitivity (for references, see Smedslund, 1969), I came to recognise a problem which seems to have no satisfactory solution within Piagetian psychology. In order to decide whether a child is behaving logically or not, one must take for granted that he has correctly understood all instructions and terms involved. On the other hand, in order to decide whether or not a child has correctly understood a given term or instruction, one must take for granted that the child is behaving logically with respect to the implications which constitute his understanding. The correct understanding of a given message is checked by observing agreement or disagreement with respect to what is equivalent to, implied by, contradicted or irrelevant to the message (Smedslund, 1970). Hence, one must presuppose logicality in such respects. There is a circular relation between logicality and understanding, each one presupposing the other, and this constraint forces the researcher to make a choice of which one to take for granted and which one to study.

I gradually came to realise that the only defensible position is always to presuppose logicality in the other person and always to treat his understanding of given situations as a matter for empirical study. From this point of view, people are always seen as logical (rational) given their own premises, and hence behaviour can, in principle, always be understood. This also applies to small children, foreigners and psychotics. The opposite position, namely, always taking understanding for granted and always treating logicality as a matter of empirical study, is taken by no one. However, an intermediate inconsistent position seems to be characteristic of much academic psychology including the Piagetian variant.

Sometimes understanding seems to be the focus of study and logicality is taken for granted and sometimes the opposite seems to be the case. Only when presence or absence of logicality is studied and understanding is taken for granted, does it become legitimate to describe children as 'non-conservers', adults as 'mad', foreigners as 'inconsistent and self-contradictory', and so on. However, it is seldom recognised clearly that such decisions about logicality presuppose that one understands properly and fully the meanings of the subject's various expressions, or that checks on such understanding again presuppose logicality on the part of the subject.

It is possible and intuitively plausible always to presuppose logicality, whereas it is clearly absurd to presuppose understanding. Intermediate positions are untenable because they have no rules for when to presuppose understanding and when to presuppose logicality, and furthermore, they always lead to infinite regressions with no rules for when to stop.

As a result of this reasoning, when I meet a small child I always take for granted that, within his limited sphere of activity and given his own premises, he is logical, and my problem is to understand what his expressions mean, and hence to grasp his existential situation. In so far as Piagetian psychologists focus on logicality as a variable (e.g. conserver or non-conserver) and give only peripheral attention to the problem of determining children's understanding of instructions and situations, I think they are making an epistemological error and are out of step with everyday human life as well as with all useful psychological practice. It may be objected that Piaget is not really denying the logicality of children at any stage, but is merely studying the various *forms* of logic they have attained. However, it is a matter of historical record that children who failed on tasks were often simply described as non-logical, and that the problem of criteria of understanding has received relatively scant attention in Piagetian literature.

The Representativeness of the Tasks

During my research work I gradually came to recognise that I presented the children with tasks that were entirely new to them and that were quite atypical compared with their normal everyday activities (Smedslund, 1966). The closest connection of these tasks with anything in children's lives was with mathematics and natural science as taught in the school systems of the technologically advanced world. It is commonly and only half jokingly said that even psychological researchers are afraid of going to Geneva because they fear they may fail on some of the tasks that the older children are given. The closed world of the school system with its competitive ideology of bookish knowledge and its emphasis on a certain conception of 'intelligence' is in many ways controversial and may be accused of neglecting other important aspects of living. As an adjunct to this system, Piagetian psychology, therefore, has some potentially questionable *political* and *practical* implications. More specifically, it may be seen as supporting a one-sidedly intellectualistic view of life and as maintaining the prestige of abstract formalism. This is true even though Piaget's psychology also has contributed new impulses to education, especially by its emphasis on *constructivism*.

Working as a practising psychologist with children's problems in a real world, I have come to experience very strongly the irrelevance of much of my Piagetian background. Major features of children's environment such as brutality, rejection, lack of contact, jealousy, lack of consistency, double communication, dependency, and in general all kinds of evil inter-actional circles dominate the picture and determine what action is to be taken. Performance and interest in school work and in theoretical tasks of the kinds favoured by Piaget, are linked in various ways with the child's family and cultural background but are also frequently strikingly unrelated to the degree of sophistication with which he behaves in his world outside the classroom. The touching and often quite complex philosophical reflections of children who fail at school and who would no doubt fail on the age-relevant Piagetian tasks, have made me very careful indeed when it comes to judging a child's capacity and potentialities. Actually, I think that the Piagetian tradition shares with the rest of academic psychology the unfortunate tendency to attribute success and failure on tasks to characteristics of the person as such instead of to characteristics of the person-in-his-total-life-situation (see Ichheiser, 1970, especially chapter 5).

In conclusion, the lack of representativeness of the tasks relative to the total *Lebenswelt* of the child is one of the reasons why Piagetian psychology is relatively useless for practical purposes. In addition, the bias towards abstract formalistic skills also has questionable political implications.

Lasting Contributions to Psychological Practice

The preceding negative evaluations explain, at least partly, why I have moved away from the Geneva tradition. Yet, the picture would be very incomplete if I did not mention at least some of the teachings of Piaget which I have brought with me, and which I regard as valid and valuable. Before I do this, let me add that I do not pretend to be in any way comprehensive in my comments. Piaget obviously is one of the giants in the history of psychology and his contributions are of an order that cannot be dealt with adequately by one person in a brief article. Let me just summarise

a few of the points that appear central from the point of view of psychological practice, in addition to the tremendous increments in factual
knowledge of children, especially in Western societies in our time that
Piaget has instigated.

(1)   I cherish Piaget's view of the interplay between assimilation and
accommodation and his constructivist position which is quite compatible
with the *hermeneutic* spiral and with the conception of a *dialectical*
psychology. It also implies an outright rejection of the still prevalent view
that psychologists gather objective and theoretically neutral data.

(2)   I believe that Piaget's support of the ancient *'méthode clinique'*
made possible most of his contributions and was an important step away
from the rigid objectivism of the traditional laboratory. It was also compatible with a recognition that the data of psychology are acquired
through acts of *communication* with a shared meaning basis presupposed.

(3)   Piaget's analysis of the notions of *centration* and *decentration*,
especially as they apply to interpersonal relations, is undoubtedly a fundamental and lasting contribution. The fruitfulness of these concepts is
especially clearly displayed in the recent analysis of Haavind and
Hartmann (1976) of the strategies of mothers as teachers and of their
children as learners.

(4)   In my view, Piaget's emphasis on the mode of *implication*, and
hence on *necessity, possibility, negation*, etc., is of crucial importance. It
underlines the role of the *subject* in psychology and rejects behaviourism's
view of man as *object*. Implication exists *for* someone, not as an objective
fact.

(5)   Finally, Piaget's accentuation of the role of *organisation* of the
person's activity is profoundly important. This leads to the characterisation of activity in terms of strategies, rather than in terms of specific
linkages between behaviour and elements in the environment. What
characterises a child, an adult layman or a professional psychologist is
not only the specific knowledge and specific skills they have, but also the
way in which they have internalised, organised and reflected upon this
knowledge and these skills. However, I do not agree with Piaget in describing organisation as approximations to formal logical structures, rather
I think organisation of behaviour should be described concretely in terms
of ordinary language and with no distinction between form and content.
Examples of general strategies described in this way would be, for
example, 'in dangerous situations, think before you act', 'in order to
control a person's behaviour, manipulate the consequences of this
behaviour', etc. Examples of therapeutic strategies described in ordinary

language are given in Smedslund (1973).

Conclusion

I have tried to describe very briefly some main points in my current evaluation of Piaget's psychology. I probably owe more to Piaget than to any other single psychologist, yet I have become increasingly critical of his theoretical system. Working with children during my Piagetian period I felt constrained to be detached, one-sidedly cognitive and entirely focused upon certain very abstract aspects of performance. What mattered to me then were the formal logical structures rather than the concrete living children in their total life situations. I tended to ignore the artificiality of the tasks and I was oblivious of the political implications of my work as supporting a one-sidedly intellectualistic and school-centred ideology. I doubt that a practitioner can be a useful psychologist if he remains wholly within that tradition. Piaget has contributed a wealth of brilliant and penetrating insights, but they must be incorporated into a view of psychology which can be lived and practised rather than merely written and talked about in academic settings.

Acknowledgements I am indebted to Karsten Hundcide for many valuable comments.

References

Haavind, H. and Hartmann, E. (1976), 'Mothers as teachers and their children as learners', unpublished manuscript, Institute of Psychology, University of Bergen, Norway.

Ichheiser, G. (1970), *Appearances and Realities: Misunderstanding in Human Relations*, San Francisco: Jossey-Bass.

Piaget, J. (1962), Introduction to Laurendau, M. and Pinard, A., *Causal Thinking in the Child. A Genetic and Experimental Approach*, New York: International University Press.

Smedslund, J. (1966), 'Les origines sociales de la decentration', in Bresson, F. and Mont-Mollin, Mde (eds.), *Psychologie et Epistémologie Génétiques*, Paris: Dunod.

Smedslund, J. (1969), 'Psychological diagnostics', *Psychol. Bull.*, 71, 237-48.

Smedslund, J. (1970), 'Circular relation between understanding and logic', *Scand. J. Psychol.*, 11, 217-19.

Smedslund, J. (1973), 'The heuristics of interpersonal transaction: A strategy for group work', work notes on small groups (no. 8). Mimeographed report, Institute of Psychology, University of Oslo.

Wason, P.C. (1976), 'The theory of formal operations – a critique', unpublished manuscript.

Wason, P.C. and Johnson-Laird, P.N. (1972), *The Psychology of Reasoning: Structure and Content*, London: Batsford.

SECTION TWO: THE PRIMARY YEARS: THEORETICAL AND EXPERIMENTAL

Introduction

There are six articles in this section, all concerned with research into various aspects of the cognitive development of children of primary school age, that is from four to eleven or twelve years old. Three of the articles go beyond this age range as well, as their concern is with development throughout the entire school period, but even in these cases the emphasis is still on the younger children.

The first two articles are both about infant-school children, aged from four to around six or seven. Both begin with a consideration of Piagetian experiments, and then continue with a critique of these and some further experiments designed by the authors in order to clarify the issues arising from their critiques. The focus of Susan Carey's article is the Piagetian work on the conservation of liquids. She argues for a closer look at the transitional period immediately prior to full conservation, and that an analysis of the reasons that children give for the judgements they make indicates that there are a number of identifiable subskills involved. In the course of her discussion of this, she suggests that a useful parallel can be drawn between the development of cognitive skills and motor skills, in that she sees both as involving a number of subskills which may be mastered in any order, and that in each instance all the relevant subskills must be co-ordinated before the overall skill is attained. Peter Bryant's article consists of a detailed examination of young children's ability or inability to make transitive inferences, that is, for example, whether when they know that Susan is taller than John and John is taller than Mark, they can automatically conclude that Susan is necessarily taller than Mark. Piaget's experiments on transitivity led him to the view that four and five year olds often cannot make such inferences. Bryant describes a series of experiments of his own which lead him to think that such children can reason in this way, provided that they can remember the necessary information.

The third article in this section is written by Efraim Fischbein, and is concerned with the development of the understanding of probability and chance. The Piagetian work on this is examined and a number of comments and criticisms are made. The whole article is to some extent informed by Fischbein's thesis that quite young children do have an intuitive

43

grasp of probabilistic concepts which their education does not always foster.

The fourth article is essentially an overview of the cognitive developmental approach to the study of moral development. In it Derek Graham considers Piaget's early work on this and the comments that have been made by other researchers in the light of their own investigations. He gives most space to Kohlberg's extension and refinement of the original Piagetian stages in moral development, together with some views on this.

The development of memory is the theme of the fifth article, written by J.W. Hagen and his colleagues. It is an overview of a wide range of experimental work on aspects of memory such as acquisition strategies, organisational and retrieval strategies, and the degree to which the child is aware of various memory characteristics. In the research they describe there is evidence of a number of developmental trends in all these areas.

This section concludes with an article by Piaget's long-standing collaborator, Bärbel Inhelder, and two of her colleagues. It is a chapter from a book whose theme is how conservation concepts can most usefully be trained and its thesis is that the secret of successful training is to build on the conservation concepts that a child has already grasped in such a way as to demonstrate to him the inadequacy of his pre-conservation judgements in the case of the concept to be trained. Thus if a child conserves number but not length, the inadequacy and inconsistency of his length judgements can be highlighted by using lengths made up of the same number of matches placed end to end, so that judgements based on number are also possible. In this way the inconsistency of his length judgements is brought home to the child and he realises that length is also conserved. This example is developed much more fully in the article.

3 COGNITIVE COMPETENCE

Susan Carey

Source: Chapter 3 in K. Connolly and J.S. Bruner (eds.), *The Growth of Competence* (Academic Press, 1974).

My purpose in this paper is to discuss the consequences of early competence in problem solving for the later cognitive and social achievements of a child. A distinction must be made between *overall* cognitive competence and *particular* cognitive achievements. The aim stated above implies that there *is* such a thing as the former — that general cognitive competence exists. I know much more about the latter, about how a child comes to master particular problems. I will therefore begin by outlining a theory of this process (A Model of Problem Solving in Early Childhood). This will provide a basis for discussing general competence in problem solving from the point of view of a child's early experience (General Competence and Early Experience).

A Model of Problem Solving in Early Childhood

I believe that a theory of the acquisition of motor skills provides the basic outlines of a theory of the acquisition of particular cognitive achievements. Such a theory of skill acquisition has been sketched by a number of authors (Bernstein, 1967; Connolly, 1973; Elliott and Connolly, 1974; Welford, 1968). The particular formulation that has influenced me most is Jerome Bruner's (Bruner, 1969), but all these theories have many common features. They all agree that skills are goal-directed and therefore any model must include means/end analyses. Skills are analysable into constituents and one of the problems in the performance of a skill is the combination of its constituents. The learning of new skills involves learning new constituents, perfecting them through practice (Bruner's 'modularization'), and the learning of new combinations. An essential component of Bruner's description of skill is that the modularization of components is a prerequisite for their combination in sequences of skilled activity. This implies that sometimes we should find *preadaptive* constituents; that is, elements of skills which have *not yet* been incorporated into successful sequentially organised acts. This is indeed the case (Bruner and Koslowski, 1972).

In order to show how such a theory of skill applies to cognitive competence, I will use the example of Piaget's conservation of quantity. Nobody

45

can deny that conservation is a cognitive achievement; furthermore, it has the dubious advantage of extreme complexity, thereby providing a framework from which to emphasize different aspects.

The basic phenomenon is this: equal quantities of water are poured into two identical beakers and one is then poured into a different shaped beaker

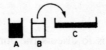

The child is then asked 'Do A and C have the same amount to drink in them, or does A have more or does C have more?' A young child, a non-conserver, maintains that C has less to drink than A. The same child, when older, judges that the two quantities are equal. It is this cognitive achievement that I want to relate to the achievement of motor skills. In order to do so, I must describe the task as the child sees it and identify its possible constituents. There are several ways in which this could be done, several levels of task description. Here, let us assume that the child's problem is answering the questions the experimenter asks. The units of analysis are each of the child's answers, each justification he gives, each prediction he makes. The constituents of these tasks are those aspects of the situation which the child takes as relevant in generating his answer.[1] What *is* relevant to any particular judgement? The correct task analysis yields at least two constituents, whether the quantities were equal or not to start with and whether any liquid had been added or subtracted during the pouring. The child, of course, may be basing his judgements on a different analysis of the task; he may think that other information is relevant, for example, relative water levels. Evidence for what he thinks is relevant can be found in the pattern of his judgements in many variations of the task and also in the justification he gives for his judgements. Development consists of changing the task analysis, including more constituents and more interrelationships between them. Granting all this, there are several possible ways in which new constituents could be added. One is that new constituents are added piecemeal, one at a time, in successive complications of the system.

Several years ago Jonckheere, Cromer and I made an observational study. We were interested in whether judgements would be easier if the quantities were, in fact, unequal than if they were equal. Therefore, we included two conditions where water was added or subtracted after the pouring was completed.

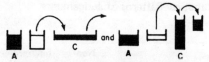

The finding that puzzled me was that several children maintained that A and C still had the same amount to drink. Notice that this finding calls into question these children's *correct* judgements on regular conservation tasks. Perhaps they had only one of the constituents of the correct answer; they knew that the original equality of the liquids was relevant but did not know that the addition or subtraction during pouring was relevant. This suggests that the development from non-conservation to conservation may be as follows:

1. Height alone is taken as relevant for amount judgements.
2. The original equality or inequality is taken as relevant.
3. The transformation (addition, subtraction or neither) is taken as relevant.

Once the child adds constituent 2 to his task analysis, he should no longer rely on constituent 1. Constituents 3 and 2 are not in that same relationship to each other; some children might pick up 2 before 3 and some others 3 before 2.[2] In the pretest of the studies summarized here, I included all cases necessary to demonstrate the piecemeal addition of the relevant constituents. Figure 3.1 shows the hypothetical patterns of judgements consistent with this view of development. The key groups are the intermediates, and the key responses are the false 'same to drink' judgements.

The pretests revealed that there were pure non-conservers and pure conservers. Also, there were intermediates, 15 per cent of whose judgements on tasks II (a and b) and III (a and b) were that A and C had the 'same amount' to drink in them. Thus, these intermediates gave false 'same to drink' judgements and might therefore have had only one of the relevant task analysis constituents.

The patterns made by the intermediates who were tested bear no resemblance to those shown in Figure 3.1. Not one of the twenty who were tested made correct 'same to drink' judgements systematically. There was no evidence for a piecemeal addition of the relevant constituents. Rather, the intermediate children had the same constituents as the conservers; they simply were not able to combine them into correct judgements and arguments. The chaotic patterns of judgements shown by all intermediates (correct judgements, judgements based on height, false

Figure 3.1: Hypothetical Patterns of Judgements

Type of task		Non-conservers, height the constituent	Intermediates, one[1] relevant constituent	Intermediates, one[2] relevant constituent	Full conservers, both relevant constituents
Regular conservation	Ia 	C has more	A = C	A = C	A = C
	Ib 	A has more	A = C	A = C	A = C
Some added or subtracted	IIa 	A has more	A = C	C has more	C has more
	IIb 	C has more	A = C	A has more	A has more
Not the same to start with	IIIa 	C has more	A has more	A = C	A has more
	IIIb 	A has more	C has more	A = C	C has more

a   These intermediates are basing their judgements on the original equality of the water *only*. Thus, they are correct on Tasks I and III, but not on II, when the transformation disturbs the original equality or inequality.

b   These intermediates are basing their judgements on the nature of the transformation *only*. Thus, they are correct on Tasks I and II, but not on III. Mistakes on III are due to the fact that none was added or subtracted does not correctly imply that A and C are equal because A and B were not equal.

'same to drink' judgements consistent with constituent 2 and also false 'same amount to drink' judgements consistent with constituent 3 were all made by each intermediate child) is only a small part of the evidence for this claim.

The child's tasks include justifying his decisions. If the intermediate child differs from the non-conserver in having more constituents in his task analysis and from the conserver in having less, then his justifications should contain more arguments than non-conservers and fewer than conservers. To look at this, we must backtrack and briefly characterize the justifications given by the two extreme groups when they are asked 'How do you know?' after a judgement. If they can think of anything at all to say, non-conservers characteristically mention only one argument — 'because it's higher', 'because it's more' (a reassertion of the judgement) being by far the most common response. In contrast, conservers' justifications are of several types, over half of which contain multiple arguments, as in 'because that one had more to start with and you only poured it. It only looks less because it's in a wider glass'. Among their justifications could be found statements of the two constituents in generating correct judgements, plus appeals to the appearance/reality distinction, suggestions of verification procedures, and explanations for changes in height in terms of width. What of the intermediate children? Their justifications were indistinguishable from the conservers — they showed all types and also gave multiple arguments on over half of their answers. But there was one important difference. In nineteen cases

Example 1:   Judgement. 'C has more to drink.'
             'How do you know?'
             'Because B had more to start with.' (false)

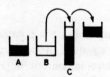

Example 2:   Judgement. 'C has more to drink.'
             'How do you know?'
             'Because you took some out of there.'
             (inconsistent with judgement)

(contributed by thirteen children) the justifications were totally in-appropriate. They were either false as in example 1 or inconsistent as in example 2.

No conserver ever made such bad arguments. Eighty per cent of these false and inconsistent arguments made by intermediates included at least one of the two constituents of the adult task analysis (inappropriately applied, of course). Thus, these children's justifications, as well as their chaotic patterns of judgements, support the view that they know what is relevant to the judgements, but simply are not skilled in putting it together correctly all the time. They do not systematically add constituents to their task analysis in a piecemeal way.

This can lead to very inconsistent behaviour. Intermediates were signi-ficantly more likely to change their judgements than either of the other two groups, both spontaneously, and when given counter-suggestions.[3] Consider the following protocol on the 'check test': Task — pour equal amounts in

Child 31. Poured the juice in the thinner glass a little higher (uninten-tionally). Said would choose the wider glass if thirsty because it had more in it. To equalize, took away some liquid from the thinner glass so they would be exactly the same level. Then said would drink the liquid in the wider glass if thirsty, because it had more. Knew that the water from the wider glass would come higher when both were poured into the identical beakers. Maintained that really the two quantities were the same and one only appeared to be more when both were in the identical glasses.

Such inconsistency is common, but the point I would like to make now is that inconsistency is not a general property of the thinking of a child at a certain age or stage of development. It is task specific. Any child (or adult) would be inconsistent on *some* task which could be devised for him. Such inconsistency is found precisely in those cases where the child or adult knows several things which are relevant to some problem but cannot keep them all straight, or does not know all the relationships between them. For example, the check test is slightly harder than the conservation tasks. A child who passes all the conservation tasks, who is a consistent conserver, may well fail the check test, contradicting himself wildly.

It is important to remember that each intermediate made some correct judgements and some incorrect judgements; gave some valid justifications and some invalid ones. The descriptions I have given of intermediates, in terms of their not being able to combine skilfully the same battery of constituent information that the conservers infer their answers from, is open to two further interpretations. Perhaps the intermediates' right answers are not different from their wrong ones — random combinations of the same basic elements. That is, they know what information is relevant but cannot distinguish the valid inferences in this information from invalid ones. This view emphasizes the differences between intermediates and conservers; the conservers have structured the relevant information differently from the intermediates. This is the Piagetian view; that conservers think that conservation is necessary while intermediates do not (cf. Smedslund, 1961). The alternative view, for which I will present evidence, states that there is no such structural watershed. First of all, the intermediates' reactions to counter-suggestions indicate that although they cannot consistently put the constituents together correctly, they recognize when they have done so. Their wavering at a counter-suggestion occurred only when their responses were incorrect and the counter-suggestions supplied correct judgements and justifications. Like conservers, intermediates never changed a judgement from right to wrong as the result of a counter-suggestion. As a second source of evidence, I would like to describe briefly an experiment which will further elucidate the skill model of cognitive competence.

The question asked in these experiments was what the reactions of children at different conservation levels would be if the water really changed in amount upon being poured into a new glass. What if a thimble-full became a bucketfull, or vice versa? I was interested in the answer to this question for two reasons. First, it provided a non-verbal way of probing for conservation. Perhaps even non-conservers would show surprise at such a violation of conservation. Secondly, it provided a direct test of whether conservers think conservation is necessary in a way that intermediates do not. Evidence for such a difference would be found if intermediates and non-conservers were not surprised when quantities changed, while conservers would indicate that they realize a trick had been played on them. Figure 3.2 shows the three tricks that were performed.

Reactions to the tricks were categorized into three categories — no reaction (level 0), a simple noting that the water level did not come to where it might have been expected (level 1), noting the discrepancy in an excited way, 'That high!', 'What happened?' (level 2). Only the level 2 reactions could be counted as 'surprise'. Figure 3.3 shows that there was very little surprise. The children's reactions to the trick where the water came to the same level in a wider or thinner glass as it had been in the

Figure 3.2: The Three Trick Problems Presented to the Children

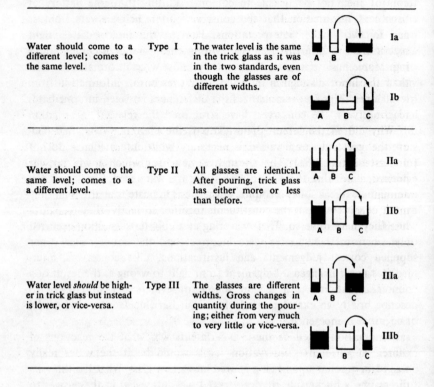

Water should come to a different level; comes to the same level.	Type I	The water level is the same in the trick glass as it was in the two standards, even though the glasses are of different widths.
Water should come to the same level; comes to a a different level.	Type II	All glasses are identical. After pouring, trick glass has either more or less than before.
Water level *should* be higher in trick glass but instead is lower, or vice-versa.	Type III	The glasses are different widths. Gross changes in quantity during the pouring; either from very much to very little or vice-versa.

Figure 3.3: Per Cent Children Showing Each Degree of Surprise to the Four Pourings (Control and Three Tricks)

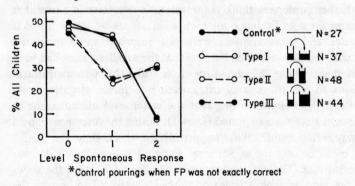

*Control pourings when FP was not exactly correct

standard (Type I trick) were indistinguishable from their reactions to a control pouring (no tricks) where the water level happened not to have been correctly predicted. There was slightly more surprise to the Type II and Type III tricks but even in these cases, 70 per cent of the children's reactions were indistinguishable from their reactions to the control pouring. More important, conservers did not show significantly more surprise than the intermediates. Sixty per cent of the conservers had at least one level 2 reaction; 44 per cent of the intermediates had at least one level 2 reaction.

Why did the conservers, who had correctly judged all six of the tasks on the pretest, accept without reaction the tricks in Figure 3.2? To understand this, it is necessary to look at what the conservers did when presented with these tricks. When asked if there was still the same amount to drink, they said yes there was. Asked to justify their statement, they produced as fine a collection of false and inconsistent justifications as ever produced by the intermediates on the pretest. For instance, several children, upon seeing

said, 'it came higher because it's so much thinner'. Others claimed they saw me add some. Some children denied that the water level was higher; others said the two quantities were still the same because the water level was higher; yet others appealed to the blueness of the water, or the lips on the glasses. This might appear to prove that conservers think conservation is necessary even though they did not show more surprise than the intermediates. But the intermediates also maintained (falsely) that the quantities were still the same (see Figure 3.4)[4] and produced a string of false and inconsistent justifications for their judgements.

These tricks present the children with a conflict between different constituents of the task analysis. First, the quantities were the same to start with and none was added or subtracted (as far as the child could see), and second, appearances dictated unambiguously that the quantities were now different. If any intermediate or conserver were shown the resultant quantities without the history, he would correctly judge the amounts unequal. Figure 3.4 shows that this conflict was not resolved in the same way on all three types of tricks. Type I tricks

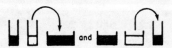

Figure 3.4: Percentage of Subjects Who said the Two still had the Same Amount to Drink on the Three Change Tricks

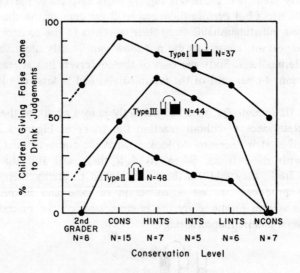

Summary:

78% of all subjects say A and C have the same amount to drink on Type I tricks

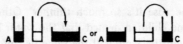

43% of all subjects say A and C have the same amount to drink on Type III tricks

21% of all subjects say A and C have the same amount to drink on Type II tricks

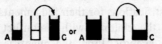

* Differences between 2nd graders and conservers sig. at 0·05 level (Fisher exact test) on Type II tricks only.

Differences between CONS, HINT, INT, LINT/ and NCONS sig. at 0·01 level (Fisher exact test) on Type III trick.

Differences between CONS, HINT, INT, LINT/ and NCONS on Type II trick not significant ($p = 0·11$ Fisher exact).

yielded 'same amount to drink' judgements 78 per cent of the time; Type III tricks

in 43 per cent of all judgements and Type II tricks

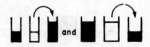

in only 21 per cent of all judgements. This provides us with a puzzle. The actual quantity change and the appearance of inequality was the strongest in Type III tricks – the dimensions of one quantity were greater in both width and height. Why, then, were children more likely to judge the quantities equal in this case than they were when the dimensions of the two quantities differed only in one dimension (Type II tricks). A clue comes from the justifications they gave. Take

as an example. Many children, having judged the quantities equal, bolstered their answer with the argument that C was wider than A and that's why the water came higher! Their reasoning apparently was as follows – C looks more than A, something must account for this difference in appearance. Glass C is different from glass A, it is wider so this difference must account for the difference in appearance of the two quantities. In Type II tricks the two glasses were identical, so this form of reasoning was not available to them. There is nothing which can explain away the apparent change in amount, so in this case the children were less likely to deny that the amounts had changed. A similar argument accounts for the preponderance of 'same to drink' judgements on Type I tricks, e.g.

The intermediates and conservers appealed to the equality of heights in bolstering their judgements that the amounts were equal.

The children were seeking local consistency. They did not immediately see that there had been a trick, so they hung on to anything which would allow them to dismiss the problem, even when they had demonstrated amply in other situations that they knew that water comes lower in wider glasses and that equal heights are not sufficient grounds for a judgement of equal amounts.

There was a difference between conservers and intermediates, an important one. After the child had made a judgement and offered a justification, I continued questioning, pointing out the inconsistencies. For example, on

one child said that the two quantities were the same because they were the same to start with and the quantity in C only looked more. Asked why it looked more, he said it was because the glass was wider. At that point I asked whether water usually comes higher in a wider glass. He said, 'Yes . . . no, I don't think so — Hey, what happened?' This child was a conserver. Conservers were significantly more likely than intermediates to realize that there was something wrong, that there had been a trick, after such a line of questioning. The intermediates saw the contradictions; they often said 'I don't know' when pressed in the above manner, but they were not sure enough of their expectancies to figure out that something impossible had happened.[5]

It is clear that even 'conservers' were 'intermediates' when compared to adults on these problems. Adults immediately see the amounts as having changed in an impossible way. I looked at some second grade[6] 'conservers' who were indistinguishable from my 5-7-year-old 'conservers' on the pretests; their data is also plotted on Figures 3.3 and 3.4. Although they are more like adults than the younger children, even they do not realize that the amounts have changed and that there has been a trick. Seeing that there was a trick was a slow process. The child had to notice that something was wrong, try to explain it away, fail, and draw the conclusion that it was not his fault that he could not explain it away. Only on the last point did the 'conservers' and 'intermediates' differ. The 'intermediates' ' judgements and their initial attempts at understanding what was happening depended upon the same task analysis that the 'conservers' made. They simply were not as sure of each of the components; their expectancies were not as firm, and therefore, they were not able to draw the same conclusions.

Let me return to the skill analogy. I am claiming that making conservation judgements and justifications is a skill, the possible constituents of which are the separable sources of relevant information in the task analysis

— original equality or inequality, the nature of the transformation, relative heights and widths of the liquid, etc. The intermediates had the same constituents as the conservers, they knew what was relevant and what inferences to draw from the relevance; they simply were less skilled in manipulating and integrating these constituents.

It is my contention that many, if not all, cognitive achievements are similar to those described above. One might ask how such intellectual skills differ from motor skills. First of all, the constituents of a motor skill are usually thought of as motoric acts (cf. Bruner's descriptions of the development of reaching). But even clear examples of motor skills require an analysis of the task, independent of the movements the person makes. Consider the game Elliott and Connolly describe (Elliott and Connolly, 1974). Part of the problem for the child is to figure out the two degrees of freedom of the apparatus and to learn to manipulate them simultaneously. Secondly, a more obvious difference between intellectual skills and motor skills is that in most motor skills there is a direct test of inappropriate task analysis or execution of the integrated act — the goal is either realized or it is not; in Elliott and Connolly's case, the ball either goes into the hole or it does not. In the conservation case, how is the child to know whether his analysis of relevant features and the inferences he draws from them is correct or not? Even on this point, there is no complete dichotomy between motor problems and intellectual problems. Most motor skills involve a constant, monitoring, feedback, but intellectual solutions must also ultimately be tested against reality. The constituents of task analysis must ultimately derive from the child's pursuits, his practical problems. Conversely, not all development of motor skills depends upon direct feedback from the environment. Consider a complex motor skill like skiing. Long after a learner is able to make it down a hill without falling, he is distinguishing good Stem Christies from bad ones — the good ones feel right, everything fits. In an intellectual task, such as making conservation judgements, the child's criterion for a good answer is his ability to make everything he thinks relevant consistent with that answer. This criterion, like that of 'feeling right', does not depend upon a constant monitoring feedback.

In the above section, I have described the development of a particular cognitive skill and discussed its relationship to the development of motor skills. How, within this framework, are we to conceive of overall cognitive development? How do we conceive of the cognitive differences between three-year-olds and seven-year-olds? My answer is that age related cognitive differences are separable into two parts, in principle distinguishable from each other. First, there is a maturational component. One can conceive of this component as absolute information processing capacity: a younger child has a shorter memory, can handle fewer constituents at once, etc. The development of this processing space follows from the maturation of the nervous system. The second component is simply a battery of individual skills, bits and pieces of acquired knowledge, that the child has mastered in the way described above. The principles of acquiring these skills are the same no matter how old the person is; my first graders wrestling with the surprise tricks were not so different from a scientist whose head is swimming in confusing data (see Hanson, 1965). This process includes learning new constituents, their modularization, and their concomitant incorporation into larger structured wholes.

There is no doubt that seven-year-olds can solve cognitive problems that three-year-olds cannot solve. Two sources are suggested for the three-year-olds' relatively immature behaviour — first, a relatively limited processing machinery, and second, relatively limited knowledge from which to extract the variables to fit into that machinery. The two sources of immaturity are independent of each other; a child will get better just by getting older, even if he is not given practice which increases or reinforces his knowledge. Within the limits of his processing machinery, he can also be helped by being given practice in the constituent skills.[7] There are several situations where a child performs worse than might be expected which also can be interpreted in terms of an interaction between processing space and knowledge. Elliott and Connolly described a case of a child's grip on a paintbrush showing a lag of over two years when compared with his grip on sticks he uses for some other purpose. Apparently, the requirement of painting with a brush reduces the degrees of freedom he can cope with in this grip (Connolly and Elliott, 1972). Anxiety also seems to reduce available processing space. This is the reason for the practice of familiarizing a child with the tester and the situation before an intelligence test.

The characterization proposed here posits no qualitative cognitive differences between children at different ages. That is, the differences between three-year-olds and seven-year-olds cannot be expressed in terms of the former being pre-operational while the latter are operational, the former being iconic while the latter are symbolic, the former being tolerant of contradictions while the latter are not. Each of these broad distinctions (and many more as well) may well apply to the stages a child goes through in solving a particular problem, but this will be true of all ages. I cannot present here my full arguments for this position; rather let us consider the implications of this view for the following question [. . .] — what effects do early problem solving experiences have on later cognitive functioning?

General Competence and Early Experience

The first question to be considered is whether there is a general problem solving cognitive skill (or set of skills) of which individuals have a differing command. If so, what is the nature of this battery of skills, and does early experience help or hinder its development? Is such experience provided differentially by different social classes? I would argue against there being any such general, overall, cognitive competence correlated with social class. The argument will proceed first by considering and rejecting candidates for such basic skills and then by giving principal reasons to doubt their existence. Finally, the consequences of early competence, or lack of competence, in problem solving will be considered.

What are candidates for the general cognitive skills we seek? I will discuss [two] suggestions that have been made:

1. Basic linguistic capacities which underly all cognitive functioning.
2. General ability in acquiring new skills (according to the theory outlined in the first section). That is, general skill in considering alternatives, structuring a task, integrating multiple constituents, etc. [...]

Intelligence cannot be considered as a basic problem-solving skill. It is the wrong kind of construct, developed as an atheoretical predictive tool. It cannot be analysed into specific, named skills which in turn could be analysed into their constituent skills.[8] Intelligence is not a specific achievement like conservation, English syntax, arithmetic, or walking. I am not denying that there are social class differences in intelligence, nor that these may be important. Rather that the question being asked [...] is whether there are specific basic cognitive achievements which are learned differentially by different people. If there are, one explanation for that difference might be intelligence differences. But, given the proper analysis of these basic skills into their constituents, the theory of skill acquisition outlined in the first section predicts that relative deficiencies in capacity, like processing space, can be compensated for by extra time and practice in the modularization of the constituent skills.

Let us begin with the first candidate — that there are basic differences in the linguistic capacities of different segments of the population. We must distinguish between true linguistic differences in language, in phonetics, syntax or semantics, and other cognitive differences which happen to be reflected in language. Linguistic differences between social classes which are supposed to have far-reaching cognitive implications are usually the latter. Most reduce to the second set of possibilities, type 2 [. . .]

In the study of linguistic differences between children the work of Turner and Pickvance (1970) is important and revealing. They found that, given problems to solve (asked questions) children from higher socio-economic backgrounds express more uncertainty (say they don't know) more often than do those from lower socio-economic backgrounds. The former show that they are aware of more alternatives, can better formulate a problem, and are more likely to ask adults for help. Turner and Pickvance themselves point out that these differences obtain even when 'verbal ability is controlled for'. Thus, they do not think these differences in language reflect true linguistic differences. Indeed, these differences are paradigm examples of the type 2 hypothesis. I believe that Bernstein's distinction between restricted and elaborated codes[†] is yet another example of this sort (Bernstein, 1961).

Working with much younger children, Tough (1970) found that three-year-olds from higher socio-economic backgrounds singled out more qualitatively different aspects of their environment, talked more about cause and effect, than did lower socio-economic three-year-olds matched in IQ and roughly for linguistic output. It is in this area that cognitive and linguistic differences overlap. What a child chooses to talk about reflects his immediate concerns and the degree to which he has structured his world. Vocabulary differentiation similarly reflects his understanding of his world – the modularization of his knowledge. Thus, these results are not simple linguistic differences. I do not want to appear to deny there are social class differences in truly linguistic development, certainly there are (Williams, 1970) [. . .]

However, I see no way that such truly linguistic differences between individuals could form the basis of important differences in cognitive functioning. Rather, there are major reasons to doubt that they could have such a role. First of all, there have now been several studies of the relationship between cognitive development and linguistic development (Carey, 1971; Cromer, 1968; Sinclair-de-Zwart, 1967) which have concluded that conceptual immaturity hampers linguistic development, rather than vice versa. Secondly, most of the phonetic, syntactic and semantic rules of language are mastered by the time a child is six years old; conceptual development never ends. Cazden (1974) and McNeill (1974) discuss the 'transparency' of language to the developing child. The child learning language appears to be learning about the world and picking up his language almost as a by-product. His parents' corrections of his speech are most often corrections of the content of his statements, of their truth or appropriateness, rather than their linguistic form. Complex as the task of formalizing the rules of a natural language is, none the less, the child easily masters it and the small differences in the rate at which individual children do so cannot be the basis of overall cognitive difference among people.

Although I reject truly linguistic differences as a viable possibility for differences in basic cognitive skills, these differences may well be very important to the learning of particular skills. Take learning to read, for example. As in the learning of any skill, learning to read places demands upon available processing space.[9] If a child's linguistic skills are relatively little modularized, then the language which is being read will occupy relatively more of his processing space, thus detracting from the development of reading. Later in this same child's school career, when reading is a source of information his relatively unmodularized reading skills would detract from the processing he would need in order to master the material he is reading. Thus, early truly linguistic differences might be expected to have a snowballing effect on a child's school performance.[10] Since language is like any cognitive achievement, such differences can theoretically be avoided by giving a young child practice in the constituent skills. There is every reason to do so, but that reason is not to prevent the child from 'thinking differently' from other children.

To summarize, I have rejected differences in truly linguistic skills as a candidate for overall, basic, cognitive differences between social classes. Furthermore, I have shown that many 'linguistic' differences that have been found between various groups of people are really examples of my second candidate for basic cognitive differences, overall competence in acquiring skill, to which we now turn. Do people differ in their ability to recognize problems, set cognitive goals for themselves, analyse, structure and modularize constituents? Are these higher order skills acquired more easily by some people than by others? I would argue that there are no differences between people in the process of acquiring skills (except perhaps in extreme pathological cases). Instead the differences that have been found reflect domain specific, local rather than global, developmental differences. Before I present this argument, I would like to give a made-up example (from Elliott and Connolly, 1974) to show the form of a very common and important mistake which I believe permeates the search for basic cognitive differences between people.

Elliott and Connolly described cross-sectional stages found in children's acquisition of motor skill – the skill of manipulating two knobs which tilt a board along two axes to make a ball go diagonally across the board. They pointed out that in the early stages of task analysis, children often expressed their frustration by saying '*it* won't do it'. In later stages, when the child understood the nature of the task (had analysed it in terms of the major constituents), failure was described as '*I* can't do it'. Now, this difference is consistent with the interpretation that the younger children have a great sense of their own powerlessness, while the older children have a sense of mastery of their environment. This difference (certainly a global one) is development – every child presumably goes through a stage of feeling powerless before feeling competent. This appears to be exactly the type of overall development hypothesis that I argued against in the first section of this paper. My position is that such a difference is task specific, it is not an overall stage in a child's development. That is, it reflects competence with respect of the particular task used by Elliott and Connolly. The child who says 'it won't do it' does not have any of the constituents of the task – doesn't have a clue as to how the apparatus works. Thus the 'sense of powerlessness' is an emotional factor caused by a local limitation of skill; it is not a general personality trait of young children. I am certain that I could find a related, slightly more complex, motor skill on which the older children would express their frustration in terms of 'it won't do it'. Furthermore, the problem becomes compounded. According to the theory of skills being proposed here, immature behaviour on a particular task results either from relatively limited processing space or relatively incomplete modularization of the constituent skills. One could assume that the children in lower class families are less comfortable with strange adults and this detracts from the processing space available to them in the Elliott and Connolly task. Or assume that they mature more slowly, or that they simply have had less experience with fine manipulatory toys, so they have less command of the constituent skills. All of these assumptions are reasonable. It follows that lower socio-economic status children will perform in a more immature way on this task than upper or middle socio-economic status children of the same age. Then, the former children will be more likely to say 'it won't do it', than the latter, who will be more likely to say 'I can't do it'. From this, our made-up experimenter would conclude that the poor have a greater sense of powerlessness than do the comfortably well off. This inference is doubly flawed. It is flawed because the general developmental difference was not an overall stage difference and it is flawed because the very same lower socio-economic status children in a few months or a year would act exactly as the upper and middle socio-economic status children do on that same task. A general sense of powerlessness cannot be attributed to lower socio-economic status children on the basis of single task evidence of this sort — it is important to check first that the difference found is not part of the developmental stages all children go through with respect to that task.[11] I hope that the form of this argument is clear, because I believe that many so-called general differences between social class are of this type [. . .]

The model of skill acquisition presented in the first section is a very weak descriptive theory. It applies to motor and cognitive achievements made by the developing child (and developed adult) minute by minute throughout his life. It simply seems unlikely to me that people can differ in functioning so fundamentally. I envisage the model of skill acquisition presented in the first section to be as basic to a cognitive theory as the concept 'reinforcement' is to behaviourism. To postulate that people differ in this functioning is anathema to me, as the postulation that people differ in their susceptibility to the law of effect[†] would be anathema to a behaviourist.[12] The skill of problem solving — that is, the skills of analysing problems, setting subgoals, making new combinations of practised constituents, etc. — is the wrong kind of theoretical construct in terms of which to expect differences among people. This is especially true because there is a perfectly sensible and simpler explanation for apparent differences in problem solving skills and that is differences in the battery of problems which have already been solved, differences in the battery of modularized skills. However, the practical consequences of both interpretations seem to me to be identical [. . .]

I have argued here that there are no basic linguistic or cognitive differences in people's problem solving or thinking. Much of the argument may have seemed of hair-splitting theoretical interest only, but I believe that it has important practical consequences. If one believes that the poor think differently from the rich because of some simple difference in linguistic or cognitive skills suitable for enshrining in a catchphrase such as Bernstein's restricted *v.* elaborated code, then one would set oneself the goal of preventing that difference in linguistic or cognitive skills from arising. I believe such approaches would prove fruitless. I have tried to show that the search for such fundamental differences in ways of problem solving is doomed to failure, at least in our present state of theorizing about cognitive functioning. We do know enough about the mechanisms involved in learning particular skills to design structured and supportive environments for the child's pre-school experiences; at present this is where our efforts should be concentrated.

Notes

1.   Since the act is generating a judgement, strictly speaking, the constituents – the child's *noticing* that water levels are different or *relating* width to height – are the actual components of that act. But it is simpler to talk as if the constituents are part of the situation.

2.   Evidence for the child's having constituent 3 but not 2 would be false 'same to drink' judgements in the following situation: the two quantities start out *unequal* but none is added or subtracted

If the child says A = C in amount, he must lack constituent 2.

3.   The standard Piagetian testing procedure includes a counter-suggestion to both correct and incorrect judgements. 'Another little boy told me that they are really the same because they were the same in there and we only poured it. Was he right?' . . . 'How could you convince him?'

4.   For the purposes of Figure 3.4, the intermediates were broken up into three sub-divisions according to how many of the questions on the pretest they got right. LINTs (low intermediates) got only one or two judgements of the six pretest tasks right. Even they think conservation is as 'necessary' as do conservers.

5.   My criterion for 'surprise' was not too stringent. All children in this sample, including non-conservers, realized that there was a trick at some point in the procedure. If they had not seen it by the end of the three tricks described above, they were shown a whole pitcher being poured into a glass whose level did not change, and then water going up and down by itself.

6.   Second grade is between ages 7-8 years.

7.   All the experiments which succeed in teaching four-year-olds to solve Piagetian concrete operational problems (e.g. Bryant and Trabasso, 1971) can be seen as examples of the latter type of improvement.

8.   There are many theories of the structure of intelligence in terms of hierarchy of capacities. But a capacity is different from a skill; a skill is content full, not content free. One can have an arithmetical capacity without knowing arithmetic; one cannot have skill in arithmetic without having practised and learned (as in the first section) multiple constituent arithmetical skills.

9.   The extreme linguistic simplicity of first texts, written in language appropriate to the speech of much younger children, is an educational device based on these considerations. Just as when a child needs to paint with a brush, his grip of it regresses a few years, so when he must read language, it is best to provide him with language modularized for years, so that the language itself makes no demands on his attention or efforts.

10.   I am indebted to Courtney Cazden for this argument.

11.   I want to re-emphasize that this is a made-up example; Elliott and Connolly did not themselves draw any such inferences from their example. I am using this as a vehicle to draw attention to an important criticism.

12.   A behaviourist would allow individual differences in the effect of a single reinforcer, but would require that all the behaviour of every person be some function of his past reinforcement history.

References

Ainsworth, M.D.S. and Bell, S.M., 1974, 'Mother-infant interaction and the development of competence', in K. Connolly and J.S. Bruner (eds.), *The Growth of Competence*, London, Academic Press.

Bee, H.L., Van Egeren, L.F., Streissguth, A.P., Nyman, B.A. and Leckie, M.S., 1969, 'Social class differences in maternal teaching strategies and speech patterns', *Develop. Psychol.*, 1, 726-34.

Bernstein, B., 1961, 'Social class and linguistic development: a theory of social learning', in A.H. Halsey, J. Floud, and C.A. Anderson (eds.), *Education economy and society*, Free Press, Glencoe, Illinois.

Bernstein, N., 1967, *The co-ordination and regulation of movements*, Pergamon Press, Oxford.

Bruner, J.S., 1969, 'Origins of problems solving strategies in skill acquisition', presented at the XIX International Congress of Psychology, London, July 1969.

Bruner, J.S., 1973, 'Nature and uses of immaturity', in K. Connolly and J.S. Bruner (eds.), *The Growth of Competence*, London, Academic Press.

Bruner, J.S. and Koslowski, B., 1972, 'Visually preadapted constituents of manipulatory action', *Perception*, 1, 3-14.

Bryant, P.E. and Trabasso, T., 1971, 'Transitive inferences and memory in young children', *Nature* (Lond.), 232, 456-8.

Carey, S.E., 1971, 'Are children little scientists with false theories of the world?', unpublished Ph.D. thesis, Harvard University.

Cazden, C., 1974, 'Two paradoxes in the acquisition of language structure and function', in K. Connolly and J.S. Bruner (eds.), *The Growth of Competence*, London, Academic Press.

Coleman, J.S. *et al.*, 1966, *Equality of educational opportunity*, US Department of Health, Education and Welfare, Office of Education, Washington, DC.

Connolly, K., 1973, 'Factors influencing the learning of manual skills by young children', in R.A. Hinde and J.S. Hinde (eds.), *Constraints on learning: limitations and predispositions*, Academic Press, London.

Connolly, K. and Elliott, J., 1972, 'The evolution and ontogeny of hand function', in N. Blurton Jones (ed.), *Ethological studies of child behaviour*, Cambridge University Press, Cambridge.

Cromer, R.F., 1968, 'The development of temporal reference during the acquisition of language', unpublished Ph.D. thesis, Harvard University.

Elliott, J. and Connolly, K., 1974, 'Hierarchical structure in skill development', in K. Connolly and J.S. Bruner (eds.), *The Growth of Competence*, London, Academic Press.

Greenfield, P.M., 1969, 'Goal as environmental variable in the development of intelligence', presented at Conference of 'Contributions to Intelligence', University of Illinois, Urbana.

Haggstrom, W., 1964, 'The power of the poor', in F. Fiessman, J. Cohen and A. Pearl (eds.), *Mental health of the poor*, Free Press, Glencoe, Illinois.

Hanson, N.R., 1965, *Patterns of discovery*, Cambridge University Press, Cambridge.

Hess, R.D. and Shipman, V., 1965, 'Early experience and socialization of cognitive modes in children', *Child Dev.*, 36, 869-86.

Klause, R. and Gray, S., 1969, 'The early training project for disadvantaged children: a report after five years', *Monog. Soc. Child Dev.*, 33.

Labov, W., 1970, 'The logic of non-standard English', in F. Williams (ed.), *Language and poverty*, Markham, Chicago.

McNeill, D., 1974, 'How to resolve two paradoxes and escape a dilemma: comments on Dr Cazden's paper', in K. Connolly and J.S. Bruner (eds.), *The Growth of Competence*, London, Academic Press.

Moffett, J., 1968, *Teaching the universe of discourse*, Houghton, Boston.

Schoggen, M., 1969, *An ecological study of three-year-olds at home*, George Peabody College for Teachers, Nashville, Tennessee.

Sinclair-de-Zwart, H., 1967, *Acquisition du langage et développement de la pensée: sous-systèmes linguistiques et opérations concrètes,* Dunod, Paris.

Smedslund, J., 1961, 'The acquisition of conservation of substance and weight in children, III. Extinction of conservation of weight acquired "normally" and by means of empirical controls on a balance', *Scand. J. Psychol.*, 2, 85-7.

Strandberg, T.E. and Griffeth, J., 1968, 'A study of the effects of training in visual literacy on verbal language behavior', Eastern Illinois University.

Tough, J., 1969, 'Language and environment: an interim report of a longitudinal study', University of Leeds, Institute of Education.

Turner, G.J. and Pickvance, R.E., 1970, 'Social class differences in the expression of uncertainty in five-year-old children', Sociological Research Unit, University of London, Institute of Education.

Weissberg, C., 'Project pathways: Harvard University; Study of high school dropouts', unpublished.

Welford, A.T., 1968, *Fundamentals of skill*, Methuen, London.

Williams, F. (ed.), 1970, *Language and poverty*, Markham, Chicago.

4 INFERENCES

Peter Bryant

Source: Chapter 3 in P.E. Bryant, *Perception and Understanding in Young Children* (Methuen, London, 1974).

The discovery that the young child is able to handle size relations fairly efficiently naturally leads one to speculate whether or not he can register that A is larger than B and that B is larger than C. Can he then go on to work out that this means that A must be larger than C?

The argument which has been developed [see Bryant, 1974, chapter 1 . . .] is that the young child is able to co-ordinate relations and that this difficulty with absolute judgements makes it a particularly urgent matter that he should. His weakness at remembering absolute properties forces him to put separate relative judgements together to produce deductive inferences.

This is a simple idea, but it is also extremely controversial. The suggestion that children can make deductive inferences goes directly against the many influential accounts of children's behaviour. In particular, it disagrees with hypotheses put forward by Piaget (1970), and by Kendler and Kendler (1967), which suggest that children are not able to co-ordinate separate judgements inferentially until they reach the age of roughly seven or eight years.

Piaget, for example, in a recent publication (1970) writes about his approach to the question of inferential ability in the following terms: 'We present two sticks to a child, stick A being smaller than stick B. Then we hide stick A and show him stick B together with a larger stick C. Then we ask him how A and C compare. Pre-operational children will say that they do not know because they have not seen them together – they have not been able to compare them.' Thus, to Piaget it seems that the young perceptually dominated child cannot compare things unless they are presented together in one perceptual event. Separate perceptual experiences can never be combined, and no deductive inference is possible.

The Kendlers, whose background is that of the American school of S-R learning theory and very different from Piaget's, draw conclusions about inferential abilities which are at least as pessimistic as his. Thus they end a review (1967) in the following way. 'Investigators have shown that rats do not solve problems that require the integration of separate habit segments. There may even be some question of whether infra-human primates would be able to solve such problems, given appropriate experimental controls. When a similar experimental paradigm is applied to a cross section of human beings we find that if we use either grade level or M.A.[†] as a developmental index solutions are very infrequent at the lower developmental levels. However, as developmental level increases solutions become increasingly frequent until at the highest level they are overwhelmingly the dominant mode of response . . . Children at the lower developmental levels do not integrate the two segments at the first opportunity because they have learned to make different responses to these compounds.' Thus, the Kendlers' opinion is that young children are as incapable as rats at making inferences, and may even be worse than monkeys or chimpanzees.

This disagreement between my theory that deductive inferences are a very basic part of the young child's behaviour and the theories of Piaget and the Kendlers, which claim that young children cannot make inferences, suggests that the evidence on the inference question should be very carefully examined. There is also another reason why this issue is important, and that is its educational significance. A child who cannot put together the information that $A > B$ and $B > C$ to produce the inference that $A > C$ clearly cannot understand even the most basic principles involved in measuring things. There will be little point, for example, in teaching such a child to use a ruler, because he will have no conception that different things could be compared with each other through their common relations to it. If, on the other hand, he can make inferences, this opens up educational possibilities for young children which may be of considerable benefit to them.

What, then, is the evidence for and against the proposition that young children can and do make deductive inferences? An examination of this evidence raises some intriguing problems to do with experimental design. The question is a delicate one, and the right controls are all-important.

Piaget and the Transitivity Problem

Piaget's original experiments on the way children cope with inference problems (Piaget and Inhelder, 1941, chapters 10 and 11; Piaget, Inhelder and Szeminska, 1960) took the form of his three-sticks example which has just been described. These experiments, which he and his colleagues called 'transitivity' experiments, involved either different sizes or different weights, and they consisted of three separate stages. First two quantities would be directly compared, A with B. Then one of these quantities, B, would be directly compared to a third, B with C. Finally, the child would be asked about the relations between the two quantities which he had not compared directly, A with C. This last stage presents the inferential problem, since in order to answer the AC question the child must combine the information from the separate direct comparisons between A and B and between B and C.

What happened in these experiments was that children below the age of approximately seven or eight years were not able to answer the inferential AC question. Above this age children generally did manage to make the inference satisfactorily. These results were consistent across several different experiments, and many other psychologists, who have repeated Piaget's three-stage transitivity experiment, have come up with the same developmental trend from consistent failure to consistent success. The most notable example is Smedslund (1963, 1966) who has done an interesting series of variations on Piaget's original experimental design and has arrived at much the same conclusions.

One of Smedslund's ingenious inferential tests is well worth describing at this point (Smedslund, 1966). The experiment was with children aged from five to seven years and again the problem was whether they could work out that $A > C$ from the information that $A > B$ and that $B > C$. The striking feature of this test, which forms only one condition in a rather complex experiment, was that the rods A and C were presented together and side by side, and were actually the same size. They were black rods, both 20 cm in length. The trick of the experiment was to have two B rods, both yellow, and yet to convince the child that there was only one B. One of the two Bs was 19.5 cm and the other 20.5 cm. The child was shown first that A was longer than B using the shorter B and next that B was longer than C using the longer B. The child, who was meant not to be aware of the switch from one B to the other, then had to work out which was the longer, A or C.

The advantage of making A and C the same length is that it gets round the difficulty of the children solving the problem, not inferentially, but simply by remembering the actual lengths. If the child is shown, for example, first a 21 cm A with a 20 cm B, and next a 20 cm B with a 19 cm C, he could perhaps solve the AC problem not by combining the two judgements inferentially but merely by remembering that A was 21 cm and that C was 19 cm. Simply remembering the absolute lengths does not involve an inference.

In fact, the experiment which included this test of what Smedslund called 'genuine measurement' produced no evidence that children below eight years were able to make transitive, deductive inferences, and Smedslund concluded that his results were very much in line with Piaget's suggestions. There is one unsatisfactory detail about this experiment. It is not at all clear why, if children could register the absolute lengths of A and C, they could not also remember the absolute lengths of the two Bs and thus realize that they had been fooled. If the control were really necessary, the test would be a bad one because children who really could make inferences might be hampered when they realized that B was not really a constant and reliable reference point. However, in view of our finding [. . .] (Lawrenson and Bryant, 1972) it seems unlikely that children can remember absolute sizes at all easily anyway, so this objection is probably not important. Moreover, the fact that this, and the rest of Smedslund's transitivity experiments, seem to support the developmental trend originally demonstrated by Piaget is certainly impressive. At first sight it does seem as though there are good reasons for believing with Piaget and Smedslund that young children do not make transitive inferences.

However, there are also good grounds for claiming that the traditional experiment has weaknesses in its design and these must be sorted out before one can reach any definite conclusions either way about the ability of young children to make inferences.

The Design of the Traditional Transitivity Experiment

No one disputes the discovery that young children generally fail and older children succeed with the traditional transitivity problems of the type administered by Piaget and by Smedslund. What is at stake is what these failures and successes mean. Two assumptions have been very widely made about the transitivity problem. The first is that the child who fails does not have the logical mechanism which is needed to co-ordinate separate items of information in an inference. The second is that a child who succeeds does possess this mechanism. It turns out that both assumptions can be criticized very severely.

We can take first the assumption about failures. The trouble with this assumption is that failures may well be caused by other factors than an inability to make inferences. An alternative possibility is that they could be due to lapses in memory. The transitivity problem is a successive one, and thus involves memory. When the child is finally asked the AC question he has to do at least two things. He must remember the AB and the BC comparisons, and he must put them together inferentially. It follows that failures could be due simply to the fact that the child does not remember the information, and that if he could remember it he could organize it in an inference perfectly well. Thus the meaning of failures in these tasks is ambiguous. They tell us nothing definite about logical ability.

This assumption about the meaning of successes is just as questionable.

It is by no means certain that the child who answers the AC question correctly does so by making a genuine logical inference. He may produce the correct answer merely by parroting a verbal label picked up in the initial training. The point here is that the correct response to A in the initial AB comparison is 'larger', while to C in the initial BC comparison it is 'smaller'. Yet 'larger' is also the correct answer to A and 'smaller' to C, when the inferential comparison has to be made between A and C. So if the child simply remembers what he said about A or about C in the initial comparisons, he will give the right answer to the AC question for quite the wrong reasons. He certainly will not have made a genuine inference.

Both these difficulties have been noticed before (Smedslund, 1969). However, the traditional transitivity experiment does not control for them, and this means that its results are uninterpretable. Until quite recently it was impossible to find an experiment on transitive inferences which simultaneously ensured that failures were not the result of forgetting and that successes could not be written off as mere parroting.

Two basic precautions are needed to ensure that failures really are inferential failures and have nothing to do with forgetting. First the child should be given a lot of experience with the initial direct comparisons so that he will probably remember these comparisons later. Secondly, at the time when the child is asked the indirect inferential question he should also be tested for his memory of the initial comparisons on which the inference has to be based. Only if he can remember the initial comparisons, but cannot manage the inference, is it fair to conclude that his failure really is an inferential one.

The control against parroting is also fairly simple. All that is needed is to increase the number of quantities involved from three to five, where $A > B > C > D > E$. With five quantities one has four initial one-step comparisons, which are $A > B$, $B > C$, $C > D$, and $D > E$. Three of the five quantities, B, C and D, each occur in two of these comparisons and each is the smaller in one initial comparison and the larger in the other. This means that by the time the child is asked the inferential questions he will have seen B, C and D equally often as the smaller and the larger stimulus. Thus he will not be able to solve any inference which is based only on B, C and D by merely repeating a specific verbal label. There is only one inference which can be based just on these three values, and that is the inferential comparison between B and D. Any other new inferential comparison based on the four initial direct AB, BC, CD and DE comparisons has to include either A or E or both, and since A is always the larger in this initial comparison and E always the smaller, these other inferences could be an unreliable test of a child's inferential ability.

The correct way to test for inferences in young children, therefore, is to have four initial direct comparisons, to make sure that the child knows these fairly thoroughly, to test the child's memory for them at the same time as testing his ability to combine them inferentially, and to make the BD question the crucial test of the child's ability to make inferences.

Alternative Transitivity Experiments

Some of these controls have been introduced by other experimenters, but none of their experiments has included all the controls in one study. For example, Braine (1959) in a well-known study with children between three and a half and seven years did make them very familiar with the material before posing the inferential problem. However, each of his problems involved only three quantities, and therefore the considerable successes obtained by the young children in this experiment could have been achieved without their ever having made an inference at all. Another study by Youniss and Murray (1970) with children of six and eight years did involve five quantities, and therefore tested genuine inferences. However, nothing was done in this study to control for memory failures. No steps were taken either to make the children reasonably familiar with the five quantities first or to check that they remembered the original direct comparison when they were asked the inferential question. Thus the consistent failures which Youniss and Murray found in their younger group could very well have been due to forgetting.

Because we could find no experiment which contained all the necessary controls, my colleague, Dr Tom Trabasso and I began a series of experiments in 1969 in order to find out as definitely as we possibly could whether young children can or cannot make deductive transitive inferences.

Our first experiment (Bryant and Trabasso, 1971) was with children of four, five and six years, and was divided into two main stages, the first a training stage and the second a test stage. In the training stage it was ensured that the children got to know the four initial direct comparisons, A > B, B > C, C > D, and D > E. In the test stage we looked at two things, whether the child could remember these initial comparisons and whether he could combine them inferentially. In particular, the test stage was concerned with the children's answers to the BD question. Every child had to deal with five rods whose lengths and colours were different. Their lengths were A = 7 inches, B = 6 inches, C = 5 inches, D = 4 inches, and E = 3 inches. The colours were blue, red, green, yellow and white, and for each child a particular colour always signalled the same length, so that, for example, for one child A would always be blue, B green, C red and so on.

We also used a black block of wood, which contained five holes and these holes had different depths. The five depths were 6 inches, 5 inches, 4 inches, 3 inches and 2 inches. The reason for having this block of wood was that it made it possible for us to show the child two rods of different lengths and yet protruding equally from the top of the block. Thus we could show the child two rods of different colours and ask him which was the longer without him being able to see which actually was the longer. This is a great help both for training the initial comparisons and for asking the inferential questions.

The training stage involved a series of trials in which the child had to make the four comparisons A > B, B > C, C > D and D > E; but the trials were arranged in such a way that the child not only made the comparisons but also learned them. In each training trial one of the four pairs of rods was shown to the child, with the two rods side by side in the block of wood, both rods protruding by 1 inch. The child, who had no way of telling which was the longer simply by looking at them in this state, was then asked which of the two was the taller (or shorter). Once he had made his choice the two rods were taken out of the box and the child was shown, and told, which was the longer. Thus each training trial ended with the child being given visual and verbal feedback about the actual lengths of the two rods involved. This training continued until the child was able to choose correctly whenever he was shown a particular pair. The child first learned each of the four pairs separately and then was given them all again but in an intermingled manner, so that on one trial he would be asked about one pair, on the next about another and so on. This second training phase continued until the child consistently chose correctly whenever he was given any of the four pairs, until, in fact, he really knew that A > B, B > C, C > D and D > E.

This training turned out to be surprisingly easy, though it sometimes took more than one session. Very few children even in the four-year-old group dropped out at this stage. Once the training had been completed they were moved on to the test stage. The same five rods and the same block of wood were used. Two things, however, were new. First, each child was asked about all ten possible comparisons (AB, BC, CD, DE, AC, AD, AE, BD, BE, CE). Notice that the first four of these are the initial comparisons, which means that the child's memory for these comparisons was being tested at this stage. The remaining six are all the possible new inferential comparisons that can be based on the four initial items. However, as has been mentioned, only one of these, the BD comparison, can be confidently regarded as genuinely inferential. Secondly, no feedback was ever given during the test phase. In each test trial a pair of rods, distinguishable as usual by the colour, was presented, again protruding 1 inch above the block of wood in which they were embedded. The child would be asked to say either which was the taller or which the shorter: but after he had made his choice he was never shown or told whether he was right or wrong. This was necessary because each of the ten pairs was presented four times during this stage, and the possibility that the child would, for example, get the BD pair right not through an inference, but simply by remembering the correct answer from the last BD trial, had to be eliminated.

This experiment produced some very consistent results, and these have since been repeated many times in many other versions of the same experimental design. All three age groups passed through the training stage fairly easily, though the older children learned the four comparisons faster than the younger ones. More important were the test scores, which showed that children at all three age levels were very well able to make transitive inferences. They remembered the initial comparisons fairly well, and they answered the crucial BD question correctly far more frequently than would be expected by chance. The percentage scores for all ten pairs are given in Table 4.1. This shows that the four-year-olds were correct in 78 per cent of the BD trials, the five-year-olds in 88 per cent and the six-year-olds in 92 per cent. So it seems that even children as young as four years can combine separate perceptual experiences inferentially,

Table 4.1: Probability of Correct Choices on Tests for Transitivity and Retention (Experiment 1) (Bryant and Trabasso, 1971)

Stimulus	B	C	D	E
4-yr-old children				
A	0.96	0.96	0.93	0.98
B	—	0.92	0.78	0.92
C	—	—	0.90	0.94
D	—	—	—	0.91
5-yr-old children				
A	1.00	0.96	1.00	0.98
B	—	0.86	0.88	1.00
C	—	—	0.92	1.00
D	—	—	—	1.00
6-yr-old children				
A	0.99	0.99	1.00	1.00
B	—	0.94	0.92	0.99
C	—	—	0.98	1.00
D	—	—	—	1.00

provided that they can remember the information which has to be combined. Moreover, their failure to answer the BD question in a few of the trials was probably due not to inferential errors, but to memory lapses. They did not recall the initial BC and CD comparisons perfectly in the test stage which means that they did not always remember the information on which the BD comparisons must be based. In fact, the BD errors made by all three age groups can quite plausibly be accounted for in terms of the extent to which they forgot the initial BC and CD comparisons (Bryant and Trabasso, 1971).

This point about memory is interesting, but the most important thing about these results is that the children's correct answers to the BD question were always significantly greater than would be expected by chance. This is strong evidence that young children can make transitive inferences very well, and therefore that Piaget's and Smedslund's hypothesis about children and inferences is far too pessimistic. There is, however, still one possible objection to concluding finally from this experiment that children can make inferences, and this concerns the possibility that they remembered the absolute lengths of B and of D. The children actually saw the full lengths of each rod at the end of every training trial, and by remembering the actual lengths they could work out that B was longer than D without having to connect B and D through their common relations with C.

It is very unlikely, in view of the great difficulty children have in remembering absolute sizes, that this is a serious objection. However, their difficulty with absolute values has not been specifically demonstrated with rods of the sort used and so the possibility that absolute memory had affected the results of our experiment could not be ruled out. We, therefore, designed another experiment to find out whether young children can make inferences even when they cannot know the absolute lengths of the rods involved.

There are various ways of eliminating absolute cues. We did it simply by cutting out the visual feedback during the training phase. In this second experiment (Bryant and Trabasso, 1971) which involved four- and five-year-old children, the procedure was identical to that of the first experiment except for one detail. At the end of each training trial, after the child had made his choice, he was only told whether he was right or wrong. He was never shown the whole length of any of the rods, and thus only saw them sticking out an inch from the top of the black block. He was, therefore, unable to learn the absolute length of the rods.

This generally made the training phase longer and more difficult, but otherwise the results were as clear cut as in the first experiment. They are presented in Table 4.2. The four-year-olds' answers to the BD question were correct 82 per cent of the time and the five-year-olds' 85 per cent. Again their few failures in the BD comparisons could be accounted for by the fact that their memory for the BC and CD initial comparisons was not perfect. This experiment demonstrates conclusively that young children are capable of making genuine transitive inferences.

Table 4.2: Probability of Correct Choices on Tests for Transitivity and Retention (Experiment 2) (Bryant and Trabasso, 1971)

Stimulus	B	C	D	E
4-yr-old children				
A	0.98	0.98	0.93	0.97
B	—	0.89	0.82	0.90
C	—	—	0.87	0.88
D	—	—	—	0.94
5-yr-old children				
A	0.98	0.92	0.95	0.97
B	—	0.87	0.85	0.98
C	—	—	0.97	0.95
D	—	—	—	0.98

Two main points follow from this conclusion. The first is that Piaget's theory about logical development must, to some extent, be wrong. His experiments did not ensure that children could remember the comparisons which they were asked to combine inferentially, and it now seems clear that children can manage this sort of inference provided that they can remember the information on which the inference has to be based. The second point is that this evidence shows that children have the logical mechanism for using framework cues as a basis for organizing and categorizing their perceptual experience through perceptual inferences.

However, as well as showing that children can make transitive inferences, these experiments also seem to show that what the child remembers may be an important factor in determining whether or not he is going to make an inference successfully. It therefore becomes important to examine the exact relationship between the child's memory for perceptual comparisons and his ability to combine them in an inference.

Inference and Memory

The two experiments, which have just been described, show that young children who do remember relative judgements can combine them inferentially. The experiments do not, however, demonstrate that the child's inferences are entirely dependent on memory. It is not possible, for example, to claim that as soon as a child had grasped and could remember the fact that B > C and C > D, he could immediately make the BD inference, because the training phase lasted some time and was kept rigidly separate from the test phase. There could have been some time during the training phase when the child had learnt and remembered that B > C and C > D, and yet was still not able to combine these two direct comparisons in an inference. Our experiments were not sufficiently sensitive to rule out this possibility of a temporary period during which the child could remember two items but could not co-ordinate them, and one cannot conclude from them that memory is a sufficient as well as a necessary condition for inferences in young children.

Another experiment was needed, therefore, to monitor the child's memory for the initial comparisons and at the same time his ability to combine them inferentially, trial by trial, right through the experiment. Suppose, for example, that the child goes through a series of trials, in each of which he is first given the basic information about the four direct comparisons A > B, B > C, C > D and D > E, and then is immediately tested both for his ability to remember these four comparisons and also for his ability to make the BD inference. Once this presentation-test sequence is finished in one trial, the next trial begins, where the same sequence is repeated, and then the next trial and so on. Thus trial by trial we can measure how well the child is grasping the four direct comparisons, and at the same time how successfully he is managing to make the BD inference. This procedure (which people who are familiar with experiments on verbal learning will recognize as very similar to paired associate learning) will show whether the child makes the inference as soon as he can remember the relevant initial comparisons, BC and CD, or whether there has to be an intervening period when he has the necessary information but cannot use it inferentially.

This trial-by-task is quite a difficult one for young children. We found (Bryant, 1973) that the easiest way to present the problem was not to use coloured rods, but to tell the child stories about how we visited a house where we met some children, and how we met different pairs of children at different times and noticed that in each case one of the two was taller than the other, that Jane, A, was taller than Tom, B, that Tom was taller than Susan, C, and so on. Having heard this story once, the child is immediately tested to see if he remembers the four pairs, and also whether he can make the BD inference. Thus in the presentation stage of each trial the child is told once about four comparisons, AB, BC, CD and DE and in the test stage he is asked five questions, four of them about the initial comparisons and the fifth about the BD inference. He is never told whether his answer to these questions is right or wrong. This procedure constitutes one trial and when it is completed another similar trial begins. The whole procedure lasts until the child is consistently correct with all five questions in the test stage.

We tried this task out with five-year-old children, and the results showed very clearly that they had only to remember the BC and CD comparisons to be able to make an inference. As soon as they began to answer the BC and the CD questions correctly, they also began to be consistently right about the BD inference. The only trouble with this experiment was that quite a few of the children never managed to be consistently correct about any of the comparisons direct or indirect. There is no doubt that the task is a particularly difficult one for young children. Nevertheless, the majority of them did eventually remember the initial comparisons, and without exception these children all also made the BD inference at the same time.

This last experiment demonstrates a clear relationship between the inferences which a child can make and the information which he can remember. The fact that children can apparently co-ordinate information they can remember does strongly suggest that when errors do occur in inference problems, these errors are most probably the result of memory failures. At any rate we can now finally reject the evidence of the traditional transitivity experiment which does not control for failures in memory. It is clear that young children can combine relative judgements which they do remember. They can make inferences.

Learning Theory and Deductive Inferences

Piaget and Smedslund are not the only psychologists who have tried to show that young children cannot make inferences. A very different theoretical background has also produced much the same hypothesis. Over the last fifteen years or so Kendler and Kendler (1967), whose background is that of S-R learning theory, have also maintained that children younger than approximately eight years of age cannot make deductive inferences.

The inference problem tackled by the Kendlers has nothing to do with relative judgements, and to that extent their work is less relevant to the central argument [. . . here] than are, for example, the experiments of

Piaget and Smedslund. Nevertheless, they have consistently argued that young children cannot combine separate experiences.

The Kendlers derived their original ideas about children's inferences from experimental work on inferences in rats. Their starting point was a series of rat experiments carried out by Maier (1939) which appeared to show that rats can to some extent combine separate and different learned routines in order to solve a problem inferentially. The Kendlers' aim was to see if young children could do any better, and they designed a series of tasks in which a child was taught two components of a problem separately and was then tested to see if he could put the two together to solve the problem.

There were some specific differences of method between their early work (1956) and their later studies (1961). However, all the experiments followed the same general pattern. In one typical experiment five-year-old and eight-year-old children and also college students were set in front of an apparatus which contained three panels side by side. There was a button in the middle of the two side panels and an open tray at the bottom of each panel. There was also a circular opening in the middle and an open tray at the bottom of the centre panel.

Initially, the child had to learn to separate things. One of these was that pressing the button on one side panel produced a marble in that panel's tray, while pressing the other panel's button produced a ball bearing. The experimenters first showed the child that one button produced the marble, the other the ball bearing, and then over a series of trials gave him sometimes a marble and sometimes a ball bearing, asking him each time to press the button which produced the thing 'like this'. The other item which the child had to learn was that dropping one of these objects (the marble for half the children, the ball bearing for the other half) into the opening in the central panel produced a reward, which was a small charm. To teach the child this the experimenters gave him both objects over a series of trials, and asked him each time to insert the correct object, that is to say, the object which produced the charm.

When the child had mastered both these items, he was simply given the three panels and told to get himself the charm. The question was whether he would be able to combine the two items, which he had already learned, by first pressing the button which produced the 'correct' object and then putting it into the hole in the central panel.

The important thing about the results of the Kendlers' experiment was that the performance of the younger children was abysmal. Many of the five-year-olds did nothing, and those who did do something responded in a haphazard manner. Even the performance of the eight-year-olds was barely above chance level, and the only people to respond with consistent success were the college students. The Kendlers concluded that young children, like rats, cannot on the whole co-ordinate separate experiences, and their explanation of this failure was that each experience involves a different response, and thus on an S-R basis has to be treated quite separately from the other.

This is a somewhat depressing conclusion and it can be questioned for two main reasons. One is that we have already seen that children can combine two judgements inferentially, and that they can do so even though they respond to the common element differently in the two judgements. For example, when they combine the information that $A > B$ and that $B > C$ to infer that $A > C$ their response to B is 'smaller' in one judgement and 'larger' in the other, and yet they clearly connect A and C through the common element, B. So, if the children cannot in the Kendlers' experiment combine different experiences their failure may have something specifically to do with the details of the actual task. Indeed, the second worry about the Kendlers' experiment is the rather artificial nature of their task. Pressing buttons to produce marbles, and putting marbles into holes to obtain a charm are not everyday experiences for a young child, and it may be that he is so bemused by the oddness of the situation that he fails to exercise his normal ability to put different experiences together in an effectively logical manner.

There is one very striking piece of evidence which supports this second criticism, albeit somewhat obliquely, since the evidence involves not a developmental but a cross-cultural experiment. Cole, Gay, Glick and Sharp (1972) repeated the Kendler study just described with three groups of non-literate Liberians whose ages were five to six years, nine to twelve years, and seventeen to nineteen years. All three groups produced conspicuously poor performances and the two older groups were vastly inferior to 'literate' control groups. However, the experimenters did not conclude that these non-literate people were unable to make inferences. They had been impressed by the fact that many of the uneducated people in the experiment had shown signs of fear or of reticence, tending in the final stage of the experiment to wait around and to do nothing, apparently looking for further instructions. Cole *et al.* concluded that the strangeness of their apparatus might have been so daunting to these people that they were reduced to an essentially passive state. 'Up to this point' their report runs 'our work provides a model of how not to do a cross-cultural experiment because we really have no way to decide among various explanations for our findings. Is it fear of the electric apparatus that makes our subjects slow to respond, or are the instructions unclear? Or is it some difficulty in making arbitrary, although seemingly simple inferences of the sort this experiment tries to elicit?'

So they designed another experiment with the same general scheme but with more familiar material. The people in this experiment were presented with two easily distinguished matchboxes, and learned that one box contained a black key, and the other a red one. They were then told that one of the two keys would open a lock of a box which contained a piece of candy which they could eat when they found it. When they had learned which was the correct key they were given the whole problem again, and the question again was whether they could combine the two separate segments of the task. The non-literate people in this second experiment were all adults and thus it is quite reasonable to compare their performance with that of the oldest non-literate group in the first experiment. The performance of the non-literate adults was well above chance in this new version of the inference task and they were therefore much better than the equivalent non-literate group in the first experiment which used the Kendlers' equipment. It seems that non-literate Liberians are able to combine separate experiences, and only fail in the rather artificial Kendler situation through some specific experimental detail which has nothing to do with inferences.

The reservations expressed by Cole *et al.* were about the reactions of Africans with little education in experimental gadgetry. However, there is no reason why these reservations should not also apply to the five-year-old Western child. Why should he not also find the equipment and the arbitrary sequence of events strange and even frightening? Some recent and unpublished work done in Oxford (Hewson, unpublished material) has shown that children as young as three years old are able to combine the separate segments of a task very like the Kendlers', provided that different material is used. For example, if instead of pressing a button the child has to open a drawer to obtain a particular reward his performance in the final inferential stage is much better.

It is, then, plausible to suggest that young children can put two learned routines together, and that their failure in the Kendlers' task is not an inferential failure. In fact, the conclusions which we have reached about the Kendlers' experimental problem and about the traditional transitivity problem are much the same. Both apparently demonstrate that young children cannot make inferences, and yet it emerges that the failures which young children typically make in both problems probably tell us nothing about their inferential ability.

One lesson to be learned from this kind of analysis is how risky it is to conclude that some ability definitely does not exist in children. One is reminded of the child who kept on meeting the man who wasn't there and wishing that he would go away. Abilities which have been definitively ruled out in young children by one psychologist have a habit of cropping up in the experiments of another. It is, on the whole, much safer to say that something is difficult than that it is impossible.

Passive Versus Active Inference Problems

The inference problems which I have described so far are essentially passive problems, in that the child is always given all the essential information on which the inference must be based. This information is handed to him on a plate. He is told, for example, that A > B and that B > C, before being asked the AC question, and he does not have to set about actively gathering the necessary information himself.

Suppose, however, that the task is turned around. The child is told first that he has to find out about how A and C compare, even though he is not allowed to compare them directly, and he is shown that B is available and is a possible means of making a connection between A and C. In this case, the child has to gather the information by himself by spontaneously using B as a ruler which will show him that A > B and B > C. This way round the inference problem is an active rather than a passive one. The child has not only to make the inference, but also to get hold of the information on which the inference must be based. It would certainly be very interesting to know how children cope with an active version of the inference problem.

We have actually had information for some time about children's reactions to a task which involves active inferences. Again we owe the information to Piaget and his colleagues. In the best known of Piaget's active, or in his terms, 'spontaneous', inference problems (Piaget, Inhelder and Szeminska, 1960; Piaget, 1953) he first showed children aged between five and nine years a tower of bricks piled on top of a small table and then asked them to build on another table another tower as tall as the first one. The two table tops were actually of different heights, and the children's task was not to line up the tops of the two towers, but to make sure that their absolute lengths were the same. A rod which was the same length as the first tower was left lying around. The point of this set-up was that the child could not compare the two towers directly because they started from bases of different heights. (One can notice incidentally again that a child with an effective absolute code for length would be able to make this comparison without the help of an inference. Piaget's covert assumption is in line with my argument that young children find it difficult to respond on the basis of absolute sizes.) So the child needed some intervening common reference point, which could be taken and compared directly to both towers and through which the two could be connected. The solution is to take the rod, B, to the first tower, A, and having found that their lengths are the same to build another tower, C, to the height of B.

In fact, the five-year-old children did not use the rod as a measure. Piaget does report that some six-year-olds tended to use their bodies as a way of comparing the two towers, and this on the whole proved a rather inefficient form of measurement. When, for example, a child put one hand on the bottom and the other at the top of one of the towers and then went over to the second tower trying to keep his hands a constant distance apart, he was almost certain to make an inaccurate comparison. Nevertheless, despite the slapstick element there is obviously evidence here of some idea of an intervening measure. From the age of seven years onwards the children began to use the rod spontaneously as a way of comparing the two towers, and thus showed quite clearly both that they could understand that A = C where A = B and B = C, and also that they knew how to gather the information needed to make such an inference.

The most important result here is the complete failure of children younger than six years to use the inference principle 'spontaneously'. Piaget himself sees this as yet another clear indication that young children cannot make inferences. However, we have already found that they can make inferences in a passive situation where they are given the information which they then have to combine. It is possible, therefore, that there is an important difference between passive and active problems, and that young children can manage in a passive situation but not in an active one.

One can quibble at Piaget's experiment which is certainly not entirely convincing. The instructions given to the children might have been unclear, and they might not, for example, have understood that the experimenter was referring to the height from the table tops and not from the floor. However, we have evidence (Bryant, 1973) which supports Piaget's contention that young children have great difficulties with active inference problems. We found that children who had actually done extremely well in our passive inference problems were quite incapable of solving an active version of this task in which they had to get hold of the right information before they made the inference. Here, then, were children who could make an inference, but who could not put their inferential ability to use in an active situation.

It would seem that there may well be a gap between potential and performance, between what a child can do and what he eventually does do. He can make inferences, but is not very good at creating a situation in which inferences can be made. This does not mean that he will never make inferences in real life, because there will be situations which are essentially passive and in which all the necessary information is provided. However, it does seem that there will be situations in which the young child will not be able to bring his inferential ability into play.

No doubt this gap diminishes with age, and it is quite possible that it does so largely as a result of the child's experiences when he is taught how to measure at school. Indeed, it may be that the aspect of the question of children's inferences which is most relevant to education is this difference between passive and active inference.

My conclusions suggest that when the child is initially being taught to measure, he needs to be told not how to make inferences but how to make his inferential ability most effective. He needs to be taught not that $A > C$ when $A > B$ and $B > C$, but how to use B as a ruler. Of course, measurement involves a great many more manoeuvres than this: and my comments apply only to the very beginnings of measurement. Nonetheless, the discovery that children can make transitive inferences provided that the situation is right may make the apparently formidable task of teaching a child how to measure seem a little less daunting.

Perceptual Inferences

The evidence presented in this chapter suggests that young children can make inferences very well indeed even though they may have some difficulty in gathering the information on which inferences can be based. Although this conclusion is obviously relevant to theories about logical development such as Piaget's, only its implications for the subject of perceptual development will be pursued here. There are two main implications, one of which concerns young children's use of perceptual frameworks, the other the relationship of perceptual to cognitive development.

The first point is that the demonstration that children can make transitive inferences means that they do have the logical basis for using frameworks when they make perceptual judgements and for basing these judgements on perceptual inferences. If a child can work out that $A = C$ whenever $A = B$ and $B = C$, he has the basis for realizing, for example, that two objects which he sees at quite different times but which are both parallel to a particular framework feature are in the same orientation. To use Piaget's example, he has the basis for working out that the level of liquid tends to stay the same by noticing that it is constantly parallel to a horizontal framework feature. Of course, to demonstrate that children can make inferences does not mean that they necessarily use these inferences when they make perceptual judgements. It only establishes that they have the logical basis to do so.

The second point concerns the passive-active inference distinction. The point is that the perceptual inferences in my hypothesis belong to the passive and not at all to the active category. If a child is given direct comparisons then, provided that he can remember them, he manages inferences well. If he has to seek out a measure, detach it from its surroundings and apply it before he makes an inference, then he is usually at a loss.

In the perceptual inferences which I have been describing the intervening measure is the background, the constant external framework. The child compares different objects which he sees at different times through their common relations to a constant background. This background is given. The child does not have to fetch it and apply it to A and to C. So the child who can manage a passive inference problem certainly ought in principle to be able to make the kind of inference which I am suggesting may be a basic feature of the perceptual judgements made by young children. Now that we have established that young children can manage passive inferences, we can go on to ask whether they rely on these inferences in perceptual situations [see Bryant, 1974, chapters 4 *et seq.*].

References

Braine, M.S. (1959), 'The ontogeny of certain logical operations: Piaget's formulation examined by non-verbal methods', *Psychological Monograph*, 75, no. 5, 1-43.

Bryant, P.E. (1973), 'What the young child has to learn about logic', in Hinde, R.A. and Hinde, J.S. (eds.), *Constraints on Learning*, London, Academic Press.

Bryant, P.E. (1974), *Perception and Understanding in Young Children*, London, Methuen.

Bryant, P.E. and Trabasso, T. (1971), 'Transitive inferences and memory in young children', *Nature*, 232, 456-8.

Cole, M., Gay, J., Glick, J.A. and Sharp, D.W. (1971), *The Cultral Context of Learning and Thinking*, London, Methuen.

Kendler, H.H. and Kendler, T.S. (1956), 'Inferential behaviour in pre-school children', *Journal of Experimental Psychology*, 51, 311-14.

Kendler, H.H. and Kendler, T.S. (1961), 'Inferential behaviour in children, II', *Journal of Experimental Psychology*, 61, 422-8.

Kendler, H.H. and Kendler, T.S. (1967), 'Inferential behaviour in young children', in Lipsitt, L.P. and Spiker, C.C. (eds.), *Advances in Child Development and Behaviour*, vol. III.

Maier, N.R.F. (1939), 'Qualitative differences in the learning of rats in a discrimination situation', *J. Comp. Psychol.*, 27, 289-332.

Piaget, J. (1953), *The Origins of Intelligence in the Child*, London, Routledge and Kegan Paul.

Piaget, J. (1970), *Genetic Epistemology*, New York, Columbia University Press.

Piaget, J., Inhelder, B. and Szeminska, A. (1960), *The Child's Conception of Geometry*, London, Routledge and Kegan Paul.

Smedslund, J. (1963), 'The development of concrete transitivity of length in children', *Child Development*, 34, 389-405.

Smedslund, J. (1966), 'Performance on measurement and pseudo-measurement tasks by 5-7 year old children', *Scandinavian Journal of Psychology*, 7, 81-92.

Youniss, J. and Murray, J.P. (1970), 'Transitive inferences with non-transitive solutions controlled', *Developmental Psychology*, 2, 169-75.

5 ESTIMATING ODDS AND THE CONCEPT OF PROBABILITY

Efraim Fischbein

Source: Chapter 6 in E. Fischbein, *The Intuitive Sources of Probabilistic Thinking in Children* (Reidel Publications, 1975).

[. . . In this chapter] we will [. . .] consider data concerning the *conceptual organisation* relevant to the ontogenesis of thinking, of the notion of chance and the estimation of odds, and the notion of probability.

From a discussion of experiments on the global estimation of odds, we will go on to consider experiments in which the elements of explicit computation appear, based on the intuitive comparison or estimation of certain relationships.

1. Chance and Necessity

According to Piaget and Inhelder (1951) the concepts of chance and necessity develop in a complementary manner: 'The discovery of chance is made gradually, as some operations fail; and it is by referring to the structure of these operations that the child grasps the notion of chance, which eventually gives rise to a system of probabilities' (Piaget and Inhelder, 1951, p. 225).

For this reason, before the age of 7-8, children do not distinguish between the possible and the necessary. Their expectations are coloured by subjective tendencies, which still express 'a lack of differentiation between notions which would be, in practice either intuitive foresight or whim' (ibid., p. 227).

The understanding that certain relations are objectively necessary, and can be thought about in a deductive manner, requires a grouped organisation of thought, characterised by commutation,[†] reversibility, and mobility. These qualities of operational thought do not, however, appear before the age of 7-8.

Piaget and Inhelder relate the notion of chance to that of *mixture*. Before the age of 7, children do not understand the irreversibility of the operation of mixing. If, for instance, a number of red and white beads are mixed in a box, many children believe that shaking the box is an operation which will separate the beads into distinct sets of red and white. The *irreversibility* characteristic of a fortuitous mixture is not understood at this age, since the child does not have an understanding of the notion of

87

reversibility (the understanding of reversibility is an essential characteristic of operational thought). The irreversibility of a fortuitous mixture can only be understood by a subject who realises that each stage of the mixture is only one among many which could be obtained with the same elements. The chances of separating a mixture into sets of elements by shaking it are very small. The idea of chance implies, therefore, according to Piaget and Inhelder, the existence of combinatorial mechanisms which the child does not possess before the age of 7.

After 7 years, children begin to accept the idea of a real and changing mixture (as the result of successively shaking the box). Not yet possessing the operational schema of permutation, however, these children still do not (before the level of formal operations) understand a mixture as only one of many possible permutations, but simply as the result of individual and isolated displacements of elements (the interaction of which displacements they do not recognise).

At the level of formal operations (after the age of 12) the child begins to assimilate the process of mixing to the schema of a set of permutations, and therefore is able to understand the interaction of individual displacements of elements (since the displacement of every individual bead can now be conceived of simultaneously). The child can now understand also that the mixture progresses as a result of successively shaking it. Thus the child comes to an intuitive understanding of the law of large numbers.[†]

The development of the notion of chance has also been considered under other experimental paradigms by Piaget and Inhelder (1951).

Throwing counters. A number of white counters have a cross on one face, and a circle on the other. Ten to 20 counters are thrown one after the other, and the child is to guess which face will land uppermost each time. Subsequently, without the child's knowledge, counters are thrown which have crosses on both faces.

From a bag containing red and blue marbles, single marbles are drawn at random. The child guesses in advance the colour of each marble to be drawn. In the second phase of this experimental paradigm, a switch is made, as above, and blue marbles only are used. Finally, the child is told that there is a 'trick', and the experimenter waits for the moment when the child realises that all the marbles are coming from a homogeneous population.

In Piaget's first stage of development, the following kinds of behaviour have been shown in children (Piaget and Inhelder, 1951, pp. 112-14): (a) *Phenomenalism* — acceptance of immediate experience, whether real or apparent; (b) *passive induction* or empirical induction (as opposed to experimental induction), which is a tendency derived directly from phenomenalism: children do not approach objective facts in a deductive manner (in this case, with a combinatorial schema). This is why they are unable to evaluate facts as being essentially either acceptable or unacceptable. They approach them from the point of view of the immediately previous experience (if there has been one), in relation to which the new phenomenon may appear natural, or perhaps merely 'odd', since it represents something new (repeated appearances of the 'cross' face of the counter). There seems, therefore, to be *an intuition of frequency and rarity*, but which has a totally empirical character. (c) A tendency to compensate, manifested in the positive and negative recency effects[†] which [. . .] also occur in probability learning.[†] (d) Belief in the personal power of whoever throws the counters. Although the children observe the random movements of the counters in the air, they believe that the final result can be controlled by the thrower.

All this demonstrates that, although preschool children possess the intuition of chance [see Fischbein, 1975] and are capable of matching behaviour, these do not derive from a conceptual schema.

After the age of 6-7 (the second developmental stage) children do not accept that the repeated appearance of the 'same' face of the counter is due to chance, and they conclude that both faces of the counter have the same sign. This is no longer a case of the purely empirical estimation of relative frequency, as in the younger children. These children judge the results with reference to a schema — even though not a very explicit one — in which 'mixture' fulfills a combinatorial role. One child explained: 'The counters can't all fall on the same side because they are too mixed up' (Piaget and Inhelder, 1951, p. 115).

The superiority of children in the third stage of development consists in the fact that these children are capable of a finer estimation of odds; '. . . probability, instead of remaining global, as in stage II, is analysed in terms of graduated judgements which indicate the existence of implicit computation' (Piaget and Inhelder, 1951, p. 121). ' "If you go on you can know . . . you are more and more certain . . . because with small numbers the chance is less" ' (ibid., p. 119).

In Piaget and Inhelder's interpretation of the concept of chance, the following aspects seem to us to be open to further discussion.

A chance result is not always the same thing as a result with a small probability of occurrence. A chance result does have a small probability of occurrence in cases where the number of possible results is great. But if, for instance, a coin is tossed, there are only two possible results. Whether heads or tails lands uppermost is still a matter of chance. Chance is equivalent to the unforeseeable, or the non-deducible. The 'unforeseeability'

[. . .] increases as the difference between the chances of either alternative occurring decreases. For any given number of possibilities, the uncertainty – and consequently the information value – is greatest when all the possibilities are equiprobable. A coin-toss, from which there are only two possible outcomes, is still a matter of chance, even though the probability of each outcome is ½.

The problem is therefore to know whether, in a situation where the number of possible states is not in itself a difficulty, the responses of the child express the same lack of understanding of chance.

Permutation, like the other combinatorial operations, does not develop until much later (after 14-15) in the stage of formal thought, according to Piaget and Inhelder (see pp. 101-3).

In cases where the design of the experiment is such that the response to a probability problem depends on correctly – or at least intuitively – solving a permutation problem, there is a risk of masking those difficulties which are specific to the concept of chance.

There is another aspect which complicates things still further. The data we have discussed [see Fischbein, 1975, chapter 3] have demonstrated that there is a strong natural tendency towards minimisation in the subjective estimate of the number of possible permutations which can be obtained with a given number of elements, even at the stage of formal operations. Thus, for example, with 5 objects (from which 120 permutations are actually possible) the mean subjective estimate of the number of possible permutations is only 16. Intuition is unable to grasp the rapid increase in the number of permutations which become possible as the number of objects increases.

These considerations lead us to doubt Piaget's and Inhelder's conclusion that the idea of chance is formed only after the age of 7, i.e. after the establishment of concrete operations.

It is necessary to distinguish between the *primary intuition* of chance and the *concept* of chance. Understanding of the concept of chance clearly presupposes an evolved conceptual system (and primarily that operational thought has been attained) and also a certain amount of familiarity with the notions of necessity, laws, causality, etc. However, if we are considering, not the scientific concept of chance, but rather the intuition of chance, in the sense in which the child arrives at the distinction between stochastic and determined phenomena, the situation is rather different.

In situations where combinatorial operations are not required, it has been observed, as we shall presently see, that the intuition of chance (in the sense of the opposite of 'determined') emerges much earlier than the previously discussed experiments of Piaget and Inhelder would indicate.

Furthermore, it is evident from the protocols cited by Piaget and Inhelder themselves that the intuition of chance emerges at the pre-operational level:

'Mon. (4.10). "Where will the marble go?" *"Perhaps there, or there"* (pointing to the two possible exits). (The trial is run, and the marble rolls toward the right-hand exit.) "And the next?" *"There"* (Trial: left-hand exit.) "What about the rest of the marbles?" *"I don't know . . ."* ' (Piaget and Inhelder, 1951, p. 44.) (The experimental apparatus consisted of five rectangular boxes placed on a slope, with a number of exits at the bottom.)

Roulette experiment: 'Mon. (4.11). "Can we tell where it will stop?" *"No, because if we say it will stop at blue, and then it goes past blue, we won't know."* ' (Ibid., p. 74.)

It is therefore possible to suggest that the intuition of chance is present even before the age of 6-7 years. There certainly exists a primary, pre-operational intuition constructed out of the day-to-day experience of the child and complementary to the intuition of necessity.

This polar pair of intuitions, chance-necessity, is largely a part of the adaptive behaviour of the child, whose cognitive reasoning is still vague and uncertain. Since they are not constrained by the coordinates which characterise the operational level, these pre-operational intuitions can be influenced by subjective or perceptual considerations.

At the concrete-operational level, the tendency to favour univocal solutions (the expression of deductive thinking) is intensified. The result is not, as might be expected, a compromise between these two possible interpretations (chance-necessity) but an oscillation between them. The growing tendency to give univocal responses leads the child into errors by invoking causal dependencies where none exists in reality.

This preference for univocal solutions is not generated by the operational structure of thought, but by the influence of the social environment, in particular that of the school. The child is taught that explanation consists in specifying a cause; that a scientific prediction must be a certainty; that ambiguity and uncertainty are not acceptable in scientific reasoning, and so on. Even if all this is not explicitly stated, it is implied in all that is taught in schools.

We have returned to the problem of determining the child's idea of chance by setting up situations in which chance operates in the simplest possible manner, starting with situations with two equiprobable alternatives (for a complete description of methods and results, see E. Fischbein, Ileana Pămpu and I. Mînzat, 'The Child's Intuition of Probability', 1967).

The subjects were children aged from 6 to 14, grouped in five age levels. The experimental apparatus consisted of inclined boards on which a set of progressively forked channels had been constructed, using thin wooden strips. The children were asked to imagine that marbles had been released in the main channel, and to say whether or not the marbles would follow any particular route in preference to the other possible ones, and, if so, to indicate the expected route. There were five different layouts of channels.

For the first three layouts, the correct response was that any route was equally probable.

Layout 1 contained two equiprobable routes, layout 2 eight, and layout 3 four equiprobable routes. In addition, layout 3 was asymmetrical. Layouts 4 and 5 contained routes which were not equiprobable.

The most surprising finding was that, for the layouts with equiprobable routes, it was the youngest children (pre-school) who gave the greatest number of *correct* responses (i.e. responses indicating the equality of chances). Older children opted more frequently for a determined route, and it was they who were most misled by the asymmetry of layout 3. They offered obviously confabulated causal explanations to justify their choices. For layouts 4 and 5, the proportion of correct responses increased with age.

The following conclusions can be drawn from these results:

(a)   Well before the operational stage, the child possesses an intuition of chance, and carries out intuitive estimation of odds, although the absence of operationally structured thought precludes the conceptual structuring of this intuition, which is complementary to the intuition of necessity.

The existence of subjective interpretations, the relative lack of differentiation between chance and caprice, and between the arbitrary and the possible at this age do not, in our view, oppose the hypothesis of an intuition of chance and probability in pre-school children.

[. . .] In *probability learning tasks* the pre-school child also demonstrates the possibility of an intuitive computation of stochastic outcomes, in the form of an intuition of relative frequencies. This is a further argument in favour of the hypothesis we are putting forward.

(b)   At the level of formal operations, according to Piaget and Inhelder, there will be an improvement in the estimation of probabilities. In fact, however, as our experiments have shown, with increasing age, *the estimations become poorer: pre-school children give the highest percentage of correct responses, when compared with 12-13 year-olds, in situations with equiprobable outcomes.* With increasing age, the responses become more erratic, more hesitant, and more frequently incorrect.

The explanation of these results would seem to lie in the fact that, as we have already mentioned, schools inculcate the notion of univocal determinism. At the operational level, the child looks for causal relations which will permit such univocal predictions, even when the objective situation provides no evidence of such relations. The most revealing of our results, in this respect, were those obtained with layout 3, in which a geometric modification to the apparatus, having no effect on the probabilities of the situation, misled particularly the older children. Evidently, chance implies to these children nothing but ambiguity and uncertainty, and thus denotes the failure of cognitive efforts. The pre-school child is less disturbed by ambiguity. The child approaching adolescence is in the habit (inculcated by instruction in physics, chemistry, mathematics, and even history and geography) of seeking causal relations which can justify univocal explanations.

This is why the intuition of chance remains outside of intellectual development, and does not benefit sufficiently from the development of operational schemas of thought, and which instead are harnessed solely to the service of deductive reasoning.

2. Estimation of Comparison of Odds, the Concept of Probability

The essential difference between the experiments carried out by Piaget and Inhelder, described above, and other experiments of the probability learning type, is that in the former case the subject makes predictions while *knowing the structure of the conditions* (for example, the composition of the urn). This involves going beyond simple conditioning (although of a different type of classical conditioning) to processes of conceptual organisation which call into play specific operational schemas.

The experiments which we shall now discuss also call into play intellectual schemas, but in addition they throw light on *the ability of the subject to compare odds*, and therefore, in the first place, *to order them according to processes of estimation.*

Experiments by Piaget and Inhelder. Piaget and Inhelder report some experiments of this type (1951, pp. 144-72).

The child is shown two sets of white counters, some of which are marked with a cross. The child is fully aware of the composition of the sets. The counters are mixed in each set, and the subject is to decide which set has the greater probability of having a marked counter drawn from it. Several kinds of questions are put to the subject: (1) Double impossibility. Neither of the two sets contains a marked counter; nevertheless the child is asked to indicate whether a marked counter can be drawn. (2) Double certainty. All the counters are marked (the sets differing in size). (3) Certainty − impossibility. (4) Possibility − certainty. (5) Possibility − impossibility. (6) Identical sets. (7) Proportionality (the sets are numerically unequal, but the proportions of marked and unmarked counters within each is the same). (8) Inequality of marked counters and equality of total counters. (9) Equality of marked counters and inequality of total counters. (10) Inequality of marked and of total counters, without proportionality.

Stage I. Children aged 4-5 frequently give incorrect responses to these questions, even in cases where the solution appears obvious − as in situations where the total number of counters is equal (3/3 : 2/3) or the number of marked counters is equal (1/2 : 1/3), and so on.

In order to respond correctly, subjects had to consider, simultaneously, both the number of marked counters and the total number of counters in each set. According to Piaget and Inhelder, they did not succeed in making this double comparison, and their responses were determined by inessential features. For example, when comparing 1/2 : 2/4, children preferred the first set, since the uniqueness of the marked counter made them believe that it would be found more easily (in fact, the probabilities are equal). When comparing 1/2 : 1/3, they estimated that the odds were equal, since the number of marked counters is the same − without taking into account, therefore, the total number of counters.

Piaget and Inhelder's explanation of these failures is as follows. At this age, the child cannot yet reason correctly on the relationships between part and whole − a difficulty which is, in turn, due to the absence of reversibility. The child does not yet understand the reciprocity between the union ($A + A' = B$) and the partitions ($B - A = A'$) and ($B - A' = A$). If a whole is analysed into parts, it ceases to exist for the child as the potential result of a union (1951, pp. 156-7).

In consequence, the logical operation of disjunction cannot be carried out, since disjunction presupposes the possibility of alternation (either A or A') and also of remembering the whole of which the two classes are parts.

Lacking the support structure of logical procedures, the child of 4-6 is unable to perform the comparisons necessary for estimating odds. Such comparisons require analysis and disjunction and, in general, the correct understanding of whole-part relationships.

Stage IB (6-7 years). At this stage, children are not yet able to resolve problems in which both the number of favourable outcomes and the number of total possible outcomes are varied together (questions 7 and

10). They can cope, though only partially, with problems in which there is only one variable. The fact that correct responses are sometimes given (though only sometimes) is explained, according to Piaget and Inhelder, by the fact that these responses are not based on operational reasoning, but purely and simply on intuitive rules (pp. 159-60).

Piaget and Inhelder therefore attribute these cases to intuition, since the responses are based solely on the perceptual configuration of the sets.

Stage IIA (7-10 years). Responses to questions involving a single variable are systematically correct, and the arguments used show cognizance of favourable outcomes, unfavourable outcomes, and total possible outcomes to an equal extent.

In contrast, problems in which the number of favourable outcomes and the total number of possible outcomes are both varied are not generally solved, although the comments of the children show concern with both aspects simultaneously.

The difficulty with two-variable problems (questions 7 and 10) is explained by the intellectual requirements of this type of problem. A comparison of two ratios is called for. It is, in fact, a double comparison which requires the ability to think about two systems at the same time − an ability which does not emerge, according to Piaget and Inhelder, before the stage of formal operations.

Stage IIB (9-12 years). At this stage, subjects are beginning to give correct solutions to two-variable questions (7 and 10). But these problems are still solved by empirical methods, and not from a base of formal reasoning. The child considers the favourable outcomes and the unfavourable outcomes alternately, and then attempts to determine the differences between them.

In the case of equal ratios (and therefore equal odds) − for example 2/6 : 1/3, if the larger set is broken down in such a way that its subsets which are each equal to the smaller set become evident, the child recognises the proportionality. But when the larger set is reconstituted, the child forgets the solution. '. . . as a double relationship, proportion therefore requires formal operations, but before these are possible, intuitive solutions are adopted which are comparable to those which precede concrete operations' (p. 169).

In Stage III, children respond correctly in estimating proportions, although they are not yet able to perform explicit calculations with fractions.

The conclusion of Piaget and Inhelder is that 'fundamental probabilistic notions are not constructed until the level of formal operations' (ibid., p. 172) for the reason that proportions require 'second-order operations',

'operations on operations', which are not available until the level of formal operations.

Comparison of odds in pre-school children. The research by Piaget and Inhelder on the concepts of chance and probability has inspired other research which has been directed mainly at the question: is it possible to speak of a concept, even a rudimentary concept, of probability in the pre-school child?

Some research work has not confined itself to the pre-school level, but has also considered older children in order to outline the evolution of the concept as well as its ontogenesis.

The data available so far from this research seem to be contradictory. On the one hand, there are data from experiments of the probability learning type which indicate that something like an intuition of probability is already beginning to manifest itself in pre-school children − an indication which is particularly strongly supported by the phenomenon of adaptation to the probability of the stimulus (probability matching behaviour). On the other hand, data obtained by Piaget and Inhelder (and also by Offenbach from a probability learning experiment, 1964, 1965) indicate that the idea of probability is not systematically established until the level of formal operations, and that, before the age of 7, the child does not even possess the concepts of mixture and chance, much less the concept of comparing odds and probability. [. . .]

Developmental aspects. The role of verbal and perceptual factors [. . .] Davies (1965) set out to test the following hypothesis:

(1)   The acquisition of the concept of probability is a progressive phenomenon.

[. . .] Davies used six age levels in her experiments, based on yearly divisions between subjects aged from 3 to 9 years, with 16 subjects in each age level.

(2)   Non-verbal probabilistic behaviour appears before verbalisation of the concept of probability. This hypothesis is suggested both by data reported in the literature (especially probability matching behaviour) and by the naturalistically observed behaviour of children at the pre-operational level, which indicates that their responses are frequently adapted to the probabilities of events (Messik and Solley, 1957). [. . .]

The investigation of non-verbal behaviour was carried out in the following manner. Two glass jars were filled with red and white beads. In one of the jars, the proportion of white to red beads was 4/5, and in the other jar the proportion was reversed. By pressing on a lever, the subject could release a single bead. The subjects were told that they could make ten lever-presses, and for each bead of a specified colour they would receive a reward; four trials of ten lever-presses were run.

The subject could choose either jar for the ten lever-presses. The apparatus was set up in such a way that the beads were not in fact delivered from the jars which could be seen, but from one which was hidden from view, and which contained 5 red and 5 white beads, the proportion of delivered beads therefore being 50 per cent — 50 per cent. The last bead delivered was always of the rewarded colour, so that the total of 5 rewarded beads had not been delivered until the end of the trial.

This experimental arrangement tested simultaneously: (a) non-verbal behaviour in probabilistic situations; and (b) the relationship between direct, perceived information and information obtained by counting the frequencies of stimuli.

The results showed that subjects responded according to the perceived proportions — that is to say, they preferred the jar in which the proportion of rewarded beads was 4/5. This preference was maintained throughout the experiment, even though the proportions of beads actually delivered pointed to a different conclusion, and should, eventually, have led to an equalisation of preference between the two jars.

The verbal test. Davies used the following procedure. Five small boxes were filled with coloured beads in the same proportions as in the non-verbal test (4/5, 1/5), though the colours were different. The child was asked to draw a bead from each of the five boxes in turn, with eyes closed, and to name the colour of the bead drawn, together with a reason for naming that particular colour. After the five draws, the child was asked which colour would be drawn if each bead was returned to its box, and again to give reasons for the answer. Scores between 1 and 10 were awarded on the basis of overall test performance (considering the correctness both of responses and explanations); if the subject had named the less numerous colour, but in explanation had said that 'sometimes' this colour could be drawn, the response was counted correct.

The following results were obtained: (1) Confirming the hypothesis that the concept of probability is a progressive phenomenon, the percentage of correct responses increased with age. The mean ages at which subjects (a) failed both tests (b) passed only the non-verbal test (c) passed both tests respectively for (a) 3.11, for (b) 4.5, and for (c) 7.4 (Davies, 1965, p. 788). (2) The non-verbal behaviour of the pre-school child proves that the child behaves in conformity with the probabilities of events.

(3) Non-verbal behaviour reflecting objective probability (event probability) appears earlier than the corresponding verbal behaviour. This conclusion is based on the comparison between the percentages of correct responses on the verbal and non-verbal tests for each age group, and the fact that no subject responded correctly on the verbal test, but incorrectly on the non-verbal test. (4) The hypothesis that there would be a sex difference was not confirmed.

The result which seems to us to have particular importance is that, in the non-verbal test, children responded throughout the session in accordance with the *perceived proportions*, and not according to the frequency of reinforcement.

From data discussed previously, we know that the child adapts its responses to the frequency of reinforcement.

In Davies' experiments, we have a situation of conflict between a directly perceived proportion and a frequency which must be computed. In such a situation, the *probability of reinforcement no longer controls the responses of the child, which come instead under the control of the directly perceived proportion.*

Comparing her results with those of Piaget and Inhelder, Davies suggests that they have based their conclusions exclusively on the verbal behaviour of the child, in so far as they claim that the concept of probability is established during the period of formal operations. (In fact, Piaget and Inhelder indicate that the concept of probability is not established as a generalised modality of thought until the level of formal operations, thereby implicating operations on proportions and combinations.)

Davies' experiments have established the fact that, in estimating odds, the child uses predominantly information which is directly perceived. If there is conflict between this and information which is obtained by computing frequencies, it is the perceptual information which will determine the child's prediction. This fact leads us to wonder whether in fact the responses of the child, at least until the age of 6-7, are only *apparently* judgements of probability, and may be reduced to comparative evaluations of sizes alone, which would be a quite different process.

Taking the experiments of [. . .] Davies (1965), [. . . and others] as their starting point, Hoemann and Ross (1971) have tried to settle this question of whether 'probabilistic' judgements by children really are probabilistic. Their hypothesis was that pre-school children do not make probabilistic judgements; their responses only *appear* to be probabilistic, because of the experimental context in which they are made, and they are in reality nothing more than perceptual comparisons.

It was therefore necessary to set up experiments which would differentiate probabilistic judgements from perceptual comparisons. Certain details of the experimental procedure will be described below, since they are crucial to a correct interpretation of the results. In all, four experiments were carried out.

Subjects in the first experiment were aged 4, 6, 7 and 10, and were divided into sets of two groups within each age level, corresponding to two experimental conditions.

On a series of paper discs were drawn circles which were segmented in black and white to differing proportions. In the probability condition, two such discs were attached to two spinners. The subject was asked to choose the spinner which would give the best chance of winning on the colour designated by the experimenter. In the proportionality condition, the subject simply had to choose the disc which contained more white (or black). In some cases, the discs had only two segments, one black and one white; in other cases the segments of black and white alternated.

The rationale behind this experiment was as follows. If there were approximately the same number of errors in both experimental conditions, it could be supposed that the judgements which were being made were not probabilistic, but perceptual. If there were fewer correct responses in the probability condition, it could be supposed that the difference was due to some probabilistic judgement, over and above perceptual judgement.

Three odds difference levels between discs were used, 1/2, 1/4 , and 1/8 (i.e. differences between proportions in which the desired colour covered the two discs which the subject had to compare. For instance: $7/8 - 3/8 = 4/8 = 1/2$).

The main finding was that there were no significant differences between the two conditions at any age level. (In fact, the data show a slightly lower percentage of correct responses in the probability condition, particularly in the case of younger subjects.)

Hoemann and Ross conclude from this experiment that the experimental design used could not differentiate between perceptual comparisons and probability judgements. The correct responses of subjects showed only their ability to perceptually compare two different sizes.

The second experiment used seven age levels, with subjects aged between 4 and 13. This time, the task involved comparisons on a single disc. In the probability condition, the subject was asked to say on which colour the pointer would stop after the spinner had started. In the proportionality condition, the subject was asked simply to compare the amounts of black and white, and say which was the greater.

The results showed significant differences between the two conditions: there were more errors in the probability judgement task. The authors conclude that this is a task which is capable of testing the ability to make probability judgements (in contrast to the two spinners task). It also emerged from the results that 4-year-old subjects are not capable of probability judgements, since the number of correct responses given by these children (56 per cent), did not differ significantly from the chance level. Between the ages of 5 and 8, there is a clear improvement in performance on the proportionality task, but performance on the probability task is still very poor.

Hoemann and Ross claim that these findings contradict the view of [. . .] Davies (1965), [. . . and others] that pre-school children are capable of probability judgement, and that they confirm the view of Piaget and Inhelder, which is that it is impossible to speak of a concept of chance and probability before the stage of concrete operations.

Hoemann and Ross's third experiment used the same conditions as the first experiment, with the difference that the subjects were asked to compare several colours on the two discs. There were two groups of 7 year-old children, each group corresponding to one experimental condition. The results were very close to those obtained in the experiment using only one spinner.

Instead of the spinners, experiment four used draws of coloured (red and green) ping-pong balls from transparent urns. The procedure was essentially the same as in similar experiments by [. . .] Goldberg (1966) and others, in which the subject, knowing the composition of the urns, must estimate which urn offers the greatest chances of drawing an item of a specified colour. The subjects were normal children at two age levels (7 and 11) and deaf children of 11 years. The same odds difference levels were used (1/2, 1/4 and 1/8).

The results of experiment four were similar to those of experiment three, showing that a task requiring comparisons of sets of discrete elements (ping-pong balls) can differentiate probabilistic from perceptual judgements. The similarity of results leads to the conclusion that the different tasks used in these two experiments are in fact analogous.

Hoemann and Ross come to the overall conclusion that their experiments two, three, and four confirm the view of Piaget and Inhelder that pre-school children do not possess concepts of chance and probability.

It also emerges from all the experiments by Hoemann and Ross that performance improves with age.

Hoemann and Ross posed the fundamental problem of differentiating between true probabilistic judgements and judgements which are simply perceptual size comparisons, which have been mistaken for true probabilistic judgements by other investigators.

Their central argument is that, in certain tasks, the results which could be obtained from estimating odds could just as easily be obtained by direct comparison of sizes, while in other tasks the difference between these two processes is made apparent.

This reasoning is vulnerable at several points. It is clear, in the first place, that size comparison enters into probabilistic judgement, since odds are represented in size relationships. This underlying comparison may be made in either perceptual or numerical terms, and in either case can be more or less complex. The transition from this initial comparison to actual estimation of odds may be direct, or it may be complicated by the nature of the problem itself.

The fact that a child asked to compare certain probabilities on two discs segmented into two colours obtains the same result for the probabilistic task and for the perceptual comparison does not necessarily prove that probabilistic judgement has not taken place. In such a task, the estimation of odds proceeds directly from the perceptual comparison, but this does not show that it can be completely reduced to this perceptual comparison. The actual wording of the test used by Hoemann and Ross was as follows: 'I want you to look at the two spinners very carefully and show me which one you will spin to make the pointer point to black (white)' (Hoemann and Ross, p. 244).

The problem as posed is in terms of estimating odds, and a correct response indicates that the child really does (although no doubt implicitly) make use of the idea of chance. Otherwise the child could not respond to this question as it is posed! The use of perceptual comparison *mediates* the response. Nothing in the formulation of the question *directly* suggests a perceptual comparison. The child is simply asked to show the spot where the spinner will stop. Without an intuition of probability, nothing suggests a quantitative comparison of the two colours. It could equally well be maintained that, in more difficult problems, where the estimation of proportions must be carried out, correct responses do not depend on probability judgements, but can be reduced to comparing proportions — whether perceptual or numerical.

It seems therefore to be the nature of the problem, including the way in which it is formulated, which will show whether the task — and the respective response — involves a probabilistic judgement or not.

There is still the problem of why, in some cases, responses to probabilistic tasks are poorer than responses to perceptual or the corresponding numerical comparisions (cf. Hoemann and Ross's second experiment). The most plausible explanation is that given by Piaget and Inhelder for an analogous situation. They found that, when sets of beads are used, better responses are obtained if two sets of beads are compared for probabilities than if two colours are compared within a single set '. . . in the case of a single set . . . the combination of elements in a single intuitive unit prevents the subject from thinking simultaneously of the whole and of the parts' (Piaget and Inhelder, 1951, p. 161).

Direct perceptual comparison is straightforward. The child simply has to show the colour which is present in larger quantity. But in order to estimate odds, the child has to relate each of the colours in turn to the total area of the disc. In the condition with *two* spinners, *there are two equal total areas* which are simultaneously perceived. In the single spinner condition, the *same total area* must serve simultaneously for both comparisons. The degree of abstraction required is greater.

Things are complicated still more when the two colours are divided into several alternating segments (as in Hoemann and Ross' experiments). In this situation, the child tends to respond at random.

The fact that inadequacy of response in probabilistic tasks can be caused by the specific nature of the task itself, i.e. by the way in which the estimation of proportions is to be carried out, rather than by the probabilistic aspect of the problem, is demonstrated also by the following result described by Hoemann and Ross. When two spinners were used, and subjects were asked to estimate chances *in a situation where several colours were winning* (third experiment), poorer responses were obtained, analogous to the responses obtained with a single disc in the first experiment.

Now, from the point of view of strict probability judgement, there is no difference between situations in which the winning elements are all of the same colour, and situations in which they are of more than one colour. *The difficulty consists in the perceptual comparison itself.*

Our conclusion is that the similarity of results obtained from probabilistic tasks and from tasks requiring numerical or perceptual comparisons does not constitute a sufficient argument for the view that there is no probabilistic judgement in these tasks. *Furthermore, the fact that subjects respond well to problems whose formulation implies the estimation of chances seems to us to constitute the proof that they are operating with the concept of chance, even if the estimation is carried out on the basis of simple perceptual comparisons.*

3. The Effect of Instruction on the Quantitative Estimation of Odds

The results obtained by Piaget and Inhelder (1951), [. . .] Davies (1965), and Goldberg (1966) have been from naive, unpractised subjects.

Together with Mînzat and Pămpu, we have approached the problem of the concept of probability in children from the point of view of the results which can be obtained by means of systematic instruction.

It will be recalled that Ojemann *et al.* (1965a, b, 1966) also used a programme of systematic instruction in order to develop probabilistic concepts, and they obtained significant improvements in children aged 11 and upwards.

We have used a similar approach (1970), but working with children aged 5, 9, and 12, in order to observe the interaction of instruction with age [. . .] We made use of a *decision-making* technique [. . .]

From two plastic boxes containing black and white marbles (for example 6 white and 2 black marbles in one box, 10 white and 5 black in the other) the child was asked to select the box which, because of its content, favoured the *chance* extraction of a marble of a specified colour.

We asked the subjects 18 questions, divided into three categories. In category C_1, the ratios between the two sets of marbles were arranged in such a way that the black and white marbles in one box were equal in number, or that the number of marbles of one colour were the same in both boxes (for example, 1 white, 2 black; 5 white, 2 black — an arrangement which clearly facilitates the choice). In C_2, no restrictions were placed on the arrangement of the marbles. C_3 consisted of 'equal' ratios, i.e. proportions. The experiments comprised three variants:

Condition I_1: the subjects received only a brief explanation of the nature of the experiment, and of the three possible responses with regard to the choice of box with the most probable favourable outcome (right, left, indifferent).

Condition I_2: the subjects received a short, but systematic explanation of how the problems could be solved. This had two stages: (a) two boxes containing, for example, 4B, 1W and 8B, 2W were presented, and after 20 draws from each box it was pointed out that the relative frequencies of black marbles which were drawn were equal (this result was arranged in advance, in order not to have to complicate the explanation); (b) the child was shown a technique of grouping which would permit the practical solution of the problems; for example, 4B, 1W and 8B, 2W become 4B, 1W and 4B, 1W + 4B, 1W — i.e. the probabilities are equal, since out of 5 marbles, 4 are black, in each box.

If there are, for example, 4B, 1W and 9B, 2W, this shows the excess of black in the second box. We used this technique for two reasons: (a) it requires no knowledge of fractions, (b) it clearly demonstrates the concept of proportionality and relative frequency.

Condition I_3: in this variant, the subjects received only explanations concerning the technique of grouping described for I_2, but with a larger number of examples.

In I_2 and I_3, subjects were taught essentially that chances cannot be estimated only by considering the number of possible favourable outcomes, but that it is necessary to relate this number to the total composition of the box.

The experiment was designed as a factorial experiment with three factors: 3 age levels x 3 instruction types x 3 question categories, with repeated measures (the same subjects) on the last factor. Twenty different subjects were assigned to each experimental condition (I_1, I_2, I_3). There was a total of 180 subjects.

In condition I_1, there were nearly as many pre-school as 9-10 year-old children who correctly solved *only C_1 tests* (which were reducible to a comparison of two terms). In contrast, 12-13 year-old subjects were able to deal with all three categories of problem, without special instruction.

In conditions I_2 and I_3, with prior instruction, there were no essential differences from condition I_1 as far as the pre-school and the older children were concerned. The pre-school children could not be induced to carry out a double comparison, or to understand the idea of proportionality, which is an essential component of the concept of probability, while the 12-13 year-old subjects gave good responses from the outset. *There were striking improvements in the responses of 9-10 year-olds, who, after brief instruction, were able to carry out the double comparison required for the evaluation of chances, and in general to operate correctly with the concept of probability.*

According to Piaget and Inhelder, such concepts are not available until the level of formal operations (after 12 years); but their data have been based exclusively on spontaneous responses of subjects. The finding that the mental mechanisms necessary for the active understanding of proportionality are already present at the level of concrete operations and can be brought into play by means of brief instruction, is of central importance to the teaching of probability.

Experimental Lessons

As a result of the findings detailed above, we proceeded, during the school year 1972-73, to investigate the effects of some experimental lessons on notions of probability and statistics with children aged 9, 10, 11, 12 and 13.

We judged that the best learning conditions could be created by pointing out simultaneously the combinatorial, statistical, and probabilistic aspects of certain practical solutions.

In our view, these notions must be learned, in the first place, from concrete experiences which demonstrate the dynamics of stochastic phenomena which are subject to statistical laws. [. . .]

We began by teaching, with the aid of examples, the notion of an *event*,[†] and the notions of a possible event, a certain event, and an impossible event. The concept of probability was presented as a measure of the foreseeable chances in a given situation (passing from the intuitive estimation of odds by the children, as described in the experiments above, to the classical definition). The fundamental notion to be conveyed by these lessons was that of *the stability of relative frequencies,* and this was attempted by means of a dual approach.

First procedure: the children were shown an urn containing beads of two colours, and the probabilities were determined by referring to the composition of the contents of the urn. One colour was designated as 'winning'. Each child drew a bead, which was thus either winning or losing. The bead was then replaced, and the result of the draw was recorded on a blackboard. The relative frequencies were indicated in blocks of 10 draws, and the children were able to follow the oscillations of frequencies. This procedure included: (a) a theoretical prediction, (b) an experiment verifying the prediction, (c) a demonstration of the oscillating frequencies, with their convergence towards a theoretical point, which is the probability.

This type of instruction is doubly attractive. The children observe with great interest the result of each draw, since it scores a loss or gain for the child concerned. They also follow the oscillations of the results very closely, to see whether or not the prediction will be borne out.

Second procedure: an urn was filled with beans, of which a few were coloured. Some of the beans were scooped out, and counted. This operation was repeated several times, and the relationship between the number of coloured beans drawn and the total drawn was commented upon each time. It was pointed out that the values expressing this relationship oscillate around the value deduced from the composition of the total contents of the urn.

From this procedure, the children accquire the important concept of the *sample*. They realise its practical significance, the way in which a sample is obtained, they begin to understand statistical inference, and they begin to grasp the inductive steps of scientific investigation. It would be possible to outline a variety of procedures which could achieve this, but it is not the teaching methods as such we wish to emphasise. What seems to us most important is that *practical experience with probabilities provides an ideal way of familiarising children with the fundamental concepts of science, such as prediction, experiment and verification, chance and necessity, laws and statistical laws, knowledge through induction, and so on.* Children show great interest in this type of activity, which has all the characteristics of a game (since it is the children themselves who make the draws, and who 'lose' or 'win') but is at the same time a true scientific experiment.

All of these lessons made use of the children's knowledge of fractions, which was in turn enhanced by relating to a multiplicity of possible situations.

Finally, a varied range of phenomena were discussed from a probabilistic perspective (physical, meteorological, biological, demographic and sociological phenomena, and the practical and scientific usefulness of sampling).

With the 11-year-old children (who had already had experimental instruction from us in previous years), the emphasis was on using combinatory ability by means of tree diagrams. Diagrams were constructed which corresponded, for instance, to two, three, four, or five draws of two or three letters (or numbers) from an urn.

A diagram like this permits us to (a) represent the concept of equiprobability (which is quite difficult for children to understand) in visual terms; (b) attach probabilities to some possible results (for example, 'what is the probability of drawing A four times in a row?' or 'what is the probability of drawing B twice in a row in four draws?', and so on); (c) show that extreme cases are rare, and that 'mixed' cases are far more frequent; (d) prepare the intuitive ground for theorems concerning the addition and multiplication of probabilities.

We have also used tree diagrams for experiments with sampling without replacement, in which the probabilities change with each draw. The children were easily able to construct the corresponding diagrams. The main aim of the exercises was to induce the essential mental skills of combinatory thinking. If this step is omitted, and the pupils exposed too suddenly to formulae and schemas, they may be able to solve standard exercises, but will not be so capable of independent and productive thought in this domain.

We also judged it necessary to introduce the *statistical dimension of probability* in this context. At the end of the second lesson, the children were given the following piece of practical homework: to write the capital letters A and B on individual slips of paper, fold them, and put them in a container; then to make four successive draws, mixing the slips of paper well each time, and to make a note of each letter drawn. This was to be done five times.

During the next lesson, a diagram of the sample space† was drawn on the blackboard, and for each event in this sample space (each event being one of the 16 possible sets of letters) the number of times it had occurred during the homework assignment was noted. If 32 children each drew 5 sets of letters, this meant that there was a total of 160 sets which must be distributed across the 16 cells of the diagram. This indicated that, in theory, each set should occur 10 times (160/16 = 10). The children were able to see that, in fact, the frequency of occurrence of each set did oscillate around this number, and that this was due purely to chance — since each child had independently drawn five sets of letters.

An experiment like this is another way of demonstrating the empirical tendency of relative frequencies to oscillate around the theoretically calculated probability, and of consolidating the children's understanding of the relationship between the empirical and theoretical components of the concept of probability. Such an experiment also has the following advantages: (a) the concept of an event is amplified; the unitary event, irreducible from the point of view of the definition of the experiment, is not, in this case, the result of a single draw, but the result of 4 draws (a set of 4 letters). (b) The children acquire an understanding of what is meant by 'possible case', 'equally possible cases', and 'total number of equally possible cases'. The sequence ABBA, for instance, is a possible case — it could occur at any time. But, in fact, *every sequence is logically possible.* They are equally possible for reasons of symmetry, since, all other things being equal, there is no reason to believe that any one sequence will occur more often than any other. The draws prove· that chance operates in such a way that each event does occur the same number of times. This is, again, a way of seeing a theoretically deduced prediction confirmed. Understanding of the fundamental concept of 'equally possible cases' requires the fusion, within the effective experimental context, of the logical and the empirical view, as described above. (c) Finally, there is the advantage that in familiarising the children with such an inventory of all possible outcomes within a given situation, one has in fact given them the concept of a sample space.

The most surprising finding was that even those children who had previously been weak in mathematics were attracted by this type of activity. Furthermore, this produced an improvement in all their mathematical abilities. We were able to confirm that these experimental lessons in statistics and probability stimulated the imagination of young adolescents, who participated naturally and enthusiastically in this game of setting up an inventory of possibilities and making predictions from it.

In order to give a more detailed picture of the content of the lessons (for the 11-year-olds) and of the results obtained, we will give below the questions in the final written test, and the percentages of correct responses.

(1)   There are 3 white beads, 2 black beads, and 5 red beads in a jar. What is the probability that the following will be drawn by chance? (a) a white bead? (b) a white bead after another white bead has been drawn? (c) either a black bead or a white bead?

(2)   A jar contains identical counters on which the numbers 1 or 2 have been marked. 4 successive draws are made, and each time the drawn counter is replaced. Draw a diagram representing the sample space. What is the probability of drawing (a) the number 2 four times in succession? (b) a set whose numbers total 6? (c) a set in which the first two numbers are 2? (d) a set in which the number 2 occurs exactly twice? (e) a set containing the number 1 at least twice?

(3)   A jar contains the letters A, E and R marked on identical counters. What is the probability of drawing: (a) a meaningful word? (b) an adjective? (c) a verb? Write down the words you have thought of in answering these questions.

(4)   How many combinations of three numbers can be formed, using the numbers from 1 to 9, if (a) the numbers can be repeated? (b) the numbers cannot be repeated?

(5)   The Ionescu family have three children. What is the probability that: (a) they are all boys? (b) there are just two boys? (c) there are at least two boys?

(6)   The numbers from 1 to 9 are placed in a jar. Four successive draws are made, replacing the drawn number each time. What is the probability of drawing a set in which none of the numbers is repeated?

The following percentages of correct responses to these questions were obtained:

(1)   (a) 93.7;   (b) 77.5;   (c) 81.9.
(2)   (a) 93.3;   (b) 84.6;   (c) 83.8;   (d) 80.8;   (e) 75.8.
(3)   (a) 53.9;   (b) 55.8;   (c) 53.7;   (d) 66.2.
(4)   (a) 78.5;   (b) 75.8.
(5)   (a) 81.7;   (b) 76.0;   (c) 72.4.
(6)   31.6.

Many children gave erroneous responses to question (3), since they had thought that letters could be repeated. A small investigation, however, led us to the discovery that it was their teachers who had wrongly advised them! We have in fact found more difficulty in making teachers understand the concepts of probability than in making their pupils understand them. The teachers had wrongly corrected the tests on several occasions; the children had given the correct responses, but the teachers had interpreted the questions wrongly. This is in fact an important finding, since it demonstrates the loss with age of certain intuitive faculties. An adolescent has better chances of rebuilding an intuitive structure than an adult.

The Intuitive Foundations of Elementary Probabilistic Operations

During the experimental lessons we have described, we became aware of certain intuitive deficiencies when we attempted to teach the probabilities of mutually exclusive and independent events. We carried out a research project with Ileana Bărbat and Ion Mînzat (1970) in order to specify the details of these deficiencies. The subjects were adolescents aged 13, 15, and 17. [. . .]

The technique we devised (and called *learning by programmed discovery*) consisted of asking subjects successive standardised questions which could be reduced to smaller items. For each problem, we started with a specialised question, depending on the field, and if the correct response was not obtained, we asked progressively more general, elementary questions which were closer to the relevant intuition. With this technique, the subjects revealed their difficulties and abilities, and in fact the whole range of mental and intuitive mechanisms, whether correct or erroneous, available to them in attempting to solve any given problem.

We were interested in the following aspects: probability as a metric of chance, the multiplication law of probabilities, the addition law (particularly in the case of mutually exclusive events) and the use of these laws, once learned.

We found, as we had done in previous investigations, that the concepts of chance and probability could be built on a natural intuitive foundation. This primary intuition also facilitated the acquisition of the basic axioms of the theory of probability. In the case of independent events, primary intuition facilitates understanding of the multiplication law (chances are reduced as more conditions are imposed), but the final calculation cannot be found intuitively.

In the case of mutually exclusive events, the probability is naturally deduced by the addition of the probabilities of the elementary events. There is, however, a difficulty in the operation of making an inventory of these elementary, equiprobable events, and, prior to this, in understanding that such a complete inventory is necessary in the first place. Generally speaking, intuition contributes nothing to these two steps.

Within the age limits investigated (13-17) there was no improvement in the primary intuitive base relevant to probability. If specific instructional procedures are not used, the intuitive base remains unchanged from the period of formal operations onward.

The Estimation of Odds: Summary

Pre-school children possess a natural intuition of chance and the quantification of chance, but, at this age, only estimations based on binary comparisons are possible. Instruction does not bring about any significant improvement in this respect.

If appropriate instruction is given at the level of concrete operations, children can learn to compare odds by means of a quantitative comparison of ratios.

At the level of formal operations, these estimations are carried out directly. The difficulties encountered by the intelligence in acquiring and using probabilistic concepts are explained in part by certain fundamental lacunae within the set of intuitions relevant to probability, and in part by an increasing tendency of maturing intelligence to seek univocal causal explanations.

References

Davies, C.M. (1965), 'Development of the probability concept in children', *Child Development*, 36 (3), 779-88.

Fischbein, E. (1975), *The Intuitive Sources of Probabilistic Thinking in Children*, Hingham, Mass., Reidel Publications.

Fischbein, E., Bărbat, I. and Mînzat, I. (1970), 'Comparison of ratios and the chance concept in children', *Child Development*, 41 (2), 377-89.

Fischbein, E., Pămpu, I. and Mînzat, I. (1967), 'The Child's Intuition of Probability', *Enfance*, 2, 193-207.

Fischbein, E., Pămpu, I. and Mînzat, I. (1970), 'Effects of age and instruction on combinatory ability in children', *Bri. Jnl. Ed. Psych.*, 40 (3), 261-70.

Goldberg, S. (1966), 'Probability judgements by pre-school children: task conditions and performance', *Child Development*, 37 (1), 157-67.

Hoemann, H.W. and Ross, B.M. (1971), 'Children's understanding of probability concepts', *Child Development*, 42 (1), 221-36.

Messick, S.J. and Solley, C.M. (1957), 'Word-association and semantic differentiation', *American Journal of Psychology*, 70, 586-93.

Offenbach, S.I. (1964), 'Studies of children's probability learning behaviour: I. Effect of reward and punishment at two age levels', *Child Development*, 35 (3), 709-16.

Offenbach, S.I. (1965), 'Studies of children's probability learning behaviour: II. Effect of method and event frequency at two age levels', *Child Development*, 36 (4), 951-62.

Ojemann, R.H., Maxey, E.J. and Snider, B.C.F. (1965a), 'Effects of guided learning experiences in developing probability concepts at the third grade level', *Jnl. Exp.*

Education, 33 (4), 321-30.

Ojemann, R.H., Maxey, E.J. and Snider, B.C.F. (1965b), 'Effects of guided learning experiences in developing probability concepts at the fifth grade level', *Perceptual and Motor Skills*, 21 (2), 415-27.

Ojemann, R.H., Maxey, E.J. and Snider, B.C.F. (1966), 'Further study of guided learning experiences in developing probability concepts in grade five', *Perceptual and Motor Skills*, 23 (1), 97-8.

Piaget, J. and Inhelder, B. (1975), *The Origin of the Idea of Chance in Children*, London, Routledge and Kegan Paul.

6 MORAL DEVELOPMENT: THE COGNITIVE-DEVELOPMENTAL APPROACH

Derek Graham

Source: Chapter 8 in V.P. Varma and P. Williams (eds.), *Piaget, Psychology and Education* (Hodder and Stoughton, 1976).

The main concern of the cognitive-developmental approach to moral development is with cognitive factors and with moral awareness and thinking. It does not deny that other aspects may be important, but its focus of interest is upon the cognitive aspect. This approach also stresses that moral development takes place in an orderly way which cannot wholly be accounted for by the specific experience of the individual as viewed from outside. Common to this approach has been the notion of stages of development, each characterised by its own particular qualities. There is no implication of discontinuity between stages. Each stage, as it were, merges into the next.

Piaget's Pioneering Work

Piaget's book, *The Moral Judgment of the Child* (1932), represents his attempt to apply the notion of stages of development, which he had already used in other ways, to the development of moral judgement. Piaget, like Kohlberg later, is primarily concerned with moral judgement rather than behaviour or affect, although no doubt he would have expected to find some relationship between these. According to Piaget, development takes place as a result of interaction between the child and the (social) environment.

1. First of all, Piaget concerns himself with children's conceptions of the 'rules of the game' — in particular the game of marbles. He says, in fact, 'The little boys who are beginning to play are gradually trained by the older ones in respect for the law: and in any case they aspire from their hearts to the virtue supremely characteristic of human dignity, which consists in making a correct use of the customary practice of a game. As to the older ones, it is in their power to alter the rules. If this is not 'morality', then where does morality begin? At least, it is respect for rules and it appertains to an enquiry like ours to begin with the study of facts of this order' (p. 2).

In the development and practice of children's application and understanding of rules, there are, Piaget proposes, three stages: (i) The stage of 'motor behaviour' when the only rules or 'regularities' the child observes are purely individual habits. The 'motor rule' thus arises out of habit, but does not include any of the obligatory nature of the social rule. Nevertheless, the 'motor rule' would seem to be necessary for the later development of social rules. (ii) the 'egocentric' stage in which the child becomes interested in the rule-regulated behaviour of older children, but does not appreciate the *social* nature and function of rules. Piaget remarks, 'Egocentrism in so far as it means confusion of the ego and the external world, and egocentrism in so far as it means lack of cooperation, constitute one and the same phenomenon. So long as the child does not dissociate his ego from the suggestions coming from the physical and from the social world, he cannot cooperate, for in order to cooperate one must be conscious of one's ego, it is necessary to liberate oneself from the thought and will of others. The coercion exercised by the adult or the older child is therefore inseparable from the unconscious egocentrism of the young child' (p. 87). The coercive rule depends upon the unilateral respect of the child for authority of the adult. Fair comment might perhaps be that the authority of the adult is likely to rest on his *power* to dispense rewards and punishments. (iii) Finally, children reach a point where they have mastered the rules of the game as such. We have here mutual respect and a concern for reciprocity, together with a degree of autonomy in the sense of the child's understanding of the nature of the decision-making, and of the mutual obligations between himself and others. Thus we find Piaget virtually distinguishing three stages in the application and appreciation of the rules of the game — an amoral stage; a stage at which rules are seen as coercive, sacrosanct, with binding power in their own right; and a stage at which rules are seen as the product of agreement and are thereby modifiable by mutual consent. The major distinction is between a 'heteronomous' attitude in which binding power rests with 'authority', and an 'autonomous' attitude which involves mutual consent.

2. Piaget believes that 'moral realism' is characteristic of childhood up to the age of about nine years. The aspect of moral realism which has attracted most attention is the notion of 'objective responsibility' versus 'subjective responsibility' or intention. If an offence is judged in terms of 'objective responsibility', the seriousness of the offence is estimated in terms of the seriousness of the consequences rather than in terms of the intentions of the actor. Piaget claims that 'the notion of objective responsibility diminishes as the child grows older' (p. 120), although he admits

that some children of only six years of age do in fact judge in terms of intention rather than in terms of consequences. Piaget seems to think that adult constraint contributes to an attitude of 'objective responsibility' because at least some adults apply their sanctions so as to suggest that it is the damage done rather than the intention which matters. But he is also careful to point out that 'those parents who try to give their children a moral education based on intention, achieve very early results, as is shown by current observation' (p. 130). Thus, according to Piaget, in at least one way parents may have a real positive influence. Piaget has not always been allowed credit for this kind of observation.

Piaget believes that his studies of moral realism suggest an advance from judgment in terms of consequences to judgment in terms of intention. He suggests that moral realism results from the nature of the child's mental development, *together with* the way in which children are treated by adults. Moral realism is thus associated with unilateral respect or heteronomy, and is also associated, in Piaget's view, with *intellectual* realism as shown in the child's tendency to draw things as he *knows* they are rather than as he sees them.

3. Piaget's third concern is with *justice*. Here, he is mainly concerned with punishment. One may regard punishment in a *retributive* way, as the dire and proper consequences of wrong-doing; or one may regard punishment as a question of reciprocity — of seeing that the transgressor puts right, or atones *appropriately* for, any wrong he commits, or at least is held responsible for the consequences of his misdeeds. Piaget himself found that the proportion of 'expiatory' punishments recommended by children decreased from six to ten years of age. Piaget may be criticised here for not being more definite in what he meant by 'reciprocity'. This seems to cover a whole range of punishments from 'an eye for an eye and a tooth for a tooth' to simply seeing that the offender appreciated the fact that he had broken the rules of mutual obligation.

Much has been made of Piaget's idea of 'immanent justice'. A belief in 'immanent justice' means that the believer feels that punishment for wrong-doing emanates from the world itself, and such a belief is, according to Piaget, widely held by younger children. Piaget believes that the belief 'originates in a transference to things of feelings acquired under the influence of adult constraint' (p. 260). Thus adult constraint is again the villain of the piece. Belief in immanent justice disappears as the child realises the relativity of adult justice, and acquires an attitude of co-operation rather than one of subservience.

Piaget does not find the *same* developmental stages in these three areas, but the major point he wishes to make is that there is progression from a 'heteronomous' to an 'autonomous' basis for moral judgment. Whereas Freud's theory emphasises — indeed overemphasises — the importance of the child's subservient relation to his parents, Piaget's theory emphasises the importance of the child's interaction with his peers, although, as we have indicated, he allows that the attitude adopted by the parents may be important. In general, however, Piaget does seem to underestimate the positive influence of parental precept and example in the development of moral judgments and attitudes. At the least, it would appear reasonable to suppose that discipline imposed from without by parents and other adults may provide the basis in control of behaviour, for the adult self-discipline and 'autonomy' upon which Piaget lays such stress. Piaget himself writes, 'Adult authority, although perhaps it constitutes a necessary moment in the moral evolution of the child, is not sufficient to create a sense of justice' (p. 319). In any event, adult authority may contribute substantially to aspects of morality other than justice. Justice is not the *only* thing that matters.

Studies Deriving from Piaget's Work

Piaget's claim that, with increasing age and social interaction with peers, the basis of judgment shifts from a consideration of *consequences* to a consideration of *intentions* has received a good deal of support (see Graham, 1972). Kugelmass and Breznitz (1968) suggest that intentionality increases slowly from the age of eleven years to the age of fourteen years, quite quickly from fourteen to seventeen years and then again less rapidly. Kugelmass and Breznitz very reasonably suggest that the cognitive ability to abstract principles is here crucial. Turner (1966), as reported by Lunzer and Morris (1968), claims that in Piaget's story about the two children, one of whom broke many cups with good intentions while the other broke only one cup but that deliberately, we have in the first case good intentions coupled with disastrous results, and in the second case bad intentions coupled with less catastrophic results. Turner holds that there must be an intermediate stage in development, in which the subject would say that the first child was *really* good and the second *really* bad, but would be unable to *retain* this judgment and would say that the 'good' child was *worse* than the 'bad' child because of the consequences when both children were judged together. The implication of the relevance of *cognitive ability* cannot be denied. A developed intelligence is necessary for the development of effective moral principles.

There has also been support for Piaget's ideas on immanent justice (see Graham, 1972), although it seems that cultural relativity may be important here.

As a matter of fact, more recent research relevant to Piaget's moral theory has mostly been concerned with 'intentionality'. Schleifer and Douglas (1973) used Piaget's 'intentionality' stories to study the effect of training. They wished to see whether the effect of training would last over time and generalise to rather different material. In their first experiment, they selected a population of six-year-old children who did not spontaneously make 'intentional' judgments on Piaget's stories. As they observed, all the pairs of Piaget stories contrasted good intentions plus a large amount of damage with bad intentions plus a small amount of damage. For their follow-up test, Schleifer and Douglas modified several pairs of stories so as to *match* bad intentions and extent of consequences. Training consisted of correcting 'low-level' ('consequences') responses and explaining why they were wrong, and also of discussing the general principles involved in *intentions*. In one group of subjects, an adult explained and discussed, while in a second group, a child of the same age as the subjects did so. Nearly all the subjects showed the effect of training in making more judgments in terms of intentionality. This advance was maintained after four weeks. One would have liked some evidence that similar, more extended training would have had effects persisting over a longer period.

In their second experiment, with children of five and a half and three and a half years of age, Schleifer and Douglas used films as visual equivalents of Piaget's stories. At these ages, both controls and trained children showed an increase in intentionality, although the trained children showed more advance.

Schleifer and Douglas incline on the whole to agree with Turiel (1969) that the effect of training is to advance the child's cognitive level rather than to bring about specific learning effects. With Turiel, they think that the operative factor is probably the presentation of alternative points of view which stimulate thinking about the issues involved. Similarly, Jensen and Larm (1970) found trained subjects superior in *explaining* their choices, and think that this indicates that they really understood the concept. They also found training by discussion superior to simple reinforcement.

Jensen and Hafen (1973) take up Piaget's suggestion that the change from immature to mature judgment (between three and nine years of age) results mainly from social interaction with peers. Young children were read pairs of stories describing an act which caused damage. They were asked to say which was the worse of the two acts. Two groups were involved. In the first group, children were rewarded when they chose the action where damage was intended. In the second group, children took part in a discussion of their choices. *Both* types of training increased the likelihood that children would take account of intentions in their judgments. Such experiments, however, while illustrating that different procedures may both have a reinforcing (short-term) effect, are scarcely relevant to the wider, long-term implications of Piaget's thinking.

Costanzo, Coie, Grumet and Farnill (1973) remark that Piaget seems to imply that children in the 'preoperational' stage do not use intention as a basis of judgment. They remark that since Piaget's stories 'covary two parameters at once, it is impossible to decide whether these children make their choice on the basis of the consequences because intentionality is considered irrelevant to the choice or whether outcome is seen as simply the more salient and identifiable cue for their moral discriminations' (p. 155). This is a good point. Costanzo *et al.* ask the question, 'How far do emergence from moral realism and the ability to take the social perspective of another reflect the same underlying cognitive processes?' This would appear indeed to be a crucial question. Costanzo *et al.* found that older children attributed more importance to intentions in respect of *harmful* consequences, but that there was little age difference in respect of *beneficial* consequences. They suggest that the *child himself* (the 'perpetrator') may well be evaluated by young children according to consequences with little attention to intentions.

In a very relevant article, Chandler, Greenspan and Barenboim (1973) argue that previous studies have suggested that children concentrate on consequences up to the age of about nine years. These authors argue that, in such studies, verbal presentations have made consequences *more salient* than intentions. In their own experiment, the authors used children of approximately six years of age. They presented their children with issues similar to those used by Piaget, and found that their children often *did* take account of intentions, *especially* when the dilemmas were presented over video-tape.

Glassco, Milgram and Youniss (1970) remark that when specific change in judgment occurs, it may be that only superficial or verbal levels are affected. As they very justly say, when training fails, it may be because the training was not the right kind of training. They seem to imply that to demonstrate the effectiveness of training contradicts the stage-developmental position. This is not necessarily so. Stage-developmental theory claims that development follows a certain sequence of stages — *not* that it cannot be advanced or retarded by, or is independent of, environmental events (reinforcements).

King (1971) studied the ability of children to distinguish intentional action from accident, and the ability to identify unconscious intentions in the behaviour of other people. Subjects were children of four and a half, six and a half and nine years of age. The oldest group was significantly superior to the two younger groups in respect of unconscious intentions. Here, the two younger groups showed no significant difference. However, one may perhaps have some doubts concerning the assessment of 'unconscious intention', however reasonable the results may appear. More obviously, the ability to discriminate between intention and accident increased with age, as we should expect.

Armsby (1971) claims that the stories used by Piaget do not adequately discriminate between the intentional and the accidental. Consequently, he used stories in which an *intentional* act was clearly contrasted with an *accidental* act. Armsby found, with children of from six to eight years of age, that there was an age progression in the proportion of judgments in terms of intentions. He noted that these children quite frequently responded to his stories in terms of intentions. (His stories were given on paper rather than verbally, so as to minimise the possible effect of memory.) Armsby also found that his children *did* consider the amount of damage resulting from an accident to be important.

Gutkin (1972), again, points out that in Piaget's stories good intentions *plus* much damage are contrasted with bad intentions *plus* little damage. In his studies, Gutkin varied both intention and damage. A scalogram analysis of his results suggested that the development of appreciation of intentions goes through four successive stages: (i) attention is paid *only* to the amount of damage; (ii) the amount of damage is still important primarily, but *some* consideration is given to intention; (iii) intentions become of primary importance, but some account is still taken of the amount of damage done; (iv) intentions become the sole criterion. It may be suspected that even in persons for whom intentions are *normally* the only criterion of judgment, in extreme cases the extent of damage may also be significant.

In general, research on the development of 'reciprocity' concepts versus 'expiatory' concepts supports Piaget, despite apparently contradictory findings by Durkin (1959a, b, c). As children get older, there would appear in general to be more feeling against fighting (unless under closely controlled conditions), and against physical retaliation. Piaget's view of this would be that fighting and retaliation constitute an unstable form of equilibrium and should tend to give way to a more *mutual* way of settling disputes: 'What is regarded as just is no longer merely reciprocal action, but primarily *behaviour that admits of indefinitely sustained reciprocity*'

(p. 323). It thus appears that what Piaget means by 'reciprocity' is not simply a matter of an eye for an eye. In fact, Piaget's use of the terms 'equality', 'equity' and 'reciprocity' is by no means clear. It is interesting that Aronfreed (1968) believes that children whose parents use 'induction' methods of discipline have more strongly internalised consciences than those whose parents use 'sensitisation' techniques. Sensitisation techniques sensitise the child to the consequences of his actions for himself (e.g. punishment for wrong-doing). Induction techniques sensitise the child to the consequences of his actions *for others*, and involve the use of reasoning and appeal to principles. Similarly, Hoffman (1963) found the use of *reasoning* to be particularly associated with the development of internal standards.

In an interesting study by Stuart (1967), an attempt was made to investigate the relation of 'decentration' to moral judgment. For Piaget, centration involves a concentration on some one striking aspect of the object or question, to the relative neglect of other features; decentration reflects the ability to take account of different aspects or points of view. If a child centres on the *height* of water in two beakers of different diameter, he will not be able to see that there may be the same amount of water in both beakers. In decentring, he is able to take account of both height and width. Stuart in fact used graphic representations of figures from different points of view in his assessment of centration. His subjects were children of from seven to nine and from eleven to thirteen years of age. Stuart did find decentration related to moral judgment (though also to age and intelligence). This is a highly interesting and provocative finding.

Rubin and Schneider (1973) likewise take up Piaget's point that the young child cannot decentre and that this leads to the egocentric thought and immature moral judgment of the preoperational child. The child is unable to take the point of view of the other, and centres entirely on his own view. It should then follow that the child who cannot decentre must fail to consider the interpersonal and reciprocal aspects of moral relationships. Rubin and Schneider hypothesise that there is a positive relationship between the capacity for decentring and the amount of altruistic behaviour to be expected from the young child. More specifically, Rubin and Schneider hypothesise that there should be a positive relationship between communication skills (absence of egocentrism) and moral judgment and altruistic behaviour (in seven-year-old children). Moral judgment was assessed by Lee's (1971) modification of the Kohlberg scale. 'Giving behaviour' was significantly correlated with lack of egocentrism and with level of moral judgment. Helping younger children was also significantly related to lack of egocentrism and to level of moral judgment. The authors concluded that there was support for a relationship between decentring (communication skills) and moral judgment and altruism.

A different kind of study by Koenig, Sulzer, Newland and Sturgeon (1973) predicted that lower-class schoolchildren should be cognitively less complex and hence show less advanced moral judgment than middle-class children. In their study they used the Barron-Welsh Figure Preference Test and the Sulzer-Koenig Moral Judgment Test. The median score for cognitive complexity was 4.7 for middle-class subjects and 2.4 for lower-class subjects. It was found that social class was related to *both* cognitive complexity and moral judgment ($P < 0.01$). Complexity and moral judgment were also found to be associated.

Criticisms of Piaget by Learning Theorists

One of the most pointed criticisms of Piaget has come from the 'social learning' school. Bandura and McDonald (1963) seemed to show that judging in terms of 'intentionality' could be reversed by social learning, and that its emergence in the first instance was probably also due to learning from adult example. Kohlberg (1969) claims that the findings of Bandura and McDonald represent only a superficial and temporary phenomenon, and further claims that the effects of learning 'downward' (according to his scheme of stages) is less stable over time than learning 'upward'.

Cowan, Langer, Heavenrich and Nathanson (1969) replicated the experiment of Bandura and McDonald. They concluded that 'neither the present study nor that of Bandura and McDonald could be used directly to affirm or deny Piaget's hypothesis. Most of the present results serve as a basis for more differentiated statements concerning the model's effects, but some of the findings raise questions which cannot yet be answered within the social learning approach' (p. 261). Bandura (1969), in a reply to this article, has said of the 1963 study by Bandura and McDonald, that 'objective and subjective judgments exist together at all age levels rather than forming successive stages that partially overlap' (p. 276). Bandura contends that findings 'consistently demonstrate that moral judgments are more variable within and between individuals, and more modifiable than Piaget's theory would lead one to expect. Furthermore, modelling influences, which receive no mention in Piaget's account of the conditions regulating judgmental behaviour, though they are obviously operative in everyday interactions, emerge as significant determinants' (p. 279). It seems to us that relatively compelling examples of behaviour must constitute part of the social or moral reality of which the child has to make some kind of sense, and that there is good ground for a future accommodation between cognitive-developmental theory and social learning theory. Both are right, both are limited.

The Contribution of Kohlberg

Kohlberg (1963) bases his work on that of Piaget, but has extended Piaget's notions in several ways. Kohlberg proposes three *levels* of development: the premoral level, the conventional level and the level of accepted principles. Each level is divided into two stages, so that Kohlberg propounds six stages of development as follows:

Level I   Premoral. At this level, the child is responsive to cultural rules and some evaluative labels, but regards them from the point of view of the pleasant or unpleasant consequences which action may entail, or from the point of view of the physical power to impose their demands, of those who impose the rules.

Stage 1. At Stage 1, the child's orientation is in terms of obedience and punishment. He feels deferential to those in power, and is concerned to avoid trouble. At this stage, he regards responsibility *objectively*, that is in terms of consequences.

Stage 2. Kohlberg refers to this stage as the stage of 'naively egoistic orientation'. What is right is what satisfies one's own needs (and perhaps sometimes the needs of others). The subject is aware that 'values' are here relative to the needs of the particular actor concerned. At this stage, there is *some* concern with exchange and reciprocity.

Level II   Conventional level. The child is here concerned with actively maintaining the expectations of his family and peers, and with justifying their expectations.

Stage 3. Kohlberg calls this the stage of the 'good boy orientation'. The child is concerned with gaining approval and with pleasing and helping others to that end. He seeks to conform to stereotyped images of what role-behaviour and intentions should be.

Stage 4. At this stage, the child is concerned to maintain the existing social authority and order. He is concerned with 'doing his duty' and with showing respect for authority. He respects expectations of others which they have properly earned.

Level III   Principled level. This is the level of principles which the individual himself accepts. The child is concerned with the definition of values and principles without direct regard to any supporting authority.

Stage 5. This stage is referred to as the stage of contractual, legalistic obligations. Duty is defined in terms of contract, avoidance of violation of the rights of others and majority will and welfare.

Stage 6. This is the stage of conscience or principles properly speaking. One's orientation is not to the actual rules and laws of society, but to self-accepted principles which involve appeal to logical universality and consistency.

Assessment of moral level is based on answers to questions relating to a series of nine moral dilemmas, verbally presented.

Studies Deriving from Kohlberg's Position

Kohlberg reports a distinct pattern of usage of his stages with increasing age in America, although Stage 6 responses remain rare. He also claims that studies in a variety of cultures justify his six stages (Kohlberg, 1966). We should expect a fair degree of internal consistency and consistency over time in Kohlberg's measures, and he does indeed claim that (a) on average, most judgments fit a single stage, (b) there are fair intercorrelations between stories and (c) there is a fair amount of consistency over time. In our own studies, we found rather less tendency for judgments to fall in one stage, and for judgments to be spread over a wider range of stages, although it must be admitted that this may conceivably have been because of uncertainties of scoring. McGeorge (1974), however, found significant variation across Kohlberg's situations, and suggests that *two* factors underlie responses, 'an emphatic or role-taking factor and one involving concepts of social rules and structures' (p. 116).

Turiel (1969) produces evidence that children are more responsive to efforts to influence them toward the stage *above* that at which they locate most of their judgments. He claims that his children did actually learn to apply a more mature form of moral reasoning rather than simply learning to apply particular answers to particular problems. Very similar findings were reported by Rest, Turiel and Kohlberg (1969), who also indicated that their children *preferred* reasoning at one stage above their own. Rest, Turiel and Kohlberg use Piaget's concept of 'décalage' to refer to the probability that in the course of their development, children *prefer* reasoning at a higher stage of judgment before they *understand* it, understand it before they fully *assimilate* it, and assimilate it before they *use* it. Moreover, as Turiel (1969) remarks, 'a child can conceptualise some issues at a higher level than others' (p. 115). This would be relevant to our own finding that children's judgments were spread over a wider range of stages than Kohlberg originally suggested. McGeorge (1974) remarks that 'presumably stage mixture in response to a single situation is occasioned by the presence of different aspects of morality within that situation' (p. 118). This again would be supported by our own findings. One would also expect, of course, that different children might conceptualise different issues at higher levels. It would indeed be rather surprising if this were not so.

Turiel and Rothman (1972) hold that moral reasoning and action are interrelated, and that, for example, subjects at Stages 5 and 6 are less likely to cheat than subjects at Stages 3 and 4, and subjects at Stages 3 and 4 less likely to cheat than subjects at Stages 1 and 2. Turiel and Rothman conducted an experiment in which subjects were exposed to reasoning at one stage above or one stage below their typical level. Subjects were initially at Stage 2, Stage 3 or Stage 4. The issue involved was whether or not to go on in an experiment in which the subjects were depriving a stooge of tokens. Turiel and Rothman report that 'Stage 2 or Stage 3 subjects persisted in this choice (continuing), regardless of the level of reasoning used to support either of the alternatives. Stage 4 subjects, however, chose to stop only when the reasoning supporting this choice was at the stage above' (p. 748).

Turiel and Rothman further comment that 'although most subjects in this study showed preference for reasoning at the stage above, nevertheless they showed little transformation in their own stage of development' (p. 750). This finding would seem to provide some measure of support for the developmental stage view. In this study, it was also found that subjects at Stage 4 decided in favour of 'stopping' when this was supported by Stage 5 reasoning. Turiel and Rothman suggest that Stage 3 subjects tended to keep behaviour and reasoning separate, while Stage 4 subjects tended to integrate them.

Grim, Kohlberg and White (1968) draw attention to 'ego-strength' factors in moral control. It is scarcely surprising that 'ego-strength' factors ('will-power') should be important. Indeed, it might well be argued that psychology has been seriously at fault in not paying more attention to such matters. After all, things like 'will-power' have long been recognised among the general public, and they should not simply be ignored without good reason. Grim, Kohlberg and White, in a factor analysis of results, found three factors: (i) a factor involving task conformity, with loadings on psychomotor measures and teachers' ratings of stable conformity to authoritative social expectations; (ii) a factor involving inner stability and related to cheating/not cheating; and (iii) a factor interpreted as 'restlessness'. Grim, Kohlberg and White note that observed moderate to high correlations between morality measures and attention measures suggest the importance of 'ego-control' factors. They pronounce the further rather obvious observation that moral behaviour is not entirely a product of conscience. These authors stress the importance of a 'slowly developing cognitive-voluntary ability of sustained attention' (p. 250). They also express the view that fully internalised moral values prohibiting cheating are a late development. This kind of interpretation, they hold, is consistent with the 'voluntaristic' view of William James, who wrote that 'the essential achievement of will is to *attend* to a difficult object and hold it fast before the mind' (James, quoted in Grim, Kohlberg and White, 1968, p. 251). The present writer is happy to see some signs of a return to a psychology where 'voluntarism' may be regarded with respect.

We have seen that Piaget stressed the importance of peer groups rather than adults for true moral development. Likewise, Kohlberg (1971) suggests that opportunities for varied role-playing ought to encourage moral development. Selman (1971) used sixty middle-class children of from eight to ten years of age. Controlling for intelligence, he gave them two role-taking tasks and Kohlberg's moral judgment measure. He found role-taking skill positively related to *conventional* moral judgment (Stages 3 and 4). After a year, a re-test of ten subjects who had been low in role-taking and in moral judgment suggested that 'the development of the ability to understand the reciprocal nature of interpersonal relations is a necessary but not a sufficient condition for the development of conventional moral thoughts' (Selman, 1971, p. 79) — as indeed one would have thought. It may perhaps be legitimate to remark that adequate tests of role-taking are difficult to devise, and that those used in Selman's study may not have been wholly adequate. The possible function of role-taking in moral development is one which deserves much more attention.

From a rather different point of view, Fishkin, Keniston and MacKinnon (1973) have investigated moral reasoning and political ideology. During May 1970, seventy-five undergraduates (a rather small number) in eight universities were given the Kohlberg material and also measures of political ideology. These authors found that subjects whose moral reasoning was at Stage 3 or Stage 4 (conventional level) tended to be politically conservative; preconventional subjects (Stages 1 and 2) tended to favour violent radicalism. There appeared in fact to be an exceptionally high relationship between Stage 4 reasoning (law and order) and conservatism, which would, indeed, in Kohlberg's terms, seem to be in accordance with expectation. Fishkin, Keniston and MacKinnon further found that *post-conventional* reasoning appeared to be associated with *rejection* of conservative views, without, however, being associated with the ideology of violent radicalism. The implication would appear to be that the postconventional subjects favoured a more individualistic view. It would indeed be interesting to see if the findings of these authors were confirmed by a similar (and preferably extended) study in Britain and possibly also elsewhere.

Fontana and Noel (1973) studied moral reasoning among students, teachers and administrators in the university. They found that administrators more frequently used Stage 4 reasoning ('law and order') than either students or teachers. Those with political leanings to the Right used more Stage 4 reasoning than those who leaned to the Left, while Leftists appeared to show more Stage 2 ('egoistic') reasoning. Teachers tended more frequently to use reasoning at Stages 5 and 6. These results, although none of them is spectacular, lend some support to Kohlberg's position. Once again, it would be interesting to see whether similar results were found in different cultures.

Again, Kohlberg (1963, 1969) reports that in American society, middle-class children go through stages faster than working-class children. We ourselves in England confirmed the superiority of middle-class children on Kohlberg's material, although the difference between the classes was rather small when verbal intelligence was controlled for. It would appear likely that such social class differences as cannot be accounted for in terms of differences in (especially) verbal intelligence are due to differences in the 'social perspective' of the two classes arising from their different roles in the occupational structure, and also perhaps to the greater use of verbal and 'induction' techniques of discipline by the middle-class parents.

Criticisms of Kohlberg's Position

In his chapter 'From is to ought', Kohlberg (1971) claims that his stages of development represent a *logically* necessary progression, and that they therefore transcend relativity and break through the myth of 'ethical neutrality'. Kohlberg claims that each of his stages of moral thinking represents a more 'integrated' and also a more 'differentiated' way of thinking, that such is the progress of all thinking, including scientific thinking, and that each successive stage is justified in that thinking at that stage is able to handle and resolve moral problems more complex than can be dealt with in terms of any lower stages of thinking. It is not entirely clear in what sense Kohlberg's stages logically follow on from one another (Peters, 1971). But even if they did, we should be inclined to agree with Alston (1971) when he says 'the mere fact that one concept logically depends on another has no tendency to show that moral thinking involving the former is superior to moral thinking involving the latter' (p. 275). We think, in other words, that despite the undoubted interest of Kohlberg's work and the future possibilities of work based thereon, given his definition of what is moral, he has not succeeded in showing that his 'moral stages' have any *absolute* application. It may turn out to be an empirical fact that Kohlberg's stages recur in all societies. But that does not *ipso facto* mean that they reflect the *only* possible concept of morality, nor dispose of 'the myth of ethical neutrality'. We feel inclined to question how far we are entitled to assume that Kohlberg's six stages do indeed represent successive approximations to moral perfection – as such stages of moral development should. The mere fact that there is so much controversy among moral philosophers as to what is 'moral' should warn us to be extremely careful in our assumptions. The present writer, in fact, has a lot of sympathy with those who attempt to distinguish in principle between 'is' and 'ought', and with those who argue that ethical neutrality is not entirely a myth.

References

Aronfreed, J. (1968), *Conduct and Conscience*, New York and London: Academic Press.
Alston, W.P. (1971), 'Comments on Kohlberg's "From is to ought" ', in Mischel, T. (ed.), *Cognitive Development and Epistemology*, New York and London: Academic Press, 269-84.
Armsby, R.E. (1971), 'A re-examination of the development of moral judgments in children', *Child Dev.*, 42, 4, 1241-8.
Bandura, A. (1969), 'Social learning of moral judgments', *J. Person. soc. Psychol.*, 11, 3, 275-9.
Bandura, A. and McDonald, F.J. (1963), 'The influence of social reinforcement and the behaviour of models in shaping children's moral judgments', *J. abnorm. soc. Psychol.*, 67, 274-81.
Chandler, M.J., Greenspan, S. and Barenboim, C. (1973), 'Judgments of intentionality in response to videotaped and verbally presented moral dilemmas: the medium and the message', *Child Dev.*, 44, 315-20.
Costanzo, P.R., Coie, J.D., Grumet, J.F. and Farnill, D. (1973), 'A re-examination of the effects of intent and consequences on children's moral judgments', *Child Dev.*, 44, 154-61.
Cowan, P.A., Langer, J., Heavenrich, J. and Nathanson, M. (1969), 'Social learning theory and Piaget's cognitive theory of moral development', *J. Person. soc. Psychol.*, 11, 3, 261-74.
Durkin, D. (1959a), 'Children's concepts of justice: a comparison with the Piaget data', *Child Dev.*, 30, 59-67.
Durkin, D. (1959b), 'Children's acceptance of reciprocity as a justice principle', *Child Dev.*, 30, 289-96.
Durkin, D. (1959c), 'Children's concepts of justice: a further comparison with the Piaget data', *J. educ. Res.*, 5, 252-7.
Fishkin, J., Keniston, K. and MacKinnon, C. (1973), 'Moral reasoning and political ideology', *J. Person. soc. Psychol.*, 27, 1, 109-19.
Fontana, A.F. and Noel, B. (1973), 'Moral reasoning in the university', *J. Person. soc. Psychol.*, 27, 3, 419-29.
Glassco, J.A., Milgram, N.A. and Youniss, J. (1970), 'Stability of training effects in intentionality in moral judgment in children', *J. Person. soc. Psychol.*, 14, 360-5.
Graham, D. (1972), *Moral Learning and Development*, London: Batsford.

Grim, P.F., Kohlberg, L. and White, S.H. (1968), 'Some relationships between conscience and attentional processes', *J. Person. soc. Psychol.*, 8, 239-53.
Gutkin, D.C. (1972), 'The effects of systematic story changes on intentionality in children's moral judgments', *Child Dev.*, 43, 1, 187-95.
Hoffman, M.L. (1963), 'Parent discipline and the child's consideration for others', *Child Dev.*, 34, 573-88.
Jensen, L.C. and Hafen, G.E. (1973), 'The effect of training children to consider intentions when making moral judgments', *J. genet. Psychol.*, 122, 223-33.
Jensen, L.C. and Larm, C., (1970), 'Effects of two training procedures on intentionality in moral judgments among children', *Dev. Psychol.*, 2, 2, 310.
King, M. (1971), 'The development of some intention concepts in young children', *Child Dev.*, 42, 1145-52.
Koenig, F., Sulzer, J., Newland, V. and Sturgeon, L. (1973), 'Cognitive complexity and moral judgment in middle and lower class children', *Child Study Journal*, 3, 1, 43-52.
Kohlberg, L. (1963), 'The development of children's orientations toward a moral order. I. Sequence in the development of moral thought', *Vita hum.*, 6, 11-33.
Kohlberg, L. (1966), 'Moral education in the schools: a developmental view', *School Rev.*, 74, 1-30.
Kohlberg, L. (1969), 'Stage and sequence: the cognitive-developmental approach to socialization', in Goslin, D.A. (ed.), *Handbook of Socialization Theory and Research*, Chicago: Rand-McNally, 347-480.
Kohlberg, L. (1971), 'From is to ought', in Mischel, T. (ed.), *Cognitive Development and Epistemology*, New York and London: Academic Press, 151-235.
Kugelmass, S. and Breznitz, S. (1968), 'Intentionality in moral judgment: adolescent development', *Child Dev.*, 39, 249-56.
Lee, L.C. (1971), 'The concomitant development of cognitive and moral modes of thought: a test of selected deductions from Piaget's theory', *Genet. Psychol. Monogr.*, 83, 93-146.
Lunzer, E.A. and Morris, J.F. (1968), 'Problems of motivation', in Lunzer, E.A., *The Regulation of Behaviour*, London: Staples Press, 304-61.
McGeorge, C. (1974), 'Situational variation in level of moral judgment', *Br. J. educ. Psychol.*, 44, 2, 116-22.
Peters, R.S. (1971), 'Moral development: a plea for pluralism', in Mischel, T. (ed.), *Cognitive Development and Epistemology*, New York and London: Academic Press, 237-67.
Piaget, J. (1932), *The Moral Judgment of the Child*, London: Routledge and Kegan Paul.
Rest, J., Turiel, E. and Kohlberg, L. (1969), 'Level of moral development as a determinant of preference and comprehension of moral judgments made by others', *J. Pers.*, 37, 225-52.
Rubin, K.H. and Schneider, F.W. (1973), 'The relationship between moral judgment, egocentrism and altruistic behaviour', *Child Dev.*, 44, 661-5.
Schleifer, M. and Douglas, V.J. (1973), 'Effects of training on the moral judgment of young children', *J. Person. soc. Psychol.*, 28, 1, 62-8.
Selman, R.L. (1971), 'The relation of role-taking to the development of moral judgment in children', *Child Dev.*, 42, 79-91.
Stuart, R.B. (1967), 'Decentration in the development of children's concepts of moral and causal judgment', *J. genet. Psychol.*, 111, 59-68.
Turiel, E. (1969), 'Developmental processes in the child's moral thinking', in Mussen, P.H. *et al.* (eds.), *Trends and Issues in Developmental Psychology*, New York: Holt, Rinehart and Winston, 92-133.
Turiel, E. and Rothman, G.R. (1972), 'The influence of reasoning on behavioural choices at different stages of moral development', *Child Dev.*, 43, 741-56.

Turner, G.N.H. (1966), 'A re-examination of certain of Piaget's inquiries on children's moral judgments in the light of his later theory', unpublished thesis, University of Manchester.

7 COGNITIVE PERSPECTIVES ON THE DEVELOPMENT OF MEMORY

J.W. Hagen, R.H. Jongeward and R.V. Kail

Source: Chapter 3 in H.W. Reese (ed.), *Advances in Child Development and Behavior*, vol. 10 (Academic Press, 1975).

A. Strategies in Acquisition and Retrieval

The developmental course of subject-employed strategies in memory has been charted in a number of different ways by various investigators (e.g. Belmont & Butterfield, 1969, 1971b; Flavell, 1970; Hagen, 1971, 1972). Various strategies have been described. While differing in many aspects they all involve some activity on the part of the subject aimed at improving subsequent recall. Children from preschool age through adolescence have been studied, and striking changes have been observed as a function of age, both in performance on a variety of memory tasks and in the use of strategies. In the remaining sections of this paper, it will be argued that these strategies are responsible for a major part of the age-related improvement in memory.

While strategies are general by their very nature, i.e. they are applicable to a range of tasks, no doubt certain task characteristics determine which strategy (or strategies) is appropriate for a particular type of task. Thus, as the child gains a repertoire of strategies he must also become proficient in linking these with the particular task he is undertaking at a given time. Further, it has been pointed out very well by Belmont and Butterfield (1969) that different strategies may or may not be used at various phases in the memorial process. Certain strategic activity may be employed during acquisition, when the to-be-remembered information is initially processed, while other strategies may be specifically suited for facilitating retrieval at the time of recall. Both of these possibilities are considered in the sections that follow.

In the course of this review, it will become clear that certain strategies for improving memory are characteristically used by older children but appear to be nonexistent in younger children's behavior. There also appears to be an identifiable transitional stage during which the child can use a strategy under certain conditions or can learn to use it during a relatively brief training session. However, the strategy is not used spontaneously nor does it show the characteristics of durability or generality. Some of our important insights have resulted from experiments that have focused on this transitional period. From the results of these studies it appears that learning, whether it be through spontaneous experience, informal education, or formal training, is critical in the development of the use of strategies. It should also be pointed out that although these periods may occur at different age levels for different strategies, our concern is not for the specific age levels but rather for the developmental progressions identified and described.

1. Acquisition

a. Verbal Mediation: Production or Mediation Deficiency?

For almost three decades there has been research aimed at demonstrating the mediational role played by verbal productions in a wide variety of cognitive tasks (for a review of this literature see Stevenson, 1972). Simple verbal labeling of stimuli was found to enhance discriminability for children at certain age levels but not others (Spiker, 1963). Furthermore, while children as young as age 4-years may have appropriate verbal responses to stimuli in their repertoire, these responses serve as mediators only for older children (Reese, 1962).

In order to explore the mediational deficiency hypothesis in a memory task, Flavell, Beach, and Chinsky (1966) showed pictures of to-be-remembered objects to 5-, 7-, and 10-year-old children. Seven pictures were shown in a circular array and the experimenter pointed to three of them as the ones to remember on that trial. A clever procedure was used to measure the child's spontaneous verbal activity during a 15-second delay period between presentation of items and the test for recall. The child wore a space helmet which had a visor that was pulled over his eyes during the delay so he could not see the pictures. However, his lips were visible and the experimenter, who could lip read, recorded lip movements during this time. After 15 seconds, the visor was lifted and the child was asked to point to the three pictures in the order in which they had been designated as the ones to remember. Only two of twenty 5-year-old children showed any evidence of verbal naming or rehearsal during the delay. However, for the older age groups, verbal activity increased so that for the ten-year-olds, 17 of the 20 showed detectable verbal activity. Further, those subjects who verbalized during the delay period typically recalled more than those who did not.

Did this verbal rehearsal actually facilitate memory? Could those children who did not rehearse be induced to do so, and would their memory be improved if they did? To answer these questions, another study (Keeney, Cannizzo, & Flavell, 1967) was performed using basically the same procedure as in the study just described. First-grade subjects were used, because it was known that some would engage in verbal activity during the delay and some would not. For those children who did engage in verbal activity, recall was higher than for those who did not. Then, those who did not show evidence of rehearsal were instructed to whisper the names of the pictures to be remembered during the delay and were tested again. These children learned to rehearse with ease and their recall was as good as the recall of those children who engaged in rehearsal spontaneously. However, upon subsequent testing, when no request to whisper was made, these 'induced' rehearsers did not continue to do so, and their recall also declined.

These findings led the authors to conclude that a production deficiency characterizes the way these children approach a memory task. They do not use skills they have available to facilitate or mediate their recall. There is no deficiency in mediation ability per se, because they do use this skill when instructed to do so, and memory is improved. Whether still younger children would have been able to show mediation when instructed to rehearse verbally is not known. It is clear, though, the children at the 6- to 7-year age level do seem to show a production deficiency in a simple short-term memory task.

b. Verbal Labeling, Rehearsal, and the Serial Recall Task. Another task has been used to study the mediational effects of verbal processes on memory. Hagen and Kingsley (1968) administered a serial recall task (adapted from Atkinson, Hansen, & Bernbach, 1964) in which a series of eight picture cards, each depicting a familiar animal, is shown to the child. The first card is shown briefly, then placed face down in front of the child. The second is then shown and placed next to the first, and this procedure is continued until all eight cards are in a row in front of the child. Then a cue card is shown by the experimenter, and the child's task is to point to the face-down card in the row that matches the cue card. On each trial, the same pictures appear but the order is varied, so it is not possible for the child to learn locations of particular pictures. Across trials, each child is tested on each of the eight card positions. Thus, it is possible to determine not only how many pictures the child remembered, but whether the order of a card's appearance in the series made a difference. The initial cards occupy the *primacy* positions, while the last cards presented just before recall is assessed occupy the *recency* positions. In the Hagen and Kingsley study (1968) children at the ages of 4, 6, 7, 8 and 10 years were included. In the label condition, the children were required to say aloud the names of the pictures as they were presented. In the no-label condition, overt naming of the pictures was not required. As

Figure 7.1: Percentage correct responses as a function of experimental group and age level: Solid line, label group; broken line, no-label group.

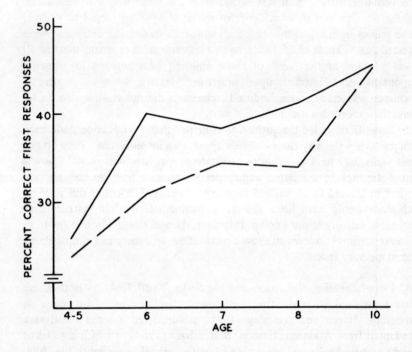

Source: J.W. Hagen and P.R. Kingsley. 'Labeling effects in short-term memory', *Child Development*, 1968, 39, 120. Figure 3. Copyright 1968 by the Society for Research in Child Development, Inc.

illustrated in Figure 7.1, recall improved sharply with age. At the middle age levels, children who labeled recalled more pictures than those who did not, but the recall by 4- and 10-year-old children was not affected. Clearly, it cannot be concluded that labeling is necessarily advantageous in recall.

Next, the serial-position data were analyzed. A score was computed for each of the eight list positions for each child. Two findings emerged that help to explain the overall findings for the labeling vs. no-labeling manipulation. First, recall for pictures in the primacy positions in Figure 7.2, the left-hand portion of each curve, was not facilitated by labeling. In fact, for the oldest age group, 10 years, recall was significantly poorer when labeling was required. Second, at the extreme right, or recency positions of each curve, it is evident that at all age levels labeling provided a decided

Figure 7.2: Percentage correct responses as a function of serial position and experimental condition for four age levels: Solid line, label group; broken line, no-label group.

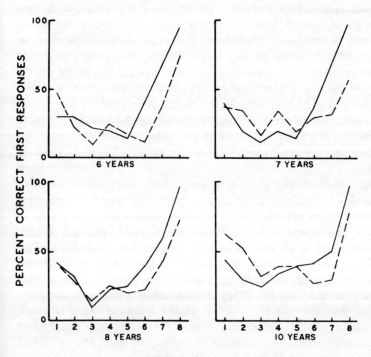

Source: J.W. Hagen and P.R. Kingsley. 'Labeling effects in short-term memory', *Child Development*, 1968, 39, 117. Fig. 1. Copyright 1968 by the Society for Research in Child Development, Inc.

advantage for correct recall. It should be noted that at age 10 years, the improvement due to labeling at the recency portion was negated by the detriment due to labeling at the primacy portion. Thus, even though overall recall was not affected, it should not be concluded that labeling had no effect on recall for the 10-year-old subjects.

From these findings, it might be argued that 4-year-old subjects displayed a *mediation* deficiency because their performance did not change even when they labeled the stimuli. At ages 6 through 8, a *production* deficiency is evident for the recall of primacy items, the same age level where this deficiency was identified by Keeney *et al.* (1967). The 10-year-old subjects performed the task considerably better than any of the younger groups. From the findings at the primacy portion of their recall curves, it was concluded that they engaged in spontaneous, covert rehearsing of the names of the pictures to be recalled. For example, as the first picture was shown, the child would say to himself, 'fish'. As the second was shown he would say, 'fish, bear'. This type of cumulative rehearsal becomes difficult as the list gets longer. Consequently, rehearsal should facilitate primarily the recall of the primacy pictures. The results for the oldest children in the no-labeling condition are consistent with this 'rehearsal strategy' hypothesis. When labeling is required, though, covert rehearsing should be more difficult, and recall at the primacy positions should suffer, which it did for those 10-year-olds.

In order to test this hypothesis more definitively, 5-year-old children, well below the age of spontaneous rehearsing, were tested in an *induced* rehearsal condition (Kingsley & Hagen, 1969). They were trained to rehearse aloud cumulatively the names of pictures as they were presented. Only five· pictures per trial were used. They learned to rehearse with no difficulty, and compared to children in the standard label and no-label conditions, their recall was facilitated. Further, they showed a striking improvement at the primacy portion of the serial-recall curve. Hence, children at this age level can be classified as exhibiting a production deficiency in this task too. They do not use rehearsal spontaneously; but when they are induced to do so, recall is improved. It appears that, while labeling has a direct facilitative effect on recency, cumulative rehearsal of the labels is responsible for the improvement in recall found at the primacy portion of the serial-position curve.

In a recent study, the properties and durability of induced rehearsal were explored further (Hagen, Hargrave, & Ross, 1973). Five- and 7-year-old subjects were given training in rehearsal similar to that used by Kingsley and Hagen (1969). It was found that this rehearsal facilitated recall at both age levels. On a post-test one week later, however, the improved recall due to induced rehearsal was found to have disappeared. This latter result is not surprising in view of the Keeney *et al.* (1967) finding of no transfer effect for induced rehearsal even in an immediate post-test.

The serial-recall task was administered to subjects at the teenage and college-age level (Hagen, Meacham, & Mesibov, 1970). Here eight serial positions were used, and it was found that required overt labeling resulted in a lower recall at the first six serial positions; only at the last two, or recency positions, did recall improve. It appears, then, that for performance at the recency positions, labeling has a direct facilitating effect, perhaps acoustical in nature. For the slightly longer-term memory for items in the primacy positions an active 'strategy for remembering' must be used in order to improve recall, and it is only this latter type of memory that shows clear developmental changes with increasing age.

A design was employed in which it was possible to manipulate the relative ease with which children could use their recall strategies or mnemonic devices (Hagen & Kail, 1973). In this study a serial position recall task, with seven items, was used. A 15-second delay between the presentation of the final to-be-remembered item and the presentation of the cue card was imposed. In the facilitation condition, the children were instructed to 'think about the pictures' during the delay period. In the distraction condition, the subjects counted aloud during the delay. Seven- and eleven-year-old children were tested in each of these two conditions, in addition to a control (no-delay) condition.

There was no difference in overall recall between the facilitation and control conditions for the 11-year-old children. However, for these children, recall of the primacy items increased in the facilitation condition, while recall of the recency items declined. In the distraction condition, where rehearsal should be difficult, recall of primacy items declined significantly for the older children but did not change for the younger children. Total recall was virtually identical for the two age groups in this condition, and their serial position curves were very similar. An additional analysis also proved revealing. The data from those younger subjects who performed as well as, or better than, the mean performance of the older subjects were analyzed separately. No evidence of a primacy effect was found even for these superior 7-year-olds. It was concluded that '. . . children in the seven year age range do not yet characteristically engage in rehearsal to improve recall, but by age eleven years children are proficient in using this strategy' (Hagen & Kail, 1973, p. 835).

The findings of another study provide supporting evidence. Locke and Fehr (1970) used electromyographical recordings to detect verbalizations in 5-year-old subjects. Electrodes were attached to their lips and chins. Pictures were shown, three at a time, followed by a 12-second delay interval. During presentation, the children did verbalize, but no verbal activity was detected during the delay interval. Rehearsing in the absence of the stimuli appears to be an activity that does not emerge until a later developmental period.

c. Evidence for Other Acquisition Strategies. While it seems clear that verbal rehearsal is a mnemonic that comes to play an important role, it is no doubt just one component in the developmental changes associated with the acquisition of information to be remembered. The child learns a complex set of skills that allows him to control, to a large degree, just what he will learn and retain. Three studies that provide additional insight into the components of these skills are now considered.

In a study by Flavell, Friedrichs, and Hoyt (1970) the children were given control of both the length of study time and the number of exposures of the to-be-remembered stimuli. Black and white drawings were shown, each of which was mounted in a window that could be illuminated by pressing a button. Children in nursery school, kindergarten, and second and fourth grade were told that their task was to learn which picture was located in each of the ten windows, and that they could expose each picture by pressing the corresponding button as long and as often as they wished. The experimenter left the room whilst the child was preparing the the recall task. When the child thought he was ready, he called the experimenter back into the room. The frequency and duration of exposure of each stimulus by the child were recorded. Even when given this opportunity to master the task, accuracy of recall was directly related to the subject's age. Further, this age-related improvement in recall was attributed in part to the finding of a dramatic increase with age in the amount of time spent in preparation for recall.

The child's verbal and nonverbal activities were also recorded by an observer viewing the child through a one-way mirror. Four different task strategies were observed. Overt naming of the pictures was done very little by the three younger groups, but was used frequently by the fourth-grade children, especially early in the study period. At the same time, rehearsal increased over the duration of the study time for the fourth graders and, to a lesser extent, for the second graders. There was no change over studying time in this measure for the two younger groups. Another strategy observed was anticipation, testing oneself prior to illuminating a picture. This technique was used primarily by fourth-grade children and to a lesser extent by some second graders. A final behavior, pointing the the actual location of the stimuli, was used increasingly over trials by the fourth-grade children only. Thus, only at the fourth-grade level were the various task-appropriate strategies used consistently to aid in subsequent recall; and only these children showed regular changes over study time in the employment of these strategies, suggesting that they were actually monitoring their performance and making corrective changes in the strategies as their study progressed toward the goal of mastery.

The use of study time was investigated in a subsequent study by Masur, McIntyre, and Flavell (1973). Seven-, nine-, and twenty-year-old subjects were given a list of pictures to memorize over a series of five trials, each trial consisting of a study period of 45 seconds followed by a recall test.

After each trial, the subjects were allowed to study half of the total number of items they were attempting to recall, and they could choose the items to include in this set from the total array. The major finding was that both the 9- and the 20-year-old subjects chose significantly more often than the 7-year-old subjects, those pictures that they had been unable to identify during the preceding recall test. In fact, the youngest group did not show this tendency at all. Other analyses indicated that, while the 9-year-old children did use this strategy (as much as the 20-year-olds), it did not appear to facilitate their recall. These findings suggest that a strategy of giving special attention to information that is less-well mastered in a task emerges with development. Further, this strategy is employed for a period of time before it is perfected. Because there was such a large difference in age between the two older groups of subjects in this study, the course of the development of this strategy cannot be described very accurately at this time.

In another task, stimuli are presented which may be grouped into common categories by the children during a study period. Moely, Olson, Halwes and Flavell (1969) presented, in a random arrangement, pictures of common objects belonging to four different categories to children from 5 years through 9 years of age. After the child named each picture, he was given 2 minutes to look at the array and to rearrange the pictures if he wished. Then the pictures were removed from view and the subject was asked to recall as many of them as possible. This procedure constituted the control condition. There were also two experimental conditions used at each age level. In the first condition, the experimenter named the four categories (animals, furniture, vehicles, and clothing) in addition to having the child name each picture. In the second experimental condition, in addition to being given the names of the categories, the child was *taught* how to sort the pictures into these groups. It was further suggested that it might be helpful if he first remembered a category and then the items in that category. During the 2-minute study period, an observer, watching through a one-way mirror, recorded the child's manual manipulations of the pictures. The child's verbalizations were tape-recorded.

The results for the 5- to 6-year-old children were very clear cut, as shown in Figure 7.3. Organizing the pictures into categories occurred with high frequency in the teaching condition, but this behavior was almost nonexistent in the other two conditions. For the 6- to 7-year-old children, the use of categories occurred with somewhat higher frequency (although not significantly) in the naming condition, but again the teaching condition resulted in their highest use. By 8 to 9 years of age, the frequency of categorization in these two experimental conditions did not differ.

Subsequent recall was found to be higher for those subjects who used manual groupings than for those who did not, regardless of age level. Further, when verbal behavior during the study period was analyzed, it was found that only the older subjects spontaneously moved pictures and verbalized in a way that permitted self-testing. A group of 10- to 11-year-old subjects was tested in the control condition only, and their spontaneous use of grouping and subsequent recall was found to be at the same level as that for the younger children in those conditions which facilitated their use of grouping during the pre-recall period. Thus, when children organized or grouped stimuli into categories during study, their recall performance was higher than that of children who did not do such organizing. These results have been replicated in a subsequent study

Figure 7.3: Prerecall organization as a function of experimental group and age level. The dependent variable is the number of times two items from the same category were placed next to each other during the study period relative to the possible number of such adjacent placements of items from the same category.

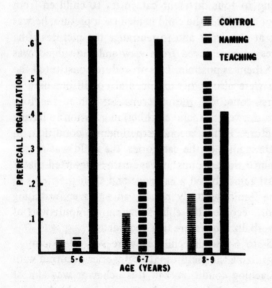

by Neimark, Slotnick, and Ulrich (1971) in which the age range of the subjects was extended to include the college-age level.

The evidence points strongly to the importance of strategies employed while information is being initially acquired for subsequent recall. These strategies show a consistent developmental progression in their implementation, and they are not well developed until several years after the onset of formal education. Just how and when strategies may be used once information has been acquired is addressed next.

2. Organization and Retrieval Processes

[. . .] Given that memory has a detectable organization, it seems reasonable that research has focused on how the subject utilizes that structure to aid him in retrieving information from memory. More recently, developmentalists have asked whether there are age-related changes in such retrieval processes.

a. Free Recall of Categorizable Stimuli. It is, of course, well established that many characteristics of stimuli affect the ability of persons to recall them, as we have seen. Words that are related to each other may be recalled together. For example, if an adult is asked to remember the words, 'apple, dog, orange, pear, snail, rabbit, plum and horse', a typical response would be, 'dog, snail, horse, apple, orange, plum'. It is evident, first of all, that his recall is not perfect. Of more interest, though, is the organization that is evidently imposed on the list, a group of animals and a group of fruits. The words were *clustered* into groups; this tendency to organize stimuli has been shown to be a typical strategy used by adults in memory tasks, and it facilitates total recall (Bousfield, 1953; Bousfield, Cohen, and Whitmarsh, 1958).[1]

To see if the presence of categories in the stimulus list would facilitate children's recall, Vaughan (1968) tested first, fourth, and seventh graders. She used two lists in her experiment. One list consisted of 16 pictures of objects bearing no particular conceptual relationship to one another. The second list included pictures of four objects from each of four different conceptual categories. Subjects were given a standard free recall test. They were asked to recall as many of the stimuli as they could in any order they wished. Overall recall increased with age; subjects recalled more words from the categorized lists; and seventh graders clustered significantly more than first graders. However, children at all ages tested showed clustering significantly greater than chance.

Rossi and Rossi (1965) have shown that the same improvement in recall with a clusterable list is obtained with subjects even younger than the school-age subjects in the Vaughan (1968) study. They presented lists of 12 pictures to subjects between the ages of 2 and 5 years. Each list consisted of three exemplars from each of four different categories. They found that both recall and the amount of clustering increased as a function of age, but even at the youngest age level, 26 of the 30 2-year-olds clustered above chance. Thus, children as young as age 2 can benefit from the presence of categories in free recall lists, but older children profit more from their presence than do younger children.

Such a developmental improvement, however, may merely be an artifact of the particular stimulus lists that were used. It is possible that younger children cluster as much as older children but according to different criteria or rules. To test this hypothesis, Rossi and Wittrock (1971) presented 12-word lists to children ranging from 2 to 5 years of age. Each list consisted of two pairs of each of three different types of pairwise relationships. Words were either phonemically similar (sun, fun), syntactically related (dogs, bark), or taxonomically related (peach, apple). Syntactic clustering in recall was not dominant at any age. Phonemic clustering was dominant for 2-year-olds but was infrequently noted thereafter. Taxonomic clustering was dominant from age 3 to age 5, where serial order (input—output correspondence) was the most frequent basis of organization. It should be noted that clustering of word *pairs* was examined in this study. Therefore, it may be more appropriate to view this task as retrieval based simply on inter-item associations than as an example of retrieval based on categorical relationships. That is, the data may reflect developmental changes in the dominant associative responses at different ages rather than changes in the hierarchical structure of information in memory.

Most of the studies of organizational processes in children's memory have confounded the categorical relationships within the stimulus list and associative relationships among items within these categories. One notable exception is a study conducted by Lange (1973) in which he presented lists of 16 items to 5½-, 11-, and 15-year-old children. The lists contained four conceptual categories but the four items within each category were not high associates of one another. For example, 'pig, squirrel, horse and giraffe' are all in the same category (animals) but are not highly inter-associated. Using such lists, only 15-year-olds demonstrated clustering significantly higher than would be expected by chance. Thus, previous demonstrations of 'categorical clustering' in very young children (see Rossi & Wittrock, 1971) may instead 'reflect skills of a lower cognitive order than has been assumed' (Lange, 1973, p. 403).

Regardless of the exact basis of organization, be it associative or based on taxonomic categorization, it seems that recall by children as young as 2 years can be increased by the presence of categorical relationships in to-be-learned lists. Several attempts have been made to enhance the child's sensitivity to the presence of such relationships. One such manipulation is to present the to-be-remembered materials in a way that increases the likelihood that the child will notice the categorical nature of the material. For instance, Cole, Frankel, and Sharp (1971) contrasted recall of lists in which all of the exemplars of a given category were presented together, in blocked fashion, with lists in which category exemplars were distributed randomly throughout the list. The children tested were in first, third, and eighth grade, and at all ages, blocked presentation resulted in higher clustering and recall. However, in testing children in the 4- to 10-year range, Yoshimura, Moely, and Shapiro (1971) found that blocked presentation of category members resulted in higher clustering than random presentation only for 9- to 10-year-olds. The reason for the discrepancy in the age level at which blocked presentation first facilitates recall is not clear at present.

In other studies, more direct means were used to draw the child's attention to the categorical structure of to-be-remembered materials. In an experiment with kindergarten, third-, and fifth-grade subjects, Kobasigawa and Middleton (1972) presented categories in either blocked or random fashion and, in addition, at each age level, half the children were told the categorical nature of the lists. At all three grades, blocked presentation resulted in higher clustering and recall performance. Telling the children about the presence of the categories, however, had no effects on clustering, nor did it interact with the type of presentation method. Apparently, if children note the presence of categories, which they seem to do quite readily, their recall improves. The relative ease with which children detect and use the categorical nature of to-be-learned materials is further illustrated by additional results from the Vaughan (1968) study introduced earlier. Half of the subjects were explicitly instructed to memorize the lists, while for the remaining subjects, the recall test came as a surprise, after they had used the words in constructing an irrelevant story. The findings of an age-related increase in recall and better recall for categorized lists than lists of unrelated words were *not* affected by the nature of the instructions.

Finally, several investigators have examined the facilitative effects on recall of presenting category cues at the time of testing. Typically, the free recall of categorized materials has been viewed as a two-step process. First, subjects must gain access to a category and second, they must recall the contents of that category. Furthermore, studies with adults (see

Cohen, 1966; Tulving & Pearlstone, 1966) have indicated that most of the variance in forgetting a categorized list is attributable to forgetting category labels or cues rather than to forgetting items within categories. For example, Cohen (1966) demonstrated that if one item is recalled from a category, then there is a high probability that the subject will recall a stable number of other items from that category, independent of list length and number of categories present (within limits). Because access to a category is such a critical factor, it seems reasonable to expect that supplying category labels at recall, given that those labels were stored with the items at the time of acquisition, will increase the amount recalled.

To test this notion, Scribner and Cole (1972) presented categorized lists of 20 items to 7-, 9-, and 11-year-olds. Half the subjects were given the category names at presentation and recall (cue condition). In addition, the remaining subjects were also required to recall all the exemplars of one category before moving on to the next (constrained condition). Recall was higher for the subjects in the constrained condition at each age, even on the fourth trial when all subjects were merely asked to recall the list without being given any category information.

In a similar study, Halperin (1974) tested 6-, 9-, and 12-year-old children on a 36-item list consisting of nine different categories. Presentation of the categories in the list was blocked and the experimenter said the category name prior to naming the exemplars. Subjects in the control condition were given standard free recall instructions. Those in the cue condition were required to recall all the items within a category after the experimenter named the category (thus replicating the constrained condition of Scribner and Cole, 1972).

When the category labels were provided, there were no differences among age groups in their recall of the different categories (recalling at least one exemplar of a category) but there were strong age differences in the noncued condition. Apparently, the categories were available to children of all ages, but only the older children were able to rely upon their own retrieval strategies to gain access to these categories when the experimenter did not provide the category cue. Further, presenting cues at the time of test facilitated category recall rather than within-category recall. While older children typically remembered more items per category, the two cuing conditions did not affect the recall of these items.

A recognition test was administered after two presentation-and-recall trials. Children in the noncued condition *recognized* seven to nine more words than they recalled on the second trial. Assuming that recognition does not involve a retrieval or search process (Kintsch, 1970), this finding suggests that there were seven to nine additional words that were available in long-term memory but that could not be recalled by the child. A similar comparison for subjects in the cued groups suggested that for the two oldest groups, all the available words were also accessible for recall. For these subjects, cued recall on the second trial approximated recognition performance (and this finding could not be attributed to a ceiling effect). However, for the 6-year-olds in the cued condition, there were approximately five words that were available but could not be recalled, as evidenced by the difference between recognition and trial 2 recall scores. Thus, the younger children, even in the cued condition, were not as adept at exhaustively recalling all words whose presence in memory was detected by a recognition test.

In summary, there are consistent developmental increases in the ability to use taxonomic and associative relationships, but it appears that the recall of children even as young as 2 years is affected, at least to a limited extent, by the presence of such relationships. It seems that children not only are sensitive to the semantic aspects of words [. . .] , but also that they are able to use these aspects to aid recall. As the child grows and his experience with the semantic relationships in language increases, his ability to make effective use of them also increases.

b. Subjective Organization.   Instead of providing the subject with an experimenter-defined categorical structure, an alternative approach to the study of organizational processes is to supply the subject with lists of 'unrelated' words, and see if he imposes a structure of his own. One method of observing such subjective organization is to present the subject a series of alternating presentation and free-recall trials with the same list of words. Each presentation is a new random order of the list. If the subject tends to recall the same words together as groups on successive trials, the groupings must be independent of the input order of the list, which varies from trial to trial. Thus, the subject must have imposed his own organization on the materials (Tulving, 1962).

In an early experiment on subjective organization (Laurence, 1966) 5- through 10-year-olds were tested as well as adults. The important finding was that adults demonstrated greater amounts of subjective organization than did any of the groups of children, which did not differ from one another. For the adults and the two oldest groups of children there was a positive correlation between the amount of subjective organization and the number of words recalled, but there was no such relationship for 5- or 6-year-olds. Thus, there is little indication that young children spontaneously impose any organization on the stimuli, and only a suggestion that the older children do so. Similar low levels of subjective organization, when compared with adult performance, were reported for subjects as old as 12 years in a study by Shapiro and Moely (1971).

In addition, attempts to induce subjective organization in young children have not been entirely successful. In one condition of a free-recall experiment, Rosner (1971) told children in the first, fifth, and ninth grades to 'chunk' items together by making up ways that the picture stimuli could go together. For first graders, instructions to chunk resulted in slightly higher subjective organization as measured by a sorting task following the recall trials, but it did not increase actual recall when compared to a standard free recall condition. Recall and subjective organization increased with chunking instructions at grades 5 and 9, although only slightly for the latter group because they were probably organizing the material even without the specific instruction to do so. The fifth graders, while they generally do not engage in such spontaneous organization, do benefit from the chunking instruction. Even though the chunking instruction increases the amount of subjective organization for first graders, it does not improve their recall performance.

In summary, although even young children are able to use experimenter-imposed categories to facilitate recall, typically they are unable to construct an organizational scheme that will aid them in recalling lists of unrelated words. The construction of such a scheme involves a more active, planful form of processing, a strategy that no doubt develops later than the ability to make use of experimenter-supplied, and usually quite obvious, relationships within the to-be-learned material.

c. Organization as Memory.   The organizational indices in both clustering studies and subjective organization studies rely on the adjacent recall of related pairs of items. Such measurements are not sensitive to higher levels of organization. To circumvent this problem Mandler and Stephens (1967) used a third approach to the study of organization and memory. Girls at ages 7, 9, 11, and 13 years were presented 15 high-frequency words. Subjects in a free-sorting condition sorted the words into two to seven categories of their own choosing on successive trials, until they had sorted the words identically on two consecutive trials. Subjects in a constrained-sorting condition were each paired with a child of the same age in the free-sorting condition and were required to duplicate their free-sorting partner's final arrangement. The placement of each word into a group by the constrained-sorting child was corrected by the experimenter if it did not correspond to the placement of that word by the child's free-sorting partner. This procedure was repeated until the subject made two errorless sorts in succession. Then all subjects were given a surprise free recall test. Children at all ages in the free-sorting condition made fewer errors and took less time in reaching the sorting criterion than the children in the constrained sorting condition. However, on the recall task, while the older subjects recalled more total words, there were no differences between the two sorting groups in the amount recalled. Once a stable organization was achieved, regardless of the number of trials necessary, the recall performance was the same.

Although Mandler and Stephens (1967) found no developmental differences in the number of categories used by the free-sorting subjects, Lange and Hultsch (1970), in a similar experiment, reported that younger subjects used more categories than older subjects. Since this number was greater than the optimal number of categories, at least for adults (Mandler, 1967), it may be that their organization was not as 'good' as that of adults. Even though they sorted to the same criterion as older subjects, the young child's organization may have been less efficient in aiding retrieval. Such a conclusion is supported in an experiment by Liberty and Ornstein (1973). The subjects were fourth graders and college students (mean ages 9.8 and 19.3 years, respectively). Each subject was presented with 28 stimuli. Half the subjects at each age were tested in a free-sorting condition similar to that employed by Mandler and Stephens (1967), except that there was a recall test after each sorting trial. Half of the remaining subjects at each age were paired with a fourth grader in the free-sorting condition and were required to reproduce their partner's sorting pattern. The other half of the remaining subjects at each grade were paired with a college student and were required to reproduce that subject's pattern of sorting. Subjects in the constrained-sorting condition also had a free recall test after each sorting trial. The important result is that at both age levels subjects in the constrained condition who were paired with college students recalled more words than subjects paired with fourth graders.

The data reported by Liberty and Ornstein suggest that the organizational schemes of younger subjects do not facilitate recall as effectively as the organizational schemes generated by older subjects. Liberty and Ornstein analyzed the structures of the groups formed by subjects during the sorting task, and found that adults grouped together words that were semantically related. Children sorted words according to meaning much less frequently and used other dimensions, such as phonemic similarity, to sort words into groups. The semantically based organization of adults may have resulted in more effective rehearsal, thereby increasing recall; alternatively, these content-oriented groups may have facilitated retrieval processes.

d. Development of Retrieval Processes.   In the preceding sections it was assumed that the contents of memory can be characterized by some form of systematic organization and that successful retrieval is dependent upon use of this structure. However, this discussion has been predicated upon the notion that subjects do, indeed, have some conception of the act of retrieval. That is, the child must be aware that he does, in fact, possess the information that is being requested of him and that his task is to retrieve that information for the experimenter. At a more advanced level, the child should be aware of the various ways that one can assist this process of retrieval other than just 'brute-force', willing the information into existence.

The development of retrieval strategies in young children was examined in a study conducted by Ritter, Kaprove, Fitch, and Flavell (1973). The subjects in this experiment were from 3 to 5 years of age. The stimuli consisted of duplicate sets of pictures of six different persons, plus six small toys, each toy being closely associated to one of the persons depicted in the pictures. There was also a row of six house—toybox units. In the first task the experimenter 'put the first picture to bed' in a house and put the associated toy in the adjacent (open) toybox. The experimenter then asked the child how the matching picture could find its twin, who was now asleep. In this task the toys were designed to serve as the retrieval cues for the location of the pictures. Prompts of varying strength (three verbal and two modeling) were given if the child did not spontaneously suggest using the toys in the boxes. After completion of the first task, the experimenter left the room with the toys and then returned to ask the subject how many names of the now-absent toys he could remember. In this second task the pictures were designed to function as retrieval cues for the names of the toys. Again, there was a series of five graded prompts to be used if the child failed to utilize the appropriate retrieval cues.

In the first task there were no age differences. More than half of the children used the toys spontaneously as cues and following the strongest prompt, only one child failed to use the toy as a retrival cue. In the second task, most of the older children (about 75 per cent of the subjects) used the pictures as retrieval cues for the toys with either no prompting or minimal prompting. In contrast, nearly half of the 3- to 4-year-olds required the strongest form of the prompt before they used the retrieval cues. In addition, approximately one-third of these younger children completely failed to use the pictures as retrieval cues in the second task. In the second task, the use of retrieval cues was not strongly suggested by the stimulus display (as was the case in the first task). Thus, the data from the second task support the hypothesis that there are developmental changes in the child's understanding of and approach to the problems of retrieval.

In a related experiment, Kobasigawa (1974) tested the hypothesis that children of different ages would differ in their utilization of retrieval cues in the recall of categorized lists. Twenty-four stimuli representing eight different categories were mounted on a board, with a picture of an appropriate retrieval cue mounted adjacent to each stimulus. For instance, a picture of a zoo accompanied each of the three animal pictures. During the presentation sequence the experimenter explicitly referred to the stimulus-cue relationship. Following presentation, 6-, 8-, and 11-year-old subjects received different recall instructions depending upon the experimental group. A control group was given typical free-recall instructions. In a cue condition, the children were given a deck of cards that were identical to the cues initially presented with each stimulus. The subjects were told that they could use these cards to help them remember. Finally, in a directive-cue condition, cards from this same deck were shown individually to the subject, who was required to name all the category exemplars related to that cue before proceeding to the next card.

Analysis of the recall data, which are presented in Figure 7.4, showed that 'the cue versus free-recall differences become progressively greater with increasing grade level, and the cue versus directive-cue recall differences become progressively smaller with increasing grade level' (Kobasigawa, 1974, p. 129). The directive-cue condition effectively eliminated developmental differences in recall, indicating that the information was stored and retrieved equally well by subjects of all ages. (Confidence intervals computed for each of the means shown in Figure 7.4 in no case included 100 per cent correct recall; thus the lack of an age effect in the directive cue condition probably is not attributable to a ceiling effect.) In contrast, a large increase in recall with age was noted in the cue condition. Even at the eight-year-old level where there is a slight (statistically insignificant) superiority of the cue condition as compared to the free-recall condition, subjects were not using the cues as efficiently as they could (directive-cue condition). However, recall by the 11-year-olds in the cue and directive-cue conditions did not differ. These subjects were able to recall exhaustively all the members of a category whether required to do so (directive-cue condition) or not (cue condition). Analysis of the clustering data for subjects in the cue condition complements these findings. High clustering scores were obtained for 11-year-olds, indicating that they recalled all the items they could from one category before moving on to the next. In contrast, younger subjects yielded low clustering scores. Kobasigawa reported that these subjects often went through the deck of cue cards several times, each time attempting to recall only one exemplar of a category before proceeding to the next.

Figure 7.4: Percentage correct responses as a function of age and recall condition: Solid line, directive-cue; broken line, cue; dotted line, free recall.

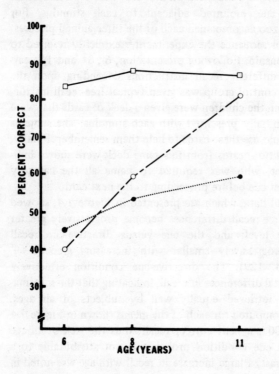

Source: Redrawn from A. Kobasigawa. 'Utilization of retrieval cues by children in recall', *Child Development,* 1974, 45, 130, Fig. 1.

That the strategy of exhaustively recalling all the exemplars of a category develops with age has been convincingly demonstrated in a study by Tumolo, Mason, and Kobasigawa (1974). A 24-item list was presented to first- and third-grade children. The list consisted of pictures of three objects from each of eight conceptual categories. The picture of an appropriate category cue accompanied each of the three pictures from that category. At the time of recall, a deck of category cue cards was given to the subject and he was told that they might be helpful for recalling the names of the pictures that had been presented. Printed on the cue cards in an informed condition, in addition to the picture of the category cue, were three blue squares indicating the number of exemplars of that category to be recalled. Subjects were told that the blue squares should remind them that there were three pictures in that category. Only the picture of the category cue appeared on each cue card for the subjects in an uninformed condition.

Overall recall was higher for third than first graders. More importantly, for third graders, there was no difference in recall between the two cuing conditions. In either situation, they were equally adept at exhaustively recalling most of the exemplars of a category. For first graders, however, recall was significantly higher in the informed condition. Without the additional information about category size, they did not exhaust their memory for the elements of one category before proceeding to the next.

The notion that many developmental differences in memory performance can be attributed to the child's increasing ability to use retrieval strategies effectively would be further supported if developmental differences did not appear in tasks in which successful performance did not require the use of such retrieval strategies. A recognition memory task is one such task in which it is assumed that retrieval processes are largely by-passed (Kintsch, 1970). Both Corsini, Jacobus, and Leonard (1969) and Brown and Scott (1971) have found very high recognition performance in preschoolers when they are asked to indicate, for each picture in a long series, whether or not that picture had appeared previously in the series.

A closely related task is one in which subjects are required to make judgments of relative recency. In this task a long list of words is first presented. Then, on a subsequent test, subjects are presented a pair of words, both of which appeared in the initial list, and they are required to indicate which word was presented more recently. Brown (1973) found that, while performance increased both as a function of the separation of the two words in the initial list and the 'nearness' of the second word to the end of the list, there were no developmental differences for subjects ranging from 7 to 18 years of age. She concluded that in a task such as this, in which no deliberate mnemonic strategy will contribute to successful performance, no developmental trend will be found. This contention was supported in a later study (Brown, Campione, & Gilliard, 1974) where an age effect was found only when the task was such that performance could be facilitated by the deliberate use of a strategy.

B. The Development of Self-awareness in Memory Skills

A paradoxical finding that has consistently reappeared in the discussion of the development of memory is that young children can perform many complex memorial activities when induced to do so by an adult, but rarely do so spontaneously. For example, young children may not spontaneously rehearse or organize, but these skills can be taught to children rather easily (see Kingsley & Hagen, 1969; Moely *et al.*, 1969). Thus we are left with the question of *why* the younger child does not engage in these behaviors, even though he is capable of doing so.

The emphasis of the information processing approach on an active, 'strategy-using' organism suggests one possible answer to this question. Presumably, the child's awareness of himself as an active organism may have its own developmental course. If the child does not view himself as an active memorizer, then he will be unlikely to initiate spontaneously the deployment of strategies in various memory tasks. In like manner, the child's knowledge of all things mnemonic probably follows some onto-genetic course. That is, the acquisition of all the facts of memory that are known to the typical adult human (either explicitly or implicitly) must occur over some developmental span. To the extent that the child does not have knowledge of either his 'mnemonic self' or of various memory phenomena, one would not expect the child to engage in any task appropriate mnemonic behavior.

One implication of this point of view is that there should be an age at which the child does not realize that a memory task demands a specific set of behaviors for its successful completion. If this hypothesis is correct, then children of this age who are given instructions merely to look at stimuli should not behave differently from children who are given more explicit instructions.

To examine this notion Appel, Cooper, McCarrell, Sims-Knight, Yussen and Flavell (1972) tested the recall of 4-, 7-, and 11-year-old children following either looking or remembering instructions. The stimuli were 15 pictures, three from each of five categories. Following presentation of the stimuli there was a 90-second study period during which the children were permitted to manipulate the still-visible stimuli in any manner they desired. Then all subjects were required to recall the pictures. The results indicated that only at the 11-year level was recall in the 'remember' condition higher than in the 'look' condition. Further, identical results were obtained when the child's clustering scores were analyzed. Observations of the child's behavior during the study period revealed that only the 11-year-olds rehearsed more in the remember condition than the looking condition.

Thus, there is support for the hypothesis that 'memorizing and perceiving are functionally undifferentiated for the young child, with deliberate memorization only gradually emerging as a separate and distinctive form of cognitive encounter with external stimuli — a form that naturally includes but also goes beyond mere perceptual contact with those data' (Appel *et al.*, 1972, p. 1365).

The differentiation of mere perceptual processing and memorizing in the older child may consist, in large part, of the acquisition of knowledge and awareness of a variety of mnemonic phenomena. Kreutzer, Leonard, and Flavell (1976) have coined the term 'metamemory' to describe this knowledge about all things mnemonic. Further, Kreutzer *et al.* suggested that children might acquire knowledge about various classes of memory phenomena. First, there is knowledge about one's abilities. With development children may become increasingly proficient at estimating their own mnemonic capabilities. Clearly, this is an important aspect because to the extent that the child is inaccurate in his assessment of his own memorial abilities, he will be less likely to realize when those abilities are being challenged, and consequently, will fail to utilize appropriate mnemonic strategies to improve his performance in such a situation.

Evidence to this effect has been provided in a study conducted by Flavell *et al.* (1970) described, in part, previously [. . .] In addition to the findings already reported, the accuracy of the child's estimate of his own memory span was assessed in these subjects of nursery school, kindergarten, second and fourth-grade levels. The child was asked first how many items he thought he could remember from a list of ten pictures. Then the actual number of pictures that the child could recall was tested. The estimates of the two younger groups of children were consistently higher than the estimates from the second and fourth graders. The percentage of subjects who predicted that they would be able to recall all of the items from the ten-item list decreased from 57 per cent at the nursery school level to 21 per cent at the fourth-grade level. The younger children were obviously much less aware of the limitations of their own memorial abilities.

Kreutzer *et al.* (1976) also pointed out that subjects acquire information about items and relationships between items that make them easier or more difficult to remember. From Section A, 2, it is evident that one of the most powerful ways of making items easier to remember is to present them in conceptual categories. Moynahan (1973) investigated the development of this knowledge of the facilitating effects of categorization upon free recall in 7, 9 and 10 year-olds. The child viewed several pairs of cards. One card of each pair contained several pictures from conceptually related classes, while items on the other card were not related. The child's task was to select the set of items that would be easier to remember, and to indicate why he believed them to be easier. Those children who failed to mention the categories in at least seven of their explanations were asked a subsequent question to determine if they had, in fact, detected the categorized nature of the cards.

The results indicated that the two older groups did not differ in the number of times they chose the categorized items more frequently than did the 7-year-olds. However, even these youngest children selected the categorized items more frequently than chance. A similar pattern of results was obtained for the explanation scores as well. Furthermore, these differences were maintained when the analyses were restricted to only those subjects who detected the categories.

The overall superiority of the older children and the greater-than-chance performance of the youngest children in the Moynahan study are similar to data obtained in the clustering experiments reviewed in Section A, 2. Consistent with the developmental differences noted in that section, it would seem plausible that a task that placed more of the burden of creating and using an organization on the child might yield more striking developmental differences. Tenney (1973) investigated the lists that kindergarten, third-, and sixth-grade children generate when asked to choose words that would be easy to remember. Children generated lists of words following one of three sets of instructions. The experimenter first told the child a key word. Then the child was asked to generate a list of words that: (a) would be easy to remember with the key word; (b) consisted of words that were members of the same category as the key word; or (c) consisted of free associates to the key word.

The analyses of these lists showed that the kindergarten children generated essentially the same list whether the instruction was to give free associates or to generate items that would be easy to remember. At the two older age levels, however, the lists of easy-to-remember words were very similar to the lists of category items. Thus, only the older children had sufficient knowledge of the effects of categorization to produce *spontaneously* such a categorized list.

By far the most comprehensive study of the child's knowledge of different memory phenomena was conducted by Kreutzer *et al.* (1976). In this study children from kindergarten, first, third, and fifth grades were interviewed to determine their knowledge about a wide range of different aspects of memory. The interview was organized around five central components that are critical for one's knowledge of memory processes. These included knowledge about (a) the individual as an habitual user of mnemonics; (b) properties of data that affect the ease with which they are remembered; (c) acquisition strategies that facilitate subsequent retrieval of stimuli; (d) ways to cope with the problem of retrieving stored information; and (e) the differing nature of the mnemonic demands placed on an individual in different retrieval situations.

Rather than review all of the data from this study, certain aspects that illustrate some of the developmental differences found in metamemory will be presented. For example, one of the facts about one's memory that has practical consequences for mnemonic behavior is the rapid decay from short-term store. To test for knowledge of this fact the child was asked, 'If you wanted to phone your friend and someone told you the phone number, would it make any difference if you called right away after you heard the number or if you got a drink of water first?' (Kreutzer *et al.*, 1976, p. 23). Children in the first through fifth grades said consistently that one should phone immediately, while kindergarteners said one could phone or get a drink of water with almost equal frequency.

In a subsequent question Kreutzer *et al.* probed the child's knowledge of the facilitating effects on paired associate learning of relationships between the paired stimuli. To insure that the child understood the requirements of the task, he first learned a list of three pairs. Then he was shown two different lists of pairs. The experimenter showed that in one list the words were opposites (e.g. boy—girl), while in the second list the pairs consisted of names of people and things they do (e.g. Mary—walk). The child then was asked which list would be easier to learn. After he had responded, the experimenter added another pair to the list that the child had judged to be easier and asked the child to select the list that was easier now. This procedure of adding items was continued until the child finally indicated that the originally more difficult list would now be easier.

The responses to this question showed striking developmental differences. Kindergarteners were more likely to say that the arbitrary pairs would be easier to learn, and the first-grade children selected the two types of pairs with equal frequency. Only the third- and fifth-grade children seemed to know that the invariant associative relationship between items in the list of opposites would facilitate learning. Furthermore, only the older children were steadfast in maintaining their selection of the earlier list. For the two younger groups, a list became automatically more difficult when just one more pair was added. Most older children did not switch their list preferences until more than three pairs had been added to the original list. They seemed to be quite certain of the importance of the relational structure in a list.

Thus, there is impressive evidence that metamemory exhibits a developmental course. It is not as clear, however, just what the relation is between the development of this self-awareness of the memory process and actual performance in memory situations. Studies should be pursued with the aim of determining whether the suspected causal links do indeed exist.

C. Concluding Remarks

Since almost the beginning of scientific psychology there has been a curiosity about the age-related changes found in memory. The early knowledge of memory development was quickly put to use in tests of intelligence; thus, almost immediately memory was considered a part of the larger sphere of intellectual functioning. However, memory was treated more or less as a unitary construct and was not analyzed further by these differential psychologists. Experimental psychology did recognize that memory performance is, to a large extent, a function of the technique of measurement; but not until the advent of the information-processing models was memory pursued vigorously as a construct in its own right.

The sheer volume of the research reviewed in [. . .] this paper attests to the magnitude of interest in recent years in the development of memory, and the orientation of this research reflects the theoretical bias that has influenced the majority of the investigations. The information-processing model suggests critical points in the memorial process where developmental changes occur — initial encoding, acquisition, storage, and retrieval — and where this process may be linked to other important aspects of cognition (see Reese, 1973).

Initial encoding, not surprisingly, involves language even in preschool-age children [. . .] Semantic information is coded for storage in a wide variety of experimental tasks across a wide age range. Other types of features of stimuli may be used depending on the circumstances. Further, children as young as 5 years can deal effectively with semantically integrated information, such as a series of short sentences. They can encode and use the semantic information presented in ways that are independent of the original formal structure. The lack of age differences, across a rather wide range (pre-school to adolescence), points to the early (and seemingly automatic) abilities children have in encoding and using considerable amounts of information.

When the focus is on the child as an active memorizer, however, the picture that emerges is very different. Age differences, across this same age range, have been found to be the rule rather than the exception when the task demands that information beyond the subject's immediate capacity must be acquired and later recalled. That young children do not attempt initially to acquire information that is presented to them for later recall is now well-established, as was argued in Section A, 1. The use of mnemonic strategies emerges over a period of years. Often younger children are able to use cues or particular mnemonic strategies when they are provided to improve recall, although the facilitation is typically transitory and does not generalize to later situations. By 10 to 11 years the child appears to have a working, flexible repertoire of these strategies from which he can draw when the situation demands. Intrinsic properties to the stimuli can be used as well as imposed devices such as rehearsing or grouping into idiosyncratic categories. The child's increased knowledge of linguistic properties and conceptual relations can and will be used if appropriate to the task at hand. These developmental differences are evident for situations involving both acquisition of new information and retrieval of already stored information, as shown in Section A, 2.

The recent studies of the child's awareness of himself as a memorizer, reviewed in Section B, provide correlational evidence for the relation between the child's self-awareness and his performance in memory tasks, and also more direct evidence that the young child is not capable of distinguishing features in a task that suggested a particular acquisition strategy. Just why the child must be well into the grade-school years before he becomes proficient in these skills is not at all evident at this time. It does seem obvious, though, that these limitations in the child are not due to the incomplete development of the structural components involved in memorizing and retrieving. Rather, the locus of age differences appears to be in the control processes used by subjects that are under the child's active direction. The importance of control processes is underscored by findings that developmental differences in memory performance can often be eliminated if young children are instructed in the use of strategies, or if the use of strategies by older children is prevented.

Since memory is a very complex phenomenon, it is not surprising that a developmental 'shift' in memory processes at a particular age level has not been identified. The shift in cognitive performance occurring at ages 5 to 7 identified by White (1965) is too narrow to encompass the changes in memory development. Instead of a well-defined shift, changes in memory between the ages 5 through 11 are a consequence of the child's gradual acquisition and mastery of sophisticated mnemonic strategies. Changes in memory performance with age reflect the development of an ever-expanding repertoire of strategies rather than a shift in the fundamental bases of cognition.

Memory is an integral component of cognition. Consequently, in some situations where a child appears to have a cognitive deficiency, the problem may lie more precisely in the child's memory processes. This point has been documented recently (Bryant & Trabasso, 1971; Riley & Trabasso,

1974). Children at the preschool age were tested in Piaget's transitive inference task, and as expected they were unable to make correct inferences when the standard testing procedures were used. However, in another condition, children were trained to criterion on the individual inequalities. The majority of these children were then able to make the correct inference. In a study of the use of hypotheses to solve a discrimination learning task, Eimas (1970) found that *if* 7-year-old children were allowed to have access to their responses on previous trials, they could eliminate systematically incorrect hypotheses as effectively as adults. In these two studies, the young child's lack of memory for important information seemed to be responsible for his deficient performance rather than an inability to perform the task per se.

The major theme in our review has been that as the child develops, he is increasingly active in his efforts to remember. The information-processing approach, with its emphasis on processes that transform and manipulate information, has proved extremely useful in identifying different components of the memorial process in children. [. . .]

As the information-processing approach continues to be applied to different age groups and other situations, there will undoubtedly be better understanding of the ways in which memory develops. Because memory plays a key role in most aspects of cognition, the study of the processes underlying memory development should provide important insights to the basic properties of cognitive development.

Notes

1. Numerous measures have been developed to indicate the amount of clustering in a subject's recall protocol. In general, these measures indicate whether the adjacent occurrence, in the protocol, of two words from the same experimenter-defined category is more frequent than would be expected by chance. Jablonski (1974) and Moely and Jeffrey (1974) have recently reviewed the various clustering measures and discussed the appropriateness of the different measures for developmental research.

References

Anastasi, A., *Psychological Testing*, New York: Macmillan, 1968.
Appel, L.F., Cooper, R.G., McCarrell, N., Sims-Knight, J., Yussen, S.R., & Flavell, J.H., 'The development of the distinction between perceiving and memorizing', *Child Development*, 1972, 43, 1365-81.
Atkinson, R.C., Hansen, D.N., & Bernbach, H.A., 'Short-term memory with young children', *Psychonomic Science*, 1964, 1, 255-6.
Atkinson, R.C. & Shiffrin, R.M., 'Human memory: A proposed system and its control processes', in K.W. Spence & J.T. Spence (eds.), *The Psychology of*

Learning and Motivation, vol. 2, New York: Academic Press, 1968.

Bach, M.J. & Underwood, B.J., 'Developmental changes in memory attributes', *Journal of Educational Psychology*, 1970, 61, 292-6.

Barclay, J.R. & Reid, M., 'Semantic integration in children's recall of discourse', *Developmental Psychology*, 1974, 10, 277-81.

Belmont, J.M. & Butterfield, E.C., 'The relations of short-term memory to development and intelligence', in L.P. Lipsett & H.W. Reese (eds.), *Advances in Child Development and Behavior*, vol. 4, New York: Academic Press, 1969.

Belmont, J.M. & Butterfield, E.C., 'Learning strategies as determinants of memory deficiencies', *Cognitive Psychology*, 1971, 2, 411-20. (a)

Belmont, J.M. & Butterfield, E.C., 'What the development of short-term memory is', *Human Development*, 1971, 14, 236-49. (b)

Benton, A.L., *Revised Visual Retention Test: Manual*, New York: Psychological Corporation, 1963.

Bjork, R.A., 'Short-term storage: The ordered output of a central processor', paper presented at the Indiana Theoretical and Cognitive Psychology Conferences, Bloomington, Indiana, April 1974.

Boring, E.G., *A History of Experimental Psychology*, New York: Appleton, 1950.

Bousfield, W.A., 'The occurrence of clustering in the recall of randomly arranged sequences', *Journal of General Psychology*, 1953, 49, 229-40.

Bousfield, W.A., Cohen, B.H., & Whitmarsh, G.A., 'Associative clustering in the recall of words of different taxonomic frequencies of occurrence', *Psychological Reports*, 1958, 4, 39-44.

Bower, G.H., 'A multi-component theory of the memory trace', in K.W. Spence & J.T. Spence (eds.), *The Psychology of Learning and Motivation*, vol. 1, New York: Academic Press, 1967.

Bransford, J.D. & Franks, J.J., 'Abstraction of linguistic ideas', *Cognitive Psychology*, 1971, 2, 331-50.

Broadbent, D.E., *Perception and Communication*, Oxford: Pergamon, 1958.

Brown, A.L., 'Judgments of recency for long sequences of pictures: The absence of a developmental trend', *Journal of Experimental Child Psychology*, 1973, 15, 473-80.

Brown, A.L., 'The role of strategic behavior in retardate memory', in N.R. Ellis (ed.), *International Review of Research in Mental Retardation*, vol. 7, New York: Academic Press, 1974.

Brown, A.L., Campione, J.C. & Gilliard, D.M., 'Recency judgments in children: A production deficiency in the use of redundant background cues', *Developmental Psychology*, 1974, 10, 303.

Brown, A.L. & Scott, M.S., 'Recognition memory for pictures in preschool children', *Journal of Experimental Child Psychology*, 1971, 11, 401-12.

Bruner, J.S., 'The course of cognitive growth', *American Psychologist*, 1964, 19, 1-15.

Bryant, P.E. & Trabasso, T., 'Transitive inferences and memory in young children', *Nature* (London), 1971, 232, 456-8.

Buehler, C. & Hetzer, H., *Testing Children's Development from Birth to School Age*, (transl. by H. Beaumont), New York: Rinehart, 1935.

Cermak, L.S., Sagotsky, G., & Moshier, C., 'Development of the ability to encode within evaluative dimensions', *Journal of Experimental Child Psychology*, 1972, 13, 210-19.

Cohen, B.H., 'Some-or-none characteristics of coding behavior', *Journal of Verbal Learning and Verbal Behavior*, 1966, 5, 182-7.

Cole, M., Frankel, F., & Sharp, D., 'Development of free recall learning in children', *Developmental Psychology*, 1971, 4, 109-23.

Corsini, D.A., 'Developmental changes in the effect of nonverbal cues on retention',

Developmental Psychology, 1969, 1, 425-35. (a)

Corsini, D.A., 'The effect of nonverbal cues on the retention of kindergarten children', *Child Development*, 1969, 40, 599-607. (b)

Corsini, D.A., Jacobus, K.A., & Leonard, S.D., 'Recognition memory of preschool children for pictures and words', *Psychonomic Science*, 1969, 16, 192-3.

Craik, F.I.M. & Lockhart, R.S., 'Levels of processing: A framework for memory research', *Journal of Verbal Learning and Verbal Behavior*, 1972, 11, 671-84.

Cramer, P., 'A developmental study of errors in memory', *Developmental Psychology*, 1972, 7, 204-9.

DiVesta, F.J., 'A developmental study of the semantic structures of children', *Journal of Verbal Learning and Verbal Behavior*, 1966, 5, 249-59.

Eimas, P.D., 'Effects of memory aids on hypothesis behavior and focusing in young children and adults', *Journal of Experimental Psychology*, 1970, 10, 319-36.

Felzen, E. & Anisfeld, M., 'Semantic and phonetic relations in the false recognition of words by third and sixth grade children', *Developmental Psychology*, 1970, 3, 163-8.

Flavell, J.H., 'Developmental studies of mediated memory', in H.W. Reese & L.P. Lipsitt (eds.), *Advances in Child Development and Behavior*, vol. 5, New York: Academic Press, 1970.

Flavell, J.H., Beach, D.R., & Chinsky, J.M., 'Spontaneous verbal rehearsal in a memory task as a function of age', *Child Development*, 1966, 37, 283-99.

Flavell, J.H., Friedrichs, A.G., & Hoyt, J.D., 'Developmental changes in memorization processes', *Cognitive Psychology*, 1970, 1, 324-40.

Freund, J.S., & Johnson, J.W., 'Changes in memory attribute dominance as a function of age', *Journal of Educational Psychology*, 1972, 63, 386-9.

Goggin, J., & Wickens, D.D., 'Proactive interference and language change in short-term memory', *Journal of Verbal Learning and Verbal Behavior*, 1971, 10, 453-8.

Hagen, J.W., 'Some thoughts on how children learn to remember', *Human Development*, 1971, 14, 262-71.

Hagen, J.W., 'Strategies for remembering', in S. Farnham-Diggory (ed.), *Information Processing in Children*, New York: Academic Press, 1972.

Hagen, J.W., Hargrave, S., & Ross, W., 'Prompting and rehearsal in short-term memory', *Child Development*, 1973, 44, 201-4.

Hagen, J.W., & Kail, R.V., 'Facilitation and distraction in short-term memory', *Child Development*, 1973, 44, 831-6.

Hagen, J.W., & Kingsley, P.R., 'Labeling effects in short-term memory', *Child Development*, 1968, 39, 113-21.

Hagen, J.W., Meacham, J.A., & Mesibov, G., 'Verbal labeling, rehearsal, and short-term memory', *Cognitive Psychology*, 1970, 1, 47-58.

Hail, J.W., & Halperin, M.S., 'The development of memory-encoding processes in young children', *Developmental Psychology*, 1972, 6, 181.

Halperin, M.S., 'Developmental changes in the recall and recognition of categorized word lists', *Child Development*, 1974, 45, 144-51.

Harlow, H.F., Uhling, H., & Maslow, A.H., 'Comparative behavior of primates. I. Delayed reaction tests on primates from the lemur to the orangutan', *Journal of Comparative Psychology*, 1932, 13, 313-44.

Hunter, W.S., 'The delayed reaction in animals and children', *Behavior Monographs*, 1913, 2, no. 1, 1-86.

Hunter, W.S., 'The delayed reaction in a child', *Psychological Review*, 1917, 24, 74-87.

Jablonski, E.M., 'Free recall in children', *Psychological Bulletin*, 1974, 81, 522-39.

James, W., *The Principles of Psychology*, New York: Holt, 1890. (reprinted: New York, Dover, 1950.)

Kail, R.V., & Levine, L., 'Encoding processes and sex-role preferences',

Developmental Reports Series, no. 48, University of Michigan, 1974.

Kail, R.V., & Schroll, J.T., 'Evaluative and taxonomic encoding in children's memory', *Journal of Experimental Child Psychology*, 1974, 18, 426-37.

Keeney, T.J., Cannizzo, S.R., & Flavell, J.H., 'Spontaneous and induced verbal rehearsal in a recall task', *Child Development*, 1967, 38, 953-66.

Keppel, G., & Underwood, B.J., 'Proactive inhibition in short-term retention of single items', *Journal of Verbal Learning and Verbal Behavior*, 1962, 1, 153-61.

Kingsley, P.R., & Hagen, J.W., 'Induced versus spontaneous rehearsal in short-term memory in nursery school children', *Developmental Psychology*, 1969, 1, 40-6.

Kintsch, W., 'Models for free recall and recognition', in D.A. Norman (eds.), *Models of Human Memory*, New York: Academic Press, 1970.

Kobasigawa, A., 'Utilization of retrieval cues by children in recall', *Child Development*, 1974, 45, 127-34.

Kobasigawa, A., & Middleton, D.B., 'Free recall of categorized items by children at three grade levels', *Child Development*, 1972, 43, 1067-72.

Kreutzer, M.A., Leonard, C., & Flavell, J.H., 'An interview study of children's knowledge about memory', *Monographs of the Society for Research in Child Development*, 1976.

Kroes, W.H., 'Conceptual encoding by sense impression', *Perceptual and Motor Skills*, 1973, 37, 432.

Lange, G.W., 'The development of conceptual and rote recall skills among school age children', *Journal of Experimental Child Psychology*, 1973, 15, 394-406.

Lange, G.W., & Hultsch, D.F., 'The development of free classification and free recall in children', *Developmental Psychology*, 1970, 3, 408.

Laurence, M.W., 'Age differences in performance and subjective organization in free-recall learning of pictorial material', *Canadian Journal of Psychology*, 1966, 20, 388-99.

Libby, W.L., & Kroes, W.H., 'Conceptual encoding and concept recall-recovery in children', *Child Development*, 1971, 42, 2089-93.

Liberty, C., & Ornstein, P.A., 'Age differences in organization and recall: The effects of training in categorization', *Journal of Experimental Child Psychology*, 1973, 15, 169-86.

Locke, J.L., & Fehr, F.S., 'Young children's use of the speech code in a recall task', *Journal of Experimental Child Psychology*, 1970, 10, 367-73.

Mandler, G., 'Organization and memory', in K.W. Spence & J.T. Spence (eds.), *The Psychology of Learning and Motivation*, vol. 1, New York: Academic Press, 1967.

Mandler, G., 'Consciousness: Respectable, useful, and probably necessary', Report No. 41, Center for Human Information Processing, University of California, San Diego, 1974. (a)

Mandler, G., 'Memory storage and retrieval: Some limits on the reach of attention and consciousness', in P.M.A. Rabbit & S. Dornic (eds.), *Attention and Performance V*, London: Academic Press, 1974. (b)

Mandler, G., & Stephens, D., 'The development of free and constrained conceptualization and subsequent verbal memory', *Journal of Experimental Child Psychology*, 1967, 5, 86-93.

Masur, E.F., McIntyre, C.W., & Flavell, J.H., 'Developmental changes in apportionment of study time among items in multitrial free recall task', *Journal of Experimental Child Psychology*, 1973, 15, 237-46.

Moely, B.E., & Jeffrey, W.E., 'The effect of organization training on children's free recall of category items', *Child Development*, 1974, 45, 135-43.

Moely, B.E., Olson, F.A., Halwes, T.G., & Flavell, J.H., 'Production deficiency in young children's clustered recall', *Developmental Psychology*, 1969, 1, 26-34.

Moynahan, E.D., 'The development of knowledge concerning the effect of categorization upon free recall', *Child Development*, 1973, 44, 238-46.

Nadelman, L., 'Sex identity in American children: Memory, knowledge, and preference tests', *Developmental Psychology*, 1974, 10, 413-17.

Neimark, E., Slotnick, N.S., & Ulrich, T., 'Development of memorization strategies', *Developmental Psychology*, 1971, 5, 427-32.

Osgood, C.E., Suci, G.J., & Tannenbaum, P.H., *The Measurement of Meaning*, Urbana: University of Illinois Press, 1957.

Paris, S.G., 'Children's constructive memory', paper presented at the biennial meeting of the Society for Research in Child Development, Philadelphia, March, 1973.

Paris, S.G., & Carter, A.Y., 'Semantic and constructive aspects of sentence memory in children', *Developmental Psychology*, 1973, 9, 109-13.

Pender, N.J., 'A developmental study of conceptual, semantic differential, and acoustical dimensions as encoding categories in short-term memory', unpublished doctoral dissertation, Northwestern University, 1969.

Reese, H.W., 'Verbal mediation as a function of age level', *Psychological Bulletin*, 1962, 59, 502-9.

Reese, H.W., 'Models of memory and models of development', *Human Development*, 1973, 16, 397-416.

Riley, C.A., & Trabasso, T., 'Comparatives, logical structures, and encoding in a transitive inference task', *Journal of Experimental Child Psychology*, 1974, 17, 187-203.

Ritter, K., Kaprove, B.H., Fitch, J.P., & Flavell, J.H., 'The development of retrieval strategies in young children', *Cognitive Psychology*, 1973, 5, 310-21.

Rosner, S.R., 'The effects of rehearsal and chunking instructions on children's multitrial free recall', *Journal of Experimental Child Psychology*, 1971, 11, 93-105.

Rossi, E.L., & Rossi, S.I., 'Conceptualization, serial order and recall in nursery school children', *Child Development*, 1965, 36, 771-8.

Rossi, S.L., & Wittrock, M.C., 'Developmental shifts in verbal recall between mental ages 2 and 5', *Child Development*, 1971, 42, 333-8.

Rubin, S.M., 'Proactive and retroactive inhibition in short-term memory as a function of sensory modality', unpublished manuscript, Human Performance Center, University of Michigan, 1967.

Scribner, S., & Cole, M., 'Effects of constrained recall training on children's performance in a verbal memory task', *Child Development*, 1972, 43, 845-57.

Shapiro, S.I., & Moely, B.E., 'Free recall, subjective organization, and learning to learn at 3 age levels', *Psychonomic Science*, 1971, 23, 189-91.

Sperling, G.A., 'The information available in brief visual presentation', *Psychological Monographs*, 1960, 74 (11, whole no. 498).

Sperling, G.A., 'A model for visual memory tasks', *Human Factors*, 1963, 5, 19-31.

Sperling, G.A., 'Successive approximations to a model for short-term memory', *Acta Psychologica*, 1967, 27, 285-92.

Spiker, C.C., 'Verbal factors in the discrimination learning of children', *Monographs of the Society for Research in Child Development*, 1963, 28 (2, whole no. 86), 53-68.

Stevenson, H.W., *Children's Learning,* New York: Appleton, 1972.

Tenney, Y.H., 'The child's conception of organization and recall: The development of cognitive strategies', unpublished doctoral dissertation, Cornell University, 1973.

Terman, L.M., *The Measurement of Intelligence,* Boston: Houghton, 1916.

Thurstone, L.L., 'Primary mental abilities', *Psychometric Monographs*, 1938, no. 1.

Tinklepaugh, O.L., 'An experimental study of representative factors in monkeys', *Journal of Comparative Psychology*, 1928, 8, 197-236.

Tulving, E., 'Subjective organization in free recall of unrelated words', *Psychological Review*, 1962, 69, 344-54.

Tulving, E., & Pearlstone, Z., 'Availability versus accessibility of information in memory for words', *Journal of Verbal Learning and Verbal Behavior*, 1966, 5, 381-91.

Tumulo, P.J., Mason, P.L., & Kobasigawa, A., 'Presenting category size information to facilitate children's recall', paper presented at the meeting of the Canadian Psychological Association, Windsor, Ontario, June, 1974.

Underwood, B.J., 'Attributes to memory', *Psychological Review*, 1969, 76, 559-77.

Underwood, B., 'Are we overloading memory?', in A.W. Melton & E. Martin (eds.), *Coding Processes in Human Memory*, Washington, D.C.: Winston, 1972.

Vaughan, M.E., 'Clustering, age, and incidental learning', *Journal of Experimental Child Psychology*, 1968, 6, 323-34.

Wagner, J.F., 'A developmental study of categorical organization in short-term memory', unpublished doctoral dissertation, University of Connecticut, 1970.

Waugh, N.C., & Norman, D.A., 'Primary memory', *Psychological Review*, 1965, 72, 89-104.

White, S., 'Evidence for a hierarchical arrangement of learning processes', in L.P. Lipsitt and C.C. Spiker (eds.), *Advances in Child Development and Behavior*, vol. 2, New York: Academic Press, 1965.

Wickens, D.D., 'Encoding categories of words: An empirical approach to meaning', *Psychological Review*, 1970, 77, 1-15.

Wickens, D.D., 'Characteristics of word encoding', in A.W. Melton & E. Martin (eds.), *Coding Processes in Human Memory*, Washington, D.C.: Winston, 1972.

Wickens, D.D., 'Some characteristics of word encoding', *Memory & Cognition*, 1973, 1, 485-90.

Wittlinger, R.P., 'Phasic arousal in short-term memory', unpublished doctoral dissertation, Ohio State University, 1967.

Yoshimura, E.K., Moely, B.E., & Shapiro, S.I., 'The influence of age and presentation order upon children's free recall and learning to learn', *Psychonomic Science*, 1971, 23, 261-3.

8 FROM ELEMENTARY NUMBER CONSERVATION TO THE CONSERVATION OF LENGTH

Bärbel Inhelder, Hermine Sinclair and Magali Bovet

Source: Chapter 6 in B. Inhelder *et al.*, *Learning and the Development of Cognition* (Routledge and Kegan Paul, 1974).

Other conservation experiments [. . . which we have carried out (see Inhelder *et al.* (1974), chapters 1-5] yielded results which make us wary of too simplistic an interpretation of a chronological order of acquisition. Clearly, the fact that elementary number is conserved well before continuous quantity does not mean that the latter concept is derived directly from the former. A complex system of interdependent relationships links the two notions. Conservation of length — a unidimensional continuous quantity — is usually acquired at a slightly later age than that of matter. Once again, the question of a link with the earlier conservation has to be explored. When elementary number conservation has been acquired, can the system of operations bearing on a (still restricted) number of elements be extended directly to the conservation of a number of elements which, when put together, form a certain 'length'? Or does conservation of length also show complex relationships with earlier conservations?

The concept of number is not equivalent to, nor contemporaneous with, that of the conservation of limited numerical quantities. Similarly, conservation of length is not equivalent to the concept of measurement. The concept of number, in the sense of an understanding of natural numbers and the operations which can be performed upon them, is slowly built up from the first elementary number conservations (see Piaget and Inhelder, 1941, and Piaget, Inhelder, and Szeminska, 1948). The concept of measurement implies several steps: first, a unit has to be partitioned off from the object to be quantified, and then this unit has to be displaced without overlaps or empty intervals; second, these continuous units form inclusions — the first bit measured is included in the bit that comprises two units, and so on. The learning experiments on conservation of length[1] were designed to explore the psychological reality underlying the theoretical parallel between number and measurement, and between numerical conservation and conservation of length.

Preliminary Experiments

In many, if not all, conservation problems one of the factors that accounts for nonconservation is the tendency to make ordinal judgments based on ideas of *going beyond, overtaking,* and so on. The level of the liquid poured into the narrow glass 'goes beyond' that of the liquid poured into the wider glass; the row of counters that have been spread out 'goes further than' the other row. In the conservation of length problems this type of judgment is particularly tenacious. When one length of wire is twisted into a zigzag and put directly underneath a straight, much shorter bit of wire, the two lengths are judged to be equal, 'because they go just as far'. Similarly, when one of two sticks, which are placed directly parallel to and underneath one another, is pushed slightly forward, that one is judged to be longer, 'because it goes further'. In a first approach to the learning experiments on length, situations were designed to assess the particular strength of the ordinal judgments as regards conservation of length. The numerical conservation problem was made more difficult by using 20 to 30 elements and by displacing the elements in one of the straight lines so as to make a zigzag. The length conservation situation was made easier by using, instead of wire or sticks, a collection of six matches put end to end (eliminating the difficulty of the partitioning operation). Apart from the fact that the matches touched each other and thus formed, in a certain sense, a continuous line, the situation used for numerical judgments appeared more complex (20-30 objects) than that used for judgments of length (six matches only).

Situations Presented

a. Number. Starting with two equal collections, A and B (see Figure 8.1), the experimenter rearranged B as shown in parts 1 and 2 of Figure 8.1,

Figure 8.1

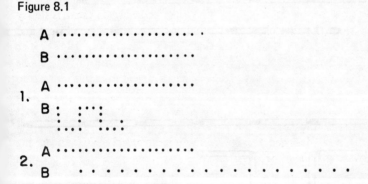

and then asked questions about the number of elements: 'Are there the same in A and B?', etc.

b. Length. Starting with two identical arrangements of matches (see Figure 8.2), the experimenter altered B as shown in parts 1 and 2 of Figure 8.2 and asked the child questions about the length of the 'roads': 'Are they the same length, or is one longer than the other?', etc.

The twelve children selected for this preliminary experiment had previously succeeded in a simple elementary number conservation problem and failed when faced with a conservation of continuous length problem involving two changes in shape of the wire.

The main results were as follows.

a) Despite the large number of objects, almost all the subjects gave con-servation judgments; a few initial errors were spontaneously corrected. They gave the same arguments as in the simple counters test, despite the particularly misleading spatial arrangements: 'Here you've pushed them into a zigzag and it's stayed straight' (compensation); 'You haven't added anything or taken anything away' (identity); and 'You can make the

Figure 8.2

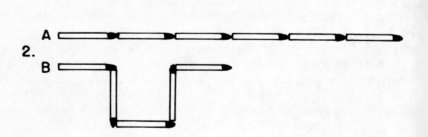

straight line zigzag as well, then that'll be the same' (reversibility).

b) For some children, questions on conservation of length in this simpli- fied situation proved easy. Focusing on the six identical matches, they quickly realized that counting the matches provided them with the correct answers, which they maintained, even when the experimenter tried to make them change their minds ('But look! That one goes much further').

For other children, however, there seemed to be no connection between the problems of number and those of length. When asked about number, the 'going beyond' aspect did not lead them into error, but when asked about length, they proved incapable of applying the same type of reasoning and continued to judge the length of the 'roads' according to whether or not they 'went just as far'. Whereas they spontaneously sug- gested that one could count the matches to check their judgments in the number tasks, it did not occur to them to do so in the length situations. Often they even declined to do so when the experimenter suggested it. Those who finally did adopt this suggestion remained unconvinced by their own findings and gave contradictory answers — changing from inequality judgments (based on the ordinal principle) to equality judg- ments (based on counting) and vice versa. Frequent returns to the number situations, where their logical convictions remained unshaken, had no effect on their answers to the length problems; the striking figural similarity of the two situations did not help them connect the two types of questions.

This preliminary experiment suggested several possibilities for further investigation. In the first place, it confirmed the persistence of ordinal judgments of the 'going beyond' type whenever questions are asked about length, even when the lengths to be compared are broken up into count- able units. This tendency to draw conclusions about respective lengths from the correspondence (or the absence thereof) between extremities appears possible only if the two lengths are arranged as in the original experiment and the experiment just described, i.e. directly underneath one another. How would the children react if roads of equal length but of different contours were presented on different corners of the table? In the second place, it seemed possible that those subjects who used the count- ing method simply shifted their attention from the extremities of the seemingly continuous lines to the individual matches and their count- ability. Their correct answers could be interpreted as pseudo-successes in conservation of length, since they might have translated the problem into a question of conservation of number. What would happen if instead of using matches of identical size, we presented them with lengths made up out of unequal elements? Finally, we wondered whether the tendency to approach questions on length in a different manner from questions on number would still be observed if questions on number and length were asked in the same situation. These considerations led to a first learning experiment where three different types of situations were used.

Initial Training Procedure

The experiment just described led to a trial training procedure, which was presented to a group of children who had succeeded in elementary number conservation and failed in conservation of length. A certain number of variations were introduced, and no effort was made to keep the procedure uniform for all the subjects: consequently, no quantitative results will be given, but the different reactions of the various situations will be described. The most interesting situations were subsequently chosen to construct a regular training procedure. Three displays were presented to the subjects.

Situation a. Two sheets of paper (40 x 30 cm) are placed in front of the subject. Either the experimenter, or the child following his instructions, lays out two roads, A and B, on the first sheet, one straight, one in a zigzag, placed directly above each other, each made up of four matches of equal size (5 cm). On the second sheet, road A is placed in the same way, but road B is laid out vertically at the extreme edge of the paper. The latter situation will be referred to as 'separate lay-out' and the former as 'close lay-out' (see Figure 8.3). The subject is asked to compare the lengths of the roads, first in the close lay-out, then in the separate lay-out. The close lay-out often leads to a judgement of inequality 'Road B is longer, it goes further'), whereas in the separate lay-out the roads are judged to be of equal length, since no comparison of points of arrival is possible and the display suggests counting of the matches. The experimenter then tries to make the subject compare these two different ways of judging. The same situation can be used as a construction task: the experimenter lays out the zigzag road, and the child is asked to construct a road of the same length either directly underneath or at the edge of the paper.

Situation b. The same close lay-out and separate lay-out are used, but the roads are made up of matches of different length (5 and 7 cm). The same questions are asked as in situation a and the same instructions are given.

Situation c. Two straight lines of sticks with tiny houses glued onto them are laid out, consisting of the same number of sticks, one directly

Figure 8.3

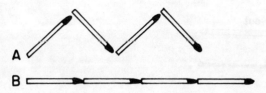

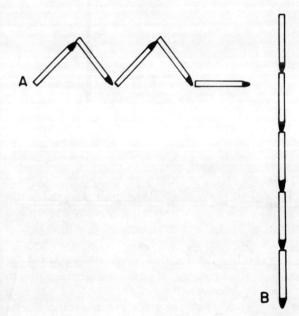

underneath the other. The experimenter rearranges the sticks of road **A**, changing its contours, and asks conservation questions regarding both the number of houses and the length of the roads: 'Are there the same number of houses here as there? Just as many? Show me, how did you find out?'; and 'Is this road just as long as the other, is there just as far to walk here as there, or is it different?' The experimenter goes back and forth between questions on length and number according to the answers the subjects give.

Figure 8.4

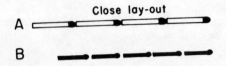

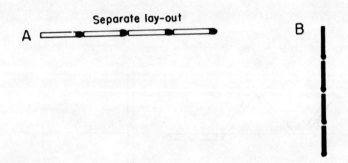

Figure 8.5

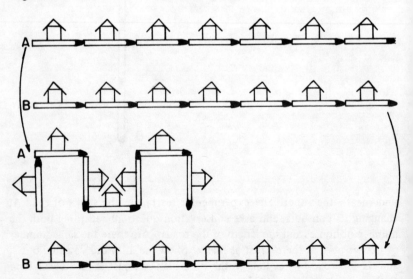

Analysis of the Responses During the Training Sessions

Various reactions were noted during this training procedure, many of which indicated an awareness on the part of the children of the inconsistency of their answers. Reasoning based on counting entered into conflict with that based on the ordinal principle; answers given to questions on number were felt to be in contradiction with answers given to questions on length. In several cases, these conflicts led to new insights. In others, the conflicts remained unsolved, and some children did not seem to be aware of the contradiction in their answers. Examples of these different reactions to the various training situations are the following.

As expected, in the separate lay-out all the subjects gave correct answers based on the number of matches. When the close lay-out was presented immediately afterward, conflicts often arose. One subject, Duv (6;6), expressed this conflict particularly clearly. Presented with a situation where four matches in the top road are in a straight line and six matches in the bottom road are in a zigzag pattern, with the beginning and end points coinciding and all matches of equal length (Figure 8.6), Duv said: 'The roads are exactly the same . . . except that you've put a bit more on the bottom one so that they're the same length.' An involved bit of reasoning, based on the coincidence of the end points, but showing awareness of the difference in the number of matches. It left the child rather perplexed; after a moment's hesitation, he said: 'But then, why are they the same? That's what I'm wondering about . . .'

Figure 8.6

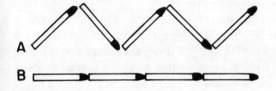

In the next situation (Figure 8.7), the same child seemed to have decided in favor of a judgment based on counting: 'The roads are the same, five matches and five matches.' When the experimenter told him that another child had said that road B was longer 'because it goes further', he was amused: 'That's really funny, there's the same number of matches and he thinks that the roads aren't the same!' But when the experimenter

Figure 8.7

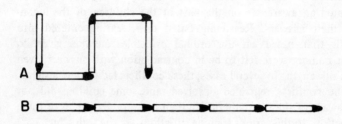

Figure 8.8

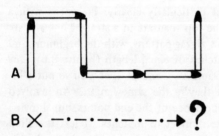

returned to the situation of Figure 8.6, the child once again returned to an ordinal estimate and maintained that the two roads were the same length. Only when he was asked to construct roads rather than give judgments did he get real insight into his own difficulties.

When in the following situation (see Figure 8.8) he had to make a straight road of the same length as the zigzag road A, starting at B, he ran his finger along the matches of A and put down the same number for his straight road, B. When he was again invited to give a judgment about length in the first situation, he proceeded in the same way, pointing to the successive pairings of the matches in both roads. Finally, he took one match away from A and said: 'Now it's the same', though B still 'goes further' than A. When the experimenter reminded him of his earlier conviction that A (five matches) and B (four matches) were the same length, he gave an explanation of the crux of his problem: 'Because I didn't count properly, because they came to the same place.' In fact, he had counted perfectly correctly, but had been incapable of reconciling the fact that the number of matches was not the same with the idea that if the ends of the roads coincided they must be of equal length.

From then on, this child appeared to have mastered the problem and gave correct answers to all questions. His post-test confirmed this acquisition.

Often children who started to count the matches when faced with the separate lay-out did not feel any conflict in the more difficult situations. For Cha (6;11), e.g., counting immediately gave way to judgments based on the order of the end points. In the construction problem in Figure 8.8 she correctly laid out her road, saying: 'Because I counted six (in A) and then six (for B).' As soon as she had finished, however, she seemed to discover the lack of coincidence between the end points and, judging the roads of different lengths, removed enough matches from B to make the ends coincide.

Other children went on to apply the counting procedure to every problem. However, they did so regardless of whether or not it was appropriate. For instance, when Cat (6;6) was asked about the lengths in situation b (Figure 8.9), she replied: 'B's got further to walk because there are seven and A's got less because there are five.' She continued to give answers based on counting to several further questions, even when these were formulated in terms of 'being just as tired or not when one walks on A and B'.

Figure 8.9

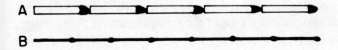

Finally, some children became increasingly confused as the experimenter passed from one situation to another. The number of possible criteria from which to choose, suggested in turn by the different situations (number of matches, coincidence of the end points of the roads, length of the individual matches, link between the original lay-out and its subsequent modification for the conservation problems), disturbed them to such an extent that they ended up by giving answers about which they themselves were clearly not happy. For example, Ann (7;3), in situation b (see Figure 8.10), when asked, 'Who's got further to walk?' after much hesitation replied: 'B's got further to go,' pointing to the five small matches, in a tone of voice which betrayed her resigned perplexity.

Situation c brought further confirmation of the fact that, for certain

Figure 8.10

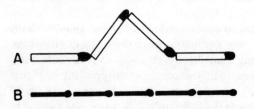

children, questions bearing on number have nothing in common with questions bearing on length. All those who had made no real progress in situations a and b gave the same response pattern in c: that is, they answered correctly all the questions about the number of houses and incorrectly all those concerning length, which they judged by the order of the ends of the roads.

Analysis of the Responses to the Post-tests

The post-tests consisted of problems of continuous length (wire). The responses were often surprising, since, in many cases, it was precisely those children who had become increasingly confused during the training sessions who made clear progress, while those who had used counting from the beginning of these sessions and shown no signs of conflict reverted to the same responses as they had given in the pre-test. There were, of course, other children who gradually grasped the various aspects of the problems; their mistakes led to an awareness of what was involved and they often gave completely correct answers in the post-tests.

The final training procedure took the findings of the preliminary experiments into account, particularly regarding the following points.

1. The responses of the children who were given the opportunity of comparing the *close* and *separate* lay-outs led us to include exercises in which all the lay-outs remain in front of the child throughout the entire training session so that at any time he can make comparisons between his solutions to the various problems.

2. Of the three types of problems used in the first experiment (i.e., the 'building' of a road of the same length as the experimenter's model; evaluation of the respective lengths of two roads both laid out by the experimenter, and problems of conservation of length), the first one ('building' a road) seemed to lead to the most interesting responses. Therefore only this type of problem was used in the training procedure for the final experiment.

3. It seemed essential to use matches of different lengths in order to obtain an accurate assessment of the children's responses. Generally, the children were given matches five-sevenths the length of those of the experimenter. The spontaneous reactions of some of the subjects, who tried to see how many times a small match could fit into a larger one, led us to include an easier situation where the children's matches were half the length of those of the experimenter.

4. In order to get a better idea of how the important principles of equal units of measurement and of compensation were handled, a situation in which the model was made up of matches of various lengths was also presented.

Final Experiment

Training Procedure, Tests, and Selection of Subjects

Problems. In the problems of the second training procedure the child is always asked to build a road 'of the same length as' or 'just as long as' the model, or to build his road 'so that there's no further to walk on it than on the other'.

Problem 1. For all the situations matches are used, those given to the child being shorter than those used in the model (exact proportion: 5:7 or 4.3 cm:6 cm).

a. Complex close lay-out. The child has to build a straight road of the same length as the zigzag model road, starting directly underneath one of the end points of the model road (see Figure 8.11). The general lay-out of this model is such that the most obvious solution is to make the end points coincide. Furthermore, as the child's matches are shorter than those

Figure 8.11

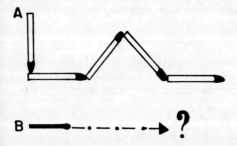

in the model (four short matches placed in his straight road 'go just as far' as the five long ones of the zigzag model), counting alone cannot result in the correct answer, although it can help the child overcome the tendency to concentrate on the end points. The correct answer can be derived from situation c.

Figure 8.12

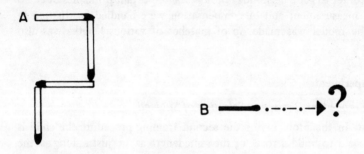

b. Separate lay-out. In this situation (see Figure 8.12), the road to be constructed is not directly underneath the model. This lay-out does not suggest the ordinal ('going just as far') criterion, but the numerical comparison; however, since the child's matches are not of the same length as those of the model road, they cannot serve as units as such. A rough visual estimate can be made, and the correct solution can be derived from situation c.

c. Simple close lay-out. In this situation, where both roads are straight with their initial end points coinciding, the ordinal criterion gives the correct solution immediately. Since the model road in a was made up of the same number of matches as that in c, the latter situation provides the answer for a if the child has grasped the principle of transitivity.

Problems a, b and c were sometimes made easier by using matches of 3 cm and 6 cm.

Figure 8.13

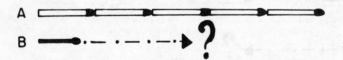

Problem 2. The model is always made up of matches of various lengths and the child is given a collection which includes five matches identical to those used by the experimenter.

a. Complex close lay-out.

Figure 8.14

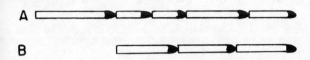

b. Separate close lay-out.

Figure 8.15

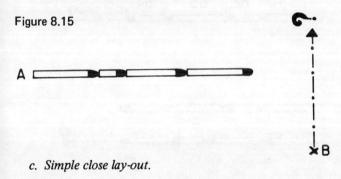

c. Simple close lay-out.

Figure 8.16

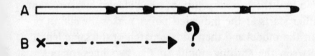

In a the child can build the correct road by three methods: (1) He can use a staggered one-to-one correspondence, starting with an identical match and following the same order (see Figure 8.17). (2) He can start with a match identical to the second one in the model (a2) and then at the end select a match identical to a1 (see Figure 8.18); (often the children chose the last match haphazardly). (3) He can use his matches in a different order (see Figure 8.19); (here, too, the choice of the last match is the most difficult).

In lay-out b the problem can be solved by a one-to-one copy.

Figure 8.17

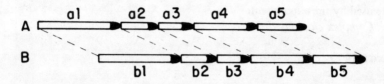

Figure 8.18

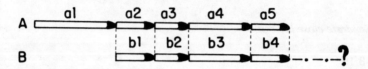

Figure 8.19

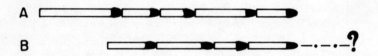

Problem 3. The mode consists of a straight length of wire, while the child has matches of various lengths and has to start his road further to the right than the model. To find the correct solution, some idea of measurement is necessary: one either starts at the indicated point, makes the end of one's road coincide with the model and then adds a match of the same length as the difference between the starting points of the two lines, or one first constructs a road directly underneath the wire and then displaces the whole construction so as to comply with the imposed starting point. For this last problem only one lay-out is used (see Figure 8.20).

Figure 8.20

For problems 1 and 2 the three lay-outs a, b and c, remain in front of the child throughout the training. After the child has proposed his initial solutions, the experimenter returns to all three lay-outs and asks for comparisons. If necessary, he points out that the child has used different and sometimes incompatible methods of solving the problems.

Selection of Subjects. Sixteen subjects were chosen, aged between 5;4 and 7;4 years. Thirteen were in the first grade and one in the second grade of a Genevan primary school and the two youngest were in the second year of a Genevan kindergarten.

The subjects were selected on the basis of two criteria.

1. A correct solution of two or three conservation of number problems. Two identical glasses, A and B, were filled with exactly the same number of beads, by the one-to-one iterative method. The contents of A were then poured into another glass, W (wider diameter) or N (narrower diameter), and the child was asked questions about the number of beads in the two glasses. After a return to the initial situation of A = B, the contents of A and B were poured simultaneously into W and N and the same conservation questions were asked. The children's answers had to be consistently correct and accompanied by clear explanations.

2. An incorrect solution of the problem of conservation of continuous lengths using two strips of modeling clay [. . .] The length problems were again presented in a first post-test immediately after training and then once more, under the same experimental conditions, in a second post-test after an interval of four to six weeks. A different version of the conservation of length test from that described by Piaget, Inhelder, and Szeminska (1948, chapter 7) was used so as to avoid presenting situations which bore too close a resemblance to those of the training situations and also so as to be able to distinguish between 'conservation' answers based on the identity of the object (on the fact that the object that had been moved was still the same) and those indicating the presence of a system of mental operations underlying a true understanding of conservation of length.

All the subjects took part in three to four training sessions given twice a week, each lasting 15-20 minutes.

Results

Comparison of Pre-Test and Post-Tests

[. . .] We distinguished between nonconservation (NC), intermediate (Int), and conservation (C) responses. In the Int category, a distinction was made between Int— responses (i.e., those in which the child is either hesitant or gives right answers regarding the first change of shape but wrong ones regarding the second) and Int+ responses (i.e. those in which the answer is completely correct for the first change in shape, but hesitant or wrong for the second) (see Table 8.1). All the subjects found it more difficult to solve the second problem than the first. A comparison of the results of the two post-tests (see Table 8.1) reveals the phenomenon of delayed progress (also observed in the other experiments). Five children (Emm, Hen, Per, Chr, Rod) improved their performance at the second post-test. At the second post-test six subjects reached complete acquisition, seven partial acquisition (four Int— and three Int+), and only two subjects remained at the NC level (one subject, Bee, was not given post-test 2).

The results of a control group who took no part in the training but were given the same pre-test and post-tests were very different from those of the experimental group. Two subjects of the control group gave conservation answers at the second post-test; they had, however, already been very close to conservation at the pre-test, where they had given arguments based on reversibility and compensation. Some of the subjects hesitated between correct and wrong answers in the pre-test, without any explanations; in the second pre-test, these children gave no correct answers at all, but they were sure of themselves and explained their answers. One child, for example, judged two roads to be of equal length 'because they go to there and there (pointing to the two final ends which coincide) . . . because they come to the same length . . . before (i.e. before the change) that didn't come up to here, but now it does . . . because I can see where the roads arrive; you don't have to look at the bends, I just look at the end'.

Apart from this change in explanations, and from the slight progress made by the two subjects mentioned above, the subjects of the control group did not modify their responses from pre-test to post-tests.

Analysis of the Responses During the Training Sessions

First of all, problems 2 and 3 will be discussed, as they turned out to be easier than problem 1. Problem 1 will be discussed more extensively since the mental processes involved in a transition from a lower to a higher level of conservation of length were most clearly revealed in the reactions to these problems.

The following responses were noted in problems 2 and 3.

The most primitive type of response was to make road B start at the imposed point, but stop in coincidence with the end point of A.

At a slightly more advanced level, the children first produced the

Table 8.1

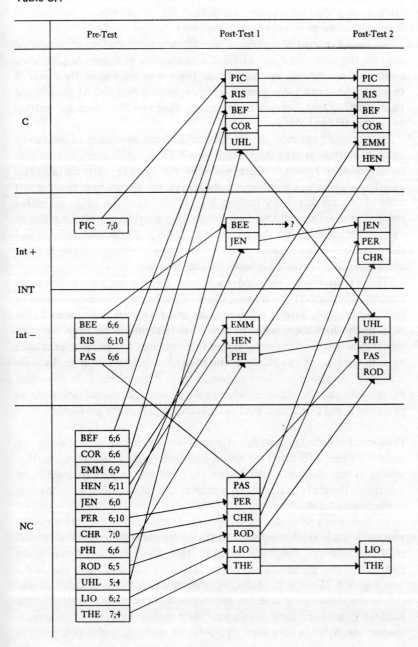

primitive solution, but then judged B too short and added another match. Having done this, they incorrectly judged that B was now longer than A. They continued to waver between the two solutions.

At the next level, the children immediately made their road go beyond road A. But since they had to work with matches of various lengths, they could not simply pick any match and place it at the end of their road B to make the correct compensation; they had to find one of exactly the right length. Several children chose their final match at random, arriving at an approximate solution.

At the most advanced levels, various methods were used to produce a correct solution, as for example in Figure 8.17.

In problem 3, where there was only the close lay-out, the accurate solution was obtained either by measuring the length between the left ends of the stocks, or by making B protrude beyond A by an estimated amount which the children then checked by moving one of the roads so that the left ends of the sticks coincided. If necessary, B was modified and then returned to its original position. This type of solution shows that the child is capable of reasoning based on conservation.

The experimenter switched back and forth from one problem to another. Throughout the session, the child's solutions remained in front of him on the table. Several children made some progress in problem 2, but only rarely does there seem to be a close relationship between the post-test results and the responses during this exercise. A correspondence does exist in the case of the children who showed no progress at all at the post-tests, and then gave low-level responses to problems 2 and 3. It also exists in the case of the children who gave the most advanced solutions to problems 2 and 3 and then made excellent progress at the post-tests.

Problem 1 elicited a variety of responses which indicated clearly the nature of the difficulties of those situations and showed the conflicts arising in the children's minds when they had to compare their different solutions. The different types of solutions can be described as follows, in developmental order.

In situation a (complex close lay-out), 14 (out of 16) subjects began by making a road which stopped exactly underneath the end of the model road, made up of five long matches (this requires four of their short matches). They declared that their roads were just as long as the model (see Figure 8.21). The experimenter then went on to the separate lay-out (b), where most of the children spontaneously counted the matches in the model and used the same number for their straight road. When the experimenter asked them how they had gone about making the two roads as equal as possible, they said they had counted: 'There were five matches in your road, so I counted five for the other one.'

Figure 8.21

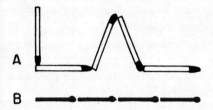

The experimenter then returned to the complex close lay-out of situation a (which was still on the table) and if the child did not spontaneously start to count the matches, counting was suggested and usually carried out correctly: four short matches and five long ones. This led to two types of reactions. Some children saw nothing wrong in using the same number of matches in A and B in lay-out b but a different number in lay-out a. At a more advanced level, others attempted to correct their construction in a by using the same number of matches as in the model. But the idea that 'going beyond' means 'being longer' is so overpowering that instead of simply adding a match to their road they invented various compromise solutions: (1) breaking the last match of their road in two pieces, so that both roads had the same number of matches, but neither went beyond the other (Figure 8.22); (2) adding a fifth match, but placing it so that it did not protrude beyond the model (Figure 8.23); (3) adding a bit of a fifth match so that the protrusion was hardly noticable (Figure 8.24).

Sometimes the children found these compromise solutions rather unsatisfactory, as for example Did (5;4), one of the subjects given the initial training procedure who, although he could not find a better solution, declared: 'It's not very much the same.'

At a more advanced level, the children added the fifth match even though this made their road go beyond the model, explaining: 'Even if it goes a bit further, there are the same number of matches here (pointing to roads A and B in lay-out b) and here (lay-out a); there are five and five.'

This last solution constitutes a step forward since the difficulty of the overpowering 'going beyond' principle is overcome; however, it is far from perfect, since the total length is simply judged by the number of matches (their quite noticeable difference in length is ignored).

Figure 8.22

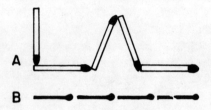

Figure 8.23

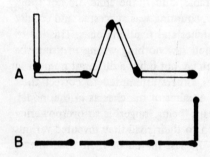

Figure 8.24

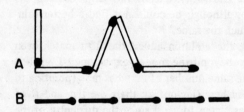

In the simple close lay-out (c) (Figure 8.13), two types of construction were made.

1. Some children immediately constructed a road of the correct length, its end points coinciding with those of the model; when asked to explain how they knew this was the right solution, they answered, quite legitimately: 'I can see that the two lines are the same: two straight roads.' However, when the experimenter asked them to count the matches in both the roads, they were reluctant to count beyond five in road B, and quite perplexed to find that there were five matches in A, but seven in B.

2. Other children started by counting the matches in A and then used the same number of matches to make B. When they discovered that using five of their matches made B shorter than A, they were puzzled and very hesitant about adding two more to B: 'I don't think it can be done . . .' (Ben, 6;5, one of the subjects given the initial training procedure).

Nevertheless, in this simple lay-out all subjects finally found the correct solution: 'There are more red matches (B), but the roads both come to the same place.' Most subjects were also able to explain why there should be more matches in road B than in road A, using a compensation argument: 'With big matches, you don't have to put so many; you have to use more of the little ones.' At this point, the experimenter returned to the separate lay-out. Now the children often 'discovered' the difference in size of the matches and added one or two matches to their road 'because my matches are smaller than yours, so I've got to put a few more, if I don't . . . if I put the same number . . . that makes a smaller road.'

If in lay-out a the child had used the same number of smaller matches for his road B as there were in A (five), so that his road already went beyond B, although it was still too short, the experimenter returned to this situation. When the children realized that in the separate lay-out (b) it was not sufficient to use five of the short matches they had taken a major step forward in understanding the problem. Consequently, it was interesting to see how this understanding would affect their responses to situation a. The following reactions were noted.

1. Having realized the need to compensate for the shorter length by a greater number, some children now added matches to their road, B. Sometimes they even exaggerated, making their own road go way beyond the model.

2. Other children became confused when situation a was repeated after situation c, and continued to hesitate between the various solutions, including the most elementary one of making the ends of the roads coincide.

3. Others hesitated between two solutions. They first used the same

number of matches as in the model, then added some more, then took them away again, etc. The experimenter then tried to help these subjects by giving them matches which were half the size of his. This often had the desired effect: the child realized that two of his matches were equivalent to one of the experimenter's and produced the correct solution. After this, a final return to the five-sevenths matches resulted in many completely correct solutions.

4. The most advanced children immediately realized the error of using the same number of matches and added one or two matches to their roads in situation a. The experimenter then asked them, once again, to compare c and a. At this point, some of these children still could not deduce the correct solution for a from situation c; but since they understood the need to compensate for the shorter length of their matches by using a greater number, they explained how they solved the problem by referring to a qualitative compensation. Others used the information about the necessary number of matches obtained in situation c to solve situation a; their arguments referred explicitly to the transitivity relationship obtaining between situations a and c. Consequently, it was not necessary to use the simpler material (matches half the size of those of the experimenter) with these subjects.

Excerpts from Protocols

The first protocol is an example of the behavior of those subjects who encounter great difficulties at an elementary level.

Lio (6;2)

In problem 1.a Lio constructs his road so that its end points coincide with those of the experimenter's road. In problem 1.b he uses the same number of matches for his road, B, as there are in A, but when he has finished he announces (correctly) that his road is shorter. However, this does not help him find a better solution, and he keeps his construction as it is, saying, 'I copied it the way it is, there are four.' In situation c he starts counting the matches he uses for his straight road, begins to hesitate when he has put down five (the number in A), but nevertheless continues until his road reaches the end point of A, then takes two matches away, explaining, 'Because there are five green ones there, and like that five red ones here,' although he adds, 'The green ones are longer than the red ones.' Lio is aware of the importance of the difference in length of the matches, but he does not know what to do about it. He proposes changing A, and agrees to look at the total length of both roads only after much hesitation, finally adding two matches.

When the experimenter goes back to situation b he once again starts counting, continues to judge his road as being shorter, but does not accept the experimenter's suggestion of adding at least one match to his road. For situation a he once again constructs a road whose end points coincide with those of A. With half the matches half the size of those of the experimenter, a slight progress is obtained for lay-out c, where Lio does agree without so much hesitation to use a different number for his road from that in the model. But in situation b he again uses the same number as in the model, and in situation a he makes the end points of his road coincide with those of the model. He is not happy with his solutions, but he can neither correct them spontaneously nor accept the experimenter's suggestions.

Lio reacts to problems 2 and 3 in the same way as to problem 1, and his results at the post-tests are exactly the same as at the pre-test.

Lio's protocol illustrates the elementary types of reactions to the problems, i.e. the alternative use of the 'going just as far' criterion and the counting method. Apart from some hesitations, Lio does not seem aware of the contradictions in his different solutions, and no progress is noted.

The next protocol illustrates the way a subject who in the second post-test reaches the Int+ level reacts to the training problems.

Per (6;10)

In situation 1.a Per spontaneously uses six of her small matches; but then she judges her road to be too long, because it goes further than the model. Her next idea is to arrange her matches in the same shape as those in A. When the experimenter reminds her that her road must be straight, she starts her construction to the left of the model road. Once again she is reminded of the instruction, and she finally opts for the solution where the end points of her road coincide with those of the model. She points out, however, that if road B were to be laid out in the same zigzag as A, A would go further. In lay-out 1.b (A made up of four matches) she uses five matches for road B, and explains that her matches are smaller than the experimenter's. However, when she counts again to check her solution, she starts to waver between the simple numerical solution and her own idea of compensating for the shorter length of her matches: 'You need more red matches and less green ones, because the red ones are smaller.' Returning to situation 1.a she gives up the compensation idea and constructs her road according to the numerical principle: five matches, as in the model. In lay-out 1.c she immediately makes a road whose end points coincide with the model, without counting, and when the experimenter attracts her attention to the difference in number, she explains without hesitation: 'The green matches are bigger, so you can put more red ones.' Throughout various comparisons between 1.a and 1.c she maintains her (correct) solution for c, but tries various compromise solutions for a. For example, she breaks some of her matches into bits, and constructs a road with the same number of matches and bits of matches as the model, without having to make it go beyond the latter. She also proposes making road B with the same zigzags as road A, or, inversely, to change the model road to a straight one. Finally she opts for a solution with the correct number in which her road starts to the left of the model and stops beyond it, and she explains: 'They are the same length, because one starts first (pointing to the first sequential match in A) and the other goes further at the end' (see Figure 8.25).

Figure 8.25

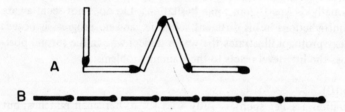

With matches half the size of the experimenter's, Per gives the same type of compromise solution. She realizes that two of her matches fill the same space as one of the experimenter's, but when she has to solve the problem of Figure 8.26 she uses three matches for her road instead of four, since with four her road 'goes too far', and then she tries to obviate the difficulty by using four matches but putting them down two by two, as is shown in Figure 8.26. These simplified solutions do not help Per, and when the situations of problem 1 are taken up once more, she continues to use compensation arguments, but never arrives at the correct solution. In situation 1.a she uses six matches (instead of seven, for the five matches in the experimenter's road) and explains: 'This one starts first, so the other one has to go a bit further and . . . and also this one has a point (a).'

Similarly, in problem 2 she makes her road go further than the model, but she cannot establish a precise relation between 'starting first'

Figure 8.26

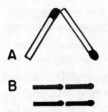

and 'going further' at the end. In problem 3 it is only after a suggestion from the experimenter that she adopts the solution of a preliminary parallel construction and then a displacement of her road. Once she has solved the problem in this way, she judges correctly that the roads are indeed of the same length.

In the first post-test she still gives wrong answers, judging by the 'going beyond' principle; but in the second post-test she reaches level Int+. Even though she does not yet give conservation judgments in all the situations, she has made notable progress in the interval between the two tests.

Per's reactions to the training procedure are intermediate between those of Lio and those of Emm (given below): she does not simply judge either by 'going beyond' or by number, but still finds only approximate solutions to problems 2 and 3, and in problem 1 tries various compromises to reconcile the numbers of matches, their difference in length, and her desire to have the two roads start and stop at the same point.

The last example illustrates the reactions of a subject who reaches the conservation level in post-test 2, but who appears to have great difficulties during the training procedure.

Emm (6;9)
In situation 1.a Emm's first reaction is to construct her road so that its end points coincide with those of the model; in 1.b, on the other hand, she explains spontaneously that she has to use more matches for her road because her matches are smaller than the experimenter's. Coming back to 1.a, she adds a match to her road, but takes it away again because 'the road goes too far'. In lay-out 1.c she first uses the same number of matches as in the model, but quickly adds two more, explaining: 'The red ones are smaller and the green ones are bigger.' When

once again asked to think about situation 1.a, she takes only number
into account, and is now so obsessed by this criterion that when presented with situation c she takes away two matches and maintains,
despite the obvious difference in length, that 'the roads are the same,
it's right, because there are five matches and five matches.' After a
comparison between one green and one red match she adds only one
match to her construction (six as against five in the model) — a compromise solution, since the difference in length is now less, and the
difference in number not too great. With the matches that are half the
size of the experimenter's Emm first constructs her road in 1.a once
again on the coincidence principle; in 1.b, however, she shows insight:
'When you have two small matches it's as if you had one big one,' and
she gives the correct solution. She manages to do the same for lay-out
1.a after much hesitation.

When the experimenter goes back to problem 1 using five-sevenths
matches, she finally admits the necessity of compensating for their
shorter length by a greater number, but the 'going beyond' principle
remains too strong, and she chooses the compromise of breaking her
matches into little bits.

In problem 2 she continues to be confused by the apparent contradiction between counting, compensation for the shorter length of her
matches, and the fact that the roads 'do not go just as far'. She
spontaneously finds the solution of making her road start from the
same point as the model and then shifting the whole construction to
the right. Even so, when she has to defend her solution against the
experimenter's argument, she is not very convinced.

Problem 3, by contrast, is immediately solved. First she chooses a
last match of approximately the right length, but when asked to
explain, she demonstrates that the last match of her road protrudes
as far beyond the end point of the model road as it lags behind the
model at the start.

In post-test 1 she is still very hesitant and reaches level Int—. In
post-test 2 she answers all the questions correctly and gives excellent
explanations.

It seems strange that a child who succeeds so well in the second post-test
should have had so much difficulty during the training sessions: at first,
Emm is convinced that the roads must have the same number of matches,
then she begins to coordinate the number with the length of the individual matches, but she can apply this only to the simple problems. In the
complex situations, her solutions are either based on a single criterion or

are the result of a compromise between several criteria. The results of Emm's first post-test tally with her reactions to the training sessions, but during the interval between the first and second post-test an internal process of reorganization seems to have occurred which results in excellent progress at post-test 2, where all her solutions are correct.[2]

Complementary Experiments

Reversal of the Order of Presentation of the Different Lay-Outs. To check whether the predominance of the counting behavior was due to the order of presentation, the order of the situations in problem 1 was reversed and lay-out c was presented first. The responses of six subjects given this order of presentation were comparable to those given above. One example will suffice to illustrate this.

Ser (6;3)
In the simple lay-out 1.c, Ser spontaneously makes a correct road B. In explanation he simply says, 'I saw (it),' and thinks there is no point in counting the matches, as suggested by the experimenter. In the separate lay-out 1.b he refers spontaneously to the number of matches − 'I counted, there are five (A) and five (B), it's the same length' − which shows that he takes no account of the size of the matches; but in 1.c he does: 'The red ones are smaller and you've got to put more.' When the experimenter goes on to the complex lay-out 1.a he stops his road to coincide with the model and comments: 'I saw by the ends, without counting.' Comparison with his solution in 1.b leads him to add another match to his road, which now has the same number of matches as the model; but since his road goes beyond the experimenter's he cannot make up his mind, taking the extra match away and then adding it again.

After a comparison between one of his matches and one of the experimenter's, Ser explains his correct solution to problem 1.c: 'The red ones are smaller, you need more.' He then manages to transpose this reasoning to b: 'I counted but I put one more (in B) because the red ones (A) are longer.' In the complex lay-out 1.a he again ends his road at the same place as the model without counting the matches. When he is reminded that for 1.b he counted, he considers that this is of no use in 1.a and answers: 'Yes (I counted in 1.b) because it was harder, here it's easier.'

Although this order of presentation might be expected to make the solution of problem 1.a (complex lay-out) easier, this did not turn out to be so. Presenting the simple lay-out first, which suggests the correct solution almost automatically and provides the right answer to problem 1.c (if the subject thinks of counting the matches), and then presenting 1.b (the separate lay-out), where almost all subjects start counting spontaneously, did not suggest an application of the counting procedure to problem 1.a. On the contrary, the same difficulties appeared, and the tendency to adopt different ways of solving the different problems seemed even stronger. The child has to realize the necessity of a compensation between the length of the individual matches and their number, and he has to become aware of the insufficiency of 'going just as far' principle. The comparison between the lengths of the different matches suggests the idea of measurement. Lay-out 1.b suggests the counting of units that make up a length. The complex lay-out demands the coordination of these aspects of comparisons of length. However, in the correct solution to this problem the straight road 'goes so far beyond' the zigzag model that even if the necessity of a compensation between the length of the units and their number is already understood many children cannot apply this principle. When they are led to make several comparisons between the different situations these children can overcome this difficulty, but the order in which the comparisons are made is immaterial.

Experiment on the Relationship between the Different Stages Observed with the Traditional Conservation of Length Task and with the Construction Tasks of the Training Procedure. An exploratory experiment was designed to determine whether, for subjects who had not followed a training procedure, the questions asked in the conservation of length task [. . .] and in the construction problems (as described in the training procedure) were of equal difficulty. For example, would one find that certain children gave conservation answers but still constructed roads on the primitive 'going just as far' principle? Or would correct answers in the conservation questions always go together with correct constructions?

The conservation of length task [. . .] and the construction problem 1.a [. . .] were presented, in a single session, to 12 subjects between the ages of 7;4 and 8;5.

Five subjects gave correct answers to both questions of the conservation of length task. Four of these subjects immediately constructed straight roads that went well beyond the end point of the zigzag model. One subject did not make his road long enough, but still made it continue beyond the end point of the model and refused the solution based on the 'going just as far' principle proposed by the experimenter.

Two subjects gave the right answer to one of the problems in the conservation task only after some hesitation. When faced with the construction problem they at first made the end points of the roads coincide, but then spontaneously judged their straight road to be shorter than the model, and added the necessary matches.

Five subjects were classified Int for the standard conservation problems: they either answered one question correctly but hesitated or gave the wrong answer to the second, or else they hesitated for both problems. These children had similar difficulties in the construction problem, i.e. they started off by making the end point of their straight road coincide with that of the model, then changed their minds as a result of the experimenter's questions, and finally made their road go beyond the model. Their hesitations, however, showed that they were not yet fully convinced of the correctness of this solution, and that the tendency to judge by the 'going beyond' principle was still strong.

This experiment showed the existence of a close correspondence between the behavior of the subjects in the two different types of problems.

Concluding Remarks

The experiments on the learning of conservation of length throw light on two connected questions. The first one concerns the nature of the connection between operatory structures dealing with discontinuous units and those that deal with a continuous quantity, i.e., length. The second concerns the ways in which children construct the concept of length and that of measurement in the case of a unidimensional quantification.

Since children seem to have the same types of difficulties in both the tasks of elementary conservation of number and those of conservation of length (i.e., there is a tendency to judge both number and length according to ordinal criteria such as 'going beyond' or 'going just as far'), one might be tempted to believe that the only additional difficulty in the length problems is that length involves a continuous quantity. According to this hypothesis, children who already possess an elementary conservation of number should have little trouble in reaching understanding of conservation of length problems if the lengths are broken down into clearly distinct units (the matches) and lined up so that they touch each other (the roads).

The preliminary experiment showed that this was not the case. The subjects were able to give correct answers to conservation questions concerning large collections of elements, even when these elements (paper balls or beads) had been placed in glasses and then poured into other glasses of different shapes and sizes. Despite these correct answers for large collections, however, some of the children could not solve the problems dealing with the length of a road, even when it was made up of a number of separate elements which were contiguous but nevertheless perceptually clearly distinct.

What is more, some of the children who managed to solve the problems in which the roads were made up of small contiguous elements of equal length did not seem to have really overcome the difficulties caused by the coincidence or noncoincidence of the end points. They appeared to have decided to pay no attention to the fact that one of the roads went beyond the other and simply counted the matches, which in the experiment happened to lead to a correct solution. When matches of different lengths were used the real character of these solutions became clear.

The results of the learning experiment therefore run counter to the hypothesis that, in children's judgments of length, the strength of the ordinal criterion is solely due to the fact that length is a continuous quantity. Moreover, the findings also show that in the case of conservation of length there is no direct developmental link between the concept of continuous quantity and that of number.

Length differs from global numerical quantity both by its continuous nature and by the fact that it has to be quantified through the use of units. A child's understanding of this second specific property is constructed by means of a differentiation between the global 'size' of the object and that of its measurable length. Length may be conserved only when its quantifiable nature is understood, and this conservation implies an understanding of the use of units of length. The results of the learning experiment provide us with some information about this problem.

Whereas at the lowest level the subjects simply used the division into units introduced by the experimenter, the more advanced subjects understood the dimensional value of the units; they knew that they could not immediately conclude that two roads were the same length if they were made of the same number of matches, but that they had to decide whether these matches were all of the same length. Moreover, the children who succeeded in the post-tests generally understood that the correct number of matches to be used in problem 1.a could be deduced from lay-out 1.c (see Figure 8.27) by using the transitivity principle. For these subjects, understanding of conservation of length appears to go together with an understanding of measurement. Their explanations, which refer, on the one hand, to the length of individual units and the total length of the road ('You need more small matches than long ones to make a road of the same length') and, on the other, refer to transitivity in order to find the correct number of matches necessary in lay-out 1.a, indicate a coordination of partition and displacement from which, in Piaget's opinion,

Figure 8.27

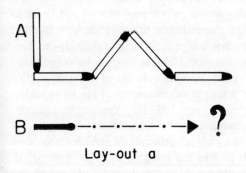

Lay-out a

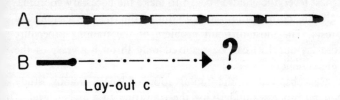

Lay-out c

derives the principle of measurement.

The training study also provides information on the processes by which a higher level of reasoning is reached.

At the lowest level, the subjects reacted to questions on number ('Are there the same number of matches, or are there more here or there?') and questions on length ('Are the two roads just as long or is one longer than the other?') as if they concerned two entirely different problems. In the construction problems, these subjects either made up their roads according to the 'going just as far' principle (in lay-out 1.a) or by the counting method (in the separate lay-out 1.b). They did not appear to feel any contradiction between their different solutions, despite the multiple comparisons between situations and despite the experimenter's suggestions.

At the second level, the comparisons between the various situations and the experimenter's questions appeared to have some effect, because the subjects became aware of the contradictions in their answers. At this level, however, they were not yet able to solve the internal conflict.

At the third level, the children started to produce what have been called 'compromise' solutions in order to solve the conflict. These solutions provide more information on the nature of the conflicts. It seems that different conceptual schemes were activated, depending on the particular question asked or the lay-out presented. In some situations, it is sufficient to use either counting or the coincidence of start and finish to obtain the correct solution (e.g., counting in the situation with matches of uniform length, or ordinal relationships in the simple close lay-out 1.c). In other situations, however, the two schemes have to be coordinated (e.g., in the complex close lay-out 1.a with matches of uniform length), while in yet other cases, the principle of measurement has to be understood (e.g., in the complex close lay-out 1.a). The compromise solutions indicate that the conflict between the two schemes was only partially resolved at this level, since the ordinal principle is sufficient to solve the problem only when both lengths are straight, and the counting, although adequate when the units are identical, is not sufficient in the situations where they are different.

At the highest level, the children began to make the necessary coordinations and to give the correct solutions both during the training sessions and at the post-tests. The most difficult problem of the training procedure (complex close lay-out 1.a) can be resolved only through a grasp of the principle of measurement.

The responses observed in the conservation of length training study clarify the general processes underlying the transition to a higher level of reasoning. Both in especially contrived situations and in normal everyday life conflicts can arise between different conceptual schemes, some of which are more developed than others. A first effort to combine and reconcile the conflicting schemes results in inadequate compromises, which indicate the beginning of a coordination between certain previously unconnected schemes. Subsequently, the various schemes are integrated into a new and more advanced cognitive structure.

The training procedure of the conservation of length study proved to be one of the most instructive, highlighting developmental processes in action. The preliminary studies showed us which schemes were used for each particular problem and, as a result, we devised exercises that we believed would activate these schemes. We also hoped that the method of switching back and forth between the problems and of giving the child the opportunity of comparing his different solutions would elicit conflicts in his mind. Once particular conceptual schemes are known to be applied in certain situations, it is possible to devise problems that activate these schemes and to induce conflicts by comparing solutions based on different principles. Questions and discussions at certain crucial points in the learning process can induce an awareness of contradictions, and provide the impetus for higher-level coordinations leading to new cognitive structures.

Notes

1. Other authors have carried out learning experiments on conservation of length (e.g. Braine [1958, 1964]. Smedslund (1963a and b, 1965] but with different aims and methods).
2. These examples were selected to illustrate particular difficulties. Other subjects gave correct answers straightaway during the training procedure and reached C at the first post-test.

References

Braine, M.D. (1958), 'The ontogeny of certain logical operations: Piaget's
    formulation examined by non-verbal methods', *Psychol. Monogr.*, 73. no. 5.
Inhelder, B., Sinclair, H. and Bovet, M. (1974), *Learning and the Development of
    Cognition*, London: Routledge and Kegan Paul.
Piaget, J. and Inhelder, B. (1941), *Le développement des quantités chez l'enfant*,
    Neufchâtel and Paris, Delachaux and Niestlé.
Piaget, J., Inhelder, B. and Szeminska, A. (1948), *La Géométric spontanée de
    l'enfant*, Paris, PUF.
Smedslund, J. (1963a), 'Development of concrete transitivity of length in children',
    Child Dev., 34, 389-405.
Smedslund, J. (1963b), 'Development of experience and the acquisition of
    conservation of length', *Scandinavian J. psychol.*, 4, 257-64.
Smedslund, J. (1965), 'The development of transitivity of length: a comment on
    Braine's reply', *Child Dev.*, 36, 577-80.

SECTION THREE: THE SECONDARY YEARS: THEORETICAL AND EXPERIMENTAL

Introduction

In this section the focus is on the secondary years of schooling, and all the articles deal with the way in which adolescent thinking develops, although in different areas. Piaget's original concept of formal-operational thought has been a major stimulus for all the five articles in this section, though they all question it to some degree.

The first article is by Piaget himself, and contains a recent assessment and revision of his earlier publications on the subject of formal reasoning. It used to be argued that the skill of formal reasoning was independent of the context, so that once the formal-operational stage had been attained, the reasoning implicit in it could be applied to any sphere of interest. Attainment of this stage was in practice measured by the performance on various scientific problems, so that if a subject did not demonstrate the systematic hypothetico-deductive approach that characterizes successful solution of such problems, he was not considered to be at the formal-operational stage. This has been criticised in a number of ways. First of all it has been argued that performance on such tests is unduly influenced by the amount and kind of scientific education that the subject happens to have had. The second criticism relates to this, but goes much further, suggesting that it is essential to look for formal reasoning in completely non-scientific contexts, and that it may well be that individuals may exhibit such reasoning in contexts with which they are familiar, but that their unfamiliarity with other areas precludes formal reasoning therein. In his article Piaget discusses such ideas and concludes that familiarity with content does seem to be a relevant factor.

The second article, by Eric Lunzer, examines the original concept of formal operational reasoning, and finds it wanting in a number of respects. Lunzer is particularly concerned with the mathematical-logical model that Piaget has used to describe the nature of formal-operational thought (known as the INRC group) arguing that this is inadequate to describe a number of examples of advanced reasoning, which he considers in some detail.

The remaining three articles in this section all belong together in many ways, as they are a set of related attempts to identify and analyse formal reasoning outside the areas of mathematics and science. The first article is written by E.A. Peel, and the other two by former students of his, W.T. Rhys and W.A. da Silva. In his article, Peel provides an overview of the work done in this area both by himself and by a number of his erstwhile students. This includes the study of the judgements adolescents make about various topical issues, the judgements they make about poems and novels, their ability to reason about geographical and historical material, and their ability to infer meanings of unfamiliar concepts from the contexts in which they occur. In all these cases there are definite developmental trends towards more advanced reasoning. The other two articles in this section consider two of these areas more fully. Rhys looks at the way in which secondary school children reason about geographical material, and da Silva examines the developmental trends in the way that such children infer the meanings of various historical concepts from their contexts.

9 INTELLECTUAL EVOLUTION FROM ADOLESCENCE

Jean Piaget

Source: *Human Development*, 15: 1-12 (1972).[1]

Abstract. Growing out of a child's cognitive developmental history, formal operations become established at about the age of 12-15 years. Reflected in his ability to reason hypothetically and independently on concrete states of affairs, these structures may be represented by reference to combinatorial systems and to 4-groups. The essence of the logic of cultured adults and the basis for elementary scientific thought are thereby provided. The rate at which a child progresses through the developmental succession may vary, especially from one culture to another. Different children also vary in terms of the areas of functioning to which they apply formal operations, according to their aptitudes and their professional specializations. Thus, although formal operations are logically independent of the reality content to which they are applied, it is best to test the young person in a field which is relevant to his career and interests.

We are relatively well informed about the important changes that take place in cognitive function and structure at adolescence. Such changes show how much this essential phase in ontogenic development concerns all aspects of mental and psychophysiological evolution and not only the more 'instinctive', emotional or social aspects to which one often limits one's consideration. In contrast, however, we know as yet very little about the period which separates adolescence from adulthood and we feel that the decision of the Institution FONEME[1] to draw the attention of various research workers to this essential problem is extremely well founded.

In this paper we would first like to recall the principal characteristics of the intellectual changes that occur during the period from 12-15 years of age. These characteristics are too frequently forgotten as one tends to reduce the psychology of adolescence to the psychology of puberty. We shall then refer to the chief problems that arise in connection with the next period (15-20 years); firstly, the diversification of aptitudes, and secondly, the degree of generality of cognitive structures acquired between 12 and 15 years and their further development.

The Structures of Formal Thought

Intellectual structures between birth and the period of 12-15 years grow slowly, but according to stages in development. The order of succession of these stages has been shown to be extremely regular and comparable to the stages of an embryogenesis. The speed of development, however, can vary from one individual to another and also from one social environment to another; consequently, we may find some children who advance quickly or others who are backward, but this does not change the order of succession of the stages through which they pass. Thus, long before the appearance of language, all normal children pass through a number of stages in the formation of sensorimotor intelligence which can be characterized by certain 'instrumental' behavior patterns; such patterns bear witness to the existence of a logic which is inherent to the coordination of the actions themselves.

With the acquisition of language and the formation of symbolic play, mental imagery, etc., that is, the formation of the symbolic function (or, in a general sense, the semiotic function†), actions are interiorized and become representations; this supposes a reconstruction and a reorganization on the new plane of representative thought. However, the logic of this period remains incomplete until the child is 7 or 8 years old. The internal actions are still 'preoperatory' if we take 'operations' to mean actions that are entirely reversible (as adding and subtracting, or judging that the distance between A and B is the same as the distance between B and A, etc.). Due to the lack of reversibility, the child lacks comprehension of the idea of transitivity ($A \leqslant C$, if $A \leqslant B$ and $B \leqslant C$), and of conservation (for a preoperatory child, if the shape of an object changes, the quantity of matter and the weight of the object change also).

Between 7-8 and 11-12 years a logic of reversible actions is constituted, characterized by the formation of a certain number of stable and coherent structures, such as a classification system, an ordering system, the construction of natural numbers, the concept of measurement of lines and surfaces, projective relations (perspectives), certain types of causality (transmission of movement through intermediaries), etc.

Several very general characteristics distinguish this logic from the one that will be constituted during the pre-adolescent period (between 12 and 15 years). Firstly, these operations are 'concrete', that is to say, in using them the child still reasons in terms of objects (classes, relations, numbers, etc.) and not in terms of hypotheses that can be thought out before knowing whether they are true or false. Secondly, these operations, which involve sorting and establishing relations between or enumerating objects, always proceed by relating an element to its neighboring element — they cannot yet link any term whatsoever to any other term, as would be the case in a combinatorial system: thus, when carrying out a classification, a child capable of concrete reasoning associates one term with the term it most resembles and there is no 'natural' class that relates two very different objects. Thirdly, these operations have two types of reversibility that are not yet linked together (in the sense that one can be joined with the other); the first type of reversibility is by inversion or negation, the result of this operation is an annulment, for example, $+ A - A = 0$ or $+ n - n = 0$; the second type of reversibility is by reciprocity and this characterizes operations of relations, for example, if $A = B$, then $B = A$, or if A is to the left of B, then B is to the right of A, etc.

On the contrary, from 11-12 years to 14-15 years a whole series of novelties highlights the arrival of a more complete logic that will attain a state of equilibrium once the child reaches adolescence at about 14-15 years. We must, therefore, analyze this new logic in order to understand what might happen between adolescence and full adulthood.

The principal novelty of this period is the capacity to reason in terms of verbally stated hypotheses and no longer merely in terms of concrete objects and their manipulation. This is a decisive turning point, because to reason hypothetically and to deduce the consequences that the hypotheses necessarily imply (independent of the intrinsic truth or falseness of the premises) is a formal reasoning process. Consequently the child can attribute a decisive value to the logical form of the deductions that was not the case in the previous stages. From 7-8 years, the child is capable of certain logical reasoning processes but only to the extent of applying particular operations to concrete objects or events in the immediate present: in other words, the operatory form of the reasoning process, at this level, is still subordinated to the concrete content that makes up the real world. In contrast, hypothetical reasoning implies the subordination of the real to the realm of the possible, and consequently the linking of all possibilities to one another by necessary implications that encompass the real, but at the same time go beyond it.

From the social point of view, there is also an important conquest. Firstly, hypothetical reasoning changes the nature of discussions; a fruitful and constructive discussion means that by using hypotheses we can adopt the point of view of the adversary (although not necessarily believing it) and draw the logical consequences it implies. In this way, we can judge its value after having verified the consequences. Secondly, the individual who becomes capable of hypothetical reasoning, by this very fact will interest himself in problems that go beyond his immediate field of experience. Hence, the adolescent's capacity to understand and even construct theories and to participate in society and the ideologies of adults; this is often, of course, accompanied by a desire to change society and even, if necessary, destroy it (in his imagination) in order to elaborate a better one.

In the field of physics and particularly in the induction of certain elementary laws (many experiments have been carried out under the direction of B. Inhelder on this particular topic), the difference in attitude between children of 12-15 years, already capable of formal reasoning, and children of 7-10 years, still at the concrete level, is very noticeable. The 7- to 10-year-old children when placed in an experimental situation (such as what laws concern the swing of a pendulum, factors involved in the flexibility of certain materials, problems of increasing acceleration on an inclined plane) act directly upon the material placed in front of them by trial and error, without dissociating the factors involved. They simply try to classify or order what happened by looking at the results of the co-variations. The formal level children, after a few similar trials stop experimenting with the material and begin to list all the possible hypotheses. It is only after having done this that they start to test them, trying progressively to dissociate the factors involved and study the effects of each one in turn — 'all other factors remaining constant'.

This type of experimental behavior, directed by hypotheses which are based on more or less refined causal models, implies the elaboration of two new structures that we find constantly in formal reasoning.

The first of these structures is a combinatorial system, an example of which is clearly seen in 'the set of all subsets', ($2n^2$ or the simplex structure). We have, in fact, previously mentioned that the reasoning process of the child at the concrete level (7-10 years old) progresses by linking an element with a neighboring one, and cannot relate any element whatsoever to any other. On the contrary, this generalized combinatorial ability (1 to 1, 2 to 2, 3 to 3, etc.) becomes effective when the subject can reason in a hypothetical manner. In fact, psychological research shows that between 12 and 15 years the pre-adolescent and adolescent start to carry out operations involving combinatorial analysis, permutation systems, etc. (independent of all school training). They cannot, of course, figure out mathematical formulas, but they can discover experimentally exhaustive methods that work for them. When a child is placed in an experimental situation where it is necessary to use combinatorial methods (for example, given 5 bottles of colorless, odorless liquid, 3 of which combine to make a colored liquid, the fourth is a reducing agent and the fifth is water), the child easily discovers the law after having worked out all the possible ways of combining the liquids in this particular case.

This combinatorial system constitutes an essential structure from the logical point of view. The elementary systems of classification and order observed between 7 and 10 years, do not yet constitute a combinatorial system. Propositional logic, however, for two propositions 'p' and 'q' and their negation, implies that we not only consider the 4-base associations (p and p, p and not q, not p and q, not p and not q) but also the 16 combinations that can be obtained by linking these base associations 1 to 1, 2 to 2, 3 to 3 (with the addition of all 4-base associations and the empty set). In this way it can be seen that implication,† inclusive disjunction† and incompatibility are fundamental propositional operations that result from the combination of 3 of these base associations.

At the level of formal operations it is extremely interesting to see that this combinatorial system of thinking is not only available and effective in all experimental fields, but that the subject also becomes capable of combining propositions: therefore, propositional logic appears to be one of the essential conquests of formal thought. When, in fact, the reasoning processes of children between 11-12 and 14-15 years are analyzed in detail it is easy to find the 16 operations or binary functions of a bivalent logic of propositions.

However, there is still more to formal thought: when we examine the way in which subjects use these 16 operations we can recognize numerous cases of the 4-group which are isomorphic† to the Klein group and which reveal themselves in the following manner. Let us take, for example, the implication $p > q$, if this stays unchanged we can say it characterized the identity transformation I. If this proposition is changed into its negation N (reversibility by negation or inversion) we obtain N = p and not q. The subject can change this same proposition into its reciprocal (reversibility by reciprocity) that is R = q > p; and it is also possible to change the statement into its correlative (or dual), namely C = not p and q. Thus, we obtain a commutative 4-group such that CR = N, CN = R, RN = C and CRN = I. This group allows the subject to combine in one operation the negation and the reciprocal which was not possible at the level of concrete operations. An example of these transformations that occurs frequently is the comprehension of the relationship between action (I and N) and reaction (R and C) in physics experiments; or again, the understanding of the relationship between two reference systems, for example: a moving object can go forwards or backwards (I and N) on a board which itself can go forwards or backwards (R and C) in relation to an exterior reference system. Generally speaking the group structure intervenes when the subject understands the difference between the cancelling or undoing of an effect (N in relation to I) and the compensation of this effect by another variable (R and its negation C) which does not eliminate but neutralizes the effect.

In concluding this first part we can see that the adolescent's logic is a complex but coherent system that is relatively different from the logic of the child, and constitutes the essence of logic of cultured adults and even provides the basis for elementary forms of scientific thought.

The Problems of the Passage from Adolescent to Adult Thought

The experiments on which the above-mentioned results are based were carried out with secondary school children, 11-15 years, taken from the better schools in Geneva. However, recent research has shown that subjects from other types of schools or different social environments sometimes give results differing more or less from the norms indicated; for the same experiments it is as though these subjects had stayed at the concrete operatory level of thinking.

Other information gathered about adults in Nancy, France, and adolescents of different levels in New York has also shown that we cannot generalize in all subjects the conclusion of our research which was, perhaps, based on a somewhat privileged population. This does not mean that our observations have not been confirmed in many cases: they seem to be true for certain populations, but the main problem is to understand why there are exceptions and also whether these are real or apparent.

A first problem is the speed of development, that is to say, the differences that can be observed in the rapidity of the temporal succession of the stages. We have distinguished 4 periods in the development of cognitive functions (see beginning of part 1): the sensorimotor period before the appearance of language; the preoperatory period which, in Geneva, seems on the average to extend from about 1½-2 to 6-7 years; the period of concrete operations from 7-8 to 11-12 years (according to research with children in Geneva and Paris) and the formal operations period from 11-12 to 14-15 years as observed in the schools studied in Geneva. However, if the order of succession has shown itself to be constant — each stage is necessary to the construction of the following one — the average age at which children go through each stage can vary considerably from one social environment to another, or from one country or even region within a country to another. In this way Canadian psychologists in Martinique have observed a systematic slowness in development; in Iran notable differences were found between children of the city of Teheran and young illiterate children of the villages. In Italy, N. Peluffo has shown that there is a significant gap between children from regions of southern Italy and those from the north; he has carried out some particularly interesting studies indicating how, in children from southern families migrating north, these differences progressively disappear. Similar comparative research is at present taking place in Indian reservations in North America, etc.

In general, a first possibility is to envisage a difference in speed of development without any modification of the order of succession of the stages. These different speeds would be due to the quality and frequency of intellectual stimulation received from adults or obtained from the possibilities available to children for spontaneous activity in their environment. In the case of poor stimulation and activity, it goes without saying that the development of the first 3 of the 4 periods mentioned above will be slowed down. When it comes to formal thought, we could propose that there will be an even greater retardation in its formation (for example, between 15 and 20 years and not 11 and 15 years); or that perhaps in extremely disadvantageous conditions, such a type of thought will never really take shape or will only develop in those individuals who change their environment while development is still possible.

This does not mean that formal structures are exclusively the result of a process of social transmission. We still have to consider the spontaneous and endogenous factors of construction proper to each normal subject. However, the formation and completion of cognitive structures imply a whole series of exchanges and a stimulating environment; the formation of operations always requires a favorable environment for 'co-operation', that is to say, operations carried out in common (e.g., the role of discussion, mutual criticism or support, problems raised as the result of exchanges of information, heightened curiosity due to the cultural influence of a social group, etc.). Briefly, our first interpretation would mean that in principle all normal individuals are capable of reaching the level of formal structures on the condition that the social environment and acquired experience provide the subject with the cognitive nourishment and intellectual stimulation necessary for such a construction.

However, a second interpretation is possible which would take into account the diversification of aptitudes with age, but this would mean excluding certain categories of normal individuals, even in favorable environments, from the possibility of attaining a formal level of thinking. It is a well-known fact that the aptitudes of individuals differentiate progressively with age. Such a model of intellectual growth would be comparable to a fully expanded hand fan, the concentric layers of which would represent the successive stages in development whereas the sectors, opening wider towards the periphery, correspond to the growing differences in aptitude.

We would go so far as to say that certain behavior patterns characteristically form stages with very general properties: this occurs until a certain level in development is reached; from this point onwards, however, individual aptitudes become more important than these general characteristics and create greater and greater differences between subjects. A good example of this type of development is the evolution of drawing. Until the stage at which the child can represent perspectives graphically, we observe a very general progress to the extent that the 'draw a man' test,[†] to cite a particular case as an example, can be used as a general test of mental development. However, surprisingly large individual differences are observed in the drawings of 13- to 14-year-old children, and even greater differences with 19-20 year olds (e.g., army recruits): the quality of the drawing no longer has anything to do with the level of intelligence. In this instance we have a good example of a behavior pattern which is, at first, subordinate to a general evolution in stages (cf. those described by Luquet and other authors for children from 2-3 until about 8-9 years) and which, afterwards, gradually becomes diversified according to criteria of individual aptitudes rather than the general development common to all individuals.

This same type of pattern occurs in several fields including those which appear to be more cognitive in nature. One example is provided by the representation of space which first depends on operatory factors with the usual 4 intellectual stages — sensorimotor (cf. the practical group of displacements), preoperatory, concrete operations (measure, perspectives, etc.) and formal operations. However, the construction of space also depends on figurative factors (perception and mental imagery) which are partially subordinated to operatory factors and which then become more and more differentiated as symbolical and representative mechanisms. The final result is that for space in general, as for drawing, we can distinguish a primary evolution characterized by the stages in the ordinary sense of the term, and then a growing diversification with age due to gradually differentiating aptitudes with regard to imaged representation and figurative instruments. We know, for example, that there exist big differences between mathematicians in the way in which they define 'geometrical intuition': Pincaré distinguishes two types of mathematicians — the 'geometricians', who think more concretely and the 'algebraists', or 'analysts', who think more abstractly.

There are many other fields in which we could also think along similar lines. It becomes possible at a certain moment, for example, to distinguish between adolescents who, on the one hand, are more talented for physics or problems dealing with causality than for logic or mathematics and those who, on the other hand, show the opposite aptitude. We can see the same tendencies in questions concerning linguistics, literature, etc.

We could, therefore, formulate the following hypothesis: if the formal structures described in part 1 do not appear in all children of 14-15 years and demonstrate a less general distribution than the concrete structures of children from 7-10 years old, this could be due to the diversification of aptitudes with age. According to this interpretation, however, we would have to admit that only individuals talented from the point of view of logic, mathematics and physics would manage to construct such formal structures whereas literary, artistic and practical individuals would be incapable of doing so. In this case it would not be a problem of under-development compared to normal development but more simply a growing diversification in individuals, the span of aptitudes being greater at the level of 12-15 years, and above all between 15 and 20 years, than at 7-10 years. In other words, our fourth period can no longer be characterized as a proper stage, but would already seem to be a structural advancement in the direction of specialization.

But there is the possibility of a third hypothesis and, in the present state of knowledge, this last interpretation seems the most probable. It allows us to reconcile the concept of stages with the idea of progressively differentiating aptitudes. In brief, our third hypothesis would state that all normal subjects attain the stage of formal operations or structuring if not between 11-12 to 14-15 years, in any case between 15 and 20 years. However, they reach this stage in different areas according to their aptitudes and their professional specializations (advanced studies or different types of apprenticeship for the various trades): the way in which these formal structures are used, however, is not necessarily the same in all cases.

In our investigation of formal structures we used rather specific types of experimental situations which were of a physical and logical-mathematical nature because these seemed to be understood by the school children we sampled. However, it is possible to question whether these situations are, fundamentally, very general and therefore applicable to any school or professional environment. Let us consider the example of apprentices to carpenters, locksmiths, or mechanics who have shown sufficient aptitudes for successful training in the trades they have chosen but whose general education is limited. It is highly likely that they will know how to reason in a hypothetical manner in their speciality, that is to say, dissociating the variables involved, relating terms in a combinatorial manner and reasoning with propositions involving negations and reci-procities. They would, therefore, be capable of thinking formally in their particular field, whereas faced with our experimental situations, their lack of knowledge or the fact they have forgotten certain ideas that are particularly familiar to children still in school or college, would hinder them from reasoning in a formal way, and they would give the appearance of being at the concrete level. Let us also consider the example of young people studying law — in the field of juridical concepts and verbal discourse their logic would be far superior to any form of logic they might use when faced with certain problems in the field of physics that involve notions they certainly once knew but have long since forgotten.

It is quite true that one of the essential characteristics of formal thought appears to us to be the independence of its form from its reality content. At the concrete operatory level a structure cannot be generalized to different heterogeneous contents but remains attached to a system of objects or to the properties of these objects (thus the concept of weight only becomes logically structured after the development of the concept of matter, and the concept of physical volume after weight); a formal structure seems, in contrast, generalizable as it deals with hypotheses. However, it is one thing to dissociate the form from the content in a field which is of interest to the subject and within which he can apply his curiosity and initiative, and it is another to be able to generalize this same spontaneity of research and comprehension to a field foreign to the subject's career and interests. To ask a future lawyer to reason on the theory of relativity or to ask a student in physics to reason on the code of civil rights is quite different from asking a child to generalize what he has discovered in the conservation of matter to a problem on the conservation of weight. In the latter instance it is the passage from one content to a different but comparable content, whereas in the former it is to go out of the subject's field of vital activities and enter a totally new field, completely foreign to his interests and projects. Briefly, we can retain the idea that formal operations are free from their concrete content, but we must add that this is true only on the condition that for the subjects the situations involve equal aptitudes or comparable vital interests.

Conclusion

If we wish to draw a general conclusion from these reflections we must first say that, from a cognitive point of view, the passage from adolescence to adulthood raises a number of unresolved questions that need to be studied in greater detail.

The period from 15 to 20 years marks the beginning of professional specialization and consequently also the construction of a life program corresponding to the aptitudes of the individual. We now ask the following critical question: Can one demonstrate, at this level of development as at previous levels, cognitive structures common to all individuals which will, however, be applied or used differently by each person according to his particular activities?

The reply will probably be positive but this must be established by the experimental methods used in psychology and sociology. Beyond that, the next essential step is to analyze the probable processes of differentiation: that is to say, whether the same structures are sufficient for the organization of many varying fields of activity but with differences in the way they are applied, or whether there will appear new and special structures that still remain to be discovered and studied.

It is to the credit of the FONEME Institution to have realized the existence of these problems and to have understood their importance and complexity, particularly as, generally speaking, developmental psychology believed that its work was completed with the study of adolescence. Fortunately, today, certain research workers are conscious of these facts and we can hope to know more about this subject in the near future.

Unfortunately the study of young adults is much more difficult than the study of the young child as they are less creative, and already part of an organized society that not only limits them and slows them down but sometimes even rouses them to revolt. We know, however, that the study of the child and the adolescent can help us understand the further development of the individual as an adult and that, in turn, the new research on young adults will retroactively throw light on what we already think we know about earlier stages.

Notes

1. A French version of the article was presented at FONEME, 3rd International Convention, Milan 1970, and published in the proceedings (FONEME, Institution for Studies and Research in Human Formation, 20135, Via Bergamo 21, Milan, Italy). The English translation was prepared by Joan Bliss and Hans Furth, to whom special thanks are due.

FORMAL REASONING: A RE-APPRAISAL

Eric Lunzer

Source: in B. Presseisen, D. Goldstein and M.H. Appel (eds.), *Topics in Cognitive Development*, vol. 2 of *Language and Operational Thought* (Plenum, 1978).

1. A Backward Look

In a paper which appeared nearly ten years ago (1965), I spoke of a 'desire to arrive at a clearer understanding of the kinds of advances in reasoning that appear as the child approaches adolescence. Are these advances sufficiently homogeneous and distinctive to warrant the use of the general term *formal reasoning* in opposition to the term *concrete reasoning* to characterise the achievements belonging to the years between 6 and 9?' The problems I would like to discuss today are exactly the same. To anticipate my conclusion right away, it is tentative, but it is opposite to that which I reached in 1965. For then my answer to the question about the unity of formal reasoning was affirmative. Today I regard it as probably more correct and almost certainly more productive to answer it in the negative.

(a) Concrete Reasoning

Before venturing into the treacherous seas of so-called formal reasoning, perhaps I may be pardoned for one brief cruise on the well-charted waters of concrete reasoning. After all, we can at least try to locate our point of departure as accurately as we can. Referring back once more to the 1965 paper, I argued then that the essential achievement of concrete operativity lay in the definability of its concepts: 'operational = operationally definable', where 'pre-operational = fluid or situationally variable'. I believe this to be quite near the truth. Its appropriateness is well brought out by the conservation experiments. In each of these the child is first presented with two objects or two arrangements which are clearly and perceptibly equal in some respect. This is followed by a transformation which alters the perceptual appearance of the things but does not affect the equivalence just established. Now if we pause to consider what we are doing when we are establishing that initial equivalence, it is clear that we are defining the concept with which we are concerned. To define weight we put objects on a balance, to define number we place them in one—one correspondence (either with other objects or with the ordered set of positive integers), to define length we put things end to end. True — in many cases these definitions can be further refined by appropriate advances in scientific and mathematical thinking. But these are the definitions that serve us well enough in the transactions of everyday living, and they are the ones with which the child must start.

Although this characterisation of concrete reasoning as reasoning in terms of precise, definable criteria is correct, it is not explanatory. I believe, on reflection, that we can go further in the direction of explanation, at least to the extent of bringing out what I take to be an important intermediate stage. Consider a well-known experiment in which the child is shown an array of objects varying in more than one dimension and asked to sort them into two groups. The objects could be red and blue circles and squares. We know that the typical four-year-old uses shifting criteria which results in complete failure. Using shifting criteria leads him to 'alignments' (Inhelder and Piaget, 1964), e.g. red square—red circle—blue circle. But this error is gradually overcome between the ages of five and six (Campbell and Young, 1968; Calvert, 1971), that is well before what Piaget and others would take to be the level of concrete operations. Moreover, there is a further development long since recognised as crucial by such writers as Reichard, Schneider and Rappaport (1944), which is the ability to 'shift' deliberately from one completed classification to another, e.g. from colour to form. It is this second development which is crucial to what Piaget terms concrete operativity. It is very close to cross-classification, the only difference being that the two classifications are successive instead of simultaneous. Likewise it is close to class inclusion, since the child must be aware of two criteria and not just one.

These considerations would lead me to revise the earlier formulation by asserting that the hallmark of concrete operativity consists in the child's awareness of the criteria of his own actions in relation to alternative opposing criteria. The child of five or six who can sort by colour *or* by shape without involuntary shifts of criteria is using a criterion correctly. At least at the level of action, his concept is precise. But his consistency is achieved by the inhibition of the alternative criteria. Conversely, the child of seven is aware of the alternative criteria, and it is precisely this awareness that enables him to shift (deliberately) or to cross-classify. This formulation (Lunzer, 1970) is more powerful than the analysis offered in 1965, for two reasons. One is that instead of several characteristics being offered (e.g. perceptual prepotence[†]), a single model is suggested, and one which is adequate to cover nearly all the acquisitions characteristic of this phase of development (cf. White, 1965; Lunzer, 1970). The other reason is that it is now apparent that for a criterion to become an object of reflection it must exist. In other words, the use of stable criteria precedes their recognition.

(b)   Formal Reasoning

Turning to the concept of 'formal reasoning' which is our chief concern for today, in 1965 I found myself quarrelling with Piaget's emphasis on the INRC group as a unifying structure underlying both the understanding of proportionality and the use of hypothesis in experimentation. Selecting one out of several characteristics provided by Piaget and giving it a personal twist which may or may not have made it simpler to apprehend, I argued that the distinctive characteristic of formal operations was the recognition of second-order relations, as in the relation of equivalence of relations between two pairs of terms linked by an analogy, or as in the equality or inequality of two ratios.

Looking back on that discussion in the light of more recent evidence as well as maturer reflection, I find the definition in terms of second order relations woefully inadequate. At the same time the critique of the INRC group as a unifying structure did not go far enough. I hope that both these comments will become clearer in what follows.

Section 2 introduces a feature which appears to be a necessary but not a sufficient condition for most forms of advanced reasoning: *acceptance of lack of closure* or ALC. Section 3 introduces a second feature of advanced thinking: *multiple interacting systems* or MIS and consists mainly in an overview, representative but not exhaustive indicating six rather disparate areas of more advanced reasoning. At least one of these does not even feature ALC. Section 4 focuses on development in logical thinking as such. The evidence appears to indicate that this is a relatively specialised skill, and one in which a high degree of efficiency is rare in the absence of specific training. Finally, Section 5 attempts to pull together some of the threads.

In this section, I suggest a formulation of the relation between thinking and logic which is very different from that of Piaget. This last section concludes with a consideration of the educational implications of the present survey.

2. ALC

In a recent paper (Lunzer, 1973) I drew a distinction between two categories of inference, simple and complex. Simple inference is said to occur whenever the information which is provided or which the subject obtains enables him to make an unambiguous inference with respect to the state of any variable about which he is concerned. Complex inference is the complementary case where such initial information does not permit of an unambiguous inference about a relevant variable, but instead permits a reduction of alternatives so that the final determination can only be made at a subsequent stage, when more information has been obtained.

The evidence for this distinction arose primarily out of an investigation carried out by Ann Pocklington which I will shortly describe, and, secondly, out of a re-consideration of certain other evidence, and especially of a seminal paper by B. Matalon (1962). However, shortly after completing the paper referred to, I read the important thesis by K. Collis (1972) who also drew on previous work by Halford (1968), and found that this author had come to a precisely similar conclusion in relation to the solution of mathematical problems. Collis defines the distinction in terms of tolerance for unclosed operations. Consider the following tasks:

(1) $3 + 4 = ?$
(2) $3 + ? = 7$
(3) $3 + 4 + 2 = ?$
(4) $3 + 4 + ? = 9$
(5) $3 + ? = 7 + 2$
(6) $? - 7 = 7 - 3$
(7) $? - 7 = 4$

It is clear that (1) and (2) require only one operation. (3) and (4) each require two operations but the first operation to be effected is clearly indicated and the result of that operation sufficiently pinpoints the second. Thus, taking the task as a whole, the sequence of operations is defined (for the average schoolchild) from the outset and each step in that sequence is closed before the solver is required to proceed to the next. By contrast (6) suggests an unclosed operation: $? - 7$ is 'some number and that number equals $7 - 3$'.

Even if $7 - 3$ is executed, it may not be immediately apparent whether the 4 is to be inserted as it stands, added to the 7, or subtracted from it. (5) and (7) may be thought of as intermediate. Collis' own results will be discussed a little more fully below.

Acceptance of lack of closure coincides exactly with the notion of complex inference described above. Because Collis' formulation is neater and more descriptive, I prefer it to my own and in the rest of this paper, it will be shortened to ALC.

The clearest and simplest illustration of the significance of ALC is the work of Pocklington just referred to. The apparatus consisted of a box with a single light and up to four buttons to press. More complex problems used all four buttons, and in this case S was told that one was a *switch*, which would cause the light to come on if it was off and vice versa, one was neutral and would have no effect, one was an *on* button and this would cause the light to come on if it was off but would have no effect if it was on already, and the last was an *off* button, the action of this being the exact opposite of the *on*. Simpler problems involved only two or three of these buttons. The task for the child was always to establish in as few moves as possible which button was which. Briefly, it was found that most children managed to solve all but the most difficult problems at all ages 5-18, but there was evidence of cognitive growth both in the progressive elimination of errors and, to a lesser extent, in the kind of error which predominated. However, the single most important observation concerned the use of alternative labels. To help them keep track of events, the children were offered a selection of eight labels for some of the problems. These could be used to tag any buttons they had identified. The labels were *on*, *off*, *change*, *neutral*, *on or change*, *on or neutral*, *off or change* and *off or neutral*. It will be seen that the last four were deliberately provided to enable the child to handle the ambiguous situations that arise when one of the buttons is pressed for the first time. At eleven years old, these were used freely whenever they were appropriate, at nine only half the children examined used them at all, and then only once on average over all the problems, at seven none of the children ever used the alternative labels. The improvement in use of alternative labels between 9 and 11 is dramatic. It is difficult to resist the conclusion that younger children fail to see the need for the alternative labels because of 'premature closure', i.e. they cannot accept, say, that a button which they have pressed could be *off or change* since it must be either one or the other. Conversely, the older children use these labels freely because of their ALC.

Perhaps one of the earliest demonstrations of the relatively late emergence of ALC is that offered by Matalon in a study of implication. He used a box with two compartments each of which could be inspected separately. One concealed a red light, the other a green. Subjects were told 'Whenever the red light is on, the green light is on.' The problem was to decide what could be said about the state of the other light after seeing the state of one. *Red on* implies *green on* is given: *green off* implies *red off* is correct, but it is also uninformative as a response, because it can be arrived at on the basis of incorrect reasoning as well as correct. The critical problems consist in showing *red off* and *green on*. In both these cases the state of the hidden light is ambiguous. Matalon found that until the age of eleven or twelve, children insist on making the inference one way or the other, usually in the direction of symmetry, as if the implication were an equivalence. [. . .]

In the following section I will review a variety of tasks, each of which may be taken as instancing more advanced thinking, and in each case I will consider the role of ALC. Anticipating a little, it may be noted that whereas ALC is a feature of most of them it is certainly not the sole feature. Its role may be thought of as an enabling one. Moreover, whereas ALC in the relatively simple tests used by Pocklington and Matalon is well nigh universal even at the age of eleven, success in the problems that follow is by no means universal and usually if it does become the rule rather than the exception this is a good deal beyond the age of eleven.

3. Varieties of Task

While Inhelder and Piaget's celebrated work on the growth of logical thinking (1958) is still the most fruitful source of ideas and of evidence compiled by a single group, it is no longer the sole source of evidence with regard to the development of more advanced thinking, as it was when it first appeared. Nor can the complex of interpretations that it contains be assimilated as an adequate theory, for it is neither sufficiently precise to function as a model, nor is it consistent with all the facts. However, I do not propose in what follows to set up an alternative and better model. I am content with the much more pedestrian task of putting together a number of task varieties each of which appears to involve a more advanced type of thinking than that which is entailed in the development of operativity between the ages of 5 and 8.

The exercise would nevertheless be relatively unproductive if it did not include some attempt to bring out what appear to be the key features of each such variety. I propose in what follows to concentrate on two such features. One is the relevance of ALC. The other is the presence of multiple interacting systems. I will define this as follows:

If a task is such that its solution can be effected by assimilation to one system of co-variations it is defined as *simple*. It is also simple if it permits of several independent objectives, provided that each of these involves an independent system of variation. However, if more than one system of co-variation is involved in the solution strategy, and successful solution depends on the interaction of the two systems, the task is *complex*. For the remainder of this paper this will be abbreviated to MIS.

By way of example, consider the action of an '*Etchasketch*'. This is a toy which allows a child to produce a drawing by manipulating two knobs, one of which causes the sketching point to move up and down while the other makes it go from side to side. In either case, the direction of movement is reversed when the relevant knob is turned backwards instead of forwards. So long as it is used for rectangular drawings etchasketch involves two non-interacting systems. But if an oblique line is required, the two systems must be brought into action simultaneously, and the task becomes complex. It should be added that because the toy itself is a concrete realisation of the combined systems designed to provide constant feedback, its manipulation as such may not involve the user in any advanced thinking. However, this is demanded when the subject is required himself to analyse oblique motion as the resultant of two orthogonal forces or motions. This is illustrated in several of the Geneva experiments, e.g. the movement of a snail (Piaget, 1946), location of a point in a rectangle (Piaget, Inhelder and Szeminska, 1960).

More generally I hope to bring out the relevance of MIS along with that of ALC in the following paragraphs. But I do not propose to end by seeking to impose an overall interpretative model designed to account for all the tasks concerned. Not only is the undertaking too difficult, I believe too, that in the present state of knowledge it is speculative and counter-productive. In particular, we know far too little about the relative effectiveness of specific training or of general 'education' with respect to each group of tasks. In the main, therefore, the present section takes the form of an annotated list.

(a)   Experimental Control of Variables

This heading is intended to subsume several of the key enquiries described in the first part of Inhelder's and Piaget's 1958 volume, notably those that require explanations of the motion of a pendulum, the bending of rods, movement on an inclined plane, the role of an invisible magnet, and the combination of liquids. These are too well known to warrant description in any detail. In each case, the subject must first discover an explanation by experimenting with the material provided. But the true test of the adequacy of his reasoning lies in his ability to prove that his explanation is the only one that is consistent with all the facts. For instance, he has to show that the oscillation of the pendulum varies with its length and is independent of other factors such as weight. The successful subject does this by the method of 'other things equal', i.e. by varying one factor at a time and holding the remainder constant.

It is clear that these behaviours feature both ALC and MIS. To take an example, when in the pendulum experiment the subject varies length and weight simultaneously, the effect that he observes may be due to either factor taken separately, or it might be contingent on their interaction. In order to select among these possibilities, he needs to carry out further controls. So far, the situation is parallel to that which obtained in the simpler Pocklington experiment. If moreover, the subject avoids the ambiguity by controlling variables from the outset, it is reasonable to infer that he is aware of the ambiguity that would arise by failing to do so. In other words, he has anticipated the possibility of lack of closure and circumvented it. The authors agree that the anticipation marks a further sub-stage in these experiments, IIIB, where a correct reading of the alternatives by itself is characteristic of the earlier IIIA. The relevance of MIS is even more obvious, since the action of any one factor is, in accordance with our definition, a system, and the task of the subject is precisely to disentangle the actions of the several systems concerned.

However, even in these experiments it is almost certainly incorrect to deduce that the subject who processes ALC and MIS is thereby a 'formal reasoner' and his success is guaranteed. Enquiries such as those of Lovell (1961) and Jackson (1965) reveal considerable intra-individual as well as intro-individual variability. It is wholly probable that familiarity with scientific experimentation in general is an exceedingly relevant factor. So also is the plausibility and hence the availability of the correct interpretation. The evidence for this latter is at present indirect, being obtained principally from studies in logical thinking as such (e.g. Roberge and Paulus, 1971, see below).

Yet another factor to be considered is the role of abstraction. This is often closely bound up with MIS. When only a single factor is involved, as in the 'spring balance' experiment† described by Inhelder and Piaget (1964), its correct elucidation is mainly a matter of categorising objects: heavier boxes depress the scale and cause the lever to project beyond the apparatus. When more than one system is involved the variables do not correspond directly with objects as given or with ready-made events. In order to test one hypothesis against alternatives the desired events and/or objects need to be constructed or reconstructed. It is the laws governing the systems that specify the mode of construction. Elements such as weight, length, etc. are to that extent abstract. They are no longer thought of simply as properties of given objects (or events) but rather as variables which can be manipulated to construct the former to any specification. The role of abstraction is clearer in the next group of behaviours.

(b) False Conservation

The false conservation tasks are fairly fully described elsewhere (Lunzer,

1968). Two situations were selected and these are illustrated in Figure 10.1. The essence of the problem is similar in the two set-ups. Starting with a square, it is possible to elongate the shape while preserving a constant perimeter (Figure 10.1A). In this case the area of the figure is progressively reduced. The apparatus consists of a board with nails appropriately placed to enable the same closed length of string to describe a square or a more or less elongated rectangle. Alternatively one can extend the perimeter while preserving a constant area by simply cutting off a more or less large portion (we used a triangle, Figure 10.1B) and transposing it. In both experiments the critical behaviour consists in recognising and explaining the non-conservation of one of the variables while allowing the conservation of the other. Characteristically, the 'concrete' reasoner insists that either both perimeter and area are conserved, and this is the model response at age 9, or if he is persuaded by E that one variable is not conserved, he argues that neither is the other. It goes without saying that there is an earlier phase (Level I) at which there is no conservation at either variable. Level II is transitional and the false conservation response is therefore characterised as Level III. It is also possible to distinguish two levels within the next phase which marks the abandonment of false conservations. At Level IV the recognition of non-conservation (especially of area) is reluctant and the subject often retains the false conservation when the deformation of the original square is minimal, even after he has allowed that it does not obtain when it is large. By contrast, at Level V although his discovery of non-conservation may be gradual, once it is attained he immediately generalises to the whole set of transformations (elongations or transpositions). At the same time he can give a correct account of the reason why only one of the variables is conserved.

The two problems offer a clear illustration of the role of MIS, since the effect of the transformation on area and on perimeter are two 'systems'. ALC is less obvious, although it can be argued that the insistence of false conservation, i.e. that area and perimeter must vary together, is an instance of 'premature closure'. However, what the enquiry illustrates most sharply is the role of abstraction. The insistence on false conservation derives from failure to consider area and perimeter in abstraction from the figures from which they are derived. The square is seen as an object which is either the same under transformation, in which case both perimeter and area are conserved, or else the object is as it were transmuted in which case both the essential properties must alter. This is well brought out by the difference in the difficulty of the two problems as illustrated in Table 10.1. Non-conservation of perimeter is accepted more readily than non-conservation of area. This is because the former notion is much less closely linked to the concept of a figure as object. It is interesting to note that despite the demand for abstraction in the analysis of area and perimeter as independent of the object from which they are derived, success in these tasks is more general at ages 14/15 than it is in most of the problems used by Inhelder and Piaget.

Figure 10.1A

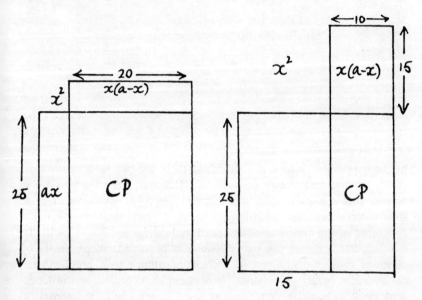

Figure 10.1B

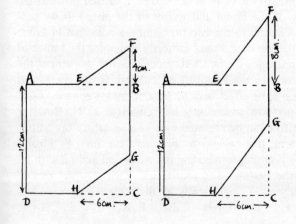

Table 10.1: Incidence of False Conservation

| | Constant Area | | | | | Constant Perimeter | | | | |
Age	I	II	III	IV	V	I	II	III	IV	V
9	1	–	6	–	–	–	–	5	1	–
10	–	1	4	1	–	–	–	4	2	–
11	–	–	3	4	–	–	–	–	–	–
12	–	–	–	5	–	–	–	–	1	1
13	–	–	–	5	1	–	–	–	2	4
14	–	–	–	4	10	–	–	–	2	10
15	–	–	–	3	5	–	–	–	1	7

From Lunzer, 1968.

(c)   Compensation and Proportionality

In the experiment I have just described there are two systems involved, change in area and change in perimeter. However, the situations are so devised that the only operations allowed are those which result in an identity transformation with respect to one of these interacting systems. A number of the experiments described by Inhelder and Piaget are similar but for the fact that the two systems can be varied independently by means of distinct operations. The 'communicating vessels' problem[†] and the hydraulic press[†] are relatively pure examples. In both cases the dependent variable, height of a column of liquid in one arm of the apparatus, may be altered by raising or levering the arm itself or by altering the position of the other arm of the U. In the second case, further variables are introduced − density of the liquid and weight of the piston. If we concentrate on what is common to the two problems we note that both are clear instances of MIS. Moreover, Piaget correctly diagnoses the source of their difficulty with reference to the INRC group. Raising one arm of the U has the effect of lowering the height of the column. If this is taken as the reference operation I, its effect may be negated by lowering the same arm, the opposite operation which may be designated as N. However the same nullifying effect can be achieved by a compensatory operation: raising the opposite arm, this being a reciprocal to the first, R. Finally the other arm can be lowered, so negating the reciprocal action, with an effect correlative to the first: C. The four actions each of which can be performed quite readily and independently by the subject are related as a group in which $N^2 = R^2 = C^2 = I$, $NR = C$, $NC = R$, $RC = N$ and $NCR = 1$.

Moreover all operations are commutative. The structure, well described by Piaget, is that of a group.

However, Piaget goes further in arguing that the INRC[†] group is *the* underlying structure which plays a crucial role in all formal thinking. I believe that MIS is far more general, although I would not argue that even this is a universal feature of problems requiring advanced thinking strategies for their solution. The false conservation experiments involve MIS but do not feature the INRC group. Neither do most of the Piagetian experiments on the experimental control of variables. Piaget argues that they do, arguing that they imply the transformation of logical propositions. However, the role of logical transformation is speculative in all these examples of reasoning. Logical reasoning as such presents problems of its own, and these will be considered separately in the next section. Meanwhile there is little warrant for an *a priori* assertion that advances in thinking are a function of advances in logic.

For the most part, the problems contained in the second part of Inhelder and Piaget's work present a compound difficulty. In addition to the compensatory structure of the several factors involved there is a requirement of quantification which takes the form of an inverse proportionality. The problems concerned are those of equilibrium in the balance[†] (law of moments), projection of shadows,[†] and motion on an inclined plane.[†] However, unlike the problems discussed in the first paragraph of this sub-section, the direction of compensations as such generally present little problem. The fact is not without interest, for it strongly supports the conclusion that complexity of structure taken by itself is an insufficient index of task difficulty. But there is abundant evidence that an understanding of proportionality comes hard.

To begin with, a distinction should be made between direct and inverse proportionality. Not surprisingly, the former is easier. Despite this several investigations have shown that even problems which involve only direct proportionality are rarely solved before the age of eleven (published studies include Lunzer (1965); Lunzer and Pumfrey (1966); and Szeminska (1968); however the first and most striking is an unpublished Genevan work by Marianne Bax). In general it appears that children prefer addition to multiplication when the latter is the correct strategy, as in reproducing to scale. The reason for this is not clear, and may be at least in part a result of bad teaching. Multiplication is usually taught as a short cut for cumulative equal addition. Although a valid interpretation, this is not the only one. An alternative and equally valid interpretation sees multiplication as a function, or one—many relation. It is the latter which is relevant to direct proportionality. Moreover, it is this aspect which is essential to a correct understanding of inverse proportionality since the mathematical inverse here takes the form of many—one relation. Unlike direct proportionality, realisations of inverse proportionality involve MIS. A simple but very clear illustration of the difficulty of these problems is provided by the large scale enquiries of Karplus (Karplus and Peterson, 1970). The problem consists simply in predicting how many large paper clips are needed to make a mannikin who will be the same shape and size as one made of small clips, given the ratio of the two sizes of clips. The percentage of subjects who gave a correct solution together with an adequate explanation rose from 6 at grade 5 to 80 at grades 11-12.

MIS may be said to feature in these problems in the sense that the relation between size and number of clips in each instance forms a simple system and the problem is to establish a relation between the two.

However, before leaving the topic of proportionality, it is worth noting that while an adequate mastery of the topic certainly entails an understanding of the whole set of relations

$$\frac{a}{b} = \frac{c}{d} \rightarrow ad = bc \rightarrow \frac{a}{c} = \frac{b}{d}$$

together with their inverses, it has not been shown that this realisation comes about spontaneously as a result of a maturing logic (Inhelder and Piaget, 1958, pp. 176 ff). It is more probable that these relations need to be taught. But the evidence suggests that even given good teaching, they will not be applied spontaneously to new problems until the subject's powers of reasoning have reached an advanced level of development.

(d)   Problem Solving in Mathematics

I pass from proportionality as a special case to mathematical reasoning in general, referring once more to the work of Collis (1972). Collis incorporates two dimensions within a single model of development. One of these relates to the form of a problem, the other to its content. When the content is both specific and intuitable it is classed as 'concrete'. In the context of mathematics this reduces to a condition that the problem must be confined to the manipulation of small integers. When the numbers are large or when they are replaced by algebraic variables, the content is 'formal'. As to the operational structure of a problem, this is concrete when it takes the form of a series of closed operations, i.e. even if the solver is required to execute more than one operation, he is always able to complete the one he is executing before proceeding to the next, and the sequence is clear from the outset. When these conditions do not obtain the structure is formal. This twofold classification leads to a two by two matrix. $8 \times 3 = 3 \times ?$ and $8 \times 4 - 4 = ?$ are examples of concrete form and concrete content. $a \times b = b \times ?$ and $428 + 517 = 517 + ?$ are examples of formal content in a concrete operational structure. $7 - 4 = ? - 7$ is an instance of concrete content in the context of a formal structure. Finally, $576 + 495 = (576 + 382) + (495 - ?)$ and $a/b = 2a/?$ are (relatively simple) instances of formal content in a formal structure. It should of course be stressed that the problems can only have a formal structure for the solver just so long as he has not been taught an algorithm for their solution. If he has, then he knows just what sequence of operations he should perform, and so, by definition, the problem ceases to be formal.

Collis predicted that the structural dimension ought, on the basis of Piagetian theory, to be more critical than content. So indeed it appeared. Thus concrete content-concrete structure problems are solved by most 9 year olds most of the time. Formal content-concrete structure adds to the difficulty of the problem, but an acceptable criterion of success is achieved about the age of ten. For concrete content-formal structure problems, a similar criterion is not reached until nearer 15, while the formal-formal problem is only solved at 16-18.

I believe this analysis to be essentially correct, and certainly productive. The difficulty of a problem is found to depend on the manipulability of the elements and on the complexity of structure. The latter is even more critical than the former. It need hardly be added that the enquiries referred to constitute no more than a beginning in relation to what must be involved in the study of development in mathematical thinking. Even if we confine ourselves to the topic of equation solving alone, at least two sets of problems require exploration.

The first is the business of writing equations. It would seem that inventing an equation to describe a state of affairs involves three sets of abstraction. One is the selection of the mathematically significant content from the circumstantial. Another is the abstraction that is entailed in selecting or accepting a mathematical symbolism to describe the elements involved. At an elementary level this entails no more than the acceptance of algebraic symbols to describe unknown quantities, and there is evidence that this presents little problem even at the age of 7-9 (Hill *et al.*, 1973). However, it is likely that the distinction between algebraic constants and variables will be far more difficult to accept. More difficult, too, would be the abstraction involved in the generalisation of operations, closely bound up with the idea of function.

A second problem concerns the use of equations. Equations are useful in the measure that they engender complete or partial solutions. The solution of equations is rarely possible without a set of transformation rules. In practice there are two ways of using such rules. The first consists in acquiring a limited number of fixed algorithms embodying a determinate sequence of transformations. Pupils who learn mathematics in this way (perhaps the majority) can pass examinations, but their mathematical understanding remains low. The alternative involves two sorts of ability: the ability to generate sequences of transformations and the ability to select those that are useful for any given problem. [. . .]

Most of the activities I have described involve ALC since they require choices in sequences of transformations. Once again, however, the role of MIS is less obvious, although it is likely to be a factor in devising and selecting suitable sequences for the solution of equations or for establishing proofs. [. . .] However the one characteristic of reasoning which figures most prominently is that of abstraction. More specifically it is an abstraction based on operations carried out by the subject himself in relation to the material i.e. what Piaget (1970) calls 'reflective abstraction'.

(e)   Explanatory Behaviour in Verbal Contexts

I turn now to a very different area, consisting of the now quite extensive group of studies carried out by Peel and his collaborators, the majority of which are reported in his most recent book (1971). These workers have been concerned with the description and measurement of development in the quality of children's explanations in such fields as history, geography and economics. The technique adopted is beautifully simple and consists in presenting the child with a passage followed by a question. The passage contains information relevant to the question, but there are usually irrelevancies besides and the evidence is always ambiguous or inadequate so that any answer demands evaluation and judgment. The following is an example (first reported in Peel, 1966):

> Only brave pilots are allowed to fly over high mountains. This summer a fighter pilot flying over the Alps collided with an aerial cable railway, and cut a main cable causing some cars to fall to the glacier below. Several people were killed and many others had to spend the night suspended above the glacier.
>
> 1. Was the pilot a careful airman?
>
> 2. Why do you think so?

The types of responses made to the two questions generally fall into one of three categories, these being:

(a) *Restricted.* Irrelevancy, tautology and inconsistency may dominate. Often the child focuses on a trivial point or he may fabricate e.g. 'Yes he was brave'; 'Yes the cable shouldn't have been there'; 'No he was a show off'.

(b) *Circumstantial.* The content as given as taken to be decisive e.g. 'No because he hit the cable'; 'No because if he was careful, he would not have cut the cable'. (Peel argues that the second of these represents a higher sub-stage.)

If two of the facts given in a passage point to opposite conclusions (as is true of most of the examples cited), the subject simply seizes on one and ignores the other.

(c) *Imaginative.* Extentuating circumstances are invoked e.g. 'You can't tell, it depends on the weather/state of the plane, etc.' More generally, the subject takes account of all the evidence as given, and in the measure that this is insufficient to settle the problem, he adduces further evidence from his store of general knowledge, or points to the need for such evidence.

It is easy to see that the chief characteristic of the second or circumstantial level is a sort of 'premature closure' due to a failure of ALC. Equally the presence of ALC at the third level enables the subject to begin to reconcile a variety of factors and this in turn entails MIS. Some of the investigations reported by Peel allow of four response categories, a distinction being made between those that merely take account of all the material given, which I would call minimal MIS, and those that offer a more thorough examination, showing a genuine grasp of the ramifications of the topic at issue. These enquiries offer clear evidence of development in the quality of children's explanations throughout the adolescent years. [. . .] [See chapters 11, 12 and 13 in this volume.]

(f) Network Problems

Mention of constraints in the last paragraph leads me to a consideration of a further class of problem, perhaps limited in scope, but interesting precisely because it is very different from all those considered so far. I refer to problems which are essentially sequential and the job is to find the right sequence of moves from a beginning state to an end state, within a given set of constraints. The moves themselves may be quite simple and easy to envisage. Moreover, if a position can be reached in several ways, it does not matter which path has been taken to reach it. The problem is to find an appropriate sequence of moves to reach the objective without breaking the rules. The particular examples we have studied are all river-crossing problems, and there were four of these:

Problem 1. Two soldiers are marching through the jungle. They come to a crocodile infested river which they must cross. There is only one small boat which belongs to two small boys. The boat is big enough to carry the two boys alone, or one soldier by himself. How do the two soldiers get across the river if the two boys are willing to help out but want their boat back again?

In order to obtain a correct solution to this problem one must be willing to allow the two boys to go across and one to return before a soldier can cross, two apparently pointless moves. One must watch the condition of the boat, either two boys or one soldier. One must ensure that the boys get the boat back; one of them must be on the far bank when the second soldier arrives.

Problem 2. A man is travelling with a wolf, a goat and a basket of cabbages. They come to a crocodile infested river over which they have to cross. There is only one small boat which will carry the man and one other thing, either the wolf, the goat or the basket of cabbages. If the goat and the cabbages are left alone together, then the goat eats the cabbages. If the wolf and the goat are left alone together, then the wolf eats the goat. How does he get across the river safely without losing any of them?

In order to obtain a correct solution to this problem one must be willing to take across the goat, go back for either the wolf or the cabbages: but on arriving on the far bank with either of these two things one must take back the goat; a backward move. The condition in the boat presents little problem, the man plus one other thing; but one needs to watch both banks carefully throughout the problem to ensure that one does not break the wolf and goat or the goat and cabbage condition.

Problem 3. Three beautiful native girls are travelling through the jungle with their husbands who are young, handsome and jealous. They come to a crocodile infested river over which they must cross. There is only one small boat which can hold no more than two people. How do they cross the river if only the men can row and no girl is ever left in the company of a man unless her husband is present?

In order to obtain a correct solution one must again be prepared to take someone across the river but later take them back again. The condition in the boat plus the fact that only men can row means that either two men or one man and his wife can be in the boat. We have also to watch the condition on both banks: a wife must never be left in the company of a man unless her husband is present.

Problem 4. Three cannibals and three missionaries want to cross a river. There is only one small boat available which can carry two people at a time. If at any time there are more cannibals than missionaries at any place then the cannibals eat the missionaries. How do all six of them get safely across the river?

In order to obtain a correct solution one must be prepared to incorporate a backward move at some stage in the solution. The condition in the boat is straightforward, two people. One also has to watch both banks in order to ensure that while two people are in the boat we never have more cannibals than missionaries. Another difficulty, however, presents itself: we have also in this case to consider the period of change from boat to bank: when the boat leaves one bank it is necessary to add together the cannibals in the boat and on the opposite bank and check that they do not outnumber the missionaries in the boat and on the opposite bank.

The four problems were set as a written test to four groups of subjects, three composed of schoolchildren and the fourth of college students. The order of the problems was varied but was not found to be a significant factor. The percentage of success achieved by each group is shown in Table 10.2.

Table 10.2: Success in River-Crossing Problems

Age	N	Problem			
		1	2	3	4
10–11	32	62	6	0	0
12–13	32	72	62	12	0
14–15	32	94	92	33	19
19+	40	87	65	17	10

One can only speculate as to the reason that the college students' performance was inferior to that of the 14-15 year olds. Presumably, however, a more highly selected group of young adults would have a higher percentage of success. It is clear that the more demanding the constraints and the larger the sequence of moves required for solution (8 crossings in problem 1, 7 in problem 2, and 11 in problems 3 and 4), the greater the difficulty of the problem. But it is no less clear that problems of this kind do not entail either ALC or MIS in the strict sense. Nor can even the more difficult problems be described as abstract, although they are certainly artificial! These considerations lead me to surmise that the identification of ALC and MIS as constituents of most of the problems that require advanced thinking is by no means definitive. Perhaps, in spite of their generality as noted in earlier paragraphs, ALC and MIS are too content-loaded to constitute specifications for thinking as such.

In order to arrive at a more embracing psychological account of thinking we may need to consider only the type of 'programme' required by the thinking subject, i.e. the number of elements to be processed and the number and structure of the rules needed for the processing.

I will return to this question in Section 5, after first considering the nature of the difficulties involved in logical problems as a separate class. Meanwhile I would re-emphasise that the problems reviewed in this section are representative, but not exhaustive. For instance I have not mentioned analogies on which I draw rather heavily in my 1965 paper, nor have I referred to the understanding of proverbs as in the familiar Terman-Newell test. However, such tests are fairly obvious instances of ALC, MIS and, perhaps, abstraction, in varying combinations of difficulty.

4. Logical Problems

One of the principal contentions of this paper is that problems of logical inference constitute a special class and should not be taken as a touchstone for the quality of thinking in general. There are two reasons for taking this stand. From the theoretical point of view, logical inference differs from most instances of reasoning because of the key importance that attaches to material implication. From an empirical standpoint we note an ever-increasing body of evidence attesting to the fact that students who are otherwise effective (though not perhaps outstanding) thinkers may nevertheless perform very poorly in tests of logical inference. A third reason is that in the present state of our knowledge, a sort of null hypothesis is a safer assumption, if only because it leaves more roads open for enquiry.

At the very least, we have to recognise that the principle of material implication plays only a very limited part either in every day thinking or in scientific thinking, yet it is crucial to most logics, and certainly to the kinds of logical problems that have been designed by myself as well as by others as tests of formal reasoning. A logic is an axiomatisation of the principles of valid inference. Within the axiomatic system, the propositional calculus holds a prior position, and with it a prior importance, since the principles that are first established within the propositional calculus are carried over into the remainder of logic. The propositional calculus is a set of rules which enables me to deduce the truth or falsehood of any compound proposition, given the truth value of all the simple propositions that enter into it. A logical truth table provides a simple algorithmic device for making such decisions. Logical, or material, implication is meaningful because it corresponds to a precise specification of entries in such a table.

Table 10.3: Material Implication

P	Q	P → Q	Q → P
T	T	T	T
T	F	F	T
F	T	T	F
F	F	T	T

The compound proposition 'P implies Q' (P → Q) is equivalent to 'Q *or* not-P', and hence to 'not-Q implies not-P'. It is asymmetrical, since the truth table for 'P → Q' differs from that for 'Q → P'. The validity of these relations is in no way dependent on the content or meaning of the simple P and Q. If P stands for the true sentence 'Piaget is a psychologist' and Q stands for the true sentence 'Piaget is a human being' then 'P implies Q' yields the true and plausible sentence 'Piaget is a psychologist implies Piaget is a human being'. But the logic is unchanged when the second sentence becomes 'Piaget is Swiss' or 'wine is intoxicating'. Moreover if we substitute the false sentence 'Piaget is French' for P, we note that P → Q is true whatever the truth value of Q (and of course whatever its content). Thus 'Piaget is French' implies 'Piaget is a psychologist' or '2 + 2 = 4' or '2 + 2 = 5' or any proposition whatever. Within logic, though not outside it, a proposition is meaningful if it is either true or false. In conformity with this requirement, any true proposition is held to imply every other true proposition and any false proposition implies any proposition whatever, be it true or false.

The assertion that 'Piaget is a psychologist implies wine is intoxicating' is true makes the logician look silly. But looking silly is a small price to pay for a watertight set of rules of inference. In practice, such sentences do not occur, but the theory is adequate for all contingencies. Alternatives are less adequate for any purpose whatever. [. . .]

The kind of logic under discussion is concerned solely with deduction or inference. It deals with the reduction of compound propositions to simple propositions, but is not at all concerned with the origin of the simple propositions themselves. In conformity with this, there is a total abstraction from content, and only the formal relations between elements are considered. The irreversibility of implications is central to formal logic, just as is the abstraction and lack of concern for causal relations. By contrast, in most cases of scientific and everyday thinking causal relations are of paramount importance. The problem is rarely one of deducing whether one compound proposition does or does not imply another by reducing both to simples. Much more often, it is one of establishing a frame of reference which will permit the formulation of fruitful hypotheses. Thus outside the field of pure logic, there is a close relation between deduction and induction.

It follows that even the irreversibility of implication plays an inconspicuous part outside logic itself. Generally speaking, a causal hypothesis asserts the dependence of a comparatively rare phenomenon q on a set of comparatively rare antecedents p. For instance the presence of a disease or an abnormality is attributed to a metabolic disturbance (e.g. phenylketonuria) or a chromosomal abnormality (e.g. Downs' syndrome) which are themselves rare. It is interesting to note that in the two cases noted, which are quite typical, the relation between the syndrome and the cause is assumed to be symmetrical: where there is a specified chromosomal abnormality the child exhibits the symptoms of mongolism and *vice versa*. Moreover, it makes sense to test the validity of the thesis by examining either chromosomal abnormalities or mongoloid children. It is much less sensible to examine all children, not-q, for chromosomal abnormality, p, simply because this would falsify the implication in a logical sense. In practice, such a procedure would be very wasteful.

Such considerations (they are by no means new, cf. Chapman and Chapman, 1959) lead one to question the role of logical inference in thinking on theoretical grounds. As to the actual levels of success attained by children of various ages on tasks of this kind, I would suggest that these permit of four general conclusions:

1. Error rates are high in logical problems and tend to remain high

at all ages. Some problems, the difficulty of which may not be obvious to the problem-setter, lead to a preponderance of error even in otherwise intelligent adults.

2. The difficulty of these problems is greatly increased when the content is either abstract or obviously false (e.g. reasoning involving the premise 'Elephants are smaller than mice').

3. Despite what has been said, there is an improvement in the solutions of logical problems over the age range with which we are concerned. However, IQ is generally a more important feature than CA.

4. The superiority of older and more intelligent subjects is often most apparent in their ability to overcome initial error.

Much of the evidence for these conclusions has been reviewed in a recent paper (Lunzer, 1973). The first part, the unsuspected difficulty of problems of pure logic is well attested by such studies as those of Sells (1936) and Chapman and Chapman (1959) in which university students obtained well under 50 per cent of correct solutions in syllogistic problems. In both experiments the content was abstracts, premises being given in the form 'All K are M', etc. However, in a more recent series of studies, O'Brien has shown that throughout high school age, children arrive at false conclusions when faced with problems of the form, 'If the car is shiny it is fast; the car is fast; therefore . . .'. Moreover, at all ages from 9 to 18, about a third of the subjects consistently tackled these problems as if the implication were reversible (O'Brien, Shapiro and Reali, 1971). There was little improvement even when medical students were chosen as subjects (Shapiro and O'Brien, 1973), and there was no apparent improvement in college students who had followed a year's course in logic (O'Brien, 1973). [. . .]

Turning to the second point, I will confine myself to three pieces of evidence. The first is the study of Roberge and Paulus already referred to. These authors found constant and highly significant differences as between conditionals or syllogisms having an abstract content, those with a 'suggestive content' (if mice are larger than elephants) and those having a plausible content (if it is raining Jane carries an umbrella) the last category being very much easier. In the area of mathematics, reference has already been made to Collis' demonstration of the greater difficulty of problems involving large numbers or algebraic symbols, and a similar conclusion was reached by Keats as early as 1955. Finally in the four-card problem just referred to, Wason and Shapiro (1971) found that the use of thematic material (train, car, Leeds, Manchester, with the sentence 'Whenever I go to Leeds I go by train') greatly reduced the difficulty and a similar result was found by Lunzer, Harrison and Davey (1972) using a concrete content (full lorry, empty lorry, red, yellow, with the sentence 'Every red lorry is full of coal'). In both experiments the problem is facilitated in the measure that the association as between the terms involved, viz. destination and mode of transport or colour of vehicle and load are plausible and even imageable, and not arbitrary, as in the original form used by Wason. In the face of this kind of evidence one is led to deny Piaget's assertion: 'In contrast with the preceding (concrete) level, the operational form is entirely disassociated from thought content' (Inhelder and Piaget, 1958, p. 265).

As to the third point, despite the fact that many logical problems permit unexpected difficulties at all ages and at most levels of intelligence, there is evidence of age-linked improvement in most cases (e.g. Roberge and Paulus, 1971). Another enquiry by Lewis is described fully in Lunzer (1973). Subjects were required to make inferences about the tribe of a 'native' encountered on 'an island' on the basis of two pieces of written information and a picture, e.g. 'All the AMLAGS have long hair'; 'None of the BRIDS have green eyes'; picture showing a short-haired man with his back to the viewer conclusion he cannot be an AMLAG; he may or may not be a BRID. Mean scores at successive ages from 11 to 15 were 13.5, 14.7, 16.4 and 21.4. At 18 the mean was 24.9, and university students achieved a mean of 34.5, the maximum score being 47. Since many of the less able children leave school before they reach the age of 18, while the university population in Britain is even more selective, one can safely conclude that over and above the age-related improvement there is an IQ effect, the variance of which is possibly greater, at least over the ages with which we are concerned. [. . .]

Finally, I can quote at least three studies which give substance to my fourth point. Two of them are extensions of the Wason four-card problem. In an earlier study (Lunzer, Harrison and Davey, 1972) we had found that a single explanation of the problem did not in general suffice to enable sixth formers and university students to solve analogous problems. Generally speaking what they did was to extract an algorithm which was applicable only when the transfer situation was maximally similar to the original problem. But a more extensive study by Abbott yielded a very different picture. Abbott gave instructions in no less than seven variants of the four-card problem and his post-test included a new problem based on the same principle, but very much more complex. At age 7-8 the lengthy teaching programme failed to produce even an algorithm for the simpler problems used in the pre-test. At 10-11 there was considerable success with these problems, but little with the new problem based on the supposedly well-established principle. However, at 13-14, there was evidence of considerable learning even to the extent of good attempts at the new problem. Another study, again by Lewis, showed that sixth formers (aged 16-18) could be led to a greater success level in the four-card problem (albeit only 37 per cent) by means of a series of simpler problems designed to alert them to the solution strategy. Younger subjects were generally unsuccessful with some of the simpler problems themselves. Finally a preliminary study by Lake used a conditional reasoning test based on those of O'Brien. Lake had two groups of subjects, one aged fifteen and the other aged nineteen. The experiment was in three stages. First the subjects were given the test of conditional reasoning. Next they were shown a worked test by an imaginary student called A. Dunce who had made the most common error in answer to each and every question and asked to discover where he had gone wrong. Finally they were given a re-test with an alternative format. It turned out that the 19 year olds were very much better than the 15 year olds, especially in explaining Dunce's errors and in improving their scores on re-test.

5. Concluding Comments

We have just seen that problems of logical inference are solved with increasing efficiency as the adolescent grows in cognitive competence. Moreover, even when initial performance remains at a relatively low level, there is an improvement in responsiveness to teaching and experience. Yet even intelligent adults often appear strikingly inept when asked to tackle formal problems, i.e. problems that require the use of inferential procedures on the basis of arbitrary associations between elements that carry no meaning for the subject. One is left to conclude that whatever it is that produces gains in scientific and everyday thinking also plays a major role in such gains as do appear in logical thinking as such. Nor will it have escaped the reader's attention that ALC (but not MIS) figures as prominently in the latter as it does in the former. But one is bound to question whether competence in logic can itself be the principal determinant in effective thinking. [. . .]

It is at least equally possible that productive thinking is primarily analogic. [. . .] Thinking is a matter of anticipating moves to enable the thinker to arrive at a desired end, setting out from a starting point that is in some way unsatisfactory, within the constraints that are imposed by nature, by society or, simply, by the rules of the game. To be successful, he must be efficient and competent in surveying the field that is his starting point and in assessing the gap that needs to be filled to arrive at his end. He must also be aware of the constraints that are operative, and also of the constraints that are not. He must, too, have a stock of analogies from which to select trial strategies. There are also effective heuristics of some generality based on a combination of forward and backward thinking. Thus one can make an imaginative anticipatory leap: if such and such were the case would the problem be solved? Nor is it irrelevant to observe that all the procedures just outlined are especially relevant to structured problems, in which at least the goal is formulated for the subjects. Much thinking has been described by Bartlett (1958) as thinking within closed systems, and he stresses the importance of a further dimension entailed in what he calls adventurous thinking, where the goals – and often the constraints – are largely unknown, and need to be clarified as the work progresses. It is this that others call creative thinking.

But all this is part of the forward looking, inductive aspect of thinking. If throughout this paper special attention has been paid to ALC and MIS it is because both belong at least as much to the inductive process as they do to the deductive process.

If there is a moral to be drawn from what has been said, it is simply that it would be inadvisable to concentrate our energies either on the study of logical process or on the teaching of logic as an aid to effective thought. Much more research is needed to clarify the role of analogy: of the origin and availability of trial rules and of trial procedures in problem solving. Why is it that some children and some adults are more effective thinkers than others? It is certainly possible, as argued by McLaughlin (1962) and Halford (1968) that the capacity of the short-term memory store imposes a limit on the complexity of problems that a man can tackle. It is possible, too, that sheer speed of information processing constitutes an important component of intelligence (Jensen, 1970). But it is highly possible that over and above the constraints that are imposed by the limitations of brain power, the ineffective thinker, like the ineffective operator, or the ineffective athlete, makes poor use of the equipment that he has. There is considerable evidence of the effectiveness of limited 'thinking programmes' in a laboratory context (cf. Covington, 1970; Peel, 1971). But there is also scope for developing such programmes on a wider scale, for experimenting with alternatives and for implementing them within the educational system.

References

Bartlett, F.C. (1958), *Thinking: An Experimental and Social Study*, London: Allen and Unwin.

Brown, R. (1970), *Psycholinguistics – Selected Papers*, New York: Free Press.

Calvert, W.M. (1971), 'A short-term longitudinal study. The development of classificatory behaviour in children at the pre-operational and concrete operational stages', M.Ed. thesis, University of Birmingham.

Campbell, R.N. and Young, B.M. (1968), 'Some aspects of classificatory behaviour in pre-school children', paper read to the Annual Congress of the British Psychological Society, Education Section, September.

Chapman, L.J. and Chapman, J.P. (1959), 'Atmosphere effect re-examined', *Experim. Psychol.*, 58, 220-6.

Collis, K.F. (1972), 'A study of concrete and formal operations in school mathematics', Ph.D. thesis, University of Newcastle, New South Wales.

Covington, M.V. (1970), 'The cognitive curriculum: a process-oriented approach to education', in J. Hellmuth (ed.), *Cognitive Studies*, vol. 1, New York: Brunner/Mazel, 491-502.

Dienes, Z.P. (1972), 'Six stages in the process of learning mathematics' (unpublished monograph).

Halford, G.S. (1968), 'An investigation of concept learning', Ph.D. thesis, University of Newcastle, New South Wales.

Herriot, P. (1970), *An Introduction to the Psychology of Language*, London: Methuen.

Hill, R., Kapadia, R., Dadds, M., Lunzer, E.A. and Armitage, V. (1973), 'The child's conception of the structure of numbers', interim report to the Social Sciences Research Council (unpublished manuscript).

Inhelder, B. and Piaget, J. (1958), *The Growth of Logical Thinking*, New York: Basic Books.

Inhelder, B. and Piaget, J. (1964), *The Early Growth of Logic in the Child*, London: Routledge.

Jackson, S. (1965), 'The growth of logical thinking in normal and subnormal children', *Brit. J. Educ. Psychol.*, 35, 255-8.

Jensen, A.R. (1970), 'Hierarchical theories of mental ability', in W.B. Dockrell (ed.), *On Intelligence*, London: Methuen.

Karplus, E.F. and Karplus, R. (1970), 'Intellectual development beyond elementary school I: deductive logic', *School Science and Mathematics*, 70, 398-406.

Karplus, R. and Peterson, R.W. (1970), 'Intellectual development beyond elementary school II: ratio, a survey', *School Science and Mathematics*, 70, 813-20.

Lovell, K. (1960), 'A follow-up study of Inhelder and Piaget's *The Growth of Logical Thinking*', *Brit. J. Psychol.*, 52, 143-53.

Lunzer, E.A. (1965), 'Problems of formal reasoning in test situations', in P.H. Mussen (ed.), 'European research in cognitive development', *Monogr. Soc. Res. Child Developm.*, 30, no. 2 (whole number 100), 19-46.

Lunzer, E.A. (1968), 'Formal reasoning', in E.A. Lunzer and J.F. Morris (eds.), *Development in Human Learning*, New York: American Elsevier.

Lunzer, E.A. (1970), *On Children's Thinking* (University of Nottingham, Inaugural lecture), London: National Foundation for Educational Research.

Lunzer, E.A. (1973), 'The development of formal reasoning: some recent experiments and their implications', in K. Frey and M. Lang (eds.), *Cognitive Processes and Science Instruction*, Bern, Stuttgart and Vienna: Huber and Baltimore: Williams and Wilkins.

Lunzer, E.A. and Pumfrey, P.D. (1966), 'Understanding proportionality', *Mathematics Teaching*, 34, 7-12.

Lunzer, E.A., Harrison, C. and Davey, M. (1972), 'The four-card problem and the generality of formal reasoning', *Quarterly Journal of Experimental Psychology*, 24, 326-39.

Matalon, B. (1962), 'Etude génétique de l'implication', in E.W. Beth *et al.*, 'Implication, formalisation et logique naturelle', *Etudes d'epistémologie génétique*, 16, 69-93 (Paris: PUF).

McLaughlin, G.H. (1963), 'Psycho-logic: a possible alternative to Piaget's formulation', *Brit. J. Educ. Psychol.*, 33, 61-7.

O'Brien, T.C. (1973), 'Logical thinking in college students', *Educational Studies in Mathematics* (in press).

O'Brien, T.C., Shapiro, B.J. and Reali, N.C. (1971), 'Logical thinking — language and context', *Educational Studies in Mathematics*, 4, 201-10.

Peel, E.A. (1966), 'A study of differences in the judgments of adolescent pupils', *Brit. J. Educ. Psychol.*, 36, 77-86.

Peel, E.A. (1967), 'A method for investigating children's understanding of certain logical connectives used in binary propositional thinking', *Brit. J. Math. and Stat. Psychol.*, 20, 81-92.

Peel, E.A. (1971), *The Nature of Adolescent Judgment*, London: Staples.

Piaget, J. (1946), *Les notions de mouvement et de vitesse chez l'enfant*, Paris: Presses Universitaires de France.

Piaget, J. (1970), 'Piaget's theory', in P.H. Mussen (ed.), *Carmichael's Manual of Child Psychology*, vol. 1, New York: Wiley, 703-32.

Piaget, J., Inhelder, B. and Szeminska, A. (1960), *The Child's Conception of Geometry*, London: Routledge.

Reichard, S., Schneider, M. and Rappaport, D. (1944), 'The development of concept formation in children', *Amer. J. Orthopsychiat.*, 14, 156-62.

Rhys, W.T. (1964), 'The development of logical thought in the adolescent with reference to the teaching of geography in the secondary school', M.Ed. thesis, University of Birmingham.

Roberge, J.J. and Paulus, D.H. (1971), 'Developmental patterns for children's class and conditional reasoning abilities', *Developmental Psychology*, 4, 191-9.

Sells, S.B. (1936), 'The atmosphere effect: an experimental study of reasoning', *Archives of Psychology*, 29, 3-72.

Shapiro, B.J. and O'Brien, T.C. (1973), 'Quasi-child logic' (in press).

Szeminska, A. (1968) in J. Piaget, J.B. Grize, A. Szeminska and Vinh Bang, 'Epistémologie et psychologie de la fonction', *Etudes d'epistémologie génétique*, 23 (Paris: PUF).

Thouless, R.H., *Map of Educational Research*, London: National Foundation for Educational Research.

Wason, P.C. and Johnson-Laird, P.N. (1972), *Psychology of Reasoning, Structure and Content*, London: Batsford.

Wason, P.C. and Shapiro, D. (1971), 'Natural and contrived experience in a reasoning problem', *Quarterly Journal of Experimental Psychology*, 23, 69-71.

White, S.A. (1965), 'Evidence for a hierarchical arrangement of learning processes', in L.P. Lipsitt and C.C. Spiker (eds.), *Advances in Child Development and Behaviour*, vol. 2, New York: Academic Press, 187-220.

11 THE THINKING AND EDUCATION OF THE ADOLESCENT

E. A. Peel

Source: Chapter 14 in V.P. Varma and P. Williams (eds.), *Piaget, Psychology and Education* (Hodder and Stoughton, 1976).

Introduction

In a publication four years ago, fresh evidence at the time was outlined on: concept formation from contextual settings; recognising superordinate classes; and the correlation between the adolescent's power to explain problems put in a textual setting and his capacity to utilise general ideas in his writing (Peel, 1972). Since then the field of study has been widened and deepened. Research on the psychology of adolescent thinking has come to fruition and its results have been linked with secondary school intellectual activity. Therefore, for the present contribution, it is proposed to paint a broader canvas.

We may set out the extended field as follows. In situations where the pupil can respond rather more spontaneously than in a classroom (even in these days), evidence can be obtained of the existence of the following phenomena, apparently involved in the path to achieving mature thought:

Organisation, through the act of classifying, of the experience of perceiving phenomena in the environment, as a development from thematic groupings of a more private nature.

Identification of the groupings as concepts, in most cases through the medium of language, which, from this point on, plays an increasingly important role in intellectual growth.

Formation of concepts from terms and cues embedded in textual settings.

Recall of past experiences and organising generalisations as potential explanation of new problem materials and situations leading to the emergence of the *possible* over and above the *actual*.

Formulation, selection and rejection of possible explanations, necessarily involving certain formal requirements and procedures in thought.

Explanation of the current here-and-now realities in terms of an optimal hypothesis.

Conversion of generalisations into abstract notions.

237

Emergence of mature forms of understanding, explaining and evaluating, involving in particular comprehension of the dynamics of stability and change in human, biological and physical situations.

In a very broad sense this list constitutes a sequence, but at any time in the adolescent's development of thought and language, several of the above trends may be operating together.

In what follows, it is proposed first to amplify some of these assertions and also to support them by fresh evidence before passing on to studies of secondary school pupils' comprehension and explanation of school material. Finally we shall discuss consequences of these findings for teaching methods and curricula in secondary schools.

Basic Characteristics of Adolescent Thinking

The intellectual progress of the adolescent is intimately interwoven with his receptive and productive powers of language, be it concerned with his vocabulary, his command of structure or his logical rigour. For this reason, language and other symbolic systems, as in mathematics and logic, are involved in higher-level thinking. We need, therefore, to research more into the adolescent's language proficiency in relation to the world he has to learn and act in. Also, estimates of his intellectual progress are probably best measured through the verbal medium. With this overall observation in mind, let us examine some of the above assertions.

By the end of childhood, the individual has acquired a vocabulary of lexical items denoting a wide range of objects and categories. We may use this vocabulary to test how far the thinker is able to organise the elements of his environment into classes of widening generality and abstraction. He has the labels to do this, but can he select appropriately from them? Using a test composed of items, some of which involved generalising, others abstracting, one investigator (Clarke, 1974) followed up this question. A person is asked to complete the third term of a series of concepts of extending generality or abstraction (not told to the solver, who is, however, guided by a model line), as for example, in

Lager	beer	alcoholic drink (model)
Anthracite	coal	*solid fuel* (test)
		fire
		power station
		mining industry
		gas

where the required response is italicised. Clarke was able to obtain the following means and standard deviations from a large sample of nine- to sixteen-year-olds, 180 in each age group. These figures provide confirmation of trends indicated earlier (Peel, 1972), namely in the ability to recognise similar relations based on increasing generality and abstraction. They show that, in the medium of *language-directed* thought, the adolescent repeats to some extent the growth in classifying from arrays of *tangible objects* revealed in earlier childhood. Clarke might have obtained an even clearer picture had he restricted the basis of all his items to that of discovering the super-ordinate class, implying the widening generality, without admixing notions of abstraction as well.

Age group (mean in years)	Mean score (max. poss. 12)	S.D.
9.25	3.37	1.77
10.28	4.46	2.00
11.29	5.29	2.05
12.23	5.49	2.22
13.35	5.36	2.14
14.30	6.38	2.35
15.21	6.10	2.21
16.16	7.01	2.59

Much concept formation of adolescence is heavily dependent upon the context of the language and symbolic representation, and does not arise solely out of lists of instances. In the sciences there are statements giving the essentials of concepts, supported by examples. The humanities utilise textual material in which the concept plays a role, but education test constructors do not overtly recognise that many of their vocabulary comprehension exercises, based on the text, are in fact assessing concept formation, as the following excerpts demonstrate:

I am too well acquainted with the generous catholicity of spirit which pervades the writing of our chief apostle of culture to identify him with these opinions; and yet one may cull from one and another of those epistles to the Philistines, which so much delight all who do not answer to that name, sentences which lend them some support.

What is the meaning of:

1. catholicity   narrowness   broadness   religiousness
2. pervades   is found throughout   escapes from   influences
3. cull   understand   gather   deduce
(extracted from a paper by T.H. Huxley entitled 'Science and Culture')
(Diederich and Palmer, 1964);

and

Alternatively, history can be conceived as a series of oscillations between worldliness and other-worldliness, or as a theatre of contest between greed and virtue, or between truth and error. Such points of view emphasise religion, morality, and contemplative habits eliciting generalisations of thought.

eliciting   *means*   giving r . . . . . . to

Comprehension itself becomes more complex (Peel, 1975a) the more advanced and difficult the text. It goes far beyond recalling the simple referent or usage meaning of words, as the above instances illustrate. It calls for a range of cognitive activity, including inferential thought, reasoning from analogy, logical rigour, interpreting the language and ideas in the text and invoking knowledge outside that given in it.

It is therefore somewhat surprising that so little has been done on concept formation from textual material, with the object of determining the *psychological* factors entering into the process. Exceptions are the work on advanced textual organisers (Ausubel, 1963) to facilitate new learning, the classical study on the meanings of words coded into sentences (Werner and Kaplan, 1952) and the similar study of history passages (de Silva, 1972). Almost all comprehension tests are educational in slant and concerned with subject-matter understanding. This has led to the limiting of responses to a multiple-choice selection or a closed completion task, as illustrated above. One looks only for the correct response and rejects the others. What we require are analyses of open responses, for in the adolescent world of thought and language there may be few blacks and whites, but many shades of intermediate greys which can give us real psychological insights into what is going on.

In textual comprehension and analysis, the mature thinker feels his way to a solution by bringing his own ideas to the task, putting them up as possibilities and then back-checking against the textual structure and content. Such complex activity can only be revealed by allowing the testee to make open, elaborated responses (Peel, 1971; de Silva, 1972). Since the thinker often brings his own ideas to textual comprehension and criticism, we may conceive two kinds of concepts: those defined in the text by the fact that it is comprehensible, and those originating in the solver. The existence of these two types of concepts has severely restricted research on textual material to the study of retention and recall, or to filling in omitted words as in the Cloze[†] technique (Taylor, 1957) or detecting foreign bits of text as in the Chunking[†] technique (Carver, 1970). In all these measures, invocation of ideas from the thinker is minimised and the testing of understanding and explanation is lost. However, an analysis of the conceptual content of responses is currently being carried out (Peel, 1975a) in terms of the connections between what are called in- and out-concepts. Counts are made of the number of the three types of connection — in-in, in-out, out-out — and indices defined which measure the amount of out-activity involved against in-activity. Connections are simply defined as subject—predicate links, but the method might permit a more sophisticated logico-linguistic analysis. What is important psychologically is that by this technique, we can ask questions on texts calling for responses at higher levels of intellectual activity.

The predisposition to shift from a generalisation to an abstraction, as implied in the change in thinking involved in the difference between a *democrat* and *democracy* or *sportsman* and *sport*, is an important tendency in higher-level thinking and discourse. Here is an example from such abstract thinking (Whitehead, 1933): 'One of the most general philosophic notions to be used in the analysis of civilised activities is to consider the effect on social life due to the variations of emphasis between individual absoluteness and individual relativity. Here "absoluteness" means the notion of release from essential dependence on other members of the community in respect to modes of activity, while "relativity" means the converse fact of essential relatedness. In one of their particularisations these ideas appear in the antagonism between notions of freedom and of social organisation.' This distinction has not been widely recognised by psychologists and only then in connection with the thought of younger children (Braine, 1962). It is interesting that language does not always provide the means of distinguishing between generalisations and abstractions as instanced above. In its stead we often have a single term, say, *poem*, which serves both purposes, often with the definite and indefinite article providing a clue. Thus a *poem* is a generalisation, the notion of *the poem* (as a literary form) is an abstraction. We may use this ambiguity to test the preference for either a generalisation or an abstraction (Peel, 1975b). Test items were composed which presented four sentences to the testee, each containing the same key word used in a general, abstract, particular, or associative sense. He was asked to select the sentence having the most significance for him. The results, some of which follow in Table 11.1, indicate a clear rise in preference for abstraction, a less marked rise for generalising and a fall in tendency to particularise, across the age range of twelve to fifteen years.

Table 11.1: Mean Tendencies to Abstract and Generalise

	Age			
	12+	13+	14+	15+
N	93	71	93	76
Tendency to:				
abstract	3.7	3.9	5.0	5.6
generalise	6.2	7.0	7.6	7.6
particularise	6.4	5.8	4.7	4.0
associate	4.7	4.3	3.7	3.8
Total number of items	21	21	21	21

Correlations between the quality of judgment in separate problem situations and the growing preference for abstraction are positive.

We may conclude this section on the psychology of adolescent thought by reproducing some definitive results on the growth of judgment and powers of explanation (Clarke, 1974). They are set out in Table 11.2 in the form of the frequency of imaginative-explanatory judgments obtained by giving nine test items to ninety subjects in lower- and higher-ability age groups. There were also included ninety higher-ability adults with a mean age of thirty-five years. The results follow on the opposite page.

Four points about these figures merit particular comment:

1. the spurt between twelve and thirteen for the lower-ability groups;
2. that between eleven and twelve for the higher-ability groups;
3. the ceiling that is reached by the end of adolescence, with apparently little change thereafter; and
4. that even in maturity not all judgments are high-level (734 out of 810).

With this conclusion of the brief pinpointing of certain features of the development of adolescent thought, we may now consider evidence of this development in the setting of secondary school material.

Table 11.2: Incidence of Imaginative-Explanatory Judgments

Age	Lower ability	Higher ability
Total no. of possible responses for each group	810	810
9:0	42	136
10:0	61	137
11:0	135	195
12:0	189	366
13:0	368	472
14:0	396	565
15:0	457	573
16:0	531	620
17:0	−	727
18:0	−	698
35:0	−	734

Understanding School Material

Research on understanding and explaining school material serves the purposes of providing further evidence on the maturation of judgment, already revealed by using non-specialist material, and also some knowledge of the pupil's insights into his subject-matter and readiness for further progress, particularly in more sophisticated material and modes of learning. With these objectives in mind, several investigations have been carried out of thinking in secondary school specialist subjects.

Two perceptive studies of thinking in geography (Rhys, 1972) and history (de Silva, 1972) [see chapters 12 and 13, this volume] have already received discussion, which need not be extended here, although the educational implications will be followed up briefly in the last section. More recent investigations have been carried out on thinking in other subjects. Of these we begin by referring to two concerned with English: one on poetry (Mason, 1974) and the other on crisis situations portrayed in prose fiction (Ellis, 1975). Then briefly we consider two on science thinking, in physical science (Wells, 1972) and biology (Pitt, 1974).

Mason (1974) tested seven year-groups of twenty comprehensive school pupils, ranging in age from eleven to seventeen-plus, the latter being a GCE 'A' level group, with four groups of four poems. The sixteen poems were short, complete and taken from school anthologies and represented a range including Haikai and, among others, poems by S. Smith, G.M.

Hopkins, T.S. Eliot and E. Dickinson. The poems were presented with the question: 'What do these poems mean to you?' This evoked a wide range of responses which it was found possible to categorise into six groups, showing:

1. lack of comprehension
2. repetition of poem content with little else
3. affective reaction, usually unfused, but sometimes with tenuous literary reference
4. cognitive awareness of a single referential element
5. coordinated generalisation, uniting cognitive and affective elements
6. explanation in terms of hypotheses linking the poem to wider human parallels.

Mason (op. cit., pp. 135-6) gives instances of these categories of responses to two poems. Marker reliability is high ($r = 0.94$).

The frequency distribution of responses in these categories according to age group is revealing (Table 11.3), where categories 1 and 2, 3 and 4, and 5 and 6 have been combined, since there is no real poetic distinction between 3 and 4 (a poem is a fusion of the affective and the cognitive) and there is little psychological distinction between 1 and 2, which are at a low intellectual level, and between 5 and 6, both of which are responses at a mature level.

Two features of these results are of particular note. First, the sharp change between domination by inadequate responses and later recognition of the affective and cognitive content of the poetry, occurring between

Table 11.3: Frequencies of Responses by Categories and Age

| Age | Response category | | | |
	1 and 2	3 and 4	5 and 6	No. of responses
11+	68	11	1	80
12+	25	51	4	80
13+	28	45	7	80
14+	27	44	9	80
15+	5	39	36	80
16+	9	44	27	80
17+	8	15	57	80

eleven and twelve-plus. This may be compared with the similar ages of Table 11.2, where the results are drawn from simple comprehension material. Second, the substantial appearance of high-level answers (5 and 6) at the age of fifteen-plus, clearly happening much later than similar changes shown in Table 11.2.

Similar changes, perhaps not so clearly marked, characterise the appearance of materials in judging human situations portrayed in literature (Ellis, 1975). The theme of sudden change in human affairs and its consequences constantly recurs in literature, and its understanding is an important element of literary comprehension and appreciation. Ellis took excerpts from several novels which embody sudden and sometime traumatic changes in the lives of characters in them and, after presenting the excerpts to his pupils, asked several questions tapping various aspects of the test situation.

One of his passages was taken from Somerset Maugham's *Of Human Bondage*, where Philip is told of his mother's death by Mr Carey. Six questions were asked in relation to the text, including the following:

Do you think Mr Carey could have done more to help Philip? Why do you think so?
What did Philip do and why at Blackstable the next day, do you think?
What was Philip doing and why a few weeks after this, do you think?

The frequencies of responses to these questions by four age groups of forty pupils in each are set out in Table 11.4 alongside the description of the category used.

Table 11.4: Frequency of Responses in Different Categories

| | Age | | | |
Response category	12+	13+	14+	15+
1 Circular, irrelevant, no response	12	19	18	9
2 Invocation of no more than two facts from the passage	193	148	111	60
3 Use of facts and possibilities but no explicit explanation	35	62	68	104
4 Explicit discussion of the dynamics of the crisis situation and possible consequences	0	11	43	67

Here we may note that mature judgments first appear markedly at the age of fourteen-plus, somewhat lower than in the judgment of the poems but higher than in the case of simple comprehension material.

The main purpose in the following brief reference to studies of thinking by adolescents in physical and biological sciences (Wells, 1972; Pitt, 1974) is to demonstrate that even when the problem situations are not encased in language, the same trends are shown, from partial, restricted thinking to mere description and finally on to imaginative explanation. This latter is characterised by verbalised concepts, covering laws and deductive activity.

Wells worked with secondary modern school boys and found comparatively few clear-cut cases of imaginative explanations, and these were associated with chronological ages of fourteen years and over. For example, the responses to his ammonia-fountain experiment, demonstrated before the pupils, were distributed as shown in Table 11.5 (op. cit., p. 216).

We may note in passing that development in thinking is shown in this research to be more positively associated with mental age.

Pitt devised eight biological problems, including the hawk-tit-greenfly food-chain problem and various biological control experiments. He tested comprehensive school pupils, age range eleven to sixteen-plus, and obtained the results shown in Table 11.6.

Again we confirm the transition to mature thinking at higher ages, this time at sixteen years of chronological age and eighteen years mental age. The sharp difference between these results and those obtained in the physical science tests is partly attributable to the sophistication and methodological bias of the biological problems.

Overall, however, all these investigations into the secondary school pupil's thinking across a wide range of subject matter confirm the trends discovered in general comprehension, with delays of up to three years in reaching mature levels of explanation and judgment.

Table 11.5: Frequency of Response by Category and Age (Ammonia-Fountain Experiment)

Category	Frequency	Mean CA	Mean MA
Restricted	15	12:9	12:8
Simple description	40	13:2	13:1
Extended description	79	13:10	14:8
Partial explanation	28	13:11	15:6
Full explanation	11	14:6	16:11

Table 11.6: Frequency of Response by Category and Age (Biological Problems)

Level	N	Mean CA	Mean MA
No response	55	13:2	12:3
Restricted	442	13:4	13:3
Simple description	517	14:0	14:11
Extended description	152	15:2	17:6
True explanation	31	16:2	18:11

Consequences for Secondary Education

The least that could come out of these studies is their power to heighten the teacher's sensitivity as to what may be going on, or not going on, in the mind of the individual pupil, beneath the regimentation of organised instruction. Then, accepting the aphorism that learning should not considerably out-pace thinking, material in all subjects should be graded accordingly, keeping in mind particularly the period of maximum growth from descriptive-repetition to imaginative-explanation.

The earlier build-up of experience and its organisation by generalisation are indispensable, not to be pursued as ends in themselves, but accepted as appropriate to their particular age levels. The ultimate aim must be imaginative thought and, for this end, experience must be made articulate through language and abstraction. The application of established ideas to new situations should be linked with this process.

Turning to specific subject areas, in English one would go a long way with Mason (1974, p. 135): 'Usefulness of the diorisms to teachers in any case can only be in terms of a starting point and guides, not as goals. An individual response to poetry, will remain a personal and, ultimately, unique matter.' We need teacher sensitivity, not instructional rigidity.

The understanding of history and geography ultimately requires competence in grasping the multiplicity of human affairs and principles of ecology. The researches encompassed in this chapter provide insights into the growth of such competence. Teaching based on them would accept partial and single explanations as a necessary lead-in to comprehensive understanding.

The lesson for science teaching and curricula may well be seen in the need 'to enlarge the pupils' store of possible explanations, i.e. to build up new concepts and to enrich and extend existing ones. There is also a need to provide experience of processing evidence and observation using both induction and deduction and to give experience of constructing and testing hypotheses' (Wells, 1972, p. 223).

Finally the changing *quality* of intelligence over the secondary school years would seem to support the notion of a spiral curriculum, where it would be possible to return to topic areas with a greater conceptual repertoire and more mature form of intellectual enquiry.

References

Ausubel, D.P. (1963), *The Psychology of Meaningful Verbal Learning*, New York: Grune and Stratton.

Braine, M.D.S. (1962), 'Piaget on reasoning: a methodological critique and alternative proposals', in 'Thought in the Young Child', *Monogr. Soc. Res. Child Dev.*, 27.

Carver, R.P. (1970), 'Analysis of "chunked" test items as measures of reading and listening comprehension', *J. educ. Measurement*, 7, 141-50.

Clarke, W.D. (1974), 'A study of the development of adolescent judgment', Ph.D. thesis, University of Birmingham.

De Silva, W.A. (1972), 'The formation of historical concepts through contextual cues', in Peel, E.A., 'The quality of thinking', *Educ. Rev.*, 24, no. 3.

Diederich, P.B. and Palmer, O.E. (1964), *Critical Thinking in Reading and Writing*, New York: Holt, Rinehart and Winston.

Ellis, J.I. (1975), Unpublished research on secondary school pupils' understanding of human situations portrayed in literature.

Mason, J.S. (1974), 'Adolescent judgment as evidenced in response to poetry', *Educ. Rev.*, 26, no. 2.

Peel, E.A. (1971), *The Nature of Adolescent Judgment*, London: Staples.

Peel, E.A. (1972), 'Some aspects of higher level learning processes during adolescence', in Wall, W.D. and Varma, V.P. (eds.), *Advances in Educational Psychology 1*, London: University of London Press.

Peel, E.A. (1975a), 'Analysis of comprehension and judgment', *Educ. Rev.*, 27, 100-13.

Peel, E.A. (1975b), 'Predilection for generalising and abstracting', *Br. J. educ. Psychol.*, 45, 177-88.

Pitt, A.W.H. (1974), 'Adolescent thinking and levels of judgment in Biology', M.Ed. thesis, University of Birmingham.

Rhys, W.T. (1972), 'Geography and the adolescent', in Peel, E.A., 'The quality of thinking', *Educ. Rev.*, 24, no. 3.

Taylor, W.L. (1957), 'Cloze readability scores as indices of individual differences on comprehension and aptitude', *J. appl. Psychol.*, 41, 12-26.

Wells, J. (1972), 'Some aspects of adolescent thinking in science', in Peel, E.A., 'The quality of thinking', *Educ. Rev.*, 24, no. 3.

Werner, H. and Kaplan, E. (1952), 'The acquisition of word meanings: a developmental study', *Monogr. Soc. Res. Child Dev.*, 15, no. 1 (whole no. 51).

12 GEOGRAPHY AND THE ADOLESCENT

W. T. Rhys

Source: *Birmingham Educational Review*, 24 (3) (June 1972), pp. 183-96.

1. The Geographical Background

Geographical analysis and interpretation at school level is focused primarily upon the study of man in relation to his environment (Scarfe, 1971). If children are to make a realistic appraisal of human activity within a spatial setting, it follows that a secure basis of concepts and skills must be established before they can go on to analyse, interpret and explain, the interaction of key elements within diverse environmental contexts.

An intensive fieldwork approach is now widely favoured as a means whereby geographical knowledge and understanding can be cultivated through direct exploration and discovery (Everson, 1969). As an essential foundation and continuing core of study, fieldwork can certainly offer much that is valuable educationally. Most secondary schools, however, range far beyond the local environment to conduct an extensive survey of the earth as a whole (Graves, 1971). Since children are called upon to examine territories which stand outside the bounds of direct personal experience, such a programme of study will inevitably give rise to certain attendant difficulties within the classroom situation.

1. In the absence of direct environmental contact pupils will have to interpret evidence presented in verbal, pictorial, cartographic or statistical form.

2. The pupil will have to orientate himself spatially within the appropriate environmental context, and take into account all the relevant factors whether they arose out of the local, the national, or the global situation.

3. The pupil will have to take note of the local decision-taking situation in the light of the knowledge, the material resources, and the preferences of the local inhabitants.

4. Finally, the factors thought to be significant will have to be inter-related to support a comprehensive explanation.

Considered in terms of Piaget's developmental psychology each of these requirements would constitute a task beyond the child's intellectual capacity prior to the period of adolescence.

1. Prior (1959) has shown that 9 and 10 year old children cannot readily interpret maps in the absence of a direct link between their concrete experience and the displayed information. Even photographs cannot be analysed to an adequate degree without disciplined experience and careful training (Long, 1961). Since pictures form a two-dimensional representation of a three-dimensional reality, it is argued that children must learn to utilise such material symbolically, in order to suggest the concepts and ideas drawn from real life (Vernon, 1962).

2. At first the child is able to orientate himself spatially in terms of direct practical action. Later he is able to structure that area which he has experienced at first hand, in a representational form, involving the coordination of known landmarks within an overall reference frame of his own construction (Piaget *et al.*, 1960). But, when the child is asked to make a systematic analysis of cartographic material, related to an environmental context which cannot be experienced directly, he is faced with a cognitive challenge of a different order. An investigation into the nature of the 'mental map' held by children of an area greater than that which they knew intimately through frequent contact, revealed that it was not until 13+ that they could contend with spatial distributions organised within an abstract frame of reference (Blair, 1964).

3. 'Decision-makers operating within an environment base their decisions on the environment as they perceive it, not as it is' (Brookfield, 1969). Human choice and action in distant parts of the world cannot be explained, therefore, without some reference to the appropriate cultural orientation. This is a sophisticated task that can confound even the skilled adult geographer. The pre-adolescent would be further handicapped by limited experience, and his limited reasoning capacity. The complexity of adult behaviour in the distant past, raises a comparable problem in history, where mature judgments are rarely expressed prior to late adolescence (Peel, 1967; Hallam, 1967).

4. The experimental investigations of Piaget and Inhelder (1958) into the powers of reasoning employed by children at different age levels, when confronted by scientific problems, have shown that an ability to deal with problems involving several elements or variables, does not come about until late adolescence. The characteristic qualities of formal-operational thought are only acquired gradually over several years, and it is unlikely that children can employ hypotheses to organise their explanations, as opposed to mere description prior to the age of 13+ (Peel, 1965; 1968).

The gradual emergence of a capacity for formal-operational thought is thus seen to be critical. In an attempt to distinguish successive levels of maturity of judgment within the overall framework of development, a set of geographical case-studies based on the criteria outlined above, were designed for presentation to a group of children spanning the age range 9 to 16 (Rhys, 1966).

2. The Investigation

1. The Subjects

The children who took part in this enquiry numbered 120 in all (CA range 9.8 to 16.3 years; MA range 8.6 to 17.6 years). The details are as follows:

a) 100 pupils were in attendance at a large urban secondary modern boys' school. Twenty were selected from each year group (years 1 to 5), evenly distributed between the 'A' and 'B' streams.
b) 20 pupils were selected from a nearby junior school, and covered a cross section of ability in the top two years.

The mental ages of each of these pupils were obtained from the Simplex Group Intelligence Test and Raven's Progressive Matrices.

2. The Experimental Method

Before a satisfactory format could be contrived a pilot-study was carried out with a limited, though representative, group of children. The study units finally selected focused attention on five major themes where the problems raised would be meaningful for the area under consideration.

1. Soil erosion in an Andes valley.
2. Masai migration in East Africa.
3. Commercial grain-growing in Manitoba.
4. Intensive rice cultivation in Japan.
5. Crofter farming in the Outer Hebrides.

Spatial remoteness was deliberately emphasised in each case, so that contact with reality was dependent upon transmitted information. The necessary data were conveyed by means of prose passages (problems 1 and 4), maps (problems 2, 4 and 5), photographs (problems 3 and 4), and statistical tables (problem 5). Provided the children could comprehend and interpret this material, it would be possible for them to identify significant elements, note key relationships, and achieve a reasoned explanation. The questions asked focused attention upon basic issues, in order to crystallize reasoning, and to compel interpretation in terms of the dominant factors operating within each problem situation.

3. Procedure

The problems were conducted on a group basis, except where the use of photographs compelled an individual presentation. It was never convenient to work through more than two problems on any given occasion, due to the length of time required. All details of the test material were checked through with the children before a single question was put. Each question was stated in a standardised form. During the individual sessions supplementary questions were employed as required to clarify any apparent ambiguity of response.

3. Response Analysis

For the purpose of analysis each problem was taken in turn, and the responses to each question were examined as an independent sequence. Responses were grouped together into categories or sub-categories whenever they conformed to a recurrent pattern, which appeared to constitute a significant stage in the overall sequence of development.

The general pattern of analysis initially applied to each response sequence was as follows:

1. An inability to comprehend the environmental context under review, where answers involved tautology, irrelevance and denial of premises. The questions were frequently related to personal experience and individual preferences, with scant consideration given to the reality of the situation.

2. A descriptive analysis conducted in terms of the presented data with gradual recognition and discovery of the essential features of the problem-situations. There was a gradual progression from unqualified inferences dependent upon circumstantial evidence, to a more adequate analysis where the children made use of concepts and generalisations standing outside the presented data to qualify or extend their answers. This very broad category embraced such a wide range of responses that it had to be subdivided. In particular, a fundamental distinction emerged between those who focused on an isolated piece of evidence, and those whose answers combined several relevant factors.

3. Here there was a difference of form dominated by variations on the following verbal pattern.

If he/they did/did not undertake a certain course of action, then a certain result would/would not follow.

Although this category could be identified at the first analysis for 10 out of the 12 response sequences, it could not be sustained as an independent category, either statistically or by the quality of judgment expressed, and it had to be fused with the most mature level of response present in category two.

4. A more sophisticated and elaborate analysis organised in terms of a positive judgment, assertion or hypothesis, to which the available evidence could be related to substantiate the general argument.

Once a response sequence had been analysed on this basis, the responses were placed in rank correlation related to chronological age, and to the mental ages derived from the two intelligence tests. Each sequence was then checked by an independent judge. The resultant correlation coefficients ranged from 0.95 to 0.98, and thus granted a high degree of reliability to the response analyses. The significance of difference between successive pairs was then calculated for each sequence. Where the derived critical ratios threw doubt upon certain of the final gradings, they were carefully reconsidered, and whenever it seemed wise to do so categories were combined.

The problems posed by the various case-studies differed in their complexity and level of difficulty. Although the final, consolidated, response sequences inevitably reflected this variety, four major response levels constantly recurred as a consistent underlying pattern (Table 12.1).

Table 12.1: Major Response Levels (Approximate Age-Levels Given in Months)

Category	CA	MA (Raven)	Principal features
1	up to 132.0	up to 144.0	Not really orientated
2	148.6	156.6	Single piece of evidence; reality oriented
3	156.6	168.6	Limited deductive analysis; items of evidence combined
4	168.6 and upwards	180.6 and upwards	Deduction from a guiding hypothesis; comprehensive judgment

Two major variants within this general pattern are worthy of note:
(i)   It was occasionally possible to subdivide category two (Table 12.3). This usually applied when a problem was presented on an individual basis. When questioned further some pupils could not develop their first limited response. On the other hand, others could sustain the direction of their response, and qualify or extend the answer first given. This distinction was normally masked when a problem was presented on a group basis.

(ii)   Where a sub-division of category four could be sustained (Table 12.2). This applied when a genuine difference in the quality of response occurred, related to an extension or refinement of the general argument.

4. Growth in the Maturity of Judgment

In contrast to the findings of Carpenter (1955) and Lodwick (1958) the results of this research displayed a closer relationship between the successive levels of development and chronological age, than with mental age. The only exceptions to this general tendency appeared to arise:

a) Between categories one and two, where the degree of comprehension displayed was inclined to fluctuate.
b) Where category four was sub-divided. Here the significant difference between successive category levels depended more on mental than on chronological age.

In an attempt to assess the relative importance of chronological as opposed to mental age, in relation to the development of thought, the final tables of analysis obtained for each of the response sequences were considered as a group. The correlation coefficients between the categories of development and the mental ages were then calculated, also those between the categories of development and the chronological ages. Chronological age was then tested for significance against the mental ages derived from Raven's Progressive Matrices,[†] producing a t-value of 2.35. Secondly, chronological age was tested for significance against the mental ages derived from the Simplex Intelligence Test, producing a t-value of 5.18. In each case the resultant difference proved to be greater than the 5 per cent level of probability.

Consequently, the general implication is that in terms of these problems the development of thought between the concrete-operational level on the one hand, and the level of hypothetico-deductive reasoning on the other, would appear to be more a function of chronological age than of intellectual maturity. This would seem to support Peel's argument that where the successive levels of thought are defined in terms of their qualitative differences, then mental age which is a measure of quantity rather than quality must, to some extent, be reduced in value 'as a criterion of growth against which to test the real temporal setting of Piaget's sequence of thought growth' (Peel, 1970, p. 177).

5. An Extended Analysis

Within an environmental context a process of dynamic interaction is at work, involving a complex of physical, social and economic forces, where all the active elements are modified over time. Geographical analysis is not related to a static situation, but has to take note of a balance of forces which is liable to change, at times approaching a state of equilibrium, at others propelled into a state of flux by some qualitative change in the total structure.

The capacity to think in terms of 'dynamic balance, involving the potentiality of action, its cancellation and possible compensation by other action', does not apparently emerge until middle or late adolescence (Peel, 1965, p. 162). The adolescent's emergent capacity to contend with equilibrium-disequilibrium situations in geography can be examined by reference to some of the response sequences derived from this enquiry. The resolution of the associated problems and their explanation is directly related to a qualitative advance in the pupil's level of intellectual functioning, and the achievement of equilibrium in a personal sense.

1. The Masai

This problem made use of a single map to display the essential information. The map showed that the tribesmen moved their cattle twice yearly from the north-west highlands to the base of the Rift Valley in the south-east. Shading indicated that the highest land had permanent water-holes and nearly 50 inches of rain per year, whilst the valley floor had an annual rainfall of under 20 inches and temporary water-holes. Arrows indicated a migration pattern tied to the heaviest rainfall periods (March–June; October–November), with movement to the valley in February and September, and a return to the highlands during July and December. The children were then asked why the Masai followed this seasonal pattern of movement.

An effective explanation would require some understanding of the extant state of dynamic equilibrium, in which they key variables (i.e. the areal and the seasonal distribution of rainfall) are interrelated on a cyclical basis to conserve the essential supplies of water and forage.

Most of the youngest children responded concretely to the dominant piece of visual evidence, namely, the area of heavy rainfall above 7000 feet. The 50 inches total was considered in isolation as a hazard ('Because . . . it would flood them'), to be offset through flight. It was evident that they could neither interpret the data meaningfully, nor consider the situation as a whole. Isohyets, like contour lines, are essentially abstract concepts expressed in symbolic form. Such material has to be interpreted at the conceptual level, whereby past learning and experience can be related to current perception.

Successive categories were more realistic, where responses were based on a descriptive analysis of the material evidence. There would be a serious attempt to relate the sequence of movement to the seasonal pattern, followed by a deduction derived from this sequence, e.g. 'they move therefore one month before the rainfall'. It was widely assumed that the possibility of flooding could be cancelled out through careful anticipation and suitable avoiding action. The fact that each area has its heaviest rainfall at the same time was ignored, and a constructive reconciliation of the underlying causative factors was not possible.

Only at the most mature level of response could the children detect and interweave the controlling variables as an integrated whole. There is now a change of form as well as a carefully reasoned reconciliation of the factors upon which the contrived state of equilibrium is dependent. Instead of following the data on a descriptive basis, a hypothesis is put forward based upon reasoned scanning of the evidence available, prior to manipulating this data to substantiate the argument.

e.g. The Masai migrate twice a year . . . to get the best seasonal rainfall they can . . . (movement details) . . . The reason why they keep moving is that the waterholes in the valley are non-permanent, but the waterholes in the highlands are. Another reason for their task is that when they are in the valley using the grass and water, the grass and water in the highlands is building up. This means that when they return to the highlands, the water and food is there for them. This method keeps repeating.

It is worthy of note that whilst every response placed in the fourth category showed deduction from a guiding hypothesis, only 11 pupils were able to break free from the 50 inches rainfall fixation and achieve an undistorted judgment (Table 12.2).

Table 12.2: Masai Migration Problem (Ages given in months)

Response category	n	CA		MA (Raven)		MA (Simplex)	
		m	$\acute{o}$	m	$\acute{o}$	m	$\acute{o}$
1	27	132.6	10.4	137.2	14.9	147.4	18.3
2	21	143.3	11.3	150.5	13.5	166.0	15.2
3	25	158.5	9.9	170.3	17.7	175.1	12.2
4i	36	179.0	10.4	186.6	19.9	185.7	13.5
4ii	11	181.7	7.5	205.2	16.6	197.0	10.8

2. The Prairie Farmers

A self-sufficient economy, as pursued by the Masai, can be considered as a closed system. But, where regional specialisation is pursued within an expanded trading system, as exemplified by the prairie farmers (unit 3), the part cannot be judged effectively if examined in isolation. The area selected for study was located on a map of the Canadian farming regions, and a set of oblique aerial photographs conveyed the essential features of the local economy. Most of the critical issues arose from a study of the first plate, which showed a small market centre surrounded by an apparently endless plain.

The children were first asked: 'Is it wise for the farmer to grow one crop only over such a very large area?'

The apparent conflict between the amount of land available and the deliberate concentration on a single crop, could only be resolved by reference to marketing and locational factors not directly attributable to the observed physical conditions. Alternative possible outcomes had to be invoked, where the economies of scale and farming efficiency might compensate for the risks attached to the controlling mode of action.

Two distinct trends were evident in the qualitative advance from the least to the most mature level of response.

(i) Egocentric answers gradually gave way to an objective appraisal of the total situation. At first human convenience was considered to be sufficient justification in itself and environmental constraints were ignored. Second level judgments were content biased, though expressed in propositional form, embodying an assumed link between the solitary element seized upon and the pattern of land-use under consideration (e.g. that the flat plain favoured mechanisation). Responses placed at the third level remained descriptive in form, though the complementary balance of cause—effect relationships were now made explicit. Thus, the profit held to accrue from mass-production could only apply 'if there's a demand for it'. Finally, at the upper level, a co-ordinated degree of deductive analysis could be derived from a carefully balanced judgment, culminating in a firm conclusion.

> e.g. Normally, No. For something could easily go wrong with the crop in a particular year, and they would lose everything. But . . . a great demand for it would be necessary before they can grow on a scale like this, and they need transportation to get it away to the world market.

(ii) This objectivity of judgment turns fundamentally upon a clear understanding of the scale of the enterprise under consideration. Many of the younger children responded perceptually to the visual evidence of space without being able to discern its geographical significance. The obvious immensity of the plains shown in the photograph did indeed provide the vital key, but only if it could call upon ideas and concepts previously acquired and independently formed to demonstrate the significance of the observed concentration on a single crop. The pupil has to be conversant with the advantages that can be derived from a concentration on a single product within the framework of international trade.

The cumulative advance in the pupil's cognitive organisation of space and his conception of relative location, could not be inferred directly from the responses made to the first question. The underlying pattern became quite explicit, however, when the children were asked:

Why has this small town grown up just here, where the main road and railway cross each other?

Two major sources of difficulty were revealed by the responses made by the younger children.

(a)   They were unable to interpret and interrelate the information conveyed within the frame of the photograph.

(b)   They regarded the area encompassed by the picture to be discrete and self-contained, unrelated to the larger area of which it formed a part.

The resolution of this degree of spatial confusion can be traced across five successive levels of response (Table 12.3).

(i)   The youngest children simply could not structure the spatial field under examination, and advantages were granted to the town's site that could apply equally well to any point on this uniform and monotonous landscape.

e.g. 'Because the land is flat and they build on flat land usually.'

(ii)   By 11 years of age both the landscape and human action could be organised within the photograph's frame of reference, in terms of the perspective granted by the camera.

e.g. 'It would be situated in the middle and have the same amount of land on either side.'

(iii)   At 12 years the camera's viewpoint is no longer held to be paramount since the town can be regarded as the destination for the crop produced by each individual farmer. The town is viewed from the stand-point of each farm within the portrayed scene, and the children are at least partially successful in coordinating perpectives from a point-of-view set within a situation wholly detached from personal experience.

> e.g. 'Because you can get the wheat here by road and rail, and seeing as how the railway goes straight through it can pick up all the wheat from the farms.'

Whilst this particular segment of space could now be related to an extended spatial plane, the area shown could not be located with complete certainty until the children could call upon external evidence to place the local area within an abstract frame of reference.

(iv) By about 13½ years the answers given made frequent reference to the Great Lakes, the St. Lawrence river, ocean transport and the British market. Thus the observed area could now be related to an extended spatial framework, through the use of landmarks culled from the reference map, or knowledge gained from classroom tuition.

(v) Finally, at 14½ years and above, the pupils displayed a secure grasp of the overall spatial context governing local action, and could relate this prairie area to the wider spatial framework of Canada as a whole, and the world beyond.

A realistic judgment was not possible, therefore, until the children could rationalize the interrelationship of the observed phenomena within the projective setting provided by the camera, and build this discrete segment of space into an extended Euclidean construct. It is considered that these closely related requirements are dependent upon the application

Table 12.3: Prairie Farmers' Problem (Question 2: Town Location)

Response category	n	CA		MA (Raven)		MA (Simplex)	
		m	o	m	o	m	o
1	16	128.1	8.4	133.4	17.4	142.5	19.6
2	14	131.7	12.7	144.7	14.1	161.8	17.7
3	21	150.2	9.5	152.2	13.9	163.8	12.2
4	36	163.4	13.7	173.5	15.9	173.8	14.8
5	33	181.6	10.1	194.9	22.2	192.7	12.9

at the formal-operational level, of those concepts of projective and Euclidean space, which would have been formed earlier at the concrete-operational level (Rhys, 1972).

6. Conclusions

The distinctive features that characterised the major category levels (Table 12.1), could be detected quite readily in each and every response sequence, even where the problem situations involved a time-related shift of equilibria (i.e. problems 1 and 5). Although this underlying pattern was consistently present it is evident that the various response sequences varied in detail. A comparision of Tables 2 and 3 is sufficient to indicate that the number of responses placed at each level differed from question to question. The answers given by individual children tended to fluctuate between one level and another when checked across all twelve response sequences, apart from a limited number who were stablised either at the first or at the fourth level. What remained invariant was the qualitative sequence of advance from the least to the most mature level of response.

The resolution of geographical problems, through a process of explanation, would seem to require objectivity on two distinct planes. First, in terms of spatial orientation, where some combination of projective and Euclidean concepts has to be employed at an abstract or symbolic level. Secondly, in terms of cutlural orientation whereby due attention is paid to local capacities and traditions when appraising the local decision-taking situation.

At the most mature level of judgment attained by the children engaged in this enquiry, whatever constituted the environmental context under review could be organised as a whole from the outset. These older pupils were able to structure and organise the total spatial field, and effectively interweave the component variables, either within a self-contained unit (e.g. problem 2) or within the context of a more extensive and elaborate structure (e.g. problem 3). At this level human action could be evaluated objectively and critically, where judgments took into account the technical resources and expectations of the local population, and the restraints imposed by their environment as they perceived it. The achievement of equilibrium with respect to symbolic representations of unencountered 'worlds' would seem to be critically dependent upon the emergence of a capacity for hypothetico-deductive reasoning.

References

Blair, D., 'A practical study of the ability of some secondary school pupils to handle the representation of spatial relationships', unpublished Dip.Ed. dissertation, Univ. Liverpool, 1964.

Brookfield, H.C., 'On the environment as perceived', in *Progress in Geography, Vol. I: International Review of Current Research*, edited by C. Board *et al.*, London: Edward Arnold, 1969.

Carpenter, T.E., 'A pilot study for a quantitative investigation of Jean Piaget's original work on concept formation', *Educ. Rev.*, vol. 7, 1955, pp. 142-9.

Everson, J., 'Some aspects of teaching geography through fieldwork', *Geography*, vol. 54, 1969, pp. 423-34.

Graves, N.J., *Geography in Secondary Education*, Geographical Association, 1971.

Hallam, R.N., 'Logical thinking in history', *Educ. Rev.*, vol. 19, 1967, pp. 183-202.

Inhelder, B. and Piaget, J., *The Growth of Logical Thinking from Childhood to Adolescence*, New York: Basic Books, 1958.

Lodwick, A.R., 'An investigation of the question whether the inferences that children draw in learning history correspond with the stages of mental development that Piaget postulates', unpublished Dip.Ed. dissertation, Univ. Birmingham, 1958.

Long, M., 'Research in picture study. The reaction of grammar school pupils to geographical pictures', *Geography*, vol. xlvi, Nov. 1961, pp. 322-37.

Peel, E.A., *The Pupil's Thinking*, London: Oldbourne, 1960.

Peel, E.A., 'Intellectual growth during adolescence', *Educ. Rev.*, vol. 17, June 1965, pp. 169-80.

Peel, E.A., 'Some problems in the psychology of teaching history', in *Studies in the Nature and Teaching of History*, edited by W.H. Burston and D. Thompson, London: Routledge and Kegan Paul, 1967.

Peel, E.A., 'Conceptual learning and explainer thinking', in *Development in Learning*, vol. 2, edited by E.A. Lunzer and J.F. Morris, London: Staples, 1968.

Piaget, J., Inhelder, B. and Szeminska, A., *The Child's Conception of Geometry*, New York: Basic Books, 1960.

Prior, F.M., 'The place of maps in the junior school', unpublished Dip.Ed. dissertation, Univ. Birmingham, 1959.

Rhys, W.T., 'The development of logical thought in the adolescent with reference to the teaching of geography in the secondary school', unpublished M.Ed. thesis, Univ. Birmingham, 1966.

Rhys, W.T., 'The development of logical thinking', in *New Movements in the Study and Teaching of Geography*, edited by N.G. Graves, London: Temple Smith, 1972.

Scarfe, N.V., 'Games, models and reality in the teaching of geography in school', *Geography*, vol. 56, July 1971, pp. 191-205.

Vernon, M.D., *The Psychology of Perception*, London: Penguin Books, 1962.

13 THE FORMATION OF HISTORICAL CONCEPTS THROUGH CONTEXTUAL CUES

W. A. da Silva

Source: *Birmingham Educational Review*, 24 (3) (June 1972), pp. 197-211.

1. Introduction

None of the declared aims of teaching history could be achieved by any means other than a proper understanding of the subject matter of history, which not yielding itself to easy experimentation on inspection compels both teacher and student to depend very heavily on language in communicating and acquiring historical knowledge.

Peel (1967, p. 166) refers to a possible major source of confusion in studying history. It would arise when 'new concepts with new unfamiliar names are introduced into connected texts and are not well defined in the process'.

In studying secondary school history, the conceptions of political and economic theory keep on constantly cropping up and they present difficulties for the immature pupil to grasp. A child's vocabulary is very limited and the words that signify these conceptions do not communicate very much. If their referents are not fully and properly explained confused and chaotic thinking is bound to result, making historical imagination impossible.

Quite apart from adequate definition and exemplification Peel (1967, p. 171) shows that there are 'other barriers to understanding caused by more involved factors', namely the initial absence and subsequent slow growth of qualities of thinking including rational thought and logico-structural process.

The only basic psychological research undertaken in this direction is the study by Werner and Kaplan (1952) on how children reached the meaning of words embedded in sentences. This pioneering study by Werner and Kaplan can be said to be only partially successful in bringing into the open the developmental aspects of the acquisition of word-meanings. The capacity to attain word-meanings cannot be said to operate alone by itself. It should depend to a great extent on the qualitative growth of the general thinking capacity. It does not appear that Werner and Kaplan in their study have fully explored the possible connections between the various stages in the acquisition of word-meanings and the growth of logico-abstract thinking.

2. The Present Study

The present study was undertaken to investigate the processes by which adolescent students ascribe meanings to coded words standing in for historical terms, going on contextual cues alone. A word-context test consisting of ten passages was administered to 160 students taken in equal proportions from those receiving selective and those receiving non-selective education in England. The subjects were also differentiated by age, the range sampled being from 12 to 16 inclusive.

The passages test was designed so as to carry one artificial word embedded in each passage. The subject reading the paragraph is expected to arrive at the meaning of the artificial word. Each of these artificial words signifies an economic or political conception arising in the learning of secondary school history. Here is one passage used in the research:

Artificial word: MALMIR (slump – depression)

The years that followed the victory of Waterloo were some of the worst that Britain ever passed through. The 'false and bloated prosperity' of the War, as Cobbett called it, gave way to a terrible malmir. The Government no longer needed to buy huge quantities of munitions and clothing for the army and the Allies; the people of Europe after more than twenty years of war, were too poor to buy the goods that British manufacturers would have liked to sell; instead the foreign governments often used their discharged soldiers to make their own goods.

The testing procedure was basically the same as that adopted by Werner and Kaplan. The subject was informed that he would be presented with ten words which he never heard before; that these words were used in a little island many thousands of miles away and were not spoken anywhere else; and that these ten words would be presented to him one at a time, each embedded in a paragraph. The interviewer concluded: 'I want you to try to find out what each of these words means.'

When faced with the task of comprehending the meaning of an unknown word embedded in a passage, subjects either made no response at all or made a response falling into one of four types which were identified as follows:

Logically restricted responses
Circumstantial conceptualisation
Logical possibilities
Deductive conceptualisation

It is only at the stage of deductive conceptualisation that a subject is able to deduce the correct meaning of the unknown word from the cues available.

3. Analysis

(i)   Logically Restricted Responses

These immature responses are not oriented to reality but are tautological, inconsistent, directly contradictory, irrelevant or otherwise irrational and display a gross lack of comprehension of the passage. The subjects responding in this category seem to be put off by irrelevancies both of form and content. The responses often take the form of casual irrelevant guesses or bizarre responses.

The following example illustrates this category of response in respect of the aforementioned passage.

Malmir: It meant a terrible disaster to the people of Britain, it gave way to a terrible disaster as it would say (age 13).

This and other similar responses seem to be solely dependent upon one single word occurring in the context, sometimes immediately preceding the unknown word.

(ii)   Circumstantial Conceptualisation

This form of signification is characterised by attempted solution in terms of one aspect of the presented data and failure to grasp the essential features of the problem. It is an attempt at understanding based on a single piece of evidence picked out from the context supporting a simple unqualified response. Subjects do not show signs of being able to use many of the material cues given and are content with making very limited trivial responses.

The following examples illustrate this category of response in respect of the aforementioned passage:

(a)   It is a disease, because the soldiers that came back from the war might have brought back diseases with them (age 14).
(b)   I think it means disaster, because the government was poor and after a war you can't come out all that prosperous after having to fork out a lot of money (age 15).
(c)   I think it is a famine, because all the money had been spent on guns and ammunitions. Therefore there was no money left to pay for

the goods (age 14).

(d)   Poverty, because they did not have any money after fighting the war (age 14).

(e)   Malmir means loss, because the people of Europe were too poor to buy the goods.

(iii)   Logical Possibilities

In this category of response subjects engage in realistic appraisal showing capacity to combine two or more pieces of evidence and ability to relate cause and effect. Possible alternatives and competing solutions are offered and possible explanations invoked. One sees here the beginnings of comprehensive exploration of the material taking account of more than one factor, as well as of generality, abstraction and penetrativeness.

The following examples illustrate this category of response in respect of the aforementioned passage:

(a)   The word 'malmir' means hardship. I think this is so because of the fact that the government couldn't sell our goods, and the countries that bought off us before now couldn't afford our goods or they now made them themselves, so Britain became a poor country (age 15).

(b)   Uprising, if Britain could not sell what the manufacturers had made then some men might be out of work. The army would not be needed for fighting and so they might get sacked. The people of Britain might think that the government had done nothing to try and improve the situation and go against the government (age 13).

(c)   Redundancy, I think so because it is said that Europe was too poor to buy things that Britain made because of twenty years of war. Also it said that European people used to make their own clothes (age 13).

(d)   Unemployment, because with the factories having been turned into munition factories they could no longer send trade to other countries who found other sources to get the products and with mass unemployment because of the men coming back from the war and the closing of the munitions factories (age 15).

(e)   Poverty; when the people from the munitions factories were discharged from it they had to find jobs elsewhere and this was hard to do. The shortage of jobs meant a rise in unemployment and poverty (age 16).

(iv)   Deductive Conceptualisation

In responses falling in this category the subject generally explores the content of the passage in almost its entirety in a deductive way and draws

266   *The Formation of Historical Concepts*

integrated and reasoned inferences taking account essentially of the problem. The primary characteristic of responses in this category is the deductive reasoning or sustained argument from the basis of assumed hypothesis resting on general rules or principles developed inductively or deduced analytically. The following instances illustrate this category in respect of the aforementioned passage:

(a)   Depression, this is probably so because after wars, etc., the government no longer needs to buy stuff and many men are unemployed so leading to a general depression of industry etc. (age 15).

(b)   Slump; after most wars the extensive munitions factories close down or are converted to make cycles and other items like this. So many people lose their jobs, which they held during the war. Secondly, a large amount of soldiers returning home from the war need jobs and there is not the demand in industry to create places in factories for ex-soldiers; so a slump occurs (age 16).

(c)   Depression, the country was in an awful state. They had been promised better wages etc. but they were denied all these privileges. After the war had finished, the country was therefore in a slump of industry as men were no longer needed to produce weapons of war (age 16).

(d)   Depression, after any war there is some sort of depression, as many new industries formed during the war were out of business when the war finished; thus many people were out of work (age 15).

(e)   Slump, after the war Britain found it could not sell the stuff it could before the war as other countries took over the market in other countries. This made industry poor. The word 'slump' fits in place of 'malmir' as this happens to most countries after the war (age 16).

4. Results

The responses were evaluated and classified by a panel of six judges including the writer and a sufficient level of agreement among the judges was established statistically.

Table 13.1 shows the frequency distribution of different response categories between grammar school and non-grammar school subjects in respect of all 10 passages.

A Pearson X^2† test was carried out to test the null hypothesis that the two attributes, type of subject and category of response, are independent. It was established beyond the .001 level of confidence that a statistical association does exist between the two attributes. Non-grammar school subjects make a high proportion of logically restricted responses while

Table 13.1: Frequency of Different Response Categories in Two Types of Subjects

Category of response	Grammar school (N = 80)	Non-grammar school (N = 80)	Total
No response	35	62	97
Logically restricted response	394	544	938
Circumstantial conceptualisation	118	76	194
Logical possibilities	62	30	92
Deductive conceptualisation	191	88	279

Table 13.2: Frequency of Different Response Categories in the Five Age Groups

Category of response	Age 12 (N = 20)	Age 13 (N = 40)	Age 14 (N = 40)	Age 15 (N = 40)	Age 16 (N = 20)
No response	8	14	26	38	11
Logically restricted response	142	275	252	189	80
Circumstantial conceptualisation	20	37	42	62	33
Logical possibilities	9	24	17	35	7
Deductive conceptualisation	21	50	63	76	69

grammar school subjects show a high proportion of instances of deductive conceptualisation.

Significant differences also exist in the frequency distributions of response categories among the five age groups tested, logically restricted responses decreasing and instances of deductive conceptualisation increasing, with age. Table 13.2 shows the number of responses falling in each category given by subjects of each age group in respect of all the passages.

The chi square for significance of difference among all age groups came out significant beyond the .001 level. The different age groups were next taken two by two and the corresponding chi-squares computed. The results of all these tests are summarised in Table 13.3. The entry in each cell relates to the result of the chi-square test for significance of difference between the age group represented by column and the age group represented by row.

Table 13.3: Results of Tests of Significance of Pairwise Differences among Composite Age Groups

Age group	13	14	15	16
12	N.S.	N.S.	P.001	P.001
13		N.S.	P.001	P.001
14			P.001	P.001
15				P.001

On this statistical evidence it seems clear that there is no real difference among the age groups 12, 13 and 14 in regard to the number of responses of different categories. However, there is a significant difference between each of the age groups 12, 13 and 14 on the one hand and each of the groups age 15 and 16 on the other. Also a significant difference exists between the two age groups of 15 and 16. The breaking point is seen to lie between the ages of 14 and 15.

The data were next examined separately for the pupils receiving selective and non-selective education respectively.

Non-Selective Education Pupils

The chi square for significance of differences among all age groups was significant beyond the .001 level. The different age levels were next taken two by two and the corresponding chi squares computed. The results of all these tests are summarised in Table 13.4. The entry in each cell relates to the test of significance of difference between the age group represented by column and that represented by row.

Once again the breaking point is seen to fall between the ages of 14 and 15.

Table 13.4: Results of Tests of Significance of Pairwise Difference among Age Groups — Non-Grammar Type

Age group	13	14	15	16
12	N.S.	N.S.	P.01	N.S.
13		N.S.	P.001	P.05
14			P.001	P.05
15				N.S.

Selective Education Pupils

The chi square for differences among all age groups was significant beyond the .001 level. Next chi squares were computed to test the significance of all pairwise differences and Table 13.5 summarises the results. The entry in each cell relates to the test of significance of difference between the age group represented by column and that represented by row.

Table 13.5: Results of Tests of Significance of Pairwise Differences among Age Groups — Grammar Type

Age groups	13	14	15	16
12	N.S.	P.05	P.001	P.001
13		P.001	P.01	P.001
14			P.01	P.001
15				P.001

In an attempt to locate the point at which the precise break occurs two more chi squares were computed, taking groups of age levels collectively, namely

(a) Age levels 12 and 13 against age levels 14, 15 and 16
(b) Age levels 12, 13 and 14 against age levels 15 and 16.

Both these chi squares are significant beyond the .001 level. However, on the strength of the magnitude of the chi square it may be said that the dividing line between the age levels of 14 and 15 is more marked and definite than the dividing line between the age levels of 13 and 14.

5. Discussion

The scheme of classification evolved here is very strikingly similar to Peel's scheme of levels in the upward progression of thought to explainer thinking. Peel's main categories of thought both as regards their respective characteristics and the total evolutionary order find confirmation in the present analysis.

The evidence from this study may be taken as strongly supporting Peel's (1967, p. 165) assertion: '. . . much of school history is taught through texts and new words are often introduced for fresh ideas and institutions mainly through contextual passages without a precise definition being given. This makes for erroneous concepts.'

Peel (1965, p. 178) succinctly points to the crux of the problem as follows: '. . . the child can receive real information by such means only if he is in a state where he can understand this information. This state requires that the new information is presented in a form demanding not more than the structure of action which the child has already formed. The child will make of the information what he can by virtue of his particular level of development — but this may not be what the adult intends. Hence the so-called discrepancy between language and thought.'

The problem may be specially present in connection with history texts written with the 'style' and not simplicity, uppermost in mind, as in a particular work where the author (left unidentified here) in the Preface writes: 'Although in general, the limitations of the youthful vocabulary have been kept in mind throughout the book, there has been no attempt to write in mono-syllables for the illiterate, a course which would have been bound to destroy all style and with it all interest.' The assumption here that the interest of the student is directly related to the verbose professional style of the author is, to say the least, highly debatable.

References

Peel, E.A. (1965), 'Intellectual growth during adolescence', *Educational Review*, vol. 17, no. 3, pp. 169-80.
Peel, E.A. (1967), 'Some problems in the psychology of history teaching, I and II', in Burston, W.H. and Thompson, D. (eds.), *Studies in the Nature and Teaching of History*, London: Routledge & Kegan Paul.
Werner, H. and Kaplan, E. (1952), 'The acquisition of word meanings: a developmental study', *Monogr. Soc. Res. Child Dev.* (1950), 15, no. I (whole no. 51).

SECTION FOUR: EDUCATIONAL APPLICATIONS

Introduction

In this final section we turn to the way in which the kinds of ideas described in earlier sections could be, and have been, applied to the classroom situation.

In the first chapter J.S. Bruner develops some general ideas about the relationship between psychology and teaching, in an attempt to move towards what he describes as a theory of instruction. The remaining four chapters are all concerned with major curriculum projects of recent years.

Ray Derricott and Alan Blyth and others were responsible for the Schools Council project on history, geography and social science for children from eight to thirteen. In this project, which came to be known as 'Time, Place and Society', they developed an approach to teaching this age-group in a way which took account of their developmental level, and this is described in the second chapter in this section.

The third and fourth chapters are both about science education, though Wynne Harlen's concerns primary school and Michael Shayer's secondary schools. Wynne Harlen was the director of the Schools Council project known as 'Progress in Learning Science', in which she attempted to devise procedures which would enable a teacher both to monitor an individual child's progress in the scientific area and to devise learning experiences for the child that were matched to his current level of understanding. In her chapter she describes these procedures and their rationale. In his chapter Michael Shayer looks at one of the Nuffield secondary science courses, the 'O' level course in physics. He argues that the kinds of reasoning demanded at various points in this course are often mismatched to the developmental level of the pupils as assessed in the Piagetian framework, and that this mismatch is a prime cause of the difficulties such pupils have with the course.

The final chapter in this section, and in the book, concerns the relationship between cognitive development and mathematics education. As well as a general discussion of the issues involved in this, Margaret Brown looks at two projects in particular. The first of these is the Nuffield maths project, during the course of which a 'concept map' was drawn up in an attempt to show the ways in which mathematical ideas appropriate to primary school children were interrelated and hence to give guidance as to the sequence in which these should be developed in the classroom. The second is the ongoing SSRC 'Concepts in Secondary Mathematics and Science' project in which both she and Michael Shayer are involved and whose mathematical swing is attempting to extend this Nuffield map upwards by finding out just what mathematical ideas secondary school children of different ages do or do not understand.

14 NOTES ON A THEORY OF INSTRUCTION

J. S. Bruner

Source: Chapter 3 (part) in J.S. Bruner, *Towards a Theory of Instruction* (Harvard University Press, 1966).

In this essay I shall attempt to develop a few simple theorems about the nature of instruction. I shall try to illustrate them by reference to the teaching and learning of mathematics. The choice of mathematics as a mode of illustration is not premised on the typicality of mathematics, for mathematics is restricted to well-formed problems and does not concern itself with empirical proof by either experiment or observation. Nor is this an attempt to elucidate mathematical teaching as such, for that would be beyond my competence. Rather, mathematics offers an accessible and simple example for what, perforce, will be a simplified set of propositions about teaching and learning. And there are data available from mathematics learning that have some bearing on our problem.

The plan is as follows. First some characteristics of a theory of instruction will be set forth, followed by a statement of some highly general theorems about the instructional process. I shall then attempt, in the light of specific observations of mathematics learning, to convert these general propositions into workable hypotheses. In conclusion, some remarks will be made on the nature of research in support of curriculum making.

The Nature of a Theory of Instruction

A theory of instruction is *prescriptive* in the sense that it sets forth rules concerning the most effective way of achieving knowledge or skill. By the same token, it provides a yardstick for criticizing or evaluating any particular way of teaching or learning.

A theory of instruction is a *normative* theory. It sets up criteria and states the conditions for meeting them. The criteria must have a high degree of generality: for example, a theory of instruction should not specify in *ad hoc* fashion the conditions for efficient learning of third-grade arithmetic; such conditions should be derivable from a more general view of mathematics learning.

One might ask why a theory of instruction is needed, since psychology already contains theories of learning and of development. But theories of learning and of development are descriptive rather than prescriptive. They

273

tell us what happened after the fact: for example, that most children of six do not yet possess the notion of reversibility. A theory of instruction, on the other hand, might attempt to set forth the best means of leading the child toward the notion of reversibility. A theory of instruction, in short, is concerned with how what one wishes to teach can best be learned, with improving rather than describing learning.

This is not to say that learning and developmental theories are irrelevant to a theory of instruction. In fact, a theory of instruction must be concerned with both learning and development and must be congruent with those theories of learning and development to which it subscribes.

A theory of instruction has four major features.

First, a theory of instruction should specify the experiences which most effectively implant in the individual a predisposition toward learning — learning in general or a particular type of learning. For example, what sorts of relationships with people and things in the preschool environment will tend to make the child willing and able to learn when he enters school?

Second, a theory of instruction must specify the ways in which a body of knowledge should be structured so that it can be most readily grasped by the learner. 'Optimal structure' refers to a set of propositions from which a larger body of knowledge can be generated, and it is characteristic that the formulation of such structure depends upon the state of advance of a particular field of knowledge. The nature of different optimal structures will be considered in more detail shortly. Here it suffices to say that since the merit of a structure depends upon its power for *simplifying information*, for *generating new propositions*, and for *increasing the manipulability of a body of knowledge*, structure must always be related to the status and gifts of the learner. Viewed in this way, the optimal structure of a body of knowledge is not absolute but relative.

Third, a theory of instruction should specify the most effective sequences in which to present the materials to be learned. Given, for example, that one wishes to teach the structure of modern physical theory, how does one proceed? Does one present concrete materials first in such a way as to elicit questions about recurrent regularities? Or does one begin with a formalized mathematical notation that makes it simpler to represent regularities later encountered? What results are in fact produced by each method? And how describe the ideal mix? The question of sequence will be treated in more detail later.

Finally, a theory of instruction should specify the nature and pacing of rewards and punishments in the process of learning and teaching. Intuitively it seems quite clear that as learning progresses there is a point at which it is better to shift away from extrinsic rewards, such as a teacher's praise, toward the intrinsic rewards inherent in solving a complex problem for oneself. So, too, there is a point at which immediate reward for performance should be replaced by deferred reward. The timing of the shift from extrinsic to intrinsic and from immediate to deferred reward is poorly understood and obviously important. Is it the case, for example, that wherever learning involves the integration of a long sequence of acts, the shift should be made as early as possible from immediate to deferred reward and from extrinsic to intrinsic reward?

It would be beyond the scope of a single essay to pursue in any detail all the four aspects of a theory of instruction set forth above. What I shall attempt to do here is to explore a major theorem concerning each of the four. The object is not comprehensiveness but illustration.

Predispositions

It has been customary, in discussing predispositions to learn, to focus upon cultural, motivational, and personal factors affecting the desire to learn and to undertake problem solving. For such factors are of deep importance. There is, for example, the relation of instructor to student — whatever the formal status of the instructor may be, whether teacher or parent. Since this is a relation between one who possesses something and one who does not, there is always a special problem of authority involved in the instructional situation. The regulation of this authority relationship affects the nature of the learning that occurs, the degree to which a learner develops an independent skill, the degree to which he is confident of his ability to perform on his own, and so on. The relations between one who instructs and one who is instructed is never indifferent in its effect upon learning. And since the instructional process is essentially social — particularly in its early stages when it involves at least a teacher and a pupil — it is clear that the child, especially if he is to cope with school, must have minimal mastery of the social skills necessary for engaging in the instructional process.

There are differing attitudes toward intellectual activity in different social classes, the two sexes, different age groups, and different ethnic groupings. These culturally transmitted attitudes also pattern the use of mind. Some cultural traditions are, by count, more successful than others in the production of scientists, scholars, and artists. Anthropology and psychology investigate the ways a 'tradition' or 'role' affects attitudes toward the use of mind. A theory of instruction concerns itself, rather, with the issue of how best to utilize a given cultural pattern in achieving particular instructional ends.

Indeed, such factors are of enormous importance. But we shall concentrate here on a more cognitive illustration: upon the predisposition to explore alternatives.

Since learning and problem solving depend upon the exploration of alternatives, instruction must facilitate and regulate the exploration of alternatives on the part of the learner.

There are three aspects to the exploration of alternatives, each of them related to the regulation of search behavior. They can be described in shorthand terms as *activation, maintenance*, and *direction*. To put it another way, exploration of alternatives requires something to get it started, something to keep it going, and something to keep it from being random.

The major condition for activating exploration of alternatives in a task is the presence of some optimal level of uncertainty. Curiosity, it has been persuasively argued,[1] is a response to uncertainty and ambiguity. A cut-and-dried routine task provokes little exploration; one that is too uncertain may arouse confusion and anxiety, with the effect of reducing exploration.

The maintenance of exploration, once it has been activated, requires that the benefits from exploring alternatives exceed the risks incurred. Learning something with the aid of an instructor should, if instruction is effective, be less dangerous or risky or painful than learning on one's own. That is to say, the consequences of error, of exploring wrong alternatives, should be rendered less grave under a regimen of instruction, and the yield from the exploration of correct alternatives should be correspondingly greater.

The appropriate direction of exploration depends upon two interacting considerations: a sense of the goal of a task and a knowledge of the relevance of tested alternatives to the achievement of that goal. For exploration to have direction, in short, the goal of the task must be known in some approximate fashion, and the testing of alternatives must yield information as to where one stands with respect to it. Put in briefest form, direction depends upon knowledge of the results of one's tests, and instruction should have an edge over 'spontaneous' learning in providing more of such knowledge.

Structure and the Form of Knowledge

Any idea or problem or body of knowledge can be presented in a form simple enough so that any particular learner can understand it in a recognizable form.

The structure of any domain of knowledge may be characterized in three ways, each affecting the ability of any learner to master it: the *mode of representation* in which it is put, its *economy*, and its effective *power*. Mode, economy, and power vary in relation to different ages, to different 'styles' among learners, and to different subject matters.

Any domain of knowledge (or any problem within that domain of knowledge) can be represented in three ways: by a set of actions appropriate for achieving a certain result (enactive representation); by a set of summary images or graphics that stand for a concept without defining it fully (iconic representation); and by a set of symbolic or logical propositions drawn from a symbolic system that is governed by rules or laws for forming and transforming propositions (symbolic representation). The distinction can most conveniently be made concretely in terms of a balance beam, for we shall have occasion later to consider the use of such an implement in teaching children quadratic functions. A quite young child can plainly act on the basis of the 'principles' of a balance beam, and indicates that he can do so by being able to handle himself on a see-saw. He knows that to get his side to go down farther he has to move out farther from the center. A somewhat older child can represent the balance beam to himself either by a model on which rings can be hung and balanced or by a drawing. The 'image' of the balance beam can be varyingly refined, with fewer and fewer irrelevant details present, as in the typical diagrams in an introductory textbook in physics. Finally, a balance beam can be described in ordinary English, without diagrammatic aids, or it can be even better described mathematically by reference to Newton's Law of Moments in inertial physics. Needless to say, actions, pictures, and symbols vary in difficulty and utility for people of different ages, different backgrounds, different styles. Moreover, a problem in the law would be hard to diagram; one in geography lends itself to imagery. Many subjects, such as mathematics, have alternative modes of representation.

Economy in representing a domain of knowledge relates to the amount of information that must be held in mind and processed to achieve comprehension. The more items of information one must carry to understand something or deal with a problem, the more successive steps one must take in processing that information to achieve a conclusion, and the less the economy. For any domain of knowledge, one can rank summaries of it in terms of their economy. It is more economical (though less powerful) to summarize the American Civil War as a 'battle over slavery' than as 'a struggle between an expanding industrial region and one built upon a class society for control of federal economic policy.' It is more economical to summarize the characteristics of free-falling bodies by the formula $S = \frac{1}{2}gt^2$ than to put a series of numbers into tabular form summarizing a vast set of observations made on different bodies dropped different distances in different gravitational fields. The matter is perhaps best epitomized by two ways of imparting information, one requiring carriage of much information, the other more a pay-as-you-go type of information processing. A highly imbedded sentence is an example of the former (This is the squirrel that the dog that the girl that the man loved fed chased); the contrast case is more economical (This is the man that loved the girl that fed the dog that chased the squirrel).

Economy, as we shall see, varies with mode of representation. But economy is also a function of the sequence in which material is presented or the manner in which it is learned. The case can be exemplified as follows (I am indebted to Dr J. Richard Hayes for this example). Suppose the domain of knowledge consists of available plane service within a twelve-hour period between five cities in the Northeast — Concord, New Hampshire, Albany, New York, Danbury, Connecticut, Elmira, New York, and Boston, Massachusetts. One of the ways in which the knowledge can be imparted is by asking the student to memorize the following list of connections:

> Boston to Concord
> Danbury to Concord
> Albany to Boston
> Concord to Elmira
> Albany to Elmira
> Concord to Danbury
> Boston to Albany
> Concord to Albany

Now we ask, 'What is the shortest way to make a round trip from Albany to Danbury?' The amount of information processing required to answer this question under such conditions is considerable. We increase economy by 'simplifying terms' in certain characteristic ways. One is to introduce an arbitrary but learned order — in this case, an alphabetical one. We rewrite the list:

> Albany to Boston
> Albany to Elmira
> Boston to Albany
> Boston to Concord
> Concord to Albany
> Concord to Danbury

Concord to Elmira
Danbury to Concord

Search then becomes easier, but there is still a somewhat trying sequential property to the task. Economy is further increased by using a diagrammatic notation, and again there are varying degrees of economy in such recourse to the iconic mode. Compare the diagram on the left and the one on the right.

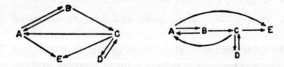

The latter contains at a glance the information that there is only one way from Albany to Danbury and return, that Elmira is a 'trap', and so on. What a difference between this diagram and the first list!

The effective power of any particular way of structuring a domain of knowledge for a particular learner refers to the generative value of *his* set of learned propositions. In the last paragraph, rote learning of a set of connections between cities resulted in a rather inert structure from which it was difficult to generate pathways through the set of cities. Or, to take an example from a recent work,[2] children who are told that 'Mary is taller than Jane, and Betty is shorter than Jane' are often unable to say whether Mary is taller than Betty. One can perfectly well remark that the answer is 'there' in the logic of transitivity. But to say this is to miss the psychological point. Effective power will, to be sure, never exceed the inherent logical generativeness of a subject — although this is an admittedly difficult statement from the point of view of epistemology. In commonsense terms, it amounts to the banality that grasp of a field of knowledge will never be better than the best that can be done with that field of knowledge. The effective power within a particular learner's grasp is what one seeks to discover by close analysis of how in fact he is going about his task of learning. Much of Piaget's research[3] seeks to discover just this property about children's learning and thinking. There is an interesting relation between economy and power. Theoretically, the two are independent: indeed, it is clear that a structure may be economical but powerless. But it is rare for a powerful structuring technique in any field to be uneconomical. This is what leads to the canon of parsimony and the faith shared by many scientists that nature is simple: perhaps it is only when nature can be made reasonably simple that it can be understood. The power of a representation can also be described as its capacity, in the hands of a learner, to connect matters that, on the surface, seem quite separate. This is especially crucial in mathematics. [. . .]

Sequence and its Uses

Instruction consists of leading the learner through a sequence of statements and restatements of a problem or body of knowledge that increase the learner's ability to grasp, transform, and transfer what he is learning. In short, the sequence in which a learner encounters materials within a domain of knowledge affects the difficulty he will have in achieving mastery.

There are usually various sequences that are equivalent in their ease and difficulty for learners. There is no unique sequence for all learners, and the optimum in any particular case will depend upon a variety of factors, including past learning, stage of development, nature of the material, and individual differences.

If it is true that the usual course of intellectual development moves from enactive through iconic to symbolic representation of the world,[4] it is likely that an optimum sequence will progress in the same direction. Obviously, this is a conservative doctrine. For when the learner has a well-developed symbolic system, it may be possible to by-pass the first two stages. But one does so with the risk that the learner may not possess the imagery to fall back on when his symbolic transformations fail to achieve a goal in problem solving.

Exploration of alternatives will necessarily be affected by the sequence in which material to be learned becomes available to the learner. When the learner should be encouraged to explore alternatives widely and when he should be encouraged to concentrate on the implications of a single alternative hypothesis is an empirical question, to which we shall return.

Reverting to the earlier discussion of activation and the maintenance of interest, it is necessary to specify in any sequences the level of uncertainty and tension that must be present to initiate problem-solving behavior, and what conditions are required to keep active problem solving going. This again is an empirical question.

Optimal sequences, as already stated, cannot be specified independently of the criterion in terms of which final learning is to be judged. A classification of such criteria will include at least the following: speed of learning; resistance to forgetting; transferability of what has been learned to new instances; form of representation in terms of which what has been learned is to be expressed; economy of what has been learned in terms of cognitive strain imposed; effective power of what has been learned in terms of its generativeness of new hypotheses and combinations. Achieving one of these goals does not necessarily bring one closer to others; speed of learning, for example, is sometimes antithetical to transfer or to economy.

The Form and Pacing of Reinforcement

Learning depends upon knowledge of results at a time when and at a place where the knowledge can be used for correction. Instruction increases the appropriate timing and placing of corrective knowledge.

'Knowledge of results' is useful or not depending upon when and where the learner receives the corrective information, under what conditions such corrective information can be used, even assuming appropriateness of time and place of receipt, and the form in which the corrective information is received.

Learning and problem solving are divisible into phases. These have been described in various ways by different writers. But all the descriptions agree on one essential feature: that there is a cycle involving the formulation of a testing procedure or trial, the operation of this testing procedure, and the comparison of the results of the test with some criterion. It has variously been called trial-and-error, means-end testing, trial-and-check, discrepancy reduction, test-operate-test-exit (TOTE), hypothesis testing, and so on. These 'units', moreover, can readily be characterized as hierarchically organized: we seek to cancel the unknowns in an equation in order to simplify the expression in order to solve the equation in order to get through the course in order to get our degree in order to get a decent job in order to lead the good life. Knowledge of results should come at that point in a problem-solving episode when the person is comparing the results of his try-out with some criterion of what he seeks to achieve. Knowledge of results given before this point either cannot be understood or must be carried as extra freight in immediate memory. Knowledge given after this point may be too late to guide the choice of a next hypothesis or trial. But knowledge of results must, to be useful, provide information not only on whether or not one's particular act produced success but also on whether the act is in fact leading one through the hierarchy of goals one is seeking to achieve. This is not to say that when we cancel the term in that equation we need to know whether it will all lead eventually to the good life. Yet there should at least be some 'lead notice' available as to whether or not cancelation is on the right general track. It is here that the tutor has a special role. For most learning starts off rather piecemeal without the integration of component acts or elements. Usually the learner can tell whether a particular cycle of activity has worked — feedback from specific events is fairly simple — but often he cannot tell whether this completed cycle is leading to the eventual goal. It is interesting that one of the nonrigorous short cuts to problem solution, basic rules of 'heuristic', stated in Polya's noted book[5] has to do with defining the overall problem. To sum up, then, instruction uniquely provides information to the learner about the higher-order relevance of his efforts. In time, to be sure, the learner must develop techniques for obtaining such higher-order corrective information on his own, for instruction and its aids must eventually come to an end. And, finally, if the problem solver is to take over this function, it is necessary for him to learn to recognize when he does not comprehend and, as Roger Brown[6] has suggested, to signal incomprehension to the tutor so that he can be helped. In time, the signaling of incomprehension becomes a self-signaling and equivalent to a temporary stop order.

The ability of problem solvers to use information correctively is known to vary as a function of their internal state. One state in which information is least useful is that of strong drive and anxiety. There is a sufficient body of research to establish this point beyond reasonable doubt.[7] Another such state has been referred to as 'functional fixedness' — a problem solver is, in effect, using corrective information exclusively for the evaluation of one single hypothesis that happens to be wrong. The usual example is treating an object in terms of its conventional significance when it must be treated in a new context — we fail to use a hammer as a bob for a pendulum because it is 'fixed' in our thinking as a hammer. Numerous studies point to the fact that during such a period there is a remarkable intractability or even incorrigibility to problem solving. There is some evidence to indicate that high drive and anxiety lead one to be more prone to functional fixedness. It is obvious that corrective information of the usual type, straight feedback, is least useful during such states, and that an adequate instructional strategy aims at terminating the interfering state by special means before continuing with the usual provision of correction. In such cases, instruction verges on a kind of therapy, and it is perhaps because of this therapeutic need that one often finds therapylike advice in lists of aids for problem solvers, like the suggestion of George Humphrey[8] that one turn away from the problem when it is proving too difficult.

If information is to be used effectively, it must be translated into the learner's way of attempting to solve a problem. If such translatability is not present, then the information is simply useless. Telling a neophyte skier to 'shift to his uphill edges' when he cannot distinguish which edges he is travelling on provides no help, whereas simply telling him to lean into the hill may succeed. Or, in the cognitive sphere, there is by now an impressive body of evidence that indicates that 'negative information' —

information about what something is *not* — is peculiarly unhelpful to a person seeking to master a concept. Though it is logically usable, it is psychologically useless. Translatability of corrective information can in principle also be applied to the form of representation and its economy. If learning or problem solving is proceeding in one mode — enactive, iconic or symbolic — corrective information must be provided either in the same mode or in one that translates into it. Corrective information that exceeds the information-processing capabilities of a learner is obviously wasteful.

Finally, it is necessary to reiterate one general point already made in passing. Instruction is a provisional state that has as its object to make the learner or problem solver self-sufficient. Any regimen of correction carries the danger that the learner may become permanently dependent upon the tutor's correction. The tutor must correct the learner in a fashion that eventually makes it possible for the learner to take over the corrective function himself. Otherwise the result of instruction is to create a form of mastery that is contingent upon the perpetual presence of a teacher.

Notes

1. D.E. Berlyne, *Conflict, Arousal, and Curiosity* (New York: McGraw-Hill, 1960).

2. Margaret Donaldson, *A Study of Children's Thinking* (London: Tavistock Publications, 1963).

3. Jean Piaget, *The Child's Conception of Number* (New York: Humanities Press, 1952).

4. Jerome S. Bruner, 'The course of cognitive growth', *American Psychologist*, 19: 1-15 (January 1964).

5. Gyorgy Polya, *How to Solve It*, 2nd edn. (New York: Doubleday, 1957).

6. Roger Brown, *Social Psychology* (New York: Free Press of Glencoe, 1965), chapter 7, 'From Codability to Coding Ability'.

7. For full documentation, see Jerome S. Bruner, 'Some Theorems on Instruction Illustrated with Reference to Mathematics', *Sixty-third Yearbook of the National Society for the Study of Education*, Part I (Chicago: University of Chicago Press, 1964), pp. 306-35.

8. George Humphrey, *Directed Thinking* (New York: Dodd, Mead, 1948).

15 COGNITIVE DEVELOPMENT:
THE SOCIAL DIMENSION

Ray Derricott and Alan Blyth

Source: Specially written for this volume.
Copyright © 1978 The Open University.

Between 1971 and 1975 we were, along with our colleagues in the team, involved in the development of the ideas of Schools Council Project, History, Geography and Social Science 8-13. The project's publications appear under the general series heading of *Place, Time and Society 8-13*. In our work over those four years one of our central concerns was to help pupils to learn purposefully about society and to make more accurate maps of themselves in relation to society. In order to do this we had to face three questions:

How do children come to learn about society?
What do we want them to learn about society?
How far can formal education affect their knowledge of society?

The first of these questions is, largely, one for the psychologists. Any account of children's learning and its development must consider how they come to perceive society. The second question is a more wide-ranging one, for it raises questions of values and rights, which are the proper concern of moral philosophers. The third question is in some ways more complex still, because it involves again both psychologists and philosophers but also sociologists, who have their own points to raise about the actual, and the desirable, relation between educational institutions and others, as well as the nature of society itself.

All of these questions are fascinating as well as critically important. In the discussion that we are to undertake, they will all be involved.

The Acquisition of Knowledge about Society

The general standpoint that will be taken here is that each child constructs his or her own idea of society as a part of their construction of reality, their process of making sense of their world. At first, it is a very limited world, usually restricted to the immediate family and locality. But as they reach their third year, approximately, they begin to be able to construct 'maps' of their world and to distinguish between the various features that they plot on their maps. In its essence, all that they subsequently learn

284

about society, during childhood, adolescence and adulthood, is a process of revision of these maps. We are all busy, always, producing new editions of our private Ordnance Surveys. Some of these revisions depend on more accurate observations, some on more extensive surveys, and some on re-interpretations and reclassifications of the information that we already have. All of them are intended to enable our maps to correspond more closely to what we perceive as reality.

Within these maps, we have to locate ourselves. Young children find this operation particularly difficult. The schools of psychology derived from Freud and Piaget alike emphasise that very young children perceive the world as an extension of themselves: the egocentric view. They find difficulty in recognising the autonomy of other people, or even of other things. Gradually, as they come to distinguish between I and not-I, they begin to place themselves in relation to others. In doing so, they develop concepts of themselves and of others, and also of the interactions that do and can take place between themselves and others. The formation of children's self-concepts has been extensively studied; their knowledge of others and of the interaction between ego and alter, self and other, has also been given much, though not quite so much, attention. There can be little doubt that the quality of self—other interaction within families, and especially between children and their mothers, is one of the principal influences on how children view themselves. Later, this interactional process is extended to other members of the family, and to other children and adults within their life space. In each instance it applies primarily to children's interaction with their *perceptions* of other people, a pheno-menon that is inaccessible to a purely behaviouristic approach. A wastrel uncle can be seen as a hero; an apparently insignificant boy from the next street can be transformed into a terrifying tyrant. And in relation to both, children develop their own self-picture, with its powerful effects upon their own emotional development and their cognitive powers.

At the same time, they learn to find their way around, first inside the home and then in the neighbourhood. Linking this knowledge with their understanding of their immediate social relationships, they come to associate places with welcome, with hostility, with resources, or with potential for adventure. As their capacity to remember relationships increases, they learn spatial patterns too: their maps acquire a genuine territorial basis.

Against this framework, too, they begin to notice changes. A family moves away; a tree is felled; a house is built; an old lady dies. These events are registered as facts; but some interpretation of their causes is sought, and perhaps unconsciously invented.

In such ways children bring themselves face to face with the realities of Society, Place and Time.

Sooner or later, in the course of revising their own maps of the world, children come into contact with the official accounts of social reality offered by adult interpreters of society. They may do so through television or even through personal encounter. They are most likely to do so in school; later, perhaps, through books encountered outside school. But school is the one place where they encountered versions of social reality specially prepared for children. These versions take account of general notions about children's own development, such as those discussed in this chapter. But they also take account of the second of the questions raised at the beginning of the chapter, namely what knowledge about society adults, or at any rate influential adults, want children to have.

These adult interpretations are significant for children's social learning in two ways. First, they become a special part of the children's environment, being both a part of their developing maps and also a key to those maps. Second, they are a part of the adult maps within which children themselves figure. We can even put these two types of significance together. A book for children about growing up in the forests of Amazonia might well contain comments on how Amerindian children learn about their own society. It is worthwhile to speculate what counterpart for children there might be to the book that you are now reading. We shall return to this point later. For the present, it may serve to emphasise the relativity of learning and of education. Nobody is always teacher, or always taught. There is no defined corpus of information that distinguishes the being-educated from the educated. All learning is by adjustment and negotiation.

The situation we have described is summarised in Figure 15.1.

Each element in this model will need some further degree of elaboration. Our task was focused on developing, in co-operation with teachers, teaching, monitoring and assessment strategies for history, geography and social science (the social subjects). These are seen as depending on and interacting with theories about how children learn and the nature of the social subjects. We link together teaching with monitoring and assessment because we believe that an effective teacher needs to know what is happening to the children he teaches; he needs to keep records to monitor their experiences and responses and this in turn helps him to assess the performance of the children. The feed-back from this monitoring and assessment, in turn, helps the teacher to pace his teaching.

Before we can make explicit some of the assumptions we make about each component of the model, we need to point out some of the

Figure 15.1

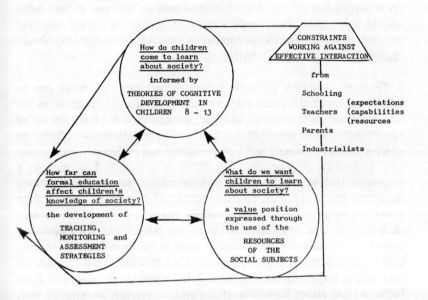

constraints that operate against the effective working of the model. These are seen to come from a variety of sources.

1. Schooling. De-schoolers are not the only people who appreciate that formal education can obstruct its own purposes. Anyone who is familiar with attempts to introduce innovations into schools is likely to know how reluctant children are to embark upon change, however well-intentioned that change may be. For not only is a part of their cognitive map marked 'School', but within that part they have roles to play. Some of these roles they learn from their parents, some from older children, some from teachers, and some from society at large. If teachers suggest that they should unlearn and restructure the pupil roles that they have already adopted, children may react through a kind of passive resistance. Only gradually is it possible to establish an amended pattern of roles.

So if children who are accustomed to learning facts about society as some-thing external to themselves, and to getting marks for right answers, find themselves expected instead to discuss topics that are not neatly wrapped up as part of 'school' and are left to find answers that are, at best, fairly satisfactory rather than 'right', then they become bewildered and resistant. But it is basic to our approach to social learning that they should engage in just this kind of activity.

2. Teachers. Teachers themselves have expectations of what can be achieved through the social subjects and the substantial literature on the dissemination of innovation and the implementation of change in an educational system indicates that teachers' expectations are difficult to alter. A teacher's training will have socialised him or her into a particular view of history or geography and its place in school. For example, a suggestion that in the teaching of these subjects process is emphasised more than the teaching of specific content, will demand of many teachers a major change of viewpoint. Similarly, suggested changes in content challenge teachers' capabilities. One of the major constraints operating against the introduction of the social sciences (anthropology, economics, politics, and sociology in particular) into the education of eight to thirteen year olds is that many teachers have little knowledge or training in these fields and are either dismissive of the ideas or insecure in terms of their own abilities to cope. This lack of capacity on the part of teachers can be explained away by them projecting their own difficulties on to the chil-dren by reasoning that the ideas of social scientists are far too complex for children of this age group.

There are examples of the research community giving support to teachers interested in experimenting in the teaching of social under-standing. The work of the Cognitive Research Trust of Cambridge (CoRT) has done much to encourage 'thinking' as a curricular subject. A recent report from the Trust (DeBono, 1976) on work in a group of primary schools which is probing children's thinking on social issues finds that:

> The thinking of younger children is much more distinct than that of older children. The mistakes are more obvious . . . Older children have usually learned the classroom techniques of giving back to the teacher what the teacher is known to expect . . . Older children are more apt to use cliches and established ideas. It is more difficult in older children to distinguish what is a personal opinion from what is a repetition of something said by the parents . . . Younger children have a much higher motivation for thinking than older children . . . younger children enjoy

thinking and are willing to think about anything that is set before them. Older children want to know why they are being asked to think about something and the relevance of the subject to their examinations. Older children often refuse to think about a subject if they do not have enough information on it. They are very concerned with being right and giving the right answer. Younger children are much less inhibited. [pp. 2-3]

Whilst we would be reluctant to be so categorical about children's responses, these findings correlate very closely with our own work in encouraging thinking on social issues. The message to teachers is clear: do not wait until adolescence before introducing into the curriculum issues that encourage children to think about social values in the world around them.

Innovations of the kind we are suggesting, require the production of resources to support teachers. The lack of suitable, available resources can be itself a major constraint on the introduction of a social science element into the middle years of schooling.

3. Other Constraints. A teaching programme which has as its general aim the development of social understanding is likely to go unnoticed or to be given tacit approval by such groups as parents and industrialists. If however, as the result of this programme, children began to ask questions at home or within the neighbourhood about existing social arrangements, about who has authority and how decisions are made, the interests of parents and other groups are likely to be aroused. Schools that encourage children in such activities run the risk of being misunderstood as being subversive of society by groups who have a more traditional view of education and some schools, in anticipation of such misunderstanding, prefer not to confront their children with controversial social issues. They indulge in a form of curricular escapism.

We can now consider each of the major elements in the model, Figure 15.1:

A. Theories of Cognitive Development in Children 8-13

Members of the project team approached the task of relating knowledge about cognitive development to the devising of teaching strategies, not as experts but as moderately well informed teachers. We were aware that our ideas needed to be grounded in theory but we were also aware, as we have seen above, that the findings of research sometimes discourage and sometimes encourage pedagogues and that 'well established relationships between laboratory phenomena and out-of-laboratory phenomena' do not exist in the social sciences. (See, for example, Satterly, 1970.)

Theories of cognitive development in children 8-13 would suggest to us the following principles:

(i)   Progression in learning is likely to be related to development from concrete to formal operations.

(ii)   There is likely to be a side range of individual difference in the pace of learning.

(iii)   Logical thinking is possible if based on direct experiences or upon experiences skilfully described or evoked in words.

(iv)   The ability to manipulate variables in the solving of problems will be limited.

(v)   Coping with the uncertainty of there not being a single 'correct' answer to many of the questions posed by study in the social subjects, will prove difficult for children in this age group.

(vi)   There will be some interest in other people but the starting point for developing understanding will often be egocentrism which is the antithesis of empathy.

B. The Resources of the Social Subjects

The social subjects offer an introduction to the *study skills* and other valued activities provide for:

(i)   Finding information.

(ii)   Evaluating information.

(iii)   Formulating and testing hypotheses.

(iv)   Developing an understanding of human actions and motivations.

(v)   Developing attitudes towards evidence; distinguishing between fact and opinion; detecting bias and distortion.

(vi)   A system for analysing value issues.

(vii)   A conceptual framework for understanding social issues.

(viii) Specific knowledge.

It will be immediately obvious here that this list represents a value position about the use of the social subjects with children in the middle years of schooling. The emphasis is skill learning; it is on process rather than content. History and geography teaching can, and does, suffer from information overload and to put a low value on specific knowledge presents a firm challenge to this situation.

However, the project team does not go all the way with those who claim that in the primary/middle years 'learning how to learn' is sufficient. We do provide some general guidelines on *what* we want children to learn about society. The use of the *key concepts* along with skill objectives is our attempt to help teachers in the task of *selecting* and *organising* content so that children can learn about man in place, time and society.

The selection of material for teaching within the social subjects must be a subtle process. To dilute it in condescending, told-to-the-children, terms, or to present it with academic aridity, would be equally unproductive. Somehow it must seem relevant and demanding, yet only just out of reach: to use McVicar Hunt's term, it must 'match' children's development. But to phrase it in this way is to formulate the problem, not to solve it. The project's approach requires each teacher to try to solve it in the unique situation in which they work, with those particular children. Apart from the immediate geographical and social environments that were already the concern of two other projects *Environmental Studies 5-13* and *Social Education*, together with the conventional terminology of the social subjects such as the globe, the atlas and the time-scale, there is virtually nothing that must be included, or excluded. Unlike mathematics or science, the social subjects present no obvious ways in which children must approach them. Attempts have been made to study them forwards, backwards, outwards, or in terms of apparently increasing complexity, but all of these present such formidable difficulties in practice that none of them can claim to be regarded as a necessary procedure. What our project suggested was that four key concepts from their common subject-matter – communication, power, values and beliefs, and conflict/consensus – together with three from the methods of study which they (but not only they) require – similarity/difference, continuity/change, causes and consequences – should guide teachers in their selection and organisation of material and that, for the rest, they should develop with each set of children an appropriate and balanced programme which should avoid random repetitiveness.

A Framework for Planning

From our admittedly non-specialist knowledge of cognitive development and from our view of resources offered by the social subjects we worked out, in co-operation with teachers, a framework for planning using *objectives* and *key concepts*. Tables 15.1 and 15.2 show these.

The list of objectives are a spelling out of the skills and attitudes valued by the team and the teachers involved. The key concepts are of two kinds. The methodological key concepts emphasise the processes involved in concept attainment. Mastering a concept involves classification in which

Table 15.1: The Project's List of Objectives

Skills			Personal qualities
Intellectual	Social	Physical	Interests, attitudes and values
1 The ability to find information from a variety of sources, in a variety of ways. 2 The ability to communicate findings through an appropriate medium. 3 The ability to interpret pictures, charts, graphs, maps, etc. 4 The ability to evaluate information. 5 The ability to organise information through concepts and generalisations. 6 The ability to formulate and test hypotheses and generalisations.	1 The ability to participate within small groups. 2 An awareness of significant groups within the community and the wider society. 3 A developing understanding of how individuals relate to such groups. 4 A willingness to consider participating constructively in the activities associated with these groups. 5 The ability to exercise empathy (i.e. the capacity to imagine accurately what it might be like to be someone else).	1 The ability to manipulate equipment. 2 The ability to manipulate equipment to find and communicate information. 3 The ability to explore the expressive powers of the human body to communicate ideas and feelings. 4 The ability to plan and execute expressive activities to communicate ideas and feelings.	1 The fostering of curiosity through the encouragement of questions. 2 The fostering of a wariness of over-commitment to one framework of explanation and the possible distortion of facts and the omission of evidence. 3 The fostering of a willingness to explore personal attitudes and values to relate these to other people's. 4 The encouraging of an openness to the possibility of change in values. 5 The encouragement of worthwhile and developing interests in human affairs.

similarities and differences are highlighted. Continuity/change is a special case of similarity/difference values, in particular, by historians. Causes and consequences is a seeking after an explanation of events. The substantive key concepts suggest content that might be studied. The list of seven is not exhaustive and no claims are made for it except that in practice it has proved useful to teachers in selecting and organising content and focusing their work in an area which is often characterised by lack of a clear emphasis. It is likely that the methodological key concepts will appear in most people's lists as representing fundamental concept-forming processes

Table 15.2: The Project's List of Key Concepts

SIMILARITY/DIFFERENCE
CONTINUITY/CHANGE   Methodological Key Concepts
CAUSES and CONSEQUENCES

COMMUNICATION
POWER   Substantive Key
VALUES and BELIEFS   Concepts
CONFLICT/CONSENSUS

---

not confined to social considerations. The substantive key concepts, on the other hand, are more likely to vary according to a particular group of teacher's perceptions of their usefulness. An example of the use of key concepts by teachers and some of the assumptions made by teachers about the ways in which children are likely to learn concepts is given below (p. 295).

Suggested Teaching Strategies

We shall now consider the final and crucial component of our model (Figure 15.1) — the development of teaching strategies and accompanying techniques for monitoring and assessment of pupil's progress. The treatment of teaching strategies in this section is necessarily selective. A fuller elaboration of our ideas is available elsewhere (Blyth *et al.*, 1976).

The first task is to identify a starting point at which the interaction between teacher and learner can begin. This is put clearly in the eminently quotable passage from Ausubel (1968):

If I had to reduce all educational psychology to one principle, I would say this: the most important single fact influencing learning is what the learner already knows. Ascertain this and teach him accordingly.

The first assumption we make then, is that children in the early middle years are unlikely to know any formal history, geography or social science. We therefore make the distinction between *pre-disciplinary* and *disciplinary* activities. Pre-disciplinary activities have as their basis, common-sense knowledge which figures already in the children's cognitive maps. They take as a starting point events from everyday life with which children may already have some familiarity. For example, in introducing children to money as a means of exchange, a starting point that we have used is the collecting and swapping habits of the children themselves. A pre-disciplinary activity may also be a story contrived by a teacher with a particular group of children in mind and which contains a number of possible starting points for discussion. An example of this kind of activity is included below.

These activities cannot be classified as history, or geography or social science but are carefully chosen for the opportunities they provide for children to practise the skills valued by subject specialists. *Disciplinary activities*, on the other hand, are drawn from the traditional content of the social subjects. The aim of the teaching strategy is to provide a progression of activities from pre-disciplinary to disciplinary which enable children to master a similar group of skills. Table 15.3 is an attempt to illustrate this with one of our objectives, the ability to evaluate information, in mind.

Table 15.3: Teaching Strategies Designed to Promote Progression in the Ability to Evaluate Information

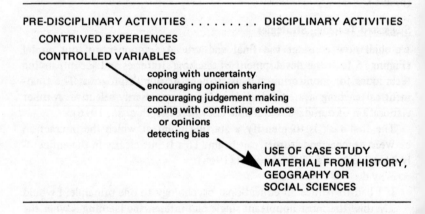

PRE-DISCIPLINARY ACTIVITIES . . . . DISCIPLINARY ACTIVITIES

CONTRIVED EXPERIENCES
CONTROLLED VARIABLES

coping with uncertainty
encouraging opinion sharing
encouraging judgement making
coping with conflicting evidence
or opinions
detecting bias

USE OF CASE STUDY
MATERIAL FROM HISTORY,
GEOGRAPHY OR
SOCIAL SCIENCES

The progression from pre-disciplinary to disciplinary activities involves the use, in the early stages, of contrived experiences in which variables are controlled before actual case study material with a disciplinary focus is used. The techniques used encourage:

coping with the uncertainty of not knowing a 'correct' answer to a problem;
encourage opinion sharing and judgement making;
give experience of coping with conflicting evidence or opinions; and
encourage the detection of bias in evidence.

All these techniques are evident in the examples that follow.

1. Examples of Pre-Disciplinary Activities

(a)   Strange Objects in the Classroom

Although much of the history and geography teaching in schools place emphasis on factual information, the social subjects cover an area of man's activity in which judgements have to be made on the basis of limited evidence; there are innumerable instances of there not being a single 'correct' answer. Young children, especially if they have been trained to believe that the teacher expects the correct answer, find it difficult to cope with the uncertainty of not knowing. We have devised a number of teaching techniques aimed at helping children to cope with this kind of intellectual uncertainty. We advise that they are only tried out in a supportive climate with teacher and children who know each other well.

The teacher introduces to a group of children several objects which are passed around and examined in detail. The objects are selected because of the unlikelihood that any of the children will know what they are. They can be from the past or from another culture. We have used a wide range of objects for this purpose, for example, a dumbell used in physical training, a button hook, a metal bed warmer, a Chinese snuff-bottle and a West African cooking implement. The children may be given limited information such as, 'this is about 100 years old' or 'this is from West Africa'. The questions asked are:

What do you think this is?
How is it used?
Why do you think that?

The children are encouraged to support their propositions about the objects. Differences of opinion are revealed and discussed. Occasionally we have encouraged children to write their thoughts as the following examples show:

One of our colleagues was co-operating with a teacher in an 8-12 middle school and encouraging her to explore children's thinking. He sent two objects to the school for the children to handle and to think about. One of these was a wooden dumbell which was about 70 years old and of the type used in some forms of physical training in elementary schools. Having handled and discussed the object this is what two of the children wrote about and what several of them drew:

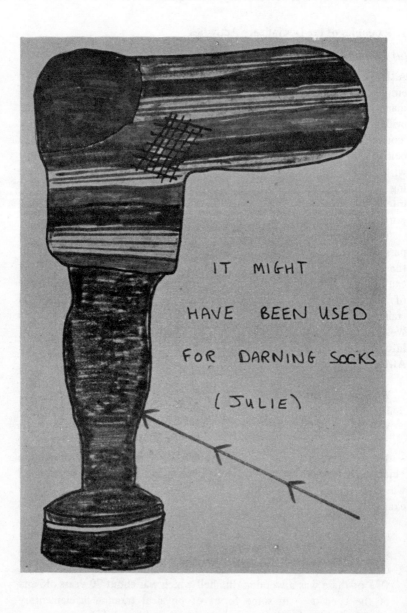

What Are They?

Mr Waplington sent us two different objects. The first object was made out of wood, it was smooth and dull. There might have been varnish on it before when it was new but now it's just a dull piece of wood. It's 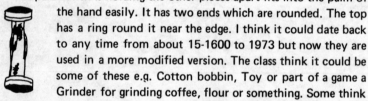 got a space in the middle where your hand would fit. The two ends have got a round edge and the middle bit is round as well. There are several things that it could be. It could be a cotton bobbin or a spinning top for a game. It could even be a slimming exerciser or a grinder.

I think it could be any of those things. Some people think it could be a baby's weightlifter or a rolling pin, an arm roller or a spinning top for a game but I don't think it will be any of those things. You could find out what it really is by going to the museum or look it up in a book.

What Are They

The wooden puzzle we got from Mr Waplington is smooth and the middle part which is holding the other pieces apart fits into the palm of the hand easily. It has two ends which are rounded. The top has a ring round it near the edge. I think it could date back to any time from about 15-1600 to 1973 but now they are used in a more modified version. The class think it could be some of these e.g. Cotton bobbin, Toy or part of a game a Grinder for grinding coffee, flour or something. Some think it could be an exerciser or a slimming aid or a thing for rolling up and down the arm, which are very good ideas but an exerciser is the real use. It is called a Dumbell. I took it home and asked my Dad what it could be. He told me and said his father used one when he was younger.

(b)   Contrived Experience – The Story of Pte Henry Rawcliffe

Often events as portrayed by historians are too complex and contain too many variables for young children to handle. As introductory pre-disciplinary activity designed to encourage the evaluation of evidence, we often use a specially written story. One such story can be found in the project's published unit called 'Clues, clues, clues, detective work in history' (Waplington, 1975). The central character in the story is Private Henry Rawcliffe. The story contains clues to his character which are limited and the variables are limited. Children are encouraged to piece together the evidence about Rawcliffe and answer the question 'What kind of man was he?'

The story is reproduced below:

John and Mary Stevenson were spending their holidays with their Uncle Tom. Uncle Tom lived in a small village.

One day they came bursting into the house.

'Uncle Tom, Uncle Tom, we've found an old house,' they shouted together.

'An old house? Oh, you mean the bungalow at the end of Spicer's Lane.'

'Who lived there? Is it anybody's? Is it haunted?'

'Steady on, steady. Some chap called Rawcliffe, or was it Radcliffe, lived there. Your Aunty May will know — wait though. If you nip down to the Old Cross you'll find Tom Bradley there. He'll be able to tell you. He's lived here all his life. Off you go, and leave me in peace.'

The children ran off to the village. They soon reached the Cross. At the side of the Cross was a wooden seat. An old man sat there puffing his pipe.

'Excuse me, are you Mr. Bradley?' John asked.

'That's me. And you're young Tom Stevenson's nephew. Don't look so amazed, young lad, there's little in this village I don't know.'

'That's why Uncle Tom sent us,' Mary interrupted.

'He said you'd know about the old house at the end of the village.'

'Oh, Rawcliffe's bungalow. A sad place, very sad.'

'Tell us,' said John.

'There's little to tell. Rawcliffe had the bungalow built just after the war — 1914-18 war, I mean. Funny chap. Never saw much of him. Kept himself to himself. Even had his groceries delivered. Strange. Doubt if I saw him twice in ten years.'

'Why didn't he talk to anyone?' Mary asked.

'No one knows.'

'What happened?' said John.

'Well, he died. Fortnight before they found his body. Couldn't find much about him, even then. No relations, not round here. Bungalow was cleared of furniture, but it was never sold. Here, look at the time. Molly's going to start nattering if I'm late for dinner.'

He got up and reached for his stick.

'When did he die? Please!' pleaded Mary.

'1928 I think. Yes, 1928, same year as Molly was born.' Mr. Bradley walked off.

'Let's go and have a look inside the house,' said John.

'Come on.'

The bungalow was deserted. It had no doors. The windows were smashed in. Grass was growing in the porch. John wasn't so keen to go in. It looked spooky.

'Come on, silly,' shouted Mary, 'it's empty.'

All the rooms were bare. Glass littered the floor.

'There,' said Mary, 'it's just an ordinary old house.'

'Wait,' said John. 'There are some bits of paper in the corner here.'

'There's something else as well. Here.'

'Put all the bits in my hanky — we'll take them home and show them to Uncle Tom. He'll know what to do with them.'

'I wonder if they'll tell us anything,' John said thoughtfully. 'They might tell us something about Rawcliffe. Fancy living all alone for all that time.'

The evidence the children find is as follows:

(i)   Rawcliffe's army discharge certificate:

(ii)   Newspaper cuttings:

The death is announced today of Mrs. Mary Rawcliffe. Mrs. Rawcliffe leaves behind a husband, Henry, and a daughter Jane.

Bradfield Chronicle, Nov. 3rd 1917.

The funeral took place yesterday of Jane Rawcliffe, aged 8, the only child of Mr. Henry Rawcliffe.

Mourners present were Miss Marion Rawcliffe (aunt), Mr. J. Henry, Mr. and Mrs. A.F. Osborne, Mrs. J. Hather. Rev. J.W.F. Wickstead officiated.

Bradfield Chronicle, Jan. 14th 1918.

(iii)   a clay pipe,
a crumpled playing card,
a knight from a chess set.

The adult thinker will quickly determine that the documents are about Rawcliffe but the objects need not necessarily be his.

Most of the children aged 9 to 11 with whom we have used this story piece together the clues about Rawcliffe which lead them to conclude that he was a lonely and unhappy man. Readers are encouraged to try for themselves children's reactions to questions such as:

Did Rawcliffe smoke a pipe?
Did he play chess?
Did he play cards?

Rarely have we found children under 11 able to categorise the evidence into:

(a)   that which is definitely about Rawcliffe,
(b)   that which might or might not be about Rawcliffe.

The evidence is not seen as a whole. Propositions are made about bits of it at a time. The same child can maintain that Rawcliffe might or might not have played chess but he did play cards. The role of the teacher in this activity is crucial. She can probe the children's thinking and reward the use of words like 'probably', 'possibly', 'might or might not have'. If children have been encouraged to cope with the uncertainty of not knowing they will often be ready to handle conflicting and inadequate evidence and be prepared to make judgements, knowing that they cannot be certain that they are right. We find considerable potential in the use of contrived, pre-disciplinary experiences of this type. The contentious issue is whether there is transfer of learning from one situation to another. Our limited experience suggests that children who have been encouraged to approach evidence in the way we have indicated can transfer this skill to the often more complex case-studies used by historians, geographers and social scientists.

2. Examples of Disciplinary Experiences

Teaching for Empathy

Our table of objectives (Table 15.1) includes the social skill, the ability to exercise empathy. We recognise that empathy contains a cognitive and an affective component but wish to highlight it as an important social skill. Empathy we take to mean the appreciation of another's viewpoint without necessarily agreeing with that viewpoint. The egocentrism of young children will make it difficult for them to empathise. The growth of empathy or person perception as they prefer to call it, is well described by Livesley and Bromley (1973).

> Gradually, egocentrism declines and cognitive and social skills develop. The child learns to take into account things other than a person's appearance, identity and possessions. He applies his growing powers of abstraction and generalisation and goes beyond the immediate stimulus situation to infer stable and constant features in a person's behaviour, referring to them in terms of trait names and general habits. At about the age of 7 or 8, the children's attempts to conceptualise persons and their behaviour are influenced by another characteristic of pre-operational thinking, traces of which remain. This is the process of identification (via mimicry and role playing) or vicarious learning whereby he 'goes through the motions' of being the other person and in this way experiences something of what it might be like (psychologically) to be another person. Naturally, he can describe peers better than he can describe adults because he finds it easier to identify with peers than with adults. A similar process of learning — a kind of empathy — may be used throughout life to solve problems in personal relationships . . . [pp. 214-15]

In devising experiences to develop empathy we assumed that:

(a)   role-play in which children are encouraged to take a variety of roles provides them with opportunities to attempt to see other people's viewpoints;

(b) explaining and justifying an opinion or a point of view to other people provides practice in adjusting to the viewpoint of the audience;

(c) formulating questions to ask of others in an interview situation requires the questioner to adjust to the respondent's viewpoint in order to communicate with him and to obtain the information required;

(d) playing rule-bound games and participating in simulations provides practice in taking roles in groups, co-operating with others, bargaining, negotiating and arguing a point of view;

(e) the development of the ability to empathise is a slow process, the range of individual differences will be wide and that occasional learning experiences cannot be expected to produce rapid results.

Table 15.4: Summarises our Ideas: The Ability to Exercise Empathy

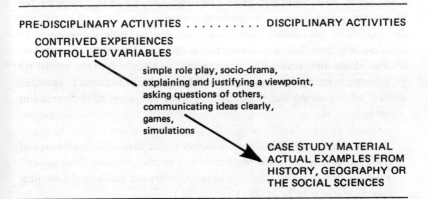

Again, we make the distinction between pre-disciplinary and disciplinary activities, the former relying mainly on contrived experiences in which the variables are controlled, moving through to the use of actual material from the social disciplines of history, geography and the social sciences. We assume that empathy is learned in the social context and we employ teaching strategies that encourage social interaction.

The work of Selman and Byrne (1974) became known to us while we were encouraging teachers to experiment in the teaching of empathy. Selman and Byrne suggest that there is a discernible sequence in the development of role taking which moves from egocentricity to empathy. The sequence is:

Level 0:   egocentric role taking,
Level 1:   subjective role taking,
Level 2:   self-selective role taking,
Level 3:   mutual role taking.

These ideas provided a welcome empirical base for what we considered to be an important part of our project. Many of our other assumptions in teaching for empathy are supported by the work of Flavell *et al.* (1968) which sees the developing ability of a child to think about his social environment not only dependent upon role-taking but also upon communicating with others. According to Flavell an effective communicator needs to adjust his message to match his perception of the receiver of the message.

We find confirmatory support of our strategies in teaching for empathy from work that appeared more recently. Geber (1977) suggests the interesting possibilities of a synthesis between the ideas of social and developmental psychology. She teases out the possible components of social interaction that are important in the development from egocentricity. From her review of a considerable body of literature Geber provides support for our assumption that children in the middle years are capable of displaying the beginnings of what can only be interpreted as empathy.

> During middle childhood and adolescence the child becomes aware of the need to pay careful attention to the characteristics of his audience when communicating with it and increasingly skilled in understanding people. (Geber, 1977, p. 224)

The assumptions we make about teaching for empathy that are outlined above suggest the range of teaching strategies that we have employed. The details of these will be found in our publications. See for example, *Games and Simulations in the Classroom* (Elliott, Sumner and Waplington, 1976) and *Themes in Outline* (Derricott *et al.*, 1977). Both these publications and some of the units contain examples of simulations designed to develop empathy.

It is impossible to do justice to many of these teaching ideas by summarising them in a few words, but the following examples will give the flavour of the work. It will be noted that these are examples of disciplinary

West Indians to Britain
Finding somewhere to live

People on the Move   **Worksheet 22**

Imagine you are a Jamaican immigrant newly arrived in Birmingham to work.
You are anxious to have your family join you in Birmingham, so you must
find somewhere for them to live. Where will you go?

Council House

*To get one of these you will have to go
on the Council's waiting list.*
You can move up the list if you can
collect extra points for:
(1) Having too few bedrooms where
   you are now.
(2) Sharing your present
   accommodation.
(3) Having poor facilities.
(4) Being short of natural light.
(5) Having to break up your family.
(6) Suffering from ill health.
(7) Being on the waiting list a long
   time.
(8) Having done war service.
BUT you cannot *join* the waiting list
until you have lived or worked in
Birmingham for 5 years. In 1960
there were already on the waiting
list thousands of families living
in lodgings.
DO YOU QUALIFY FOR A
COUNCIL HOUSE?

Private house

You can have one of these if you can
(1) Put down many hundreds of
   pounds as a deposit.
(2) Show that you have a large
   enough income to pay off the
   mortgage.
(3) Convince the building society,
   which lends the money, that your
   job is really secure.
(4) Convince the building society
   that you can keep the property in
   a good state of repair.
(5) Convince them that your way of
   life is not likely to upset the
   people in the district.
(6) Promise not to sublet to anyone
   else.
CAN YOU DO THESE THINGS?

experiences, one geographical and one sociological.

In a theme entitled *Locating a Factory*, children took part in a simulation in which one group (the industrialists) was encouraged to think of the most effective ways of communicating to a public enquiry (the rest of the class) the advantages that their factory would bring to the area. Members of the enquiry were encouraged to formulate and ask questions which they thought would provide them with sufficient data to make a decision. Each group therefore, was expected to anticipate the other's thinking and motives and thus to exercise empathy.

The unit *People on the Move* (1976) is one that focuses on the concept of migration. It is designed with 11 to 13 year olds in mind. Case-studies are used to illustrate factors that cause people to move from one place to another. *The Irish to Liverpool* considers the migration caused by the failure of the Irish potato crops in the 1840s and uses mainly historical sources. *The West Indians to Birmingham* has a sociological emphasis and follows the fortunes of a West Indian family — the Clarkes — as they attempt to establish themselves in Birmingham. Slides and an illustrated booklet show the Clarkes at home, at work, at leisure, at school and at church. An attempt is made to establish a story identity with this family. Some of the worksheets indicate the kinds of problems immigrants face when settling in a new community. The worksheet on p. 305 is one of a series that attempts to get pupils to appreciate the problems that immigrants face in finding a house.

3. Using Concepts

Concepts are neither good nor bad, they are only more or less useful. [Easton, 1965, p. 33]

The examples of our work that we have used so far all illustrate ways in which we have attempted to develop skills in children. We also advocate the use of key concepts. Our ideas on the use of key concepts in curriculum planning are detailed in Blyth *et al.* (1976), Derricott *et al.* (1977), and Elliott (1976). A philosophical analysis, by an outsider, of the project's use of key concepts will be found in Kingdom (1975).

There are a number of essential points we need to make clear about our advocacy of key concepts:

1. We *do not* claim that the list of seven key concepts is an exhaustive one. Neither is the list exclusive to the social subjects. We do not claim that the list has any epistemological status. It has not been arrived at by a rigorous process of philosophical analysis. The key concepts were chosen

because, in our judgement, they would prove useful to teachers in guiding their selection and organisation of content. They were chosen for their potential in being useful to historians, geographers and social scientists who were planning to teach their separate subjects and at the same time they might provide a common focus for interrelating or integrating the social subjects. We claim then, that key concepts are useful procedural devices for teachers.

2. What about pupils? We *do not* claim that children between eight and thirteen will attain an adequate understanding of each of the key concepts. Some children, particularly in the later middle years, can be expected to use terms such as communication and power. We do not expect however, that children will learn glib definitions of these concepts. Over the years, if they are subject to the kinds of questions that the key concepts provoke, and experiences that are structured with ideas about (say) power and communication in mind, they will begin on the road to understanding and using these concepts.

In recommending the use of key concepts by teachers it was incumbent upon us also to offer them helpful guidelines. There are no universally accepted conceptual maps for the social subjects. Indeed for many historians, teaching for concepts is considered to be quite inappropriate. We should, of course, have set up longitudinal studies of concept development in children to provide an empirical basis for our work but involvement in a curriculum development project does not allow for such a luxury. We therefore had to be content with drawing what inferences we could from the general literature on concept learning and encouraging teachers to experiment with our embryonic ideas. Tables 15.5 and 15.6 are an attempt to convey some of our suggestions.

We postulate that a conceptual map for the social subjects can be conceived as being hierarchical. We envisage there to be three levels in this hierarchy. At *Level I* are the hundreds or even thousands of *specific concepts* that are used by historians, geographers and social scientists. Some examples of these are queen, war, army, costume, uniform, money, market, site, transport, newspaper, family, church, route. All these specific concepts satisfy most of the criteria at Level I in that they are closed and easy to define, narrow in scope, can be experienced through the senses or through carefully evoked experiences using language, movement and drama.

Each specific concept is capable of being illuminated and its meaning enriched by one or more *subordinate concept*. Subordinate concepts

Table 15.5: Criteria for Assessing the Appropriateness of Concepts for Children 8-11

Type of concept	Criteria	Distance from child's experience	Complexity	Scope concept	Open-endedness	Age
Specific concepts ↑	3 Level I	Directly related	Can be experienced through senses	Narrow in scope	Closed and easy to define	8 ↑
Sub-ordinate concepts	p o i n Level II t s					
↓ Key concepts	c a l Level III e	Unrelated	Abstract notion	Broad in scope	Open to disagreement about interpretation and meaning	13

occupy *Level II* and are less directly related to children's experience, more difficult to experience through the senses or through drama and movement or other vicarious experiences, they are less narrow and more difficult to define. Above the subordinate concepts, at Level III, are the *key concepts* with their high level of abstraction, broad scope and openness to differing interpretations and meaning. These overarching key concepts are capable of being used to further illuminate and enrich the individual's understanding of the subordinate and specific concepts from the lower levels.

Analysis of this kind is speculative but if we are to move from speculation to something approaching fantasy, we can envisage a series of concept trees made up of concepts from all three kinds. There must be many of these trees but whether, in the social subjects, they go together to form the neatly defined regimentation of a Forestry Commission plantation or are more akin to the unfathomed patterns of a natural woodland we will not conjecture. One of the concept trees based on the key concept power might be as shown on p. 310.

Table 15.5 is offered to teachers as a set of guidelines for judging the appropriateness of concepts for the children they teach. Table 15.6 shows the responses of one group of teachers to the use of key concepts in

Table 15.6: Sequencing of Content Using Key Concepts

	Communication	Power	Values/ Beliefs	Conflict/ Consensus	Methodological Key Concepts
8+	Transport in a local setting. Local road patterns. Local transport services.	Preserving law and order. The Police Service past and present.	Rules: safety rules, highway code, rules in games. Belonging to groups with rules, Scouts, etc.	Simulation: setting up an Island Society.	
					Similarity/ Difference
9+	National network of motorways. Railways. Airports. Why is the pattern as it is?	Simulation: The siting of a new airport. Who decides?	Families in different cultures. Comparison of roles of individuals in families.	Conflict over the use of domestic space, local space.	
					Continuity/ Change
10+	Barriers to communication and how these are overcome. Crossing rivers, estuaries. Tunnels, the Channel Tunnel.	Floods: living with the threat of floods.	Going to school. Ways in which the young are taught in different cultures.	Providing for leisure need — conflicts of interest. Tourist v. Conservationist.	
11+	Communication through the media. Newspapers, radio, TV.	Working in a factory. Trades Unions. Strikes.	Victorian life.	Life during the Second World War.	
					Causes and Consequences
12+	Advertising. Can we believe all we are told?	The Oil Crisis. Who has the power?	Culture clash. Aborigines of Australia.	Enclosures: Simulations.	

(From Blyth *et al.*, 1976, pp. 136-7.)

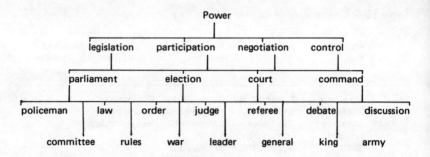

developing a sequence of themes for children from 8 to 13. The methodological key concepts are themselves sequenced. It is assumed that activities that emphasise *similarity/difference* precede those that emphasise *continuity/change* and that *causes and consequences* as a key concept offers challenges at a higher level of difficulty than the other two and is therefore not emphasised until late in the middle years. The table also shows that the teachers have taken the four substantive key concepts and from these have derived a series of themes and experiences which they consider to be appropriate at each age level.

Communication is illuminated by ideas containing many specific and subordinate concepts that move from local transport through national transport to physical barriers to communication (estuaries). The communication of ideas is not considered until the later years.

Power is considered by starting with specific concepts in a local setting (the police). The airport simulation is used to introduce the idea of decision-making. The theme of 'Floods' explores the dangers man faces from natural disasters and how man tries to control and alter his environment to avoid disasters.

Values and Beliefs show a sequence which begins with themes that are rooted firmly within the child's experience. A similar set of sequencing principles is found under the key concept *Conflict/Consensus*.

When looking for support from the research community it is also possible to pick up negative or constraining signals. Modgil and Modgil (1976) in their summary of Piagetian researches related to social studies offer the judgement that:

When it is realised . . . that children of this age are only beginning to appreciate the rules governing the game of marbles, in which all the physical elements are present, expectations of the amount of real understanding of the role of adults in the community outside must be small indeed. (p. 54)

Whether inferences drawn from children's reactions to a game of marbles can have wider application is open to debate. Smedslund (1977) questions the representative nature of many of the Piagetian tasks, claiming that they are alien to the total *Lebenswelt* of the child. Anthony (1977) suggests that there may be a danger in a search for a universal and content free set of structures to explain cognitive development. He recommends for consideration an alternative *skill integration* model of development. Model skills are taken to be sets of procedures deployed in particular settings. The integration of these skills involves increasing generalisation to new situations. While we feel that Anthony's ideas need clearer elaboration and systematic testing, they do offer us encouragement. As teachers we have arrived at what appears to be a similar viewpoint. To us, the place where an investigation of children's developing social understanding should be held, is in the classroom or the neighbourhood, in the social context of a small group under the guidance of a skilled teacher who in her probing of children's thinking takes on something of the role of a clinician.

This brings us to the one element in our model (Figure 15.1) to which we have not yet made direct reference. The model refers to the development of teaching, *monitoring and assessment strategies*. The clinician is an astute and perceptive observer; he is a master of probing interaction in an atmosphere created to be supportive and encouraging; he keeps systematic case-notes and records and he is prepared to share his perceptions with, and take the advice of colleagues. We see the teacher in a similar role as he explores children's thinking and provides them with matching activity and experience. One of our colleagues (Cooper, 1977) refers to this approach as diagnostic teaching. Its effectiveness depends upon the teacher knowing as much as possible about the individual children he teaches and on having clear objectives.

Keeping records that are useful in monitoring children's progress is a time consuming affair. The procedures involved have to be simple to operate and easy to interpret. The technique we have used and are still developing, is to take one of our objectives as a starting point and to elaborate the range of ways in which the achievement of that objective might manifest itself in a child's behaviour. The objectives are thus used as a checklist which provide one element in building up the profile of an individual child. It is impracticable for a teacher to keep a daily record but a check on each child twice a term can furnish the teacher with a guide to individual progress and a salutary record of the emphasis and

General objective: *the ability to evaluate information*

name of pupil.............................   age................   teacher............

	Date				
1. Can cope with the uncertainty of there not being a correct answer					
2. Is prepared to make a judgement about a situation					
3. Is prepared to share a judgement with others					
4. Is prepared to comment on other people's ideas, opinions					
5. Is prepared to have his own ideas, opinions commented on					
6. When discussing evidence, uses words like 'probably', 'possibly', 'might'					
7. Can distinguish between fact and opinion					
8. Can cope with evidence from a number of sources					
9. Can recognise conflicting evidence					
10. Shows a wariness of possible bias or distortion in evidence					
11. Shows a wariness of possible omission of evidence					

Respond   Y = Yes
               S = Sometimes
               N = No

direction of his own teaching. Two illustrative examples of this technique are included on pages 312 and 313.

We do not claim that these checklists exhaust the range of all possible behaviours related to the objectives. Neither do we claim that the behaviours, as listed, represent any kind of established hierarchy. Our work with teachers on these ideas is still in its infancy but we include here what can only be described as crude schedules, in order to encourage discussion and experimentation. One of the major problems we face in trying to implement these ideas is that teachers tend to make global assessments of the children they teach. We are trying to provide guidelines that encourage teachers to make explicit the bases of these global assessments and to examine the 'coarse-grain' elements in the behaviours they observe. We believe that when teachers become aware of this 'coarse-graining' they become more effective and diagnostic teachers and are better able to pace

General objective: *the ability to exercise empathy*

name of pupil................................. age........ teacher..........

	Date					
1. In playing a simple guessing game (e.g. 'Guess which hand') shows signs of the ability to interpret and anticipate partner's behaviour						
2. Can take part in a rule-bound game which involves co-operation with partner						
3. Can identify with a character from a story he/she has heard						
4. In describing another person (orally or in writing) can go beyond descriptions of appearance, size and general physical features to include trait names (e.g. kind, helpful) and general habits						
5. Can think of appropriate questions to ask when conducting an interview						
6. Can take an effective part in a simulation						

Respond　　　Y = Yes
　　　　　　　S = Sometimes
　　　　　　　N = No

the development of their pupils by providing appropriate activities and experiences.

Concluding Comments

From these examples it is possible to draw together a few general threads. First, it is clear that children can learn to handle evidence in such a way as to distinguish the true from the false and the relevant from the irrelevant. This they can begin to do in everyday or fictional 'pre-disciplinary' situations, later transferring their skills to situations which lie outside their immediate maps of experience and which therefore require the use of the techniques of the social subjects. This is what could be expected of children between 8 and 13 in the light of the general theories associated with Piaget, and of instruction associated with Gagné. The more interesting and unusual issue is that children need to accept that some problems do not admit of complete answers. Parents and employers, and teachers themselves, are liable to assume that education is about certainty, about questions with the right answers at the back of the book. It would be easier, but less human, if the world were like that. Bertrand Russell once pointed out that it was a task of education to enable people to make decisions without adequate evidence. According to the Piagetian view of cognitive development, it is scarcely possible for children to accept such uncertainty either cognitively or emotionally before mid-adolescence; the experience of the project suggests that, given suitable circumstances, it may be possible to begin teaching for uncertainty sooner than that. If so, it means that children can bring themselves to insert 'unknown' on parts of their maps even when their yearning is for certainty.

A more general outcome of the project's experience in relation to the asking of questions indicates that they can develop confidence through increasing capacity to ask, as well as to answer, questions. Indeed, social learning can be seen to be largely a matter of learning how to ask the right questions: right, that is, because they are relevant for the reconstruction of experience, a point which Dewey would surely have approved. The development of critical thinking skills emerged as an important thread in cognitive growth and a further guiding principle in the selection of appropriate content.

Alongside this can be placed a second important consideration, namely the way in which empathy figures in cognitive development. It is difficult for children to develop clear ideas about social situations remote in place or time or social organisation or to learn to imagine, accurately, what it is like to be somebody else. Yet this is just how personal experience can and must be extended. Unless children and young people can strenuously attempt to see other points of view and other problems, then their social horizons remain limited. In face of the great pressure exerted by society and by subcultural influences, it is a considerable achievement on the part of formal education if the habit of empathy can be seriously encouraged. It is clearly a matter of cognitive as well as of emotional growth, one about which a great deal more needs to be known, despite the lip-service regularly paid to it.

Taken together, these observations throw a little more light on the questions from which we began. We can see some further possibilities for understanding how children learn about society. We can discern the kinds of decisions we are making when we give our views about what we want them to learn about society. Finally, we have a few further indicators which suggest the effective part that formal education can play in this process of learning.

Other Patterns of Social Learning

The observations on social learning outlined in this chapter apply only to our own culture, and in particular to the culture of England and Wales. Even in the Western world, different patterns are found where closer governmental control of education is accepted. Many countries embody in their formal educational systems an explicit study of their constitutions or of their ideology. Often with considerable success. In England and Wales this would be ineffective, though there are cultural groups within the country which attempt it on their own account. But outside the confines of the Western world, the whole patterns of social learning differ markedly. Tribal societies in Africa, the caste society of India, and most clearly of all, fully Marxist regimes, have evolved means of social learning which operate on entirely different lines from those with which we are familiar. Even for those within our own culture who admire these other patterns from afar, it requires a very great effort of empathy to conceive in concrete terms of the ways in which children in those other societies learn. It is not the purpose of this chapter to explore those ways. For those who wish to do so, there are standard books which constitute useful introductions.

It is, however, the purpose of this chapter to remind its readers that the context of social learning in our own society, however complex and imperfectly understood it is, constitutes only one of many environments within which children of the world today make maps with which to perceive each other. It is a stimulating, but a potentially perilous diversity.

References

Anthony, W.S. (1977), 'Activity in the learning of Piagetian operational thinking', *BJEP*, vol. 47, part 1, pp. 18-24.

Ausubel, D.P. (1968), *Educational psychology: a cognitive view*, New York, Holt, Rinehart and Winston.

Blyth, W.A.L., Cooper, K.R., Derricott, R., Elliott, G., Sumner, H., Waplington, A. (1976), *Curriculum Planning in History, Geography and Social Science*, Collins, ESL Bristol.

Cooper, K.R. (1976) , *Evaluation, Assessment and Record-Keeping in History, Geography and Social Science*, Collins, ESL Bristol.

Cooper, K.R. (1977), 'Diagnostic teaching', *Education 3-13*, vol. 5, no. 1, pp. 12-16.

Cooper, K.R. and Harlen, Wynne (1977), 'A stronger teacher role in curriculum development', *Journal of Curriculum Studies*, vol. 9, no. 1, pp. 21-29.

De Bono, E. (1976), *Some content and patterns of thinking in primary school children*, Report HR2327 from SSRC Projects, available from British Library Lending Division.

Derricott, R., Elliott, G., Sumner, H., Waplington, A. (1977), *Themes in Outline*, Collins, ESL Bristol.

Easton, D. (1965), *A Framework for Political Analysis*, Engelwood Cliffs, Prentice-Hall.

Elliott, G. (1976), *Teaching for Concepts*, Collins, ESL Bristol.

Elliott, G., Sumner, H., Waplington, A. (1976), *People on the Move (pupil's unit)*, Collins, ESL Bristol.

Flavell, J.H., Botkin, R.T., Fry, C.L., Wright, J.W., Jarvis, P.E. (1968), *The Development of Role-Taking and Communication Skills in Children*, New York, Wiley.

Geber, B.A. (ed.) (1977), *Piaget and Knowing*, Routledge and Kegan Paul.

Kingdom, E. (1975), *Key concepts and curriculum content*, Schools Council Project, occasional paper no. 5, School of Education, University of Liverpool.

Livesley, J. and Bromley, D.B. (1973), *Person Perception in Childhood and Adolescence*, London, John Wiley.

Modgil, S. and Modgil, C. (1976), *Piagetian Research: compilation and commentary*, vol. 4, Windsor, NFER Publishing Company.

Satterly, D.J.H. (1970), *A study of cognitive styles and their implications for curriculum development*, unpublished PhD. thesis, University of Bristol.

Selman, R. and Byrne, D.F. (1974), 'Structural developmental analysis of levels of role-taking in middle childhood', *Child Development*, vol. 45, pp. 803-6.

Smedslund, J. (1977), 'Piaget's psychology in practice', *Br. J.E. Psychol.*, 47, 1-6.

16 MATCHING THE LEARNING ENVIRONMENT TO CHILDREN'S DEVELOPMENT: THE PROGRESS IN LEARNING SCIENCE PROJECT

Wynne Harlen

Source: Specially written for this volume.

One of the comments most commonly made about the project 'Progress in Learning Science' is that it would be more appropriately named if the word 'science' were dropped from the title. This, in some respects, is true, in others not, for the project has indeed a double focus. It is centrally concerned to help teachers with the process of making decisions about activities and approaches most likely to benefit their particular pupils, and the strategies suggested for this are relevant to learning across the curriculum. At the same time the examples and detailed discussion of the issues involved focus on one area of the curriculum, science, and the problems encountered by teachers of five to thirteen year olds. Reasons for choosing science rather than any other area are to be found partly in the background provided by previous curriculum development projects and partly in the priorities of the project's sponsoring body, the Schools Council.

Systematic curriculum innovation began in this country with recognition of the need to update science education. Though secondary science projects were the first to be started, supported by the Nuffield Foundation before the Schools Council was set up, primary science was also under scrutiny. The idea that primary schools should do more than the traditional nature study was already being actively discussed in the late 1950s and was given public support in 1961 by the inspectorate[1] and by the Association for Science Education,[2] which established a Primary Schools Committee in 1963. The Nuffield Junior Science project[3] began in January 1964, and meanwhile the Ministry of Education[4] and the Froebel Foundation[5] sponsored projects to study the development of scientific ideas in children. These groups shared the view that science for young children should mean first hand experience of observing and manipulating objects and materials; they rejected any idea of a simplified version of the science taught in secondary schools, and stressed the importance of science as a way of working rather than a body of knowledge to be mastered. In its initial policy statement the ASE's Primary Committee clearly supported the emphasis upon learning processes and not on content:

'At this level we are concerned more with the developing of an enquiring attitude of mind than with the learning of facts' and 'at no time is the imparting of factual knowledge to be regarded as an end in itself'.[2] Many echoes of this statement can be found in the publications of the Nuffield Junior Science project. Coverage of a certain content was not to be the factor dictating children's activities but rather the project urged that children should find their own problems to study, ones of significance to them, not those handed to them by others.

The work of Piaget had a strong influence on these early publications about primary science. Piaget provided from his research sound arguments for stressing the involvement of children in practical investigations. But whilst these findings formed the theoretical underpinning for the methods of teaching and learning advocated it was felt in some quarters that there remained a large gulf between researchers and teachers. It was a desire to provide, or strengthen, a link between research findings and the advice given to teachers that motivated a proposal to the Schools Council for a project on 'The development of scientific and mathematical concepts in children between the ages of 7 and 11'. This project was set up in 1968 at the University College of North Wales at Bangor, where it lasted until 1973. It originally intended to examine a wide range of concepts relevant to maths and science, but then decided to focus its work in the three fundamental concepts of area, weight and volume.

The Bangor project produced a research report[6] and a book for teachers,[7] separate sections on the three concepts forming the main bulk of the latter. Within each section the detailed treatment of various aspects of the development of the concept begins with the presentation of a series of tests for the teacher to use to find out the child's existing ideas, followed by teaching suggestions tailored to what is found. The project team claimed that they 'do not wish this guide to be thought of as a recipe for teaching various topics', but at the same time, they argue, there is a need for a certain amount of prescription: 'if we are to aim for understanding rather than rote responses by the pupils we believe that the presentation of practical work requires a sequential treatment and a considerable degree of structure'.[8] Kits of materials for use in carrying out the tests and for the teaching sequences have been produced to accompany the teachers' guide. This project thus gives a very thorough treatment to a small number of concepts and is in sharp contrast to the Nuffield project both in the nature and range of materials produced. Yet both projects were aiming to promote the classroom implementation of Piaget's ideas; perhaps their differences illustrate the difficulties of attempting to do this.

Soon after the end of the Nuffield project the Schools Council set up Science 5/13[9] to provide further help for teachers in the primary and middle years. Science 5/13 endorsed the same basic child-centred approach to learning science as its predecessor and the conviction that: 'In general children work best when trying to find answers to problems they have themselves chosen to investigate'.[10] As with the Nuffield project it was impossible to implement this approach by producing anything like a course, a list of experiments, or a programme of work. Instead Science 5/13 produced a large and rich resource of ideas and examples for activities relating to a number of different topics, from which teachers can choose, take suggestions, or adapt, to suit their own pupils. There are no pupil books and no kits of equipment, since these would necessarily restrict the freedom of pupils to work on problems of their own finding.

The main differences between the two projects are that Science 5/13 gives more background information for teachers about topics and activities described, suggests an explicit statement of objectives and provides a structure for building up skills and concepts progressively. The Nuffield project team held that stating objectives might needlessly set limits to the children's achievement rather than assist it, whereas Science 5/13 considered that the statement of objectives was necessary for teachers to guide children's work effectively. By stating objectives at three stages of development Science 5/13 aimed to provide a structure for building up skills, concepts and attitudes progressively. However despite the extra support the Science 5/13 units provide, the task remaining to teachers is to decide which of the many possible activities and approaches is most appropriate for individuals or groups in their care.

It is unavoidable that this decision-making is left to the teacher if a learner-centred approach – one which begins from the learner's present ideas and interests – is to be implemented. The teacher is undoubtedly in the best position to find out 'where a child is' and start from there, but the difficulties of doing this are not to be minimised. It requires knowledge of the child's ideas and skills, a clear idea of goals for development of these things, knowledge of the course this development is likely to take and awareness of the kinds of experiences which foster the development. The Bangor project was in its own way providing some help with this, but only in respect of three concepts. That teachers needed additional guidance in this decision-making was recognised during the work of the Science 5/13[9] project and the present author, then evaluator of Science 5/13, attempted to supply help with at least part of the process. This took the form of a series of 'diagnostic statements'[11] derived from the Science 5/13 objectives, intended to help teachers find out about the children's development by observing aspects of behaviour in their day-to-day activities. Trials showed that the attempt was useful in principle, though the form it took was too rough and clumsy for easy use, and really tackled only part of the problem. No more could be done within the terms of reference of Science 5/13, therefore a new project, which eventually was called 'Progress in Learning Science' was proposed to the Schools Council.

The problems of decision-making in relation to teaching science have their counterpart in all other areas of the curriculum, as was acknowledged by the Plowden Committee:

> Teachers face the difficult task of assessing individual differences, appraising effort in relation to them and avoiding the twin pitfalls of demanding too much and expecting too little.[12]

However, though central to a great deal of teachers' work, there are reasons why the task presents particular difficulties in science. Science activities generally call upon a combination of a number of different skills, ideas and attitudes, making the recognition of development in any one of these attributes more difficult than in cases where individual skills are more easily picked out, as perhaps in mathematics or reading. Also the degree to which development in certain abilities is evident depends on the content of the activity, the opportunities it provides; this interaction of content and process complicates the assessment of either.

Primary school teachers may also find difficulty in assessing science because of uncertain personal knowledge of the subject, which not only reduces confidence but may also mean that they have not the necessary understanding themselves to recognise aspects of scientific development in children. Teachers of science in secondary schools on the other hand may find that assessing development is not easy because of unfamiliarity with the progressive stages in development in children's ideas, and the course of gradual formation of basic concepts. Specialist science teachers also have the problem of facing many different classes each week with a consequent reduction in opportunity to find out about each individual.

These were, then, some of the reasons for focusing on science whilst dealing with a set of more general issues. The project was thus set up with the general aim of providing teachers with help in assessing children's development in scientific ideas, skills and attitudes and using this information in making decisions about experiences appropriate to children at different stages of development. In contrast with the earlier projects it was not concerned with producing teaching materials or ideas for activities, an abundance of these being already available in the products of

Science 5/13, the Nuffield project and other publications. The purpose was rather to concentrate on the teaching strategy which would hopefully enable teachers to use these existing resources to greater advantage.

Theoretical Basis

At the centre of ideas held and developed by the project was the notion that in making decisions about learning experiences the aim should be to match these to the pupils' development in the skills, ideas and attitudes involved. This was directly in line with the child-centred philosophies underpinning the Science 5/13 and the Nuffield project, but these earlier projects had not spelled out the reasons for this nor its consequences for the way teachers made decisions in the classroom. PLS thought it necessary to answer the question 'Why is matching so important?' before going into the details of attempting to put it into practice.

Three reasons were proposed for considering that matching is an essential part of an effective teaching strategy. The first called on theories of children's learning. The project made considerable use of Piaget's description of mental development as a basis for discussing the pattern of children's changing ideas, but pointed out that Piaget was not the only person to have stressed matching.

> The importance of using methods and modes of communication which fit the point a child has reached is widely acknowledged by experts, who may differ on other matters, but not on this. A child can only use the ways of thinking and reacting which he has built up himself to help him make sense of new experience. If the new experience is too far beyond the reach of his present ideas he not only fails to make sense of it but also misses a chance of advancing his ways of thinking. On the other hand when his activities *are* at a level at which he can make sense of them they enlarge his knowledge and help to strengthen, or perhaps modify, his abilities and ideas. It is through modifying existing ways of thinking to take account of new experience that mental development takes place: thus the notion of 'matching' also embraces that of 'stretching'; it is not a static but a dynamic process.[13]

The second reason was deduced from evidence of 'mismatching'.

> The mismatch can arise either when experiences require more advanced ideas than a child possesses or when they are at too simple a level and give no opportunity for mental stretching. In these circumstances children *do* learn something, but it is not what we intend them

to learn; instead they may be learning that school is a boring place, or a place where they are bewildered and never able to do what is expected of them. Repeated experience of failure may set up a vicious circle in which both teacher and child reach the conclusion that the child is never going to succeed, and this in itself makes further failure more likely. Of course occasional failure, and unavoidable mismatching which must occur at certain times, will not be damaging; it is when repeated failure is the general pattern that a child will inevitably regard his work in a negative way and come to dislike school and all that is associated with it, and may even develop a negative attitude towards himself.[14]

Thirdly, the opinions of experienced teachers were cited, as exemplified in the Plowden report from which the following passage was quoted:

There has to be the right mixture of the familiar and the novel, the right match to the stage of learning the child has reached. If the material is too familiar or the learning skills too easy the children will become inattentive and bored. If too great maturity is demanded of them, they fall back on half remembered formulae and become concerned only to give the reply the teacher wants. Children can think and form concepts so long as they work at their own level and are not made to feel that they are failures.[15]

However convincing the arguments in favour of matching may be it has to be admitted that in practice complete matching is an ideal unattainable in practice. This can easily be appreciated by looking at what it involves. The first ideas about this are introduced schematically in the project's material:

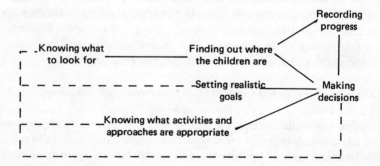

The three arrows from the left pointing towards 'decision making' suggest the processes on which the latter depends if there is to be any attempt to start from the child's ideas. Finding out where the children are depends upon having in mind what to look for, which will be influenced by the teacher's long-term goals. Setting realistic short-term goals depends on appreciating the course of development towards the goals and the size of step a particular child is likely to be able to take. The loop to 'recording progress' suggests that the build up of a cumulative record of 'where the children are' can reveal evidence of progress, or lack of it, and help in making decisions about how to help them.

It is immediately necessary to face the uncertainty of all the information on which a decision is based. We never know exactly 'where a child is'; even if we did, at any one time, he would very soon have changed. Neither can we be sure what are realistic goals; there are no universal guidelines about the right size of step a child can be asked to take in his thinking. Even if we did know these things there would still be uncertainty about the activities and approaches which would help a child take the next step. Any decision can at best be an approximation based on the experience of ourselves and others and on whatever relevant research has been carried out.

There are therefore no rules to follow for matching; no prescriptions can be given for the 'best' decisions in particular instances. But though the decision will be different in each instance the strategy for arriving at it is the same in each case. The key element in the strategy is *feedback* about the effect of one decision which is immediately used in further decisions, producing a closer approximation to matching. The process is thus seen to be essentially dynamic, one in which information about the changing situation is constantly being gathered and used. Matching considered in this way is not a matter of employing certain techniques for assessing children or guidelines to choosing activities, but a teaching strategy with consequences for many aspects of teachers' behaviour and interaction with their pupils.

One of these consequences brought out is the need to cater for children as individuals. Since each child will be at different points in development with respect to the range of attributes involved in learning and will have a unique set of background and personal factors affecting his responses, it follows that it will not be possible to 'match' if the teacher makes decisions for a class as a whole. The concept of matching demands that information is gathered about individual children and decisions are made for children as individuals.

This catering for children as individuals does not mean that they have separate activities or learn on their own. In some cases the difference between the experiences of one child and the next in a group may be only in the teacher's expectations of each of them, or in the parts they are encouraged to take in group activity. In other cases children apparently engaged in the same activity can be working at quite different levels, one widening his experience by seeing what happens, another pursuing enquiries to find out why it happens. With these variations the children can each be learning quite different things and at the same time interacting with each other and each helping another's thinking.

In order to help teachers implement the strategy for matching which has been described the project produced materials which attempt to give help with the three processes involved: gathering information about the children, interpreting this in terms of development so that realistic goals can be identified and knowing what activities and approaches are likely to promote progress at different points in development. The form these take and the way in which they were produced is now described.

The Project's Development

It is often the case that problems take on a changed character as one begins to grapple with them, certain aspects are revealed only in the course of trying intended solutions; it is as though the act of investigation is a necessary part of understanding a problem. This is certainly what happened in PLS; over the course of the four and a half years of the project there were various changes in emphasis, different approaches tried, ideas modified. Commenting on this in one of the later 'information papers' produced by the project it was stated: 'We like to think that these shifts have shown flexibility in responding to emerging issues rather than an inability to know our own minds.'[16]

The background to the project has already been described, so the story is taken up from when the work began, in April 1973. The project had a small team, of two and a half at its greatest, and that for only one of the years of its life. It was not however for this reason only that much of the work has been done in collaboration with groups of teachers. The involvement of teachers was prompted by strong convictions that a curriculum development project should be directed towards central concerns of teachers, that teachers have the right to take a part in determining the problems to be tackled and the kinds of solutions provided, and that they have the ability and experience to take this part. The project saw itself as working in partnership with teachers; the team members had the time, the kind of experience to give a broad view, and access to research that most teachers probably did not have, whilst the teachers had closer involvement and insight into the classroom problems than the team. Decisions about the initial focus and content of the work had, of course, to be taken by the project director, working alone in the first year, but the hope was to keep these decisions open to change as found necessary.

Work was begun first on devising means of helping teachers gather information about their children's ideas and abilities. The context of use for day-to-day decision making places great demands upon the method used for obtaining information about the children. What is needed is a method which is flexible, gives immediate results, can be used repeatedly, as frequently as necessary, does not consume teaching and learning time and is capable of providing information about a wide range of abilities, attitudes, skills and concepts. A form of assessment with these ideal properties was not to be found by looking at conventional tests. However we realised that it could be found in what teachers already do. In the normal course of their work teachers are constantly observing individual children's reactions and responses and this observation could provide an ideal channel for the kind of feedback wanted. But much of what teachers observe may not seem to them very helpful for recognising development in relation to science if they are not aware of behaviours which are significant. The clues are there, but many teachers are not picking them up because they do not realise what to look for. It seemed likely, therefore, that the most suitable form of help would be an observation check-list which would focus attention on relevant aspects of children's behaviour.

The first step in devising check-lists to provide a framework for observing was to answer the question – what do we need to know about children to help their learning? Several groups of teachers were formed, in various parts of the country, to tackle this question. At first we thought of devising three check-lists, covering the 5 to 13 age range in three overlapping sections: 5 to 9, 7 to 11 and 9 to 13. Therefore separate groups of teachers concerned with these smaller age ranges were formed. At different times there were series of meetings with three groups of infants, two groups of juniors, two of middle school and one of lower secondary teachers.

Before beginning to answer the question of what were the attitudes, concepts, abilities, etc. about which teachers may need information, it was necessary to consider what was meant by 'science'. There was agreement to a surprising degree amongst all teachers consulted with the statement that in the age range considered, science could be described as 'a way of learning involving first hand experience, enquiry, problem solving, the interpretation and communication of findings and the encouragement of attitudes which promote this way of working'.[17] Evidently this refers to the kind of activity carried out in many areas of the curriculum and in relation to content other than that generally studied in 'science'. This interpretation of science is much the same as that underlying the Nuffield Junior Science Project and Science 5/13.

This statement about the meaning of science may well be criticised for what it omits rather than what it includes. There are those who, whilst agreeing with its emphasis on process rather than content, point out that some essential elements of scientific processes are missing. Science is centrally concerned with making sense of the world around through the proposition and testing of hypotheses, which can never be proved to be correct but are used until shown to be incorrect and are then replaced by alternative hypotheses. The project justifies the omission of this aspect of the scientific process on the grounds that its concern is the learning of science, not the fully developed scientific behaviour as conceived by philosophers. In the years from five to thirteen it is only possible to build up those aspects of scientific behaviour which are accessible to the ways of thinking of children in this age range, those which are essentially concrete, deriving patterns from observations and exploring the extent of their patterns. To entertain hypotheses and to test them by attempting to disprove them demands a greater ability to think in abstract terms; this aspect of science is most appropriately developed at the later stage of formal thought.

Criticism of a different kind comes from those who object that the statement apparently neglects the content of science. Factual knowledge will of course be accumulated whilst children are helped to explore their environment and make sense of their experience in a scientific way, but the question is whether there are some items of knowledge which should be specified as being important to cover before the age of thirteen. The Nuffield and Science 5/13 projects had set themselves against specifying content, mainly on the grounds that to do so would tend to restrict children's freedom to pursue problems of their own, prevent integration of science with work in other areas of the curriculum and reduce the motivation for learning skills and developing ideas which is so strong when children can work on what interests them. The importance of a progressive build up of a body of knowledge was not ignored but it was felt that this became of more importance from the age of thirteen onwards.

The answer which PLS gave on the question of content came at the next stage, of identifying in more detail the way of learning and the attitudes referred to in its statement about science. As well as enquiry skills and attitudes a number of basic concepts, or generalisations, were included, indicating a minimum set of ideas about things in their environment which children should build up whilst learning to explore and experiment. These are attainable through a great range of different experiences and therefore do not dictate children's activities.

In the course of discussions with the various groups about details of items for the three age ranges it became clear that the distinctions we were trying to make between one age range and another were too fine and were likely to give an unwanted impression of linking age to developmental stage. The idea of two lists, not linked to age but simply to 'earlier' and 'later' development was found more workable. From the consensus of views from different groups and after many drafts, further discussions and revision, the following lists of goals emerged:

For Earlier Development	*For Later Development*
Curiosity	Curiosity
Originality	Originality
Perseverance	Perseverance
Openmindedness	Openmindedness
Self-criticism	Self-criticism
Responsibility	Responsibility
Willingness to co-operate	Willingness to co-operate
Independence in thinking	Independence in thinking
Observing	Observing
Raising questions	Proposing enquiries
Exploring	Experimenting/investigating
Problem solving	Communicating verbally
Finding patterns in observations	Communicating non-verbally
Communicating verbally	Finding patterns in observations
Communicating non-verbally	Critical reasoning
Applying learning	Applying learning
Classifying	Concept of causality
Concept of causality	Concept of measurement
Concept of time	Concept of volume
Concept of weight	Concept of force
Concept of length	Concept of energy
Concept of area	Concept of change
Concept of volume	Concept of interdependence of living things
Concept of life cycle	Concept of adaptation of living things

For the purpose of helping teachers' observations, however, it was not sufficient to list the goals and suggest looking at how observant a child is, or whether or not he displays openmindedness. Such an approach would give the teacher little help in knowing what to look for and would be open to a variety of interpretations of the meaning of observation, openmindedness, and so on. Instead the project produced check-lists which attempt to do two things: to provide agreed meanings for each goal and to suggest behavioural indications of different points in development towards each goal. The intention was to draw attention to particular aspects of children's actions and responses and at the same time provide a structure for interpreting what was observed in terms of the development of particular attributes. For example for the ability of 'finding patterns in observations' the statements suggesting progressive levels for the 'earlier' development are:

1. Rarely goes beyond a straight report of observations showing little sign of appreciation of any patterns within them which could have been discerned.
2. Makes rather sweeping statements about his observations, suggesting patterns which are not justified by the evidence.
3. He puts 'two and two together' and attempts to find patterns in his findings which are justified by what he has observed.

For the concept of cause and effect:

1. Accepts that things happen and mechanical things work without seeking for a cause, or suggests reasons in terms of fantasy or mystery.
2. Gives explanations in terms of the presence of some component or feature which may play some part in the process but is not itself the cause. Has difficulty predicting what he thinks may happen when certain changes are made.
3. Seeks to explain physical effects in terms of physical causes even though the correct causal relationship may not be found. Uses the cause-effect relationship observed to suggest what will be the result of certain changes.

For openmindedness:

1. Tends to stick to preconceived ideas ignoring contrary evidence.
2. Will take notice of some opinions and ideas different from his own but not others, being influenced by the authority behind alternative

views rather than the strength of the evidence or argument.

3. Generally listens to and considers all points of view and relevant evidence; accepts new ideas if the evidence is convincing.

The course of development described by the statements for many of the goals draws on the findings of Piaget and others, such as the work of the Bangor project (see pages 2 and 3). The results of relevant research were used where these existed, as in the case of basic concepts and some attitudes linked to cognitive development, to produce first drafts. The draft statements were compared with empirical observations on children carried out by working groups of teachers helping the project. In the case of several goals — particularly those relating to enquiry skills — there was little previous work to use as a guide and the statements were developed by observation. Experienced teachers were asked to record behaviour of children whom they judged to have little, moderate or well developed skill in, say, ability to propose enquiries. Discussions of the criteria being used enabled more generalised statements to be framed from the specific examples provided. These were then tried and discussed by other teachers and modified to produce successive drafts. One statistical tool used in revising the statements was a form of cluster analysis. This showed up such things as overlap between statements relating to different goals and inconsistency in the relationship of supposedly progressive levels of development.

Information for revising the check-lists was not the only kind of result from the trials of the early drafts. It was immediately clear that there were striking differences in reactions of teachers who had taken part earlier and of those who had not helped to produce the drafts. The former group saw the check-list in the context of matching, and of examining how well they themselves were catering for the children's development. The latter, however, despite an introductory discussion, saw it as a complex way of assessing children and keeping records; they failed to grasp its relevance to their teaching. This kind of experience was repeated at later stages, and eventually was a major factor in altering the form of the project's products.

In parallel with the production of the check-lists, work began on guidelines to the sorts of experience likely to be beneficial to children at different points in development. This was also carried out with the help of groups of teachers, who provided a large number of examples to illustrate children's behaviour at different points in development of each goal and to communicate ideas about ways of helping children make progress. Guides for each of the goals were drafted separately and later put together as a book called 'Finding Answers: Guide to Diagnosis and Development'. Guidelines to the kinds of experiences which have been found effective in helping children's progress are described — in broad terms and illustrated by examples. They vary in nature according to the kind of goal being discussed. In the case of development of concepts they refer to kinds of activities which should be provided and others which should be avoided for children according to their existing ideas. For example in the case of the concept of Time:

Children's Ideas	*Appropriate Activities*
Behaves as if he has his own time which is only occasionally linked to the time of others.	1, 2, 3, 4, 5.
Uses events in his daily routine to mark the time and judge time intervals.	1, 2, 3, 4, 5.
Appreciates time is the same for everyone and knows the sequence of common events in his experience.	3, 4, 5, 6, 7.
Unable to take into account differences in speed when comparing the time or distance of travel of moving objects.	4, 5, 6, 7, 8.
Recognises that two equal time intervals remain the same regardless of the speed, frequency or nature of events taking place in them.	6, 7, 8, 9, 10, 11.
Takes distance and time into account when comparing speeds.	8, 9, 10, 11, 12.

Some of the activities listed 1-12 are:

1. Sand and water play with containers with holes at varying levels and of different sizes, using words quick, slow, fast, etc.
2. Ordering daily activities in sequence, using words before, after, sooner, later, etc.
3. Re-telling simple stories, putting events in order of sequence, using dramatic play.
4. Keeping a calendar, with names of days and months. Marking events on a calendar.
5. Celebrating birthdays, discussing age, getting older, etc.
6. Playing with mobile toys on slopes of varying gradients. Comparing rates of movement of clockwork toys.

7.   Telling the time, using words minute, hour, quarter to, etc.

8.   Dramatic play and story writing to develop an appreciation of succession of events.

10.   Constructing and calibrating timing devices, e.g. sand, shadow, water clocks.

11.   Working out time intervals and duration of a series of events: timetables, cooking, automatic timing devices, 24 hour clock.

12.   Timing events and activities, e.g. pendulum swing, races, personal activities, heart beats.

In the case of attitudes the guidelines do not refer to activities but to approaches, relationships and opportunities which can encourage development of more mature attitudes. For instance, for 'Responsibility' the main elements in fostering this attitude are described under the headings: providing appropriate opportunities for taking responsibility, recognising variation between children, providing a safe framework, providing an example and encouraging accountability. There is a different scheme again for the enquiry skills. After a brief discussion of the development of the skill three short sections give suggestions for encouraging it at the three levels described in the check-list statements.

During the development of the guides it was clear that, as in the case of the check-lists, they were not enough help on their own. Teachers in our working groups had fully discussed the issues which had to be resolved in producing the check-lists and guides and were aware of the context in which they were intended to be of use, but those without this experience found the materials much less relevant and helpful. It seemed that the *products* were perhaps no more important than the *processes* of discussing the notion of matching, considering the need to have information about children's progress, working out the goals of learning in science, identifying aspects of the learning environment which foster the development of certain ideas, attitudes and skills. Consequently the project decided to devise ways of enabling teachers to study aspects of these and other relevant topics.

A collection of materials for discussion during in-service meetings was assembled, consisting of notes, information on audio-tape, child-studies to illustrate matching in action, examples on video-tape of various behaviours both of teachers and children; evidence and arguments in favour of matching were presented and information was given about children's development before the check-lists were introduced. The major effort went into the preparation of this material eighteen months after the beginning of the project, when the team was at full strength. Development trials of the first draft took place in seven schools in Oxfordshire, where the teachers met in school-based discussion groups for nine sessions throughout one term. Feedback from a variety of sources was gathered and used to revise and reorganise the materials.

The changes found necessary in writing the final version were extensive, more than a little revision here and there but rather a complete reshaping and remaking of much of the content. A major reason for this was the realisation that we had failed to 'match' the in-service work to the teachers. As one Head, who had been leader of a group in her school, put it 'It's exactly the same with the grown-ups as it is with the children. If you try to take them further than they are ready to go you just get disaster, you'd do better to leave them alone.' The teachers were at various stages in their appreciation of ideas about matching and indeed in their understanding of children's development and a way of catering for this diversity had to be found.

To give this needed flexibility, the main content was re-arranged in three 'themes' which can be used separately, or in any sequence. The three themes reflect the three aspects of the process of matching:

Making and recording observations about children.
Children's development and learning.
Making decisions about the learning environment.

Each theme is divided into six topics which can be treated in varying degrees of depth, rather as in the example just given in the section about Piaget. 'Supplementary material' provides a collection of further ideas for discussion and additional examples which can be used by those who wish to go beyond the level of practicality of the main sections. In addition to the three themes there are two introductory topics which give an overview of the problems addressed in the project's products as a whole and in the in-service material in particular. Introductory material in the trial version was felt to be inadequate, so these two topics were produced to help to give teachers an idea of what to expect in the material and what they were likely to get from it.

Differences in teachers' reactions were particularly marked in relation to the discussion of Piaget's description of development. In the trial material Piaget's stages were presented on video-tape, where the commentary described the main characteristics of the stages and sequences showed children engaged in normal activities displaying behaviour which seemed to illustrate the characteristics. The written material for teachers consisted only of summary notes about each stage, linking the stages of thinking with appropriate activities. This treatment seemed to satisfy very few, but the reasons for dissatisfaction were diverse.

There were those who 'tuned out' at the first mention of Piaget — it has always seemed too theoretical and complex for them. There were those who felt this was going over ground they had covered at college and expected something 'new'. There were those who intuitively agreed with the developmental description but wanted to understand the details and the consequences in a much less hurried and summary manner.

The approach decided upon in relation to this aspect of the material illustrates the compromise adopted throughout in rewriting. The subject of development in thinking is introduced through examining children's ideas about one particular subject, 'time' being chosen for this. Examples are given to show a gradual development, in terms familiar to teachers of primary children. A pattern in this development is then drawn out and linked with development of children's other ideas. Piaget's description is then brought in to fill out details of the general pattern of development, the more theoretical parts being provided not in the main text but the 'supplementary material'. Piaget's ideas are also used to suggest a way of helping a child progress from one point in his thinking to another. A section on audio-tape, and in transcript, describes the four factors which Piaget identified as affecting the development of children's ideas: maturation, experience of objects and actions, social transmission and the process of accommodating ways of thinking to new experiences. These four factors are drawn together to conclude that

> providing there are experiences which a child can take in with his already formed ideas, then challenge to these ideas from experiences which do not entirely fit them is a good way to encourage progress. The child then proceeds by small degrees, from one level to a slightly more powerful way of thinking, but he cannot jump several levels at a time.[20]

These ideas are applied in a later section where it is pointed out that in practice there can be no guarantee of progress from certain experiences, the teacher has to try a rather 'hit or miss' approach:

> . . . we can find out through observation about . . . how well a child has developed a certain skill or way of thinking. Although we don't know exactly how or when to help him make the next step, we can make use of this knowledge that we have about where he is at present. Acting on this information we can give him plenty of opportunity for

enjoying and using his present skills with success. If he then encounters more complex situations in which he has to extend these ideas and skills he will be more able to attempt these and to succeed if he has consolidated the ideas and skills in the first place. If he begins to fail too often then we know the situations are too far ahead of him and he should return to the level of activity where he can succeed.[21]

It is intended that these broad principles are kept in mind when using the suggestions on activities suitable at different points given in 'Finding Answers'.

The Products and their Use

The project's materials have been published under the overall title 'Match and Mismatch' in acknowledgement of their relevance to many areas of learning, not just to science. Between them the products have two purposes, for use during in-service course and use in the classroom as a resource. Schematically the purposes and products are related as follows:

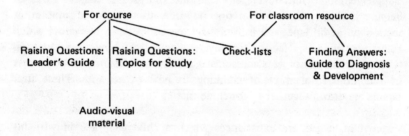

In summary the project has produced two books for teachers, one of topics for in-service study (entitled 'Raising Questions') and one of guidelines to selecting activities and approaches according to children's development (entitled 'Finding Answers: A Guide to Diagnosis and Development'). The Leader's Guide contains all the material in 'Raising Questions' plus notes for in-service group leaders. The two check-lists are included in 'Raising Questions'.

We now take a closer look at 'Raising Questions' to give some idea of the nature of the in-service materials and what follows from using them. Space allows for only one of the three themes to be considered in any detail, and the one entitled 'Making and Recording Observations' has been chosen since it introduces the check-lists and brings out some implementations problems and approaches.

The first of the six topics in this theme begins from the methods teachers already use for assessing children's attributes, since such assessments are being made all the time, often subconsciously. Issues of 'subjectivity' and 'objectivity' are raised in relation to the kinds of information teachers need for the purpose of helping children's learning as opposed to other purposes. There are some notes of the 'Pros and cons of testing' in the 'Supplementary material', for use if desired. A case study is presented on tape and film strip of a ten year old boy, a child who is very quick to pick up new ideas and demonstrates orally a real understanding of complex relationships, yet is a poor reader and has great difficulties in writing, introduces discussion on the breadth of information required about individual children. The focus is then narrowed to the kinds of information relevant to learning science and to the ways in which progress towards various goals can be observed. There is opportunity to apply one set of check-list statements to children seen on video-tape before the whole lists are introduced. An input on tape and film strip opens up the topic of 'What is observing?' This suggests that it is much more than just looking at children but involves the relationship between teacher and pupils. Ways in which teachers can examine and perhaps improve their observation are proposed. Finally there is some discussion of different ways in which observations can be recorded and the records used.

During this series of discussions teachers are asked to make a study of one child in their class and apply to him or her the various ideas which emerge. When the check-list statements are introduced it is suggested that the criteria stated for three goals — problem solving, the concept of length, and curiosity — are kept in mind in relation to this one child. Some problems are then faced before the task is made overwhelming by attempting to use the whole list.

A common problem at this early stage is that of knowing just what to look for. This arises particularly in relation to concept development as, for example, the concept of length with young children. One of the project team members working with a small group of teachers found it helpful to set up special situations in order to observe the children's behaviour relating to the concept of length. They watched a child engaged on activities which called upon the notion of length, listened while the team member asked the child questions which drew out his ideas and then discussed the behaviour they had seen in terms of the criteria given in the check-list statements for this concept. After repeating for themselves the activities and questioning with other children they began to recognise the significant things which the children were doing. The account of this, recorded in the 'Supplementary Material' goes on: 'Then they said that they wouldn't need to go through the special activities again. Before they couldn't relate the check-list statements to the children at all, and now they could do this and they are trying to match the children's activities to the development which they now see.'[22] The special situations served to focus the teachers' observations and once this was done they saw things happening which they had not noticed before in the children's normal work and it was no longer necessary to structure this for observation. For the teacher this is a stage of internalising the criteria and two things seem to help in this process; to keep to a small number of statements, and, where possible, to discuss observations of one child with another teacher who has also observed the child. In some cases the small number of statements has been selected from the project's list, while in other cases teachers have preferred to use a few broader goals, such as 'enquiry skills', 'concentration', 'willingness to listen', for which they have worked out criteria for describing development.

After some time, perhaps a month or more, of using a restricted list with one or only a few children, observations can be gradually extended to the whole set of goals and to more children. Experience has shown it to be more helpful to extend the range of observations in relation to a few children rather than to use the partial list with all the pupils, or to attempt to do both at once. The reason is that the immediate goal is for the teacher to learn to use the check-list as a mental framework. This framework is the same for all the children, so once it has been set up it can readily be used for any number. Some teachers have found that during this time it has been necessary to have the check-list fairly close at hand and to look through it frequently as a check on what is being noticed.

At this stage of attempting to use the whole check-list two different strategies have emerged; they can be described as 'starting from the check-list' and 'starting from the child'. In the former the teacher sets out to look for behaviour relating to particular criteria (as in the special situations described above) and records, mentally or on paper, only observations relevant to these. In the other strategy the observer examines the child's behaviour more as a whole and then attempts to relate it to the criteria. Often teachers have found that they have changed from one strategy to the other with increasing familiarity with the criteria; they begin of necessity by starting from the check-list but later change to starting from the child. The latter is probably to be preferred since it is more likely to reveal deficiencies in the check-list and to preserve the whole view of the child.

The other two themes in 'Raising Questions' can be only briefly outlined. Each is divided into six topics. The theme 'Making decisions about the learning environment' concerns the response to information about children's development when deciding about activities, organisation, interventions, relationships — all parts of the learning environment which have to be considered when attempting to match. The starting point is the identification of the many factors which influence children's learning and discussion of the ones which teachers can vary to suit individuals. Taking first the factors relating to classroom organisation and constraints the relationship between forms of organisation and goals is explored. Examples of four studies of classrooms presented on tape and film strip initiate discussion, not of whether one organisation is 'better' than another, but whether an organisation is helping or hindering progress towards particular kinds of achievement. Similarly methods of organising activities in different ways, along a continuum from teacher-directed to activities developed from children's interests, is discussed in terms of the strength and limitations of each for achieving a range of goals. Teachers are invited to examine the range of methods they use and if some extension of existing procedures seems required there are some ideas for doing this in the 'supplementary material'. The next two topics in this theme concern the selection of activities, introduced through a detailed examination of activities related to 'floating and sinking'. Consideration of the demands of an activity and of its potential for developing ideas is proposed as a way of assessing the likelihood of a match with children's ideas. Video-taped examples enable the points arising to be tested out. The discussion is broadened to other activities and the book 'Finding Answers' is introduced. Material relating to the teachers' role in supporting progress in both cognitive development and promoting positive attitudes completes this theme.

The theme about 'Children's development and learning' looks first at how children's feelings and attitudes affect their learning. Several pieces of evidence are provided in writing or on video-tape to suggest that it is as important to consider development in attitudes as it is to take account of intellectual development. The discussion of the encouragement of particular attitudes is linked with sections in 'Finding Answers'. Piaget's description of development is approached (as mentioned on page 333) from the particular discussion of children's changing notions of 'time' to the general pattern of cognitive growth, and the consequences of different ways of thinking for decisions about suitable activities are brought out. A taped discussion of 'What influences mental development' describes the four factors identified by Piaget as influencing cognitive growth, in which lies the strongest argument of all for the importance of 'matching'. The main attempt to bring out the practical implications is made in the final topic of the theme.

Again the teacher's role is seen as crucial, for many mismatches may well be made in a teacher's mind if inappropriate goals or expectations are set. Four approaches to active work are exemplified, from free choice to work cards, and the question is posed as to how well each provides for 'matching' of the various factors influencing learning which were earlier discussed. There are of course no blanket answers given. The answers are those which teachers work out for themselves after examining self-critically the extent to which potential for matching or mismatching exists in the provision they make for their children's learning.

Notes and references

1.   Ministry of Education Pamphlet No. 42, *Science in the Primary School*, London, HMSO, 1961.
2.   Association for Science Education, *Policy Statement*, prepared by the Primary Schools Science Committee, 1963.
3.   Nuffield Junior Science Project materials, *Teacher's Guide 1, Teacher's Guide 2, Animals and Plants, Apparatus*, published by Collins, Edinburgh, 1967.
4.   The DES supported the Oxford Junior Science Project 1963-7. The project team produced a report to the DES and also a book entitled *An Approach to Primary Science*, by Redman, S., Brereton, A. and Boyers, P., London, Macmillan Educational, 1969.
5.   The Froebel Foundation, supported by the British Association, ran a research project into scientific development in children, directed by Nathan Isaacs. A report, *Children learning through scientific experience*, was published by the Froebel Foundation in 1966.
6.   Research Report by E. Rothwell-Hughes published by Macmillan Education in the Schools Council Research Series, 1977.
7.   Bell *et al.*, *Area, weight and volume: monitoring and encouraging children's conceptual development*, London, Nelson, 1975.
8.   Ibid., p. 10.
9.   The Science 5/13 project was supported from 1967 to 1975. It produced twenty-six units for teachers, published by MacDonald Educational (London) from 1972-5.
10.   L.F. Ennever and W. Harlen, *With Objectives in Mind*, Guide to Science 5/13, p. 4.
11.   See W. Harlen, *Science 5/13: A Formative Evaluation*, London, Macmillan Educational 1975, pp. 66-8.
12.   *Children and their Primary Schools* (Plowden Report), London, HMSO, 1967, para. 874.
13.   *Match and Mismatch. Raising Questions*, topics for in-service study by teachers produced by 'Progress in Learning Science', Edinburgh, Oliver and Boyd, 1977, p. 8.
14.   Ibid., p. 8.
15.   *Children and their Primary Schools* (Plowden Report), London, HMSO, 1967, para. 533.

16.   At regular intervals during its lifetime the project circulated information papers summarising its current ideas and progress. Seven information papers were written, all now out of print. The quotation was in the opening paragraph of No. 6, June 1976.

17.   Ibid., p. 2.

18.   From 'Check-list for earlier development', pp. 239-47 of *Match and Mismatch. Raising Questions*, Edinburgh, Oliver and Boyd, 1977.

19.   *Match and Mismatch. Finding Answers*. Guide to diagnosis and development produced by 'Progress in Learning Science', Edinburgh, Oliver and Boyd, 1977.

20.   *Match and Mismatch. Raising Questions*, Edinburgh, Oliver and Boyd, 1977, pp. 104 and 105.

21.   Ibid., pp. 118, 119.

22.   Ibid., pp. 201, 204.

17 CONCEPTUAL DEMANDS IN THE NUFFIELD O-LEVEL PHYSICS COURSE

Michael Shayer

Source: *School Science Review*, 54 (186), p. 26 (1972).

In an article in *Education in Chemistry*[1] a technique of assessment of science courses based on Piaget's conceptual stages was described. In a subsequent article[2] it was applied to the Nuffield O-level chemistry course. In this application its language is used to suggest some conclusions about the style and structure of the O-level physics course.

For each experiment in the *Guide to Experiments* an attempt has been made to answer two questions. What is the minimum conceptual level that the pupil must have attained without which his interest cannot be sustained? And what conceptual level is needed to enable the pupil to extract from the experiment what is suggested in the *Teacher's Guide*? Answers to these questions are shown by circles and triangles in Figure 17.1. On the graph three dotted lines have been superimposed representing estimates of the ages at which three different types of pupil will gain access to the conceptual stages as described by Piaget. IQ 125+ is taken to represent the top one-fifth of the grammar and public school populations, IQ 115 is taken to represent normal grammar school pupils, and IQ 100 for the average comprehensive pupil. The lowest points in Year I and II have been joined to indicate the route of a possible minimal course, whereas for part of Year III, they have been joined to indicate the route suggested by the *Teacher's Guide* — the normal course.

Note on IQs

If someone has an IQ of 100 it means that, at the age of 10, say, his performance on a battery of specified tests is just average of a large representative sample of English children aged 10. If he has an IQ of 125+ at the age of 10, he performs on test as well as, or better than the average of the population perform at 12½. It is the ratio, expressed as a percentage, of his mental age to his chronological age. The value of 115 was chosen because half the selective school population have IQs within ± 3 of this: it thus seemed a fair characterization of the normal grammar school child.

Piaget's developmental stages are found to correlate quite well with mental ages rather than chronological ages;[3] this, taken together with the known normal distribution of mental age in the child population, enables one to estimate at what ages children will be capable of the different stages of conceptualization which Piaget describes.

Conceptual Stages Described by Piaget

The two stages which are of concern in the secondary school are the second and third: the *concrete* and the *formal*. Each of these takes about four years to work through, and is subdivided A and B: B marking the end of a stage, when its conceptual style has become freely available, and A representing a more loosely defined period when some of its strategies are

Figure 17.1

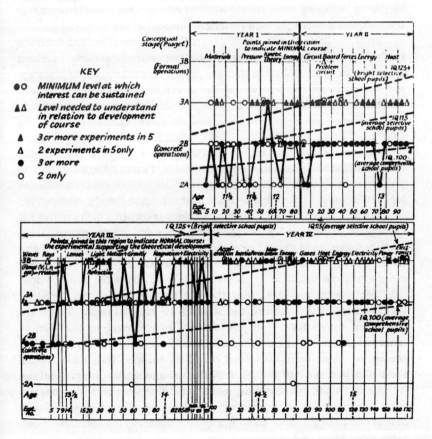

used, but not consistently, or with confidence.

The *concrete operations* stage is characterized in speech by repetition rather than analysis: reported conversation is necessarily of the 'I said to him' and 'he said to me' type — the bulk of the ordinary conversation of adolescent girls. In games or morality it is when the *rule* or the *law* is the important thing. Someone at this stage will not see that a different situation requires modification of the rule, and that real sanction is derived from mutual respect and adjustment between persons. In number work, numbers regarded as things can be manipulated as a series, but not in the abstract as in algebra or deductive geometry. Simple and double classification is possible (animals as vertebrates/invertebrates *and* land or sea creatures), allowing some simple work in biology, but hypothesis-making is *not* available as an approach (certainly someone at this stage can use trial and error to discover something of what is happening, but the scientific method requires more than this). Curiosity is certainly present — perhaps the more so as any relations that are perceived, as the name of the stage suggests, can only be observed as the direct properties of the apparatus which is being handled or the situation in which they occur. And, even in the intelligent adult, it is at this level that new experience would be assimilated first.

The *formal operations* stage enables the pupil to make use of a far more flexible relationship to the world in that the necessity for action can be postponed while the situation is translated into some symbolic form of representation — be it verbal or mathematical — and thereby manipulated to a possible outcome. As a speculative example, when a rugby player has become so experienced in the *obvious* moves and countermoves taking place between his body and movement, and that of others, that he begins to see (either in discussing game strategies, or in a flash in the game itself) more subtle combinations of moves that involve taking the more obvious ones for granted and then using them in combination to 'get through', then, perhaps, he has reached this stage in the game of rugby. Or when a car driver can perform 'four-wheel drift'. In conversation the form of 'reported speech' can be used, sparing one the agony of having to hear the whole sequence through. Matters of ethics become discussable on the more complex plane of the reconciliation of interests and responsibilities of people. This is sometimes expressed thus: that whereas at the concrete stage *relations* (like ratios) can be observed, at the formal stage *relations between relations* can be seen (like proportionality, the relation of one ratio to another). But this is only half the story. A perception involves a field or a medium, and relations between relations presuppose some language of symbols in which they can be successfully manipulated. Hence the term *formal* — rather than *logical* — operations, to denote some formal language or reversible symbolizing in which the relating takes place (in the car driver's mind the various possibilities that can happen to the car would be present as very strong kinaesthetic-visual images rather than words). The abstract manipulations of algebra and set theory become possible; and, in relation to science, since the possession of a formal apparatus allows the consideration of the *possible*, hypothesis-making becomes an available strategy. In Table 17.1, examples of the stages and sub-stages are given.

Table 17.1

Concrete operations		Formal operations	
2A	2B	3A	3B
	Conversation repeated in detail.	'Reported speech'	
Games involving reality. Making working models. Perception of patterns, classifying, and labelling. Number games (battleships). 'The rules' inflexibly kept to.			
	Morality is obeying the law.	Morality involves recognition of others' viewpoints and interests.	
Conservation of 'substance'.	Conservation of mass.	Conservation of volume.	Density as relationship between different volumes of different liquids.
	Number work involving seriation, i.e. the 4 rules: Addition, Subtraction, Multiplication, Division. Simple causation — 'this' causes that.	Long division. Equations and simple algebra.	3-dimensional imagination. Manipulative algebra involving proportion. Equilibrium. Probability and chance.

If one teaches science in a highly selective school, and rarely below the third year at that, one will rarely meet any pupils below the 3A stage of formal operations: if one teaches science to average classes in a comprehensive school, and rarely *above* the fourth year, one is unlikely to have met any pupils whose thinking goes beyond the concrete operations stage.

If you try to make someone participate in a process which is taking place at a more complex level than that to which they have access, communication breaks down. Your words may be simple, but the relationships they point to are not. But the feeling is unmistakable, as of the floor having given way without warning. In girls, particularly, it can cause either acute anxiety, or resentment, or both.

The Estimation of Conceptual Levels

This has been made the easier in that, when Piaget came to study the higher conceptual levels which develop in middle and late adolescence, it seemed that these were either more evident, or at least more readily tested, in the context of science experiments than in any other kind of activity. So in *The Growth of Logical Thinking* the tests cover a wide span of representative physics experiments. In each, Inhelder and Piaget list examples of response at each of the four levels (Concrete: 2A and 2B; Formal: 3A and 3B) used in Figure 17.1. So these were tabulated, and compared with the experiment details and *Teacher's Guide* recommendations. Where a section of work had no equivalent in *The Growth of Logical Thinking*, the mathematical operations involved and the style of reasoning were inspected — was it simple classification or seriation? Was a proportionality schema involved? etc. A rule of thumb used frequently (derived from Piaget's work, but not expressed explicitly there) was that if a theoretical model was involved — as, say, in the kinetic theory work — this could not be handled as an operative tool at all if the pupil was still at the concrete stage, but could be handled, if given and explained, for making some predictions if the pupil was at stage 3A. And that the active search for, and possible discovery of an explanatory and predictive model was only to be expected at stage 3B. In Table 17.2, the full list of Inhelder and Piaget's experiments is given, and details of two of them, together with the other criteria of assessment used. The reader is invited to use this table in looking at Figure 17.2, where details of part of Year 3 are given, and to compare them both with their own assessment of the experiments, and estimate of their difficulty from having taught them.

No Year V work is included on the graph, because the details of the work, and the explicit intention of the course developers, as expressed in the *Guide*, are that this should be a year in which all the work done — both new and the old seen in retrospect — is to be done as a perception of the integrating theories of physics, all of which involves 3B operations.

Figure 17.2

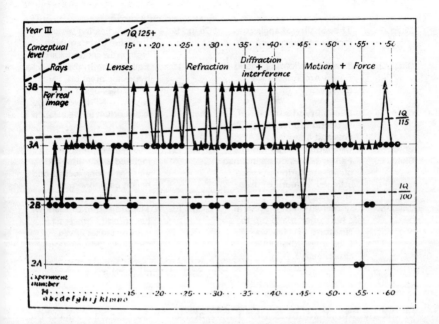

Conclusions

It is clear both from the spirit and the detail of the Nuffield physics course, particularly in the first three years, that the fact of conceptual development in children was both known and allowed for in a more conscious way than in the planning of the chemistry or biology courses. Not only is there a smoothly progressing standard of complexity visible from the first year to about half way through the fourth, but the principle is consistently observed throughout that any abstract or symbolizing work is introduced via the experimental situation to which it refers, and by which the situation is interpreted or correlated with other experience. This characteristic style — so different from traditional physics teaching — can be seen as one that allows the maximum of integration, for the pupil, of experience gained concretely with the formal or abstract language developed to handle deeper relationships, whereas much traditional physics teaching could more properly be classified under the pathology of thinking — the handling of formal relationships as symbolic games hardly related to experience at all. Indeed, when analysed in Piaget's terms, some

Table 17.2: (a) Physics Experiments used in Inhelder and Piaget: Growth of Logical Thinking

Chap. 1.	The equality of angles of incidence and reflection.	Chap. 9.	Communicating vessels (pressure differentiated from cross-sectional area).
Chap. 2.	The law of floating bodies (up to Archimedes via density).	Chap. 10.	Equilibrium in the hydraulic press (cf. force in syringes of different widths — NP I, exp. 396).
Chap. 3.	Flexibility of a metal rod, in relation to length, thickness and material.	Chap. 11.	Equilibrium in the balance.
Chap. 4.	Oscillation of a pendulum.	Chap. 12.	Hauling weight on an inclined plane (idea of work as having weight and height components).
Chap. 5.	Falling bodies on an inclined plane, in relation to speed attained, amount of drop, and weight of ball.		
Chap. 8.	Conservation of motion in a horizontal plane (up to Newton's first law via frictionless 'thought-experiment').	Chap. 13.	The projection of shadows (variation of image sizes with distances, given rectilinear propagation).

of the traditional routines which may at least have seemed to have the merit of being efficient ways to theoretical competence, can be seen to be regressions — short circuits rather than short cuts. For example, someone who has memorized some easy 'proof' of the $pv = 1/3\ nmc^2$ relationship could be only handling it as a child handles numbers on a page as things (reifying relationships, as the philosophers put it), remembering only the rules of addition and subtraction across the equality sign (2B). Or someone who can 'prove' from it that p is directly proportional to T could merely be operating in terms of substitution rules (3A). Whereas to see it as a summarizing operation across a large number of applications, each of which have been imagined through in terms of the kinetic theory model (surely a built-in result of the Nuffield course) is alone enough for it to be a 'formal operation' (3B) as Piaget describes.

Yet it would seem from Figure 17.1 that the course as it stands and is intended to be handled as a five-year process, is accessible at all points only to the 125+ IQ range of pupils. The third-year work is the crunch-point. This represents the top 5 per cent of the school population as a whole, or about the top quarter of the selective school population. A good half of the selective school population would only be expected to 'gear-in' with the course as it stands during the fourth year, and even if much

Table 17.2: (b) Criteria of Assessment Used: Capabilities of Pupil at each Stage

2A	2B	3A	3B	
To verbalize at all about angle relationships.	To establish an ordering of slope relationships — 'if *this* is sharper, *that* will be sharper'.	To begin to investigate the situation by making hypotheses.	To establish an equal angle law which covers all cases.	Inhelder and Piaget: Chap. 1, 'Incidence and Reflection'.
To find small weight more effective at large distances.	Can formulate weight-distance relationship qualitatively — 'the heavier it is the closer the middle' (for balance).	Can formulate relationship quantitatively — 'for distances 1 and 1/3 you need weights 1 and 3'.	Can explain relationship in 'work' terms (see Chap. 12).	Chap. 11, 'Equilibrium in the Balance'.
Not possible.	Sees 'model', sees 'situation' — cannot relate them.	If use of 'model' clearly explained, can make some simple predictions from it.	Can actively search for an explanatory 'model', or can extend one that has been given.	Use of 'model' as in kinetic theory work.
	Finding out *what* happens only.	Finds further interest in beginning to look for *why*.	Can be interested in *checking* a 'why' solution.	'Interest'.
As 2B, but incomplete, and not immediately perceivable.	Seriation: A > B > C. Classification and double classification.	A proportionality relationship in a concrete situation.	Proportionality and inverse proportionality.	Abstractions.
Will investigate what happens.	Will find out what happens, including seriation and classification as tools of perception.	Can see the point of making hypotheses, and can deduce relationships if situation is simplified to one variable at a time.	Knows that, in a system with several variables, he must 'hold all other things equal' while investigating one thing at a time.	Investigation style.

traditional physics teaching was based on an intensive fourth- and fifth-year approach to O-level, the Nuffield course must suffer more than they from such cramming. One would imagine that many teachers of average grammar school pupils have used their own judgements and dodged some of the integrating theory in the first three years, perhaps even have omitted some of the experiments. Indeed, a possible use for this article might be to suggest informed ways of doing this, that do as little harm as possible to the structure of the course.

By contrast, though, because of the thinking about learning and development which went into the course, much of the Year I and II work is accessible to a much wider range of the school population: I know of comprehensive schools in London which are using it. Many of the routines involved with *Materials* in the first year could form just the bridging work between primary school work in maths (and science) and the secondary school that people have been looking for. It was to point to this that I joined the points on Figure 17.1 to indicate a possible minimal course. However, there is a problem. There are *two* Year I and II Nuffield physics courses: the one written by the authors of the *Teacher's Guide* and *Guide to Experiments*, and the one, involving just the same material and experiments, but written by the compilers of the *Questions Book*. In Figures 17.3 and 17.4 I have added 'density-maps' of the accompanying questions to a magnified slice, as in Figure 17.2, of part of Year I and Year II work. The difference in level is apparent. You *can*, by doing Year I and II in the spirit of the *Guide*, and by dropping the occasional reference to 'models' — as in the kinetic theory section, and some of the circuit-board work — keep a very high proportion at the concrete operational level.

On the other hand, by not only squeezing every bit of intellectual imagining that is referred to in the *Guides*, but also using the *Question Book*, you could obviously take your very able pupils to the point where the last three years was almost a downhill run, so well prepared would they be by having met each strand of the course twice.

It seems obvious that if minimal use of the early part of the Nuffield physics course is desirable (it does not form part of the terms of reference for the developers of the course, but it *is* taking place), a totally different questions book would need to be written; and, I suspect also — as is indeed already being discussed in London in relation to CSE physics exams — a far less ambitious fourth- and fifth-year course would need to be written, putting the roof on in a different way.

To the remarks about how well structured and evenly progressing the course is, one reservation might be added. The intelligent pupil gets the stimulus of the integrating theory so that he can 'see where he is going',

Figure 17.3

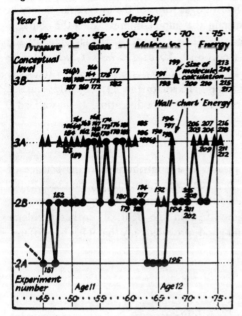

Figure 17.4

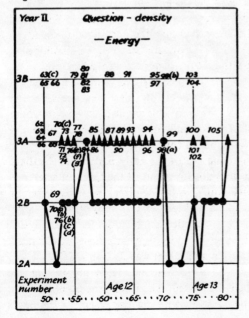

or at least see how things are beginning to link up. But if the teacher of the average selective school•child dodges some of the integrating theory in the first three years, can he sustain the pupil's interest when the course is not being progressively linked up? This reservation is suggested by the course organizers themselves (see pp. 9, 10 of *Teachers' Guide V*). The reader is invited mentally to shift the whole course one year to the *right* in relation to the development line marked for the IQ 115 child, and see if he finds it suggestive in comparison with modifications he has already, perhaps, made.

To conclude, this article is meant as a contribution to the science of science teaching. It is meant as a tool which can quickly be used, hypothetically , when experience tells that something is wrong with a teaching situation. If it needs to be modified in the light of further problems revealed by experience, well and good, provided only that it has been of use.

Notes

1. Shayer, M., *Educ. in Chem.*, 1970, 7, 182-6.
2. Ingle, R.B. and Shayer, M., *Educ. in Chem.*, 1971, 8, 182-3.
3. Mealings, R.J., *Educ. Rev.*, 1963, 15, 194-207.

18 COGNITIVE DEVELOPMENT AND THE LEARNING OF MATHEMATICS

Margaret Brown

Source: Specially written for this volume.
Copyright © 1978 The Open University.

1. Introduction: The Problem

We have recently experienced an upsurge of public concern, expressed by parents, employers and teachers in further education, about the apparently low levels of mathematical achievement of many children in both primary and secondary schools. There is evidence to show that these criticisms have at least some justification and that there are indeed a large number of children, maybe the majority, who are without what are usually considered to be basic numerical skills (Rees, 1972; Levy, 1977). There is also some data which suggests that this phenomenon is not a new one, and pre-dates the introduction of both modern mathematics and comprehensive schooling (Pidgeon, 1967).

And yet most children spend around 1500 hours (the equivalent of about 1½ years) learning mathematics. How is it possible that at the end of this so many of them seem to have absorbed so little of what they have experienced in that time?

The simplistic answer is to blame the teachers, and the methods of teaching, but this fails to explain the almost universal nature of this phenomenon of failure in different regions of Britain, and indeed in different countries (Husen, 1967; Karplus et al., 1975) over a long period of time. There is also evidence that it exists whether courses are modern or traditional in flavour (Skemp and Mellin-Olsen, 1974; Engineering Industry Training Board, 1977). The fact that there is known to be a wide spread of attainment among individual children within classes which have had the same teaching also suggests that large scale teacher incompetence is not the major factor.

Perhaps we should focus on the children rather than on the teachers, and consider the relationship between mathematical knowledge and what we know of children's thinking.

2. Types of Mathematical Learning

Gagné (1970) and Bloom et al. (1956) each suggest ways of classifying types of learning, and many others (e.g. Romberg and Wilson, 1966; Husen, 1967; University of London, 1970) have offered variations on them.

For simplicity we shall consider a model of mathematical learning which distinguishes between four aspects: simple recall, algorithmic learning, conceptual learning, and problem-solving strategies.

Public debate is often confused since society at large tends to identify achievement in mathematics with attainment in the first two aspects, teachers mainly concentrate on the second and third, and educationists value especially the third and fourth.

(a)   Simple Recall

This is referred to by Gagné (1970) as 'stimulus-response learning', and is classified by Bloom (1956) under the separate headings of 'knowledge of terminology', 'knowledge of specific facts', and 'knowledge of principles and generalisations'. It plays a relatively small part in mathematics, and is mainly restricted to the memorising of number bonds and multiplication tables, terminology and units, and simple formulae.

Since this content is reasonably small, most of children's shortcomings in this area could be remedied by more frequent practice (Lovell, 1970). One has to remember though that children vary greatly in their capacity to recall information, so that it is difficult for teachers to estimate for each individual the amount of practice which is necessary without becoming tedious and time-wasting.

Also, since recall is known to be more effective when the material is meaningful to the subject (Lovell, 1970) teachers can claim justification in delaying memorisation until sufficient conceptual foundations are available for any particular child.

(b)   Algorithmic Learning

This is referred to as 'rule-learning' by Gagné (1970) and would probably be considered as an aspect of 'comprehension' by Bloom (1956). Skemp (1976) gives a detailed and interesting discussion of the pros and cons of algorithmic learning, which he terms 'instrumental understanding', a little misleadingly as most people prefer to reserve the term 'understanding' to refer to conceptual learning.

Algorithmic learning can be thought of as the memorising of a store of well-defined procedures e.g. how to do long multiplication, how to solve simultaneous equations, how to convert from miles per gallon to litres per 100 kilometres, and so on. Thus the individual is acting like a computer; provided he is told which programme to access he will recall it and put it into operation on any set of data which may be provided in the form specified in the programme. This is a rather more complex function than that of recall, where the individual is acting merely as a data store. In the case of mathematics, poor recall of facts and formulae could be remedied by carrying round a written reminder which for everyday use would scarcely run to two sides of paper, and which even for active mathematicians and scientists would hardly exceed a small booklet. However to remedy shortcomings in algorithmic learning one would need a reasonably sized book containing sequences of instructions.

(c) Conceptual Learning

This has some aspects of Gagné's (1970) categories of 'concept learning' and 'rule learning', and of Bloom's (1956) 'comprehension' although it also includes aspects of 'application'; it is referred to by Skemp (1976) as 'relational understanding'.

Conceptual learning is rather harder to define than recall or algorithmic learning; although we recognise when someone exhibits 'understanding' we find it a difficult phenomenon to either describe or explain. A 'concept' is certainly not an isolated entity which can be 'learned', but is rather a 'junction', in a whole 'network' of relationships; without the 'network' there could be no 'junction'.

For instance we would agree that someone had a well-developed concept of 'fraction' if he could apply this idea in a wide variety of situations (e.g. if I earn £36 a week and you earn £48 then my salary is 3/4 of yours, if I divide 3 apples among 4 people they will get 3/4 of an apple each, which is the same amount as would result if I divided one apple into eight pieces and took 6 of them etc.). In addition it would require a knowledge of the relationships between different fractions (e.g. 3/4 is twice 3/8, equivalent to 12/16, the sum of 5/12 and 1/3; if my salary is 3/4 of yours, then yours is 4/3 of mine, or 4/7 of the total, etc.). It would also include a knowledge of the relationship between concepts, for instance between fractions and ratio, rate, percentage, decimals in both general terms and in particular cases (e.g. 3/4 = .75 = 75%, etc.). Although any of these operations could be taught as an isolated algorithm, the strength of conceptual learning is in the interconnections between them all, and in particular in the ability of selection and of flexible interchange between different operations. Since conceptual learning is obviously fundamental in mathematics, it seems likely that it is in these terms that the apparent difficulties of learning mathematics can be explained; conceptual structures and learning hierarchies are therefore discussed in much greater depth in the next section.

(d) Problem-Solving Strategies

These are referred to as 'problem-solving' in Gagné (1970) and cover aspects of 'application', 'analysis' and 'synthesis' in Bloom (1956). They are also the subject of much of the work of de Bono (1970); on the mathematics side Polya (1954, 1962, 1963) has probably done more than anyone to try to list them explicitly.

It is doubtful whether problem-solving strategies should be listed separately, for they are in effect algorithms, albeit rather more generalised ones than those referred to earlier. They include various lines of attack which can be put into operation in order to try to identify a means of solution to a problem where the method is not recognised immediately by the solver.

Many but not all of these strategies are not specific to mathematics, but obviously in any given mathematical problem an ability to operate within the relevant parts of the conceptual structure is essential before any general strategy can be effective.

It seems possible that many of these strategies can be taught (de Bono, 1970; Polya, 1963) but since the area is not well charted, and since the general problem of mathematical failure seems likely to arise from the conceptual learning rather than the problem-solving area, we will not concern ourselves with this aspect here.

Relationships between Types of Learning

A mathematical task cannot be classified according to which type of learning it requires without a knowledge of the previous learning experiences and present conceptual structure of the learner. For instance a task like 'Express 3/8 as a decimal' may be solved using any one type of learning:

(a)   By simple recall, taking a second or so, provided the information 3/8 = 0.375 is readily accessible from the personal data-store.
(b)   By accessing a suitable algorithmic procedure, stored in the long-term memory, for changing fractions into decimals, e.g. performing the division sum 3.000 ÷ 8 = 0.375. (This can be performed by someone with no conceptual knowledge about either decimals or fractions.)
(c)   In a number of different ways using a conceptual structure which has strong and flexible interconnections between fractions and decimals, e.g. recall that 1/4 = 0.25, calculation that since 1/8 is 1/2 of 1/4, then 1/8 = 0.125, and so 3/8 = 3 × 0.125 = 0.375. (This also utilises very simple problem-solving strategies.)
(d)   By using problem-solving strategies in cases where the person has some knowledge of the properties of decimals and fractions as

separate entities, but may have no idea initially of how to relate them.

It is clear that pupils have failed to remember many of the mathematics algorithms they have been taught. This is perhaps not surprising since there are a great many even in common use, and each has 'branching procedures' which depend on variations in the data or in the results of previous steps. As with recall of facts, recall of algorithms obviously becomes easier when as many steps as possible lose their arbitrariness and are meaningfully related to concepts the child already possesses. In addition, of course, if sufficient conceptual knowledge is available, any steps which are forgotten can be filled in from first principles, even if this takes rather more time. In fact professional mathematicians would generally not bother to recall many formulae and procedures which are taught to school children (e.g. that for inverting 2 x 2 matrices), finding it easier to derive them from scratch on the occasions when they may need them rather than to overburden their memories. However for many children these algorithms are learned largely in isolation from concepts, sometimes because the teacher makes no effort to relate them, sometimes because although this effort is made the conceptual foundations either do not exist in the child's mind, or only exist in a way which makes it difficult for such links to be made.

It is also true that algorithmic learning may stimulate conceptual learning by encouraging a child to create further links between the concepts he already has in order to make sense of an algorithm. However this process is unlikely to happen unless the child already has a sufficiently developed conceptual structure to make such adjustments possible, and even then it is not automatic.

Even if a child has a fair-sized repertoire of algorithms and 'facts', without some conceptual background he is unlikely to be able to apply them in practical situations. Such isolated knowledge is as useful as is a computer or calculator without an operator; the choice of programme can rarely be completely reduced to algorithmic procedures.

For instance a child may be able to solve

$$\begin{array}{r} 94 \\ - 78 \\ \hline \end{array}$$

but be unable to cope with 94 − 78, and totally helpless when asked 'If a plastic beaker has a mass 78 gm, and when some water is poured in it the total mass is 94 gm, what is the mass of the water?'

As part of the Social Science Research Council programme 'Concepts in Secondary Mathematics and Science (CSMS)' at Chelsea College, University of London, we have been investigating children's conceptual structures in different areas of secondary mathematics, and in some cases have examined the relationship between this and the knowledge of related algorithms.

In the field of simple number operations on whole numbers, for instance, we confirmed that although children with a greater degree of conceptual understanding were more likely to remember computational algorithms (r = .69, n = 557, for a representative sample of 11 to 12 year old children, between 'conceptual' and 'algorithmic' tests), there were a few individual children who managed to perform well on computational algorithms with very little conceptual background, presumably because they had had a great deal of practice.

In fact children find it quite difficult to identify the algorithms required for solving simple practical problems; for instance one third of a representative sample of 1,089 children aged 11 to 12 did not recognise that a multiplication algorithm was required in the problem: 'An oven tray used for cooking little cakes will hold 56 cakes. A baker fills 28 trays. How many cakes will he cook?' When asked to look at it from the other side, less than one third of the children could think of any practical problem they could solve by multiplying 56 by 28.

On the other hand some children who could not recall the 'official' algorithm for subtraction of 3-digit numbers managed to solve practical subtraction problems quickly and efficiently using their own private procedures resulting from a good conceptual understanding of the operations involved.

In general it seems that more emphasis should be put on building up conceptual understanding to enable algorithms both to be remembered and utilised appropriately, even if this means delaying their teaching until a sufficient conceptual structure exists. However there may well be a few algorithms which are so important in everyday life, or future employment, to justify the time necessary for practising them without this conceptual background.

It certainly seems likely that children's problems with learning mathematics are rooted in their difficulties in forming conceptual structures; indeed while there are a number of theories prescribing how children should be taught mathematics (e.g. Dienes, 1973; Gagné, 1970), it seems that Piaget's theory involving the formation of such structures is the only one which can even begin to explain the causes of mathematical failure.

The major difficulty, at least for secondary school mathematics teachers, is our present lack of knowledge of the nature of these structures, including both the order in which and the processes by which such structures are formed. We also have only the most primitive of methods for determining the levels of development of individual children. It is the major aim of the CSMS project to at least make a start on providing such information in order that future mathematics curricula will better be able to avoid the waste of time involved in trying to teach relations or operations or algorithms when children's conceptual structures are not sufficiently developed to assimilate them.

3. Conceptual Structures in Mathematics and Piagetian Stages

A major attempt to try to plot the order of children's conceptual development at primary school level was made as part of the Nuffield Mathematics Project (1973), and is shown in Figure 18.1.

Although it is often known as a 'concept map', this is perhaps misleading for two reasons. First, if 'concepts' are thought of as 'junctions' in the cognitive structure, they can only be built up gradually by the formation of the operational schemes (or 'relations') which connect the concepts together; indeed it is doubtful whether it is possible to speak meaningfully of *completely* acquiring a concept as this would imply that all possible links with other concepts had been formed. Thus it cannot be said that the concept of a 'fraction' is acquired before that of a 'decimal', although certain operational schemes involving fractions may be acquired in advance of certain others involving decimals. Any map such as the Nuffield one must therefore represent the order of acquisition of operational schemes, and not 'concepts'.

The second point to keep clear is that the 'map' does not try to show the nature of a cognitive structure itself, but merely to indicate a likely order of chronological development of the schemes which form part of the structure.

Thus a child will not arrive at the idea of sorting by several attributes (see column on lefthand side) until he has perceived that the number of elements in a set remains invariant even if the spatial configuration is changed, and this in turn is preceded by the ability to match the elements of two sets. However since 'matching' and 'neighbourhoods' appear on separate branches, it would be possible for a child to arrive at either of these two operations first. The map is therefore known as a 'partially ordered network'. The map was drawn up in conjunction with Piaget and the Geneva School, and many of the entries on the map represent operations the exact nature of which can be defined by reference to the Piagetian literature. For instance 'inclusion' denotes the ability to relate

Figure 18.1

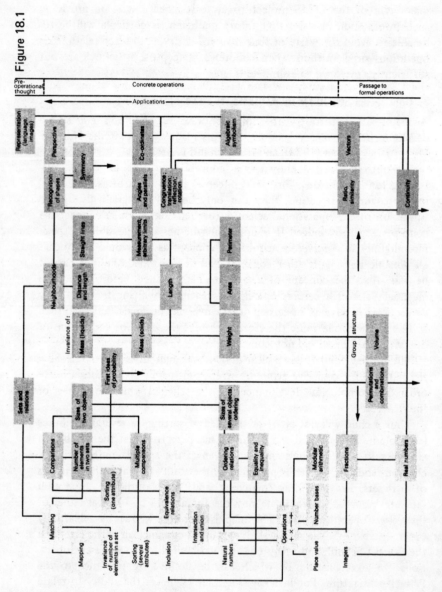

a set to one of its subsets, e.g. to recognise that while all tulips are flowers, not all flowers are tulips, so that in a set of daisies and tulips, there are more flowers than tulips (Inhelder and Piaget, 1964). Such Piagetian operational descriptions exist for many of the entries, especially those in the earlier (top) part of the network.

However other entries on the map cannot be so defined; for instance Piaget did no work on place value or algebraic symbolism. In such cases the label in fact covers a number of operational schemes which obviously spread over many different levels of cognitive functioning (e.g. results of the CSMS algebra study indicate that there are probably at least four distinct levels of thinking involved in algebraic symbolism and that these would span virtually the whole range of the map, from top to bottom).

One of the aims of the CSMS project is therefore to extend the Nuffield map into the area of secondary mathematics, which will include the clarification of many of these items which appear especially in the latter (lower) sections of the tree which are at the moment operationally undefined.

In many of these cases, the possession of the operational scheme is difficult to isolate from the use of conventional mathematical language and the use of algorithms which have been learned by rote. It is for instance difficult to ascertain whether a child understands certain aspects of fractions without recourse to either symbols or terminology (3/4, three-quarters) which demand prior acquaintance, if not direct teaching. Such operations, where linguistic conventions are virtually unavoidable, were specifically avoided by the Geneva school; Piaget preferred to limit his work to those operations which appear to depend only on experience with the manipulation of concrete objects, although he would agree that the development of many of these operations is dependent on the child's previous physical experience, if not on the conceptual structure of the mother-tongue.

Piagetian Stages

On the right hand side of the Nuffield 'map' is a reference line dividing levels of the tree between 'pre-operations', 'concrete operations' and 'formal operations' stages. This classification is possible at the earlier levels of the map since these entries relate directly to operational schemes investigated by Piaget and his associates within his structure of stages, but there are difficulties, both methodological and philosophical, in extending the mathematics map within the same framework.

The implications of the existence of Piagetian stages for the teaching of mathematics are too often summed up simplistically as 'children should

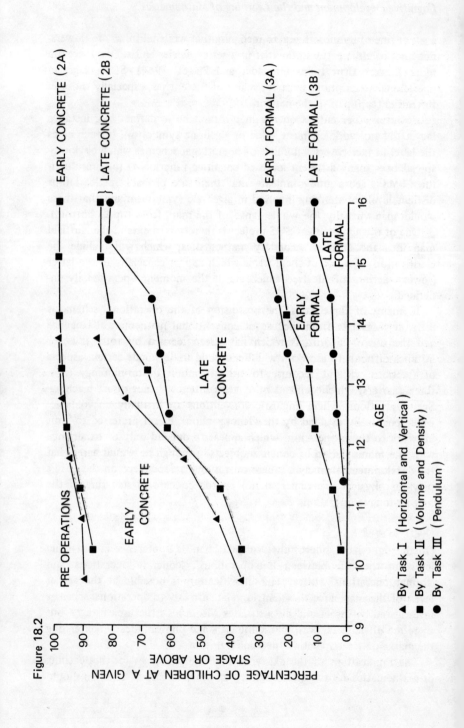

Figure 18.2

PERCENTAGE OF CHILDREN AT A GIVEN STAGE OR ABOVE

AGE

PRE OPERATIONS
EARLY CONCRETE
LATE CONCRETE
EARLY CONCRETE (2A)
LATE CONCRETE (2B)
EARLY FORMAL (3A)
LATE FORMAL (3B)
LATE FORMAL
EARLY FORMAL

▲ By Task I (Horizontal and Vertical)
■ By Task II (Volume and Density)
● By Task III (Pendulum)

use concrete apparatus to learn mathematics until they reach the formal stage at around 11 years of age, when it can be assumed that they are able to work with abstract symbols'.

This type of statement misses the point for three reasons:

(a) the distinctions between concrete and formal operations made by Piaget are much more subtle than those between the modes of teaching using apparatus and symbols;

(b) the degree of confidence implied by such a statement is unjustified by the experimental evidence; not only is it far from proven that a child's development progresses in stages rather than continuously, but the nature of any such stages is a matter of contention (e.g. Lunzer, 1973; Brown and Desforges, 1977);

(c) even if the stages are shown to provide a good model of development, the ages at which children progress from stage to stage cover a wide range, and in particular the onset of formal operations seems less likely to occur on average much later than 11 years. Indeed a survey of Piagetian stages in a representative sample of over 10,000 English school children, undertaken by the CSMS project using class versions of original Piagetian tasks related to scientific concepts, produced the results shown in Figure 18.2 (Shayer, Kuchemann and Wylam, 1976). This indicates for instance that at age 12 only about 10 to 15 per cent of children give responses classified as early formal (3A), with only a small proportion of those assessed as late formal (3B); around 45 per cent are late concrete (2B), 35 to 40 per cent early concrete (2A), and the remaining 5 per cent of the responses of the normal school population would be classified as pre-operational. The results shown on the graph would seem to indicate that the vast majority of secondary school children are progressing through the concrete operations stage, with only a minority attaining even early formal operational reasoning.

There can be no simple statement of the implications of Piaget's stage hypothesis for the learning of mathematics. However, assuming for the moment that the hypothesis is valid, there are some conclusions that can be tentatively drawn from his work.

Pre-Operations. A major characteristic of the pre-operations stage is that of shifting of criteria; thus children, unable to either repeat their reasoning or reverse their operations, give answers which frequently seem either irrelevant or illogical. Since mathematics is a subject where consistency is an essential property of even the most primitive operations, it follows that the most one can hope to achieve mathematically with pre-operational children is the accumulation of useful physical and linguistic experience which will eventually lead to reversibility. (Piaget implies this conclusion by describing concrete operations as 'logico-mathematical' operations.)

In the CSMS work on 'number operations', referred to earlier, we found a few children in the 11-12 year old age group who during an interview gave responses which appeared to be typically pre-operational. For instance, in answer to the question:

A gardener has 391 daffodils. These are to be planted in 23 flowerbeds. Each flowerbed is to have the same number of daffodils. How do you work out how many daffodils will be planted in each flowerbed?

Two responses were as follows:

YG   You er . . . I know what to do but I can't say it . . .
MB   Yes, well you do it then. Can you do it?
YG   Those are daffodils and these are flowerbeds, large you see . . . Oh! they're being planted in different flowerbeds, you'd have to put them in groups . . .
MB   Yes, how many would you have in each group? What would you do with 23 and 391, if you had to find out?
YG   See if I had them, I'd count them up . . . say I had 20 of each . . . I'd put 20 in that one, 20 in that one . . .
MB   Suppose you had some left over at the end when you've got to 23 flowerbeds?
YG   I'd plant them in a pot (!!)

DPi   About 200.
MB   About 200. How did you work it out?
DPi   Just guessed.
MB   Just guessed, OK. Which of those did you do? (subject shown various arithmetic expressions, e.g. 391 ÷ 23, 391 + 23, etc.).
DPi   No.
MB   No. OK.

It is important to realise that such responses are not 'stupid', in fact they can sometimes be quite sensible; they are simply not 'logical' in a mathematical sense.

It was clear from interviews where such responses were found, that these children had picked up very little from six or seven years of mathematical education.

Early Concrete Operations. Children at this stage are beginning to recognise logical properties which remain invariant when the perception of the physical situation changes, e.g. that the number seven is a property of a set of seven objects and does not depend either on whether they are buns or bananas, or on whether they are arranged in a pile or a long row. Similarly if a set of three objects and a set of five objects are combined into a new set, this will contain eight objects, again independent of the nature and spatial distribution of the objects. Having formed these operational schemes, the child will have little trouble in using the symbolism $3 + 5 = 8$ to represent the equivalence; for the use of mathematical symbolism only causes difficulties when the operations and entities it represents are not properly assimilated into the cognitive structure. (This was confirmed during the CSMS number operations interviews, where children who claimed to have 'forgotten the names' of the symbols X or − invariably proved unable to recognise applications of these operations even after the meanings had been explained by the interviewer.)

Piaget (1952) seems to suggest that an understanding of multiplication is acquired along with addition at the early concrete stage; yet in another study (Inhelder and Piaget, 1964) evidence is presented that multiplicative classification (i.e. classifying simultaneously by two attributes) does not develop until the late concrete stage. CSMS results showed that 80 per cent of 11-12 year olds recognised as a multiplication problem:

A bucket holds 8 litres of water, 4 buckets of water are emptied into a bath. How do you work out how many litres of water are in the bath?

whereas only 50 per cent of this age group recognised as a multiplication problem:

A shop makes sandwiches. You can choose from 3 sorts of bread and 6 sorts of filling. How do you work out how many different sandwiches you would choose?

This, taken in conjunction with the graph in Figure 18.2 seems to confirm the Genevan results, for in the former problem multiplication can be perceived as a repeated addition process, while the latter requires an appreciation of multiplicative classification (known mathematically as a 'cartesian product' or 'cross product'), since a sandwich has to be classified simultaneously as containing both 'brown bread' and 'ham'.

The following interview response (to the daffodil item given on page 362) was thought to be typical of a child at the early concrete operations stage, since the operation of subtraction, and hence addition, seemed to be established but not that of division (or multiplication).

MB (Reads question) What would you do with those two numbers to work it out?

SB 23 there, take away 23, 23, 23 . . .

MB Keep on taking away 23?

SB Yes.

MB Can you think of any of those that would be right? (Child is shown a number of arithmetic expressions $391 \div 23, 23 - 391$, etc.)

SB That one. ($23 - 391$)

MB 23 take away 391. Any others?

SB That one. ($391 - 23$)

MB 391 take away 23.

Another response, this time to the sandwiches item above, also seemed to typify this stage:

MB (Reads question.)

YG (Reads question again) What must I do?

MB You want to know how many different sorts of sandwiches you could choose. If you can choose 6 sorts of filling and you can have 3 different sorts of bread — you can have white, brown or rye bread, say. Now if you could have each of those sorts of bread and also there are 6 different sorts of filling you could have in them, how many different sandwiches could you have altogether?

YG . . . 9.

MB How did you get the 9?

YG Because if you put them together, that makes 9. (Indicates $6 + 3$ is the correct expression.)

Of course, other operational schemes are being attained around this stage which are of importance in the learning of mathematics, e.g. ordering, inclusion, and the invariance of properties such as length.

Late Concrete Operations. Throughout the concrete operations period there occurs the phenomenon of vertical decalage, i.e. the development of operations which have basically the same logical structure as those which are acquired earlier, but which are more difficult to generalise from concrete experience due to the presence of more perceptual 'noise'.

Thus the property of area is recognised as invariant even when a shape is cut up and rearranged, and the use of numbers and number operations is extended to cover not only a set of discrete objects, but also the number of standard measurement units in a particular length or area.

The graph in Figure 18.2 would suggest that a significant proportion of secondary school children would not yet have reached the stage of late concrete operations and hence may not have a sufficient understanding of area and the nature of measurement in general. Initial CSMS results on this topic confirm that this is so; in particular, when presented with the situation below only 65 per cent of children of 11-12 thought that D and K had equal areas:

I cut a square D and arrange the pieces to make a new shape K like this:

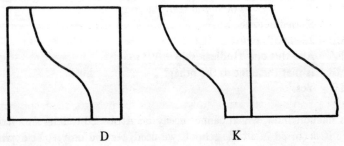

D   K

The attainment of multiplicative classification is accompanied by not only a fuller appreciation of multiplication and division including the use of ratio and proportion (provided that the numerical ratios are simple, e.g. 1:2, 1:3, 1:5, etc.); it also enables points to be identified on graphs by a pair of co-ordinates. Early CSMS results in the areas of ratio and graphical interpretation confirm both these predictions.

Collis (1975) suggests that children who are, according to the Piagetian scheme, late concrete operational are able to extend their numerical operations to large non-intuitable numbers (e.g. 372) and to repetitions of operations (e.g. 3 + 4 + 7). The CSMS study on number operations did indeed show that the use of large numbers rather than small ones in a problem tended to depress the percentage of children recognising the operation involved by about 10-15 per cent. The fact that the exception where there was little difference was on the cartesian product items (e.g. the sandwiches problems) also seemed to support Collis's hypothesis, since children who could cope with that were in any case thought to be at a late concrete operational stage.

During the CSMS interviews the children who seemed to be at this stage gave quick, decisive answers to the number operations problems, but interestingly enough did not necessarily recognise the non-commutativity of division (or sometimes subtraction) e.g. in answer to the 'daffodils' problem on page 362.

MB	(Reads question) I don't expect you to work it out, not in your head, but can you tell me what you'd do with 391 and 23 to tell you what the answer would be.
TZ	Shall I work it out?
MB	If you want to, or you can tell me how you would work it out.
TZ	Um . . . 391 divided by 23 . . . you share the . . .
MB	That's all right, OK. Which of those would it be then?
TZ	That one. (Indicates 391 ÷ 23)
MB	391 . . . how would you read that out? 391 . . .
TZ	Shared between . . .
MB	23. That's right.
TZ	And this one. (Indicates 23 ÷ 391)
MB	Is that the same as the other?
TZ	Yes.

This phenomenon, which cannot easily be attributed to school experience since it occurred in all the schools we used, seemed only to be explicable if one assumed that the operation of division was still related very closely to experience involving whole numbers. Thus a division problem involving 3 and 12 was perceived to involve 12 objects being split into 3 groups (or groups of 3), giving the unambiguous answer 4. The order of recording this in symbolism was therefore seen as unimportant.

Of course there are other operations which develop during the concrete operations stage which are of importance to mathematical learning, e.g. invariance of shape under geometrical transformations, the use of place value, the use of algebraic symbolism to refer to an identifiable object or length, and so on.

Formal Operations. It is at this level that it becomes most difficult to interpret Piaget's theory and apply it to mathematics learning; indeed his assertion that there is a qualitative difference between concrete and formal operations but that each of these types has itself a basic common structure, is often questioned (e.g. Lunzer, 1973; Brown and Desforges, 1977).

One very common set of operations in mathematics is those related to ratio and proportion, which underlie also the use of fractions and decimals, enlargement and similarity, rate and gradient, and so on. Piaget's assertion that the proportionality scheme develops during the formal operational period (Inhelder and Piaget, 1958) has been confirmed by many other works (e.g. Karplus *et al.*, 1965; Lovell and Butterworth, 1966; Pumfrey, 1967). The CSMS results also confirm this, except in cases already referred to where the multiplying factor is a whole number, in which case proportionality is reduced to an aspect of whole-number multiplication, and can thus be understood by children at the late concrete operations stage.

Two of the questions used in the CSMS study of ratio are given below; the first is adapted from Genevan work; the second is similar in structure except that it necessarily involves fractions and deals with geometrical enlargement.

(a)   Two eels X (25 cm long) and Y (15 cm long) are fed with fishfingers, the length of fishfinger depending on the length of the eel. X gets a fishfinger 10 cm long. How long should the fishfinger given to Y be?

(b)

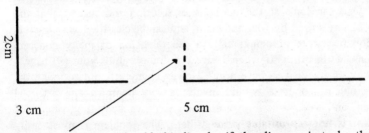

How long should this line be if the diagram is to be the same shape as the other one but bigger?

The first question was answered correctly by 23 per cent of children at the end of their second year in secondary school (age 13), 28 per cent of third year children, and 33 per cent of fourth year children; whereas the second was answered correctly by 8, 11 and 20 per cent respectively. (As in the case of all CSMS data, these samples were representative of the English population of their age, and included in each age group children from different schools in a variety of areas.) Thus these results, taken in conjunction with the graph in Figure 18.2, tend to confirm Piaget's contention that the idea of proportionality develops during the formal operations period.

A recent study by Ruth Rees (1972) on the mathematical difficulties of trainee apprentices revealed a core of items which caused trouble not only at this level, but also among student teachers. Every single one of these items can be shown to require the use of proportionality.

Other mathematical operations which are classified as formal by Piaget are those involving combinations and permutations (Piaget and Inhelder, 1975), and deductive logic, which is used in the framing of mathematical proofs (Inhelder and Piaget, 1958). However, it is difficult to apply the Piagetian criteria to other mathematical areas. For instance, at what cognitive levels are the two problems:

(a)   What can you say about x if $x + 5 = 8$?
(b)   What can you say about x if $x + 5 = 8 - 3x$?

The first of these can be solved by children around the middle stage of concrete operations (86 per cent of second year secondary children gave correct answers), but most people would predict that the second would require formal operations. Yet one cannot easily analyse its structure in terms of the INRC group, or propositional logic of hypothetico-deductive thought, which are the criteria laid down by Piaget (Inhelder and Piaget, 1958). One can look at the methods of solution and suggest that the former can be solved by trial and error, and can be classified as a concrete operation by virtue of being really a generalisation of many concrete situations of the form 'If when I give you 5 more dolls you will have 8 dolls, how many do you have now?' However, any attempt to make the latter problem 'concrete' would involve a very complex and artificial statement and would in a   e not lead easily to a solution, since trial and error is not a profitable strategy here. The problem is most easily solved by operating with expressions like x and $3x$ as if they were numbers. Although they do in fact stand for particular numbers, they can only be operated on at this stage as generalised numbers, and hence the child has to be able to work with something which is generalised from a number, the number having itself been generalised from concrete situations. This would come within Piaget's definition of formal operations as 'second degree operations', i.e. operations on operations (Inhelder and Piaget, 1958, p. 254) and therefore a case for the formal operational nature of the second question could be made on those grounds, although there are few precedents for this type of argument in the Piagetian literature. Malpas and Brown (1974) have attempted to develop this type of analysis and apply it to questions in mathematics examinations.

Another easier criterion to apply to the above algebra questions is Collis's notion of 'acceptance of lack of closure' (ALC), as referred to by Collis (1972) and Lunzer (1973). It is clear that in the first example the child can immediately 'close' the situation by substituting a small number, whereas in the second one several operations have to be performed before a numerical answer is in sight.

It is certainly true that in the CSMS algebra study many children demonstrated a desire for speedy closure; for instance, when asked how they could write the number which was 5 larger than n, many gave the answer 19, presumably because they were prepared to try anything to find a numerical answer (n is the 14th letter of the alphabet). Similarly in another example:

What can you say about c if c + d = 10 and c is less than d?

44 per cent of second year secondary children, 41 per cent of third years and 36 per cent of fourth years gave only one number (usually c = 4), again illustrating a desire to arrive in a single step at a unique and un-ambiguous answer.

The concept of a numerical variable (i.e. a generalised entity which can take any numerical value) is necessary to operate with functional relationships expressed either in letters, e.g. $y = 3x^2$, or as a continuous line on a graph. In two of the CSMS studies, those concerned with algebra and graphs respectively, questions involving relationships between numerical variables were found to be extremely difficult, with less than 20 per cent and sometimes less than 10 per cent of fourth year secondary pupils demonstrating any real understanding, and correspondingly lower percentages of second and third years.

Some examples are given below:

(a) Mary's basic wage is £20 per week. She is also paid £2 for each hour of overtime that she works.
(i) If h stands for the number of hours of overtime that she works and if W stands for her total wage (in £s) write down an equation connecting W and h.

(ii) What would Mary's total be if she worked 4 hours overtime?

(b)   f = 3g + 1. What happens to f if g is increased by 2?

(c)

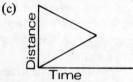

Does this graph represent a journey? Explain your answer.

(d)

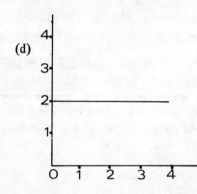

What is the equation of this line? (This is a standard part of the mathematics curriculum for many children in the first two years of secondary school; the testing took place at the end of the school year.)

Percentages in each year with correct answers

		2nd	3rd	4th
a	(i)	2	5	8
	(ii)	65	77	76
b		3	7	13
c		12	9	16
d		14	10	14

Such examples can be argued to be formal operational in the same way as the second algebra question referred to above since they involve 'second degree operations'; indeed (a), (b) and (d) involve relationships between two variables, each requiring second degree operations. ALC is a little harder to justify here than in the previous example since the lack of closure in (a), for example, lies not in the solution process but in the algebraic nature of the answer.

There do however still seem to be some mathematical operations which cannot easily be related to any of the above criteria for formal operations. Subtraction and multiplication of negative numbers are two such operations which are of particular interest since mathematics teachers continue to argue over when and how they should be introduced.

It may be, of course, that attempts at providing alternative theories of learning to Piaget's will eventually prove more fruitful for the analysis of mathematical operations. At present there is considerable activity in the field of information processing, where simulation of conceptual processes is being attempted using techniques from the theory of computing (e.g. Klahr and Wallace, 1970, 1972). This is however still at too early a stage to judge its practical value. The Piagetian theory may be incomplete, indeed it may even be mistaken; however it does enjoy some predictive success, and it is at present undoubtedly the best theory we have available to help us understand the difficulties children experience in learning mathematical concepts.

Summary

1. The fact that many children find it difficult to learn mathematics would seem to be attributable to their difficulties in building up a conceptual structure, since this is a crucial factor in all aspects of mathematical learning, including the learning of algorithms and the application of problem solving strategies.

2. The major theory of conceptual learning is that of Piaget. In cases where the theory is both clear and applicable, its predictions in mathematical education seems to be born out by empirical evidence. In particular the slow pace at which many children seem to progress through the concrete operations stage can often be used to explain their failure to assimilate mathematical ideas.

3. The nature of formal operations is not at the moment clearly defined, nor does it seem to be comprehensive; both these features render it difficult to apply to examples of mathematical operations. In addition, the notion of formal operations is theoretically unsatisfactory due to the lack of a unifying criterion.

4. It may prove possible to extend and refine the theory, which after all has many strengths and previous successes even in an incomplete form. The alternative, of constructing a totally new theory, seems a long way off at present.

5. Meanwhile the 'Concepts in Secondary Mathematics and Science' Project is attempting to complete a learning hierarchy covering the major areas of school mathematics (and science) which will both accord with empirical results and, wherever possible, contain an underlying theoretical rationale. This should be of help to teachers and other curriculum developers in giving insight into the way children learn mathematics, and thus provide a basis for improving the quality of mathematical education in schools.

References

Bloom, B.S. *et al.* (1956), *A Taxonomy of Educational Objectives*, Vol. 1, Longman.
Brown, G. and Desforges, C. (1977), 'Piagetian psychology and education: time for revision', *Br. J. Educ. Psychol.*, 47, 7-17.
Collis, K.F. (1972), 'A study of concrete and formal operations in school mathematics', Ph.D. thesis, University of Newcastle, New South Wales.
Collis, K.F. (1975), *A study of concrete and formal operations in school mathematics: a Piagetian viewpoint*, Australian Council for Educational Research.
de Bono, E. (1970), *Lateral Thinking: a textbook of creativity*, Ward Lock Educational.
Dienes, Z.P. (1973), *The six stages in the process of learning mathematics*, National Foundation for Educational Research.
Engineering Industry Training Board (1977), *School learning and training*, EITB publication.
Gagné, R.M. (1970), *The Conditions of Learning*, Holt, Rinehart and Winston.
Husen, T. (ed.) (1967), *International Study of Achievement in Mathematics*, Vols. I and II, Wiley.
Inhelder, B. and Piaget, J. (1958), *The Growth of Logical Thinking from Childhood to Adolescence*, Routledge and Kegan Paul.
Inhelder, B. and Piaget, J. (1964), *The Early Growth of Logic in the Child*, Routledge and Kegan Paul.
Karplus, R. *et al.* (1975), 'Proportional reasoning and control of variables in seven countries', working paper of AESOP, University of Berkeley.
Klahr, D. and Wallace, J.G. (1970), 'An information processing analysis of some Piagetian experimental tasks', *Cogn. Psychol.*, 1, 358-87.
Klahr, D. and Wallace, J.G. (1972), 'Class inclusion processes', in Farnham-Diggory, S. (ed.), *Information Processing in Children*.
Levy, A. (1977), 'Decline in mathematics', in Cox, C.B. and Boyson, R. (eds.), *Black Paper 1977*, Temple Smith.
Lovell, K. and Butterworth, I.B. (1966), 'Abilities underlying the understanding of proportionality', *Mathematics Teaching*, 37, 5-9.
Lovell, K. (1970), *Educational Psychology and Children*, University of London Press.
Lunzer, E.A. (1973), 'Formal reasoning: a reappraisal', PMEW paper, Chelsea College, University of London.
Malpas, A.J. and Brown, M. (1974), 'Cognitive demand and difficulty of GCE O.level pretest items', *Br. J. Educ. Psychol.*, 44, 2, 155-64.
Nuffield Mathematics Project (1973), *Checking Up III*, John Murray and W.R. Chambers.
Piaget, J. (1952), *The Child's conception of Number*, Routledge and Kegan Paul.
Piaget, J. and Inhelder, B. (1975), *The Origin of the Idea of Chance in Children*, Routledge and Kegan Paul.
Pidgeon, D.A. (1967), *Achievement in mathematics: a national study of secondary schools*, National Foundation for Educational Research.
Polya, G. (1954), *Mathematics and Plausible Reasoning*, Vols. I and II, Princeton University Press.
Polya, G. (1962, 1965), *Mathematical Discovery*, Vols. I and II, Wiley.
Polya, G. (1963), *How to Solve It*, Doubleday.
Pumfrey, P. (1967), 'The growth of the scheme of proportionality', *Br. J. Educ. Psychol.*, 37, 202-4.
Rees, R.M. (1972), 'Mathematics in further education: difficulties experienced by craft and technician students', Brunel Further Education Monograph, no. 5, Hutchinson Educational.

Romberg, T.A. and Wilson, J.W. (1966), 'The development of mathematics achievement tests for the National Longitudinal Study of Mathematics Achievement', School Mathematics Study Group, Stanford, California.

Shayer, M., Kuchemann, D.E. and Wylam, H. (1976), 'The distribution of Piagetian stages of thinking in British middle and secondary school children', *Br. J. Educ. Psychol.*, 44, 2, 155-64.

Skemp, R.R. and Mellin-Olsen, S. (1974), 'Qualitative differences in mathematical thinking', unpublished paper.

Skemp, R.R. (1976), 'Relational understanding and instrumental understanding', *Mathematics Teaching*, 77, 20-6.

University of London (1970), *General Certificate of Education, Mathematics Syllabus C. Teacher's Booklet*, University of London.

GLOSSARY OF TECHNICAL TERMS

Accommodation: the process whereby a scheme adapts itself to the demands of a new situation.

Algorithm: a procedure for solving a problem, usually a calculation. The 'borrowing' and 'carrying' rules in subtraction and addition are examples.

Assimilation: the process of adapting the new situation to the schemes already possessed.

Asynchronism: See synchrony.

Categoric concepts: concepts which are defined in terms of the attributes the objects possess: redness, squareness, sharpness, etc.

Centration: paying attention exclusively to one aspect of a situation, and hence ignoring the relevance of other aspects. One of Piaget's examples is in the context of the conservation of liquids experiments. The child only uses the heights of two glasses in comparing the amount of liquid they contain, and ignores the width, or vice versa.

Communicating vessels problem: the child has to explain the way in which the liquid levels in two vessels linked by a tube fluctuate when the vessels are raised or lowered relative to each other.

Commutation: this is a property of some actions, or operations and not of others. Operations are the combination of two elements in some way. Thus addition is an operation in which two numbers a and b are combined in a particular way. If it makes no difference to the answer if a and b are put in reverse order, then the operation is said to be commutative. Thus addition is commutative ($8 + 4$ yields the same result as $4 + 8$) whereas subtraction is not ($8 - 4$ is not the same as $4 - 8$).

Conflict-equilibration: a strategy for bringing about a development in an individual's schemes, arising out of Piagetian theory. The individual is put into a situation in which two different schemes of his lead to contradictory results, because of the inadequacy of one or both of them. This sets up an imbalance in his cognitive structures, which is the kind of situation that leads to development because of the need for equilibration, or balance.

Decentration: the converse of centration. (See 'centration'.)

Draw-a-man test: a test in which children are asked to draw a picture of a man, their levels of performance being assessed according to such criteria as presence or absence of fingers, number of fingers, position

374

of eyes relative to nose and so on.

Equilibration: a central construct in Piagetian theory. Just as nature is said to abhor a vacuum and so adjusts to remedy one whenever it occurs, so cognitive structures are said to abhor an imbalance between themselves and the environment and so accommodate themselves in such a way as to reduce or eliminate this imbalance. It is because of this basic drive that cognitive growth occurs at all.

Event: here this term is being used in a technical way in the context of probability theory. An event is the outcome of a particular action, e.g. if the action is throwing a dice, the possible outcomes are 1, 2, 3, 4, 5, and 6. So possible events are 1, 2, 3, 4, 5, and 6. Other possible events are 'even number', number less than 3, 'odd number', any number other than 1, and so on. The probability of any such event occurring can be calculated, at least in this finite context. For example the probability of an even number is 1/2, and the probability of a number less than 3 is 1/3.

Functional-relational concepts: these are concepts which group objects not according to their physical attributes but according to the way they are used. A man, lawn-mower and grass are grouped together because the man uses the mower to cut the grass.

Hydraulic press experiment: here a weighted piston exerts pressure on the liquid in one arm of a U-shaped tube, thus forcing the liquid to rise up in the other arm. Different liquids can be tried, and different weights can be put on the piston. The child has to explain the way the liquid rises and falls.

Implication: consider the two propositions:

> p: this switch is off
> q: the washing machine is not working.

In propositional logic, implication is a way of combining these two propositions. p (this switch is off) implies q (the washing machine is not working) is a true statement if the washing machine never works when the switch is off. Put symbolically we never get p and *not* q together (*not* q being the negation of q: i.e. the washing machine is working) so p is said to imply q, $(p \Rightarrow q)$, if the only situations that are ever found are p and q, not p and q, not p and not q. $p \Rightarrow q$ is not true if we ever get p and not q.

Represented in a truth table we have

$$p$$

		True	False
q	True	True	True
	False	False	True

Truth table
for
p implies q

Inclusive disjunction: this is another concept from propositional logic (see the previous glossary item). In this case though the inclusive disjunction of p and q is said to be true as long as one or other or both of p and q is true. Its truth table is as below

$$p$$

		True	False
q	True	True	True
	False	True	False

Truth table for the
inclusive disjunction
p and q

Isomorphism: essentially this means a transformation which preserves shape and structure. Each element before transformation has a unique parallel with an element after transformation. For instance, if a map contained every detail that existed, drawing the map would be an isomorphism.

INRC group: this is a model borrowed from propositional logic which is considered to be isomorphic with the structures of formal operational thought, in Piagetian theory.

Laws of effect: any response to a situation which is followed by satisfaction of some kind will be more firmly linked to the situation than responses which are not so followed; and hence be more likely to recur. Conversely, those which are followed by discomfort will be less likely to recur.

Morphism: here another word for transformation. An isomorphism is one in which no detail is lost and relationships between the parts are preserved. A homomorphism is a transformation in which detail is lost in the process.

Motion on an inclined plane experiment: there is a plane whose gradient can be altered. A ball can be rolled down the plane, rebounding when it hits a springboard at the bottom. The problem is to find the relationship between the height at which the ball is released and the length of its rebound.

MA (mental age): this concept is derived from intelligence test scores. If a child performs at a level that is the norm for 10-year-olds, then he is said to have a mental age of 10, regardless of his chronological age.

Pearson's χ^2 *(chi-squared):* this is a statistic used to compare frequencies actually obtained in a study with those that could occur by chance.

Perceptual prepotence: being dominated by immediate perception, and the expense of incorporating what is perceived in its context. Susceptibility to visual illusions is a manifestation of this.

Postive and negative recency effects: being influenced by what happened in the immediate past, rather than taking a longer view. Suppose heads have been obtained in the last three tosses of a coin, although prior to that there were many heads and tails. The positive recency effect would be to choose heads again, as that has won the last few times, while the negative recency argument would lead one to choose tails, as it must be tails' turn now. In fact the probability of heads or tails in any one throw is completely unaffected by what has gone before. However both kinds of recency effects are commonly found.

Probability learning: probability learning is said to occur when a subject is in an experimental situation in which he has to predict the outcome of a probabilistic experiment, repeated over large numbers of trials. For example if a coin is loaded in such a way that it will yield heads 60 per cent of the time and tails 40 per cent of the time, over a long period, and then the subject is allowed to toss the coin over and over again, each time predicting whether it will be heads or tails, the pattern of his predictions gradually changes in the light of his experience. This learning is called probability learning.

Projection of shadows experiment: here rings of varying diameters are placed between a light source and a screen. The problem is to find two shadows which cover each other exactly, using two unequal rings.

Restricted/elaborated code: these are terms coined by Bernstein to describe different kinds of language use. The restricted code is one in which language is grammatically simple; statements are made without being qualified or explained in any way. The elaborated code is a use of languages which does have these properties.

Schemes: this is a central Piagetian construct. It is the schemes which assimilate new situations and accommodate to them due to the equilibration process.

Sample space: this is a term from probability theory and is closely related to the concept of 'event' described in this glossary. The sample space is the set of all possible outcomes to an experiment e.g. the set (1, 2, 3, 4, 5, 6) when a die is thrown.

Semiotic function: this is a term which Piaget now uses instead of 'symbolic function'. The symbolic function was the ability to construct a symbol to represent something which is absent. These symbols may be idiosyncratic to the symboliser, or they may be conventional linguistic ones. 'Symbolic function' was sometimes taken to refer only to the idiosyncratic symbols, so the term was changed to 'semiotic function', to make it clear that both these and conventional symbols were included.

Structuralism: often contrasted with behaviourism, it is concerned with such problems as the structure of knowledge, the structure of memory and the rules which govern the use of these.

Structure d'ensemble: as the climax of a stage, the structure of the child's thinking should have a completeness and a unity at its level. The INRC group is proposed as such a structure at the formal stage, and 'groupings' for the concrete operational stage. These structures are very general and abstract and the intention is to capture the essence of the thinking at that stage.

Synchrony: here used to mean that different components of a cognitive skill are mastered at the same time. If they are described as asynchronous, they are out of step with each other.